Critical Approaches to Information Retrieval Research

Muhammad Sarfraz
Kuwait University, Kuwait

A volume in the Advances in Library and
Information Science (ALIS) Book Series

Published in the United States of America by
IGI Global
Information Science Reference (an imprint of IGI Global)
701 E. Chocolate Avenue
Hershey PA, USA 17033
Tel: 717-533-8845
Fax: 717-533-8661
E-mail: cust@igi-global.com
Web site: http://www.igi-global.com

Library of Congress Cataloging-in-Publication Data

Names: Sarfraz, Muhammad, editor.
Title: Critical approaches to information retrieval research / Muhammad
   Sarfraz, editor.
Description: Hershey, PA : Information Science Reference, [2020] | Includes
   bibliographical references and index. | Summary: "This book examines
   interdisciplinary and multidisciplinary applications in data, text,
   image, sound, and document retrieval"--Provided by publisher-- Provided
   by publisher.
Identifiers: LCCN 2019023685 (print) | LCCN 2019023686 (ebook) | ISBN
   9781799810216 (hardcover) | ISBN 9781799810223 (paperback) | ISBN
   9781799810230 (ebook)
Subjects: LCSH: Information retrieval. | Information storage and retrieval
   systems.
Classification: LCC ZA3075 .C747 2020 (print) | LCC ZA3075 (ebook) | DDC
   025.5/24--dc23
LC record available at https://lccn.loc.gov/2019023685
LC ebook record available at https://lccn.loc.gov/2019023686

This book is published in the IGI Global book series Advances in Library and Information Science (ALIS) (ISSN: 2326-4136; eISSN: 2326-4144)

British Cataloguing in Publication Data
A Cataloguing in Publication record for this book is available from the British Library.

The views expressed in this book are those of the authors, but not necessarily of the publisher.

For electronic access to this publication, please contact: eresources@igi-global.com.

Advances in Library and Information Science (ALIS) Book Series

Alfonso Ippolito
Sapienza University-Rome, Italy
Carlo Inglese
Sapienza University-Rome, Italy

ISSN:2326-4136
EISSN:2326-4144

MISSION

The **Advances in Library and Information Science (ALIS) Book Series** is comprised of high quality, research-oriented publications on the continuing developments and trends affecting the public, school, and academic fields, as well as specialized libraries and librarians globally. These discussions on professional and organizational considerations in library and information resource development and management assist in showcasing the latest methodologies and tools in the field.

The **ALIS Book Series** aims to expand the body of library science literature by covering a wide range of topics affecting the profession and field at large. The series also seeks to provide readers with an essential resource for uncovering the latest research in library and information science management, development, and technologies.

COVERAGE

- Librarian Education
- Journal Collections
- E-Books in Libraries
- Corporate Libraries
- User Experience (UX)
- Collaborative Learning and Libraries
- Library Performance and Service
- Patents/Trademark Services
- Library Buildings and Design
- Archive Management

IGI Global is currently accepting manuscripts for publication within this series. To submit a proposal for a volume in this series, please contact our Acquisition Editors at Acquisitions@igi-global.com or visit: http://www.igi-global.com/publish/.

Titles in this Series

For a list of additional titles in this series, please visit: www.igi-global.com/book-series

Research Data Access and Management in Modern Libraries
Raj Kumar Bhardwaj (University of Delhi, India) and Paul Banks (The Royal Society of Medicine, UK)
Information Science Reference • ©2019 • 418pp • H/C (ISBN: 9781522584377) • US $195.00

Handbook of Research on Transdisciplinary Knowledge Generation
Victor X. Wang (Liberty University, USA)
Information Science Reference • ©2019 • 475pp • H/C (ISBN: 9781522595311) • US $285.00

Social Media for Communication and Instruction in Academic Libraries
Jennifer Joe (University of Toledo, USA) and Elisabeth Knight (Western Kentucky University, USA)
Information Science Reference • ©2019 • 319pp • H/C (ISBN: 9781522580973) • US $195.00

Enhancing the Role of ICT in Doctoral Research Processes
Kwong Nui Sim (Victoria University of Wellington, New Zealand)
Information Science Reference • ©2019 • 278pp • H/C (ISBN: 9781522570653) • US $185.00

Social Research Methodology and New Techniques in Analysis, Interpretation, and Writing
M. Rezaul Islam (University of Dhaka, Bangladesh & University of Malaya, Malaysia)
Information Science Reference • ©2019 • 320pp • H/C (ISBN: 9781522578970) • US $195.00

Ethics in Research Practice and Innovation
Antonio Sandu (Stefan cel Mare University of Suceava, Romania) Ana Frunza (LUMEN Research Center in Social and Humanistic Sciences, Romania) and Elena Unguru (University of Oradea, Romania)
Information Science Reference • ©2019 • 373pp • H/C (ISBN: 9781522563105) • US $195.00

Marginalia in Modern Learning Contexts
Alan J. Reid (Coastal Carolina University, USA)
Information Science Reference • ©2019 • 250pp • H/C (ISBN: 9781522571834) • US $175.00

Scholarly Publishing and Research Methods Across Disciplines
Victor C.X. Wang (Grand Canyon University, USA)
Information Science Reference • ©2019 • 372pp • H/C (ISBN: 9781522577300) • US $195.00

701 East Chocolate Avenue, Hershey, PA 17033, USA
Tel: 717-533-8845 x100 • Fax: 717-533-8661
E-Mail: cust@igi-global.com • www.igi-global.com

Table of Contents

Detailed Table of Contents

Ilyes Khennak, University of Science and Technology Houari Boumediene, Algeria
Habiba Drias, University of Science and Technology Houari Boumediene, Algeria

Query expansion (QE) is one of the most effective techniques to enhance the retrieval performance and to retrieve more relevant information. It attempts to build more useful queries by enriching the original queries with additional expansion terms that best characterize the users' information needs. In this chapter, the authors propose a new correlation measure for query expansion to evaluate the degree of similarity between the expansion term candidates and the original query terms. The proposed correlation measure is a hybrid of two correlation measures. The first one is considered as an external correlation and it is based on the term co-occurrence, and the second one is considered as an internal correlation and it is based on the term proximity. Extensive experiments have been performed on MEDLINE, a real dataset from a large online medical database. The results show the effectiveness of the proposed approach compared to prior state-of-the-art approaches.

Fatiha Naouar, MARS Research Laboratory, Tunisia
Lobna Hlaoua, MARS Research Laboratory, Tunisia
Mohamed Nazih Omri, MARS Research Laboratory, Tunisia

Collaborative retrieval allows increasing the amount of relevant information found and sharing history with others. The collaborative retrieval can reduce the retrieval time performed by the users of the same profile. This chapter proposes a new relevance feedback algorithm to collaborative information retrieval based on a confidence network, which performs propagation relevance between annotations terms. The main contribution in this work is the extraction of relevant terms to reformulate the initial user query considering the annotations as an information source. The proposed model introduces the concept of necessity that allows determining the terms that have strong association relationships estimated to the measure of a confidence. Since the user is overwhelmed by a variety of contradictory annotations, another contribution consists of determining the relevant annotations for a given evidence source. The experimental study gives very encouraging results.

In today's competitive world, each company is required to change software to meet changing customer requirements. At the same time, an efficient information retrieval system is required as changes made to software in different versions can lead to complicated retrieval systems. This research aims to find the association between changes and object-oriented metrics using different versions of open source software. Earlier researchers have used various techniques such as statistical methods for the prediction of change-prone classes. This research uses execution time, frequency, run time information, popularity, and class dependency in prediction of change-prone classes. For evaluating the performance of the prediction model, sensitivity, specificity, and ROC curve are used. Higher values of AUC indicate the prediction model gives accurate results. Results are validated in two phases: Experimental Analysis I validates results using OpenClinic software and OpenHospital software and Experimental Analysis II validates result using Neuroph 2.9.2 and Neuroph 2.6.

Chapter 4

As information becomes increasingly abundant and accessible on the web, researchers do not have a need to go to excavate books in the libraries. These require a knowledge extraction system from the text (KEST). The goal of authors in this chapter is to identify the needs of a person to do a search in a text, which can be unstructured, and retrieve the terms of information related to the subject of research then structure them into classes of useful information. These may subsequently identify the general architecture of an information retrieval system from text documents in order to develop it and finally identify the parameters to evaluate its performance and the results retrieved.

Chapter 5

Document indexing is an active domain, which is interesting a lot of researchers. Generally, it is used in the information retrieval systems. Document indexing encompasses a set of approaches that can be applied to index a document using a corpus. This treatment has several advantages, like accelerating the research process, finding the pertinent contains related to a query, reducing storage space, etc. The use of the entire document in the indexing process affects several parameters, such as indexing time, research time, storage space of treatment, etc. The focus of this chapter is to improve all parameters (cited above) related to the indexing process by proposing a new indexing approach. The goal of proposed approach is to use a summarization to minimize the size of documents without affecting the meaning.

This chapter discusses how text summaries could be generated by using a high-level semantic representation. The semantic representation is built using the discourse structure which is comprised of three text representation techniques, namely, universal networking language (UNL), rhetorical structure theory (RST), and Saṅgatis. Sangati is an ancient concept that is used in Sanskrit language literature to capture coherence. This discourse structure is indexed using a concept called sūtra which has been used in both Tamil language and Sanskrit literatures. The chapter mainly focusses on how summary could be generated by using this unique discourse structure and the indexing technique concept, sūtra. Forum for information retreival (FIRE) corpus has been used to test the system and a performance comparison has been done with the one of the state-of-art summary generation systems that is built on discourse structure.

World wide web has information resources even on unthinkable subjects. This information may be available instantly to anyone having Internet connection. This web is growing exponentially, and it is becoming difficult to locate useful information in such a sheer volume of information. Semantic web extends the current web by emphasizing on interoperable ontologies which are capable of processing high quality information so that the agents placed on top of semantic web can automate the work or curate the content for the user. In this chapter, an extensive research in the area of ontology construction is presented, and after having a critical look over the work done in this field and considering the limitation of each, it has been observed that constructing ontology automatically is a challenging task as this task faces difficulties due to unstructured text and ambiguities in English text. In this work an ontology generation technique is devised covering all important aspects missing in the existing works giving better performance as compared to another system.

Emotion detection from voice is a complex task, whereas from the facial expression it is easy. In this chapter, an attempt is taken to detect the emotion through machine using neural network-based models and compared. As no complete database is available for different age groups, a small database is generated. To know the emotion of different age groups substantially, three groups have been generated with each group of 20 subjects. The efficient prosodic features are considered initially. Further, the combination of those features are taken. Each set of features are fed to the models for classification and detection. Angry, happy, and sad are the three emotions verified for different group of persons. It is found that the classifier provides 96% of accuracy. In earlier work, cluster-based techniques with simple features pitch, speech rate, and log energy were verified. As an extension, the combination of features along with machine learning model is verified in this work.

Emotions are age, gender, culture, speaker, and situationally dependent. Due to an underdeveloped vocal tract or the vocal folds of children and a weak or aged speech production mechanism of older adults, the acoustic properties differ with the age of a person. In this sense, the features describing the age and emotionally relevant information of human voice also differ. This motivates the authors to investigate a number of issues related to database collection, feature extraction, and clustering algorithms for effective characterization and identification of human age of his or her paralanguage information. The prosodic features such as the speech rate, pitch, log energy, and spectral parameters have been explored to characterize the chosen emotional utterances whereas the efficient K-means and Fuzzy C-means clustering algorithms have been used to partition age-related emotional features for a better understanding of the related issues.

Reliability of loosely coupled services through the paradigm of service-oriented computing and observing their fault tolerance against massive load in clustered load balancing web server plays an important role while evaluating the quality aspects of software-as-a-service (SaaS), grid, and distributed systems. This chapter shows some aspects of service execution while observing their failure records against massive execution of server-side instruction. A novel reliability estimation framework is proposed that can be deployed for evaluating the reliability of service execution over clustered load balancing web server. A load generating tool is used to generate massive load over the service execution. In this study we will discuss an experimental system and its architecture by using clustered load balancing web server, the reliability estimation framework along with the goodness of fit study through statistical analysis. The overall assessment of the work will validate the applicability of the proposed framework for the loosely coupled service in clustered load balancing web server.

Recently, data mining and intelligent agents have emerged as two domains with tremendous potential for research. The capacity of agents to learn from their experience complements the data mining process. This chapter aims to study a multi-agent system that evaluates the performance of three well-known data mining algorithms—artificial neural network (ANN), support vector machines (SVM), and logistic regression or logit model (LR)—based on breast cancer data (WBCD). Then the system aggregates the classifications of these algorithms with a controller agent to increase the accuracy of the classification using a majority vote. Extensive studies are performed to evaluate the performance of these algorithms using various differential performance metrics such as classification rate, sensitivity, and specificity using different software modules. In the end, the authors see that this system gives more autonomy and initiative in the medical diagnosis and the agent can dialogue to share their knowledge.

Chapter 12

Breast cancer is the most frequent cancer in morocco with 36.1%. It is the second leading cause of death for women all over the world. The effective way to diagnose and treat breast cancer is the early detection because it increases the success of treatment and the chances of survival. Digitized mammographic images are one of the frequently used diagnosis tools to detect and classify the breast cancer at the early stage. To improve the diagnosis accuracy, computer-aided diagnosis (CAD) systems are beneficial for detection. Generally, a CAD system consists of four stages: pretreatment, segmentation, features extraction, and classification. In this chapter, the authors present some work in the development of a CAD system in order to segment a breast tumor (microcalcifications) on mammographic images and classify it by choosing the algorithm that gives a good rate using a technique of a vote.

This chapter explores diagnosis of the breast tissues as normal, benign, or malignant in digital mammography, using computer-aided diagnosis (CAD). System for the early diagnosis of breast cancer can be used to assist radiologists in mammographic mass detection and classification. This chapter presents an evaluation about performance of extracted features, using gray-level co-occurrence matrix applied to all detailed coefficients. The nonsubsampled contourlet transform (NSCT) of the region of interest (ROI) of a mammogram were used to be decomposed in several levels. Detecting masses is more difficult than detecting microcalcifications due to the similarity between masses and background tissue such as F) fatty, G) fatty-glandular, and D) dense-glandular. To evaluate the system of classification in which k-nearest neighbors (KNN) and support vector machine (SVM) used the accuracy for classifying the mammograms of MIAS database between normal and abnormal. The accuracy measures through the classifier were 94.12% and 88.89% sequentially by SVM and KNN with NSCT.

HE stain images play a crucial role in the medical imaging process. Often these images are regarded as of golden standards by physicians for the quality and accuracy. These images are fuzzy by nature, and hence, traditional hard-based techniques are not able to deal with this. Thereby, a decrease in the accuracy of the analysis process may be experienced. Preprocessing of these images is utmost needed so that the fuzziness may be removed to a satisfactory level. A new approach for tackling this problem is introduced in this chapter. The proposed technique is soft computing-based advanced adaptive ameliorated CLAHE. The experimental results demonstrate the superiority of the proposed approach than the other traditional techniques.

Chapter 15

Classification algorithms are widely applied in medical domain to classify the data for diagnosis. The datasets have considerable irrelevant attributes. Diagnosis of the diseases is costly because many tests are required to predict a disease. Feature selection is one of the significant tasks of the preprocessing phase for the data. It can extract a subset of attributes from a large set and exclude redundant, irrelevant, or noisy attributes. The authors can decrease the cost of diagnosis by avoiding numerous tests by selection of features, which are important for prediction of disease. Applied to the task of supervised classification, the authors construct a robust learning model for disease prediction. The search for a subset of features is an NP-hard problem, which can be solved by the metaheuristics. In this chapter, a wrapper approach by hybridization between ant colony algorithm and adaboost with decision trees to ameliorate the classification is proposed. The authors use an enhanced global pheromone updating rule. With the experimental results, this approach gives good results.

Chapter 16

Cloud computing is an effective alternative information technology paradigm with its on-demand resource provisioning and high reliability. This technology has the potential to offer virtualized, distributed, and elastic resources as utilities to users. Cloud computing offers numerous types of computing and storage means by connecting to a vast pool of systems. However, because of its large data handling property, the major issue the technology facing is the load balancing problem. Load balancing is the maximum resource utilization with effective management of load imbalance. This chapter shares information about logical and physical resources, load balancing metrics, challenges and techniques, and also gives some suggestions that could be helpful for future studies.

Preface

Information retrieval (IR) is an active and important area of study and research today. It is the activity of obtaining resources relevant to an information need from a collection of information resources. IR is considered as the science of searching for information from a variety of information sources related to texts, images, sounds, or multimedia. Due to high need of the time, this book is a motivation to explore theoretical innovations and methods in the retrieval of information. A compilation of latest advances in IR research may be a source revolutionizing for facilitating and enhancing the exchange of information among researchers involved in both the theoretical and practical aspects.

The chapters in this comprehensive reference explore the latest developments, methods, approaches and applications of IR in a wide variety of fields and endeavors. This book is compiled with a view to provide researchers, academicians, and readers of backgrounds and methods with an in-depth discussion of the latest advances. It consists of sixteen chapters from academicians, practitioners and researchers from different disciplines of life.

The target audience of this book are professionals and researchers working in the field of information retrieval in various disciplines, e.g. computer science, information technology, information and communication sciences, education, Health, library and others. The book is also targeted to information engineers, scientists, researchers, practitioners, academicians, related industry professionals for an in-depth discussion of the latest advances.

Khennak and Drias begin the book with a discussion on a novel hybrid correlation measure for query expansion (QE) based information retrieval. QE is one of the most effective techniques to enhance the retrieval performance and to retrieve more relevant information. It attempts to build more useful queries by enriching the original queries with additional expansion terms that best characterize the users' information needs. In this chapter, the authors propose a new correlation measure for query expansion to evaluate the degree of similarity between the expansion term candidates and the original query terms. The proposed correlation measure is a hybrid of two correlation measures. The first one is considered as an external correlation and it is based on the term co-occurrence. The second one is considered as an internal correlation and it is based on the term proximity. Extensive experiments have been performed on MEDLINE, a real dataset from a large online medical database. The results show the effectiveness of the proposed approach compared to prior state-of-the-art approaches.

Naouar et al., in Chapter 2 of the book, follow with a discussion of "Uncertain Confidence's Network-Based Collaborative Information Retrieval Relevance Feedback Algorithm." Their work aims at presenting an algorithm for Collaborative retrieval. Collaborative retrieval allows increasing the number of relevant information found and share historical with others. The collaborative retrieval can reduce the retrieval time performed by the users of the same profile. This chapter proposes a new relevance feedback algorithm to collaborative information retrieval based on a confidence's network. It performs propagation relevance between annotations terms. The main contribution in this work is the extraction of relevant terms to reformulate the initial user query considering the annotations as an information source. The proposed model introduces the concept of necessity that allows determining the terms that have strong association relationships estimated to the measure of a confidence. Another contribution consists on determining the relevant annotations for a given evidence source as the user is over whelmed by a variety of contradictory annotations which are far from the original subject. The experimental study gives very encouraging results.

In today's competitive world, each company requires to change the software, to meet with changing customer's requirements. At the same time, efficient information retrieval system is required, as changes made to software in different versions can lead to complicated retrieval system. Chapter 3, "Enhancing Information Retrieval System Using Change Prone Classes" by Bura and Choudhary, aims to find out association between changes and object oriented metrics using different versions of open source software. Earlier researchers have used various techniques such as statistical methods for the prediction of change prone classes. This research uses execution time, frequency, run time information, popularity and class dependency in prediction of change prone classes. For evaluating the performance of the prediction model, the authors have used the following methods: Sensitivity, Specificity and Receiver Operating Characteristics (ROC) Curve. Higher values of AUC (the area under relative operating characteristic) indicate the prediction model gives significant accurate results. Results are validated in two phases: Experimental analysis I validates results using OpenClinic software and OpenHospital software and Experimental analysis II validates result using Neuroph 2.9.2 and Neuroph 2.6.

Much of the information become increasingly abundant and accessible on the Web. The researchers do not have needs to go to excavate in the books and the libraries, these require a knowledge extraction system from the text (KEST). In the next chapter, "Search for Information in Text Files," Hassani et al. aim to identify the needs of a person to do a search in a text. This search can be unstructured and retrieve the terms of information related to the subject of research then structure them into classes of useful information. This may subsequently identify the general architecture of an information retrieval system from text documents in order to develop it and finally identify the parameters to evaluate its performance and the results retrieved.

This is followed by "An Approach of Documents Indexing Using Summarization" introduced by Khalloufi et al. Document indexing is an active domain, which is of great interest to a lot of researchers. Generally, it is used in the Information Retrieval Systems. Document indexing encompasses a set of approaches that can be applied to index a document using a corpus. This treatment has several advantages, like accelerate the research process, find the pertinent contains related to a query, reduce of space storage, and others. The use of the entire document in the indexing process affects several parameters such as: indexing time, research time, storage space of treatment, etc. The focus of this chapter is to improve all parameters (cited above) related to the indexing process by proposing a new indexing approach. The goal of proposed approach is to use a summarization to minimize the size of documents without affecting the meaning.

Motivated by recent results in Text Summary Generation System, Chapter 6, "Building Text Summary Generation System Using Universal Networking Language, Rhetorical Structure Theory, Sangatis and Sutra: Summary Generation Using Discourse Structures" by Subalalitha, addresses the issue about how text summaries could be generated by using a high level semantic representation. The semantic representation is built using the discourse structure which is comprised of three text representation techniques, namely: Universal Networking Language (UNL); Rhetorical Structure Theory (RST); and Saṅgatis. Sangati is an ancient concept that is used in Sanskrit language literature to capture coherence. This discourse structure is indexed using a concept called sūtra which has been used in both Tamil language and Sanskrit literatures. This chapter mainly focusses on how summary could be generated by using this unique discourse structure and the indexing technique concept, sūtra. Forum for Information REtrieval (FIRE) corpus has been used to test the system and a performance comparison has been done with the one of the state-of-art summary generation systems that is built on discourse structure.

World Wide Web has information resources even on unthinkable subjects. This information may be available instantly to anyone having Internet connection. This web is growing exponentially and it is becoming difficult to locate useful information in such a sheer volume of information. Semantic web extends the current web by emphasizing on interoperable ontologies which are capable of processing high quality information so that the agents placed on top of semantic web can automate the work or curate the content for the user. In the following chapter, Arora has described "Automatic Ontology Construction: Ontology From Plain Text Using Conceptualization and Semantic Roles." This chapter presents an extensive research in the area of ontology construction. After having a critical look over the work done in this field and considering the limitation of each, it has observed that constructing ontology automatically is a challenging task as this task faces difficulties due to unstructured text and ambiguities in English text. In this work an ontology generation technique is devised covering all important aspects missing in the existing works giving better performance as compared to another system.

Emotion detection from voice is a complex task, whereas from the facial expression it is easy. Mohanty, in Chapter 8, "Emotion Analysis of Different Age Group From Voice Using Machine Learning Approach," has attempted to detect the emotion through machine using neural network based models and compared. As no complete database is available for different age group, a small database is generated. Thus, to know the emotion of different age groups substantially, three groups have been generated with each group of 20 subjects in this chapter. The efficient prosodic features are considered initially. Further the combination of those features are taken. Each set of features are fed to the models for classification and detection. Angry, Happy, and Sad are the three emotions verified for different group of persons. It is found that the classifier provides 96% of accuracy. In earlier work, cluster based techniques with simple features pitch, speech rate, and log energy were verified. As an extension the combination of features along with machine learning model is verified in this chapter.

Acoustic features describing human speech, emotions are age, gender, culture, speakers, and are situational dependent. Due to an underdeveloped vocal tract or the vocal folds of the children, and a weak or aged speech production mechanism of the older adults, these acoustic properties differ with the age of a person. In this sense, the features describing the age and emotional relevant information of human voice also differ besides being discriminating and reliable. Chapter 9, "Analysis of Speaker's Age Using Clustering Approaches With Emotional Dependent Speech Features" by Palo and Behera, investigates a number of issues related to the database collection, feature extraction, and clustering algorithms for effective characterization and identification of human age of his or her paralanguage information. The prosodic features such as the speech rate, pitch, log energy and spectral parameters have been explored to characterize the chosen emotional utterances. K-means and Fuzzy C-means clustering algorithms have been used to partition age-related emotional features for a better understanding of the related issues.

Reliability of loosely coupled services through the paradigm of service-oriented computing and observing their fault tolerance against massive load in clustered load balancing web server plays an important role while evaluating the quality aspects of software-as-a-service (SaaS), grid and distributed systems. In Chapter 10, "Some Aspects of Reliability Estimation of Loosely Coupled Web Services in Clustered Load Balancing Web Server," Bora and Bezboruah present some aspects of service execution while observing their failure records against massive execution of server side instruction. A novel reliability estimation framework is proposed that can be deployed for evaluating the reliability of service execution over clustered load balancing web server. A load generating tool is used to generate massive load over the service execution. This chapter discusses an experimental system and its architecture using clustered load balancing web server, the reliability estimation framework along with the goodness of fit study through statistical analysis. The overall assessment of the chapter validates the applicability of the proposed framework for the loosely coupled service in clustered load balancing web server.

Recently, Data mining and intelligent agents have emerged as two domains with tremendous potential for research. The capacity of agents to learn from their experience complements the data mining process. Chakour et al., in Chapter 11, propose a multi-agent system that evaluates the performance of three well-known data mining algorithms: Artificial Neural Network (ANN), Support Vector Machines (SVM) and logistic regression or logit model (LR), based on breast cancer data (WBCD). The, the proposed system aggregates the classifications of these algorithms with a controller agent to increase the accuracy of the classification using a majority vote. The chapter consists of extensive studies made to evaluate the performance of these algorithms using various differential performance metrics such as classification rate, sensitivity, and specificity using different software modules. The proposed system gives more autonomy and initiative in the medical diagnosis and its agents can dialogue to share the their knowledge as human experts.

Breast cancer is the most frequent cancer in morocco with 36.1%. It is the second leading cause of death for women all over the world. The effective way to diagnose and treat breast cancer is the early detection because it increases the success of treatment and the chances to survive. Digitized Mammographic images is the one of the frequently used diagnosis tools to detect and classify the breast cancer at the early stage. To improve the diagnosis accuracy, computer aided diagnosis (CAD) systems are beneficial for detection and also it can reduce the rate among women with breast cancer. Generally, a CAD system consists of four stages: Pretreatment, Segmentation, Features Extraction and Classification. In Chapter 12, "Split and Merge-Based Breast Cancer Segmentation and Classification," Khoulqi and Idrissi have presented some work in the development of a CAD system in order to segment a breast tumor (microcalcifications) on mammographic images and classify it by choosing the algorithm that gives a good rate using a technique of a vote.

Diagnosis of the breast tissues as normal, benign, or malignant in digital mammography, using Computer-aided Diagnosis (CAD) is a very important area of study today. System for the early diagnosis of breast cancer can be used to assist radiologists in mammographic mass detection and classification. Nonsubsampled contourlet transform (NSCT) based diagnosis methods are effective to accomplish this task. Taifi et al., in the next chapter, discovers an evaluation about performance of extracted features, using Gray-Level Co-occurrence Matrix applied to all detailed coefficients the NSCT of the region of interest (ROI) of a mammogram. They were used to be decomposed in several levels. Detecting masses is more difficult than detecting microcalcifications due to the similarity between masses and background tissue as F - Fatty, G - Fatty-glandular and D - Dense-glandular. To evaluate the system of classification, the authors have utilized the ideas of K- nearest neighbors (KNN) and Support Vector Machine (SVM). They ahve used the accuracy for classifying the mammograms of MIAS database between normal and abnormal. The accuracy measures through the classifier are 94.12% and 88.89% sequentially by SVM and KNN with NSCT.

Next in Chapter 14, Bora presents "Enhancing HE Stain Images Through an Advanced Soft Computing-Based Adaptive Ameliorated CLAHE." HE stain images play a crucial role in the medical imaging process. Often these images are regarded as of golden standards by physicians for the quality and accuracy. These images are fuzzy by nature and hence, traditional hard based techniques are not able to deal with this, thereby a decrease in the accuracy of the analysis process may be experienced. Preprocessing of these images is utmost needed so that the fuzziness may be removed to a satisfactory level. A new approach for tackling this problem is introduced in this chapter. The proposed technique is soft computing based Advanced Adaptive Ameliorated CLAHE. The experimental results demonstrate the superiority of the proposed approach than the other traditional techniques.

Alaoui and Elberrichi, then, introduce "Enhanced Ant Colony Algorithm for Best Features Selection for a Decision Tree Classification of Medical Data" in Chapter 15. Classification algorithms are widely applied in medical domain to classify the data for diagnosis. The datasets have considerable irrelevant attributes. Diagnosis of the diseases is costly as various tests are required to predict a disease. Feature selection is one of the significant tasks of the preprocessing phase for the data. It can extract a subset of attributes from a large set and exclude redundant, irrelevant or noisy attributes. The authors, in this chapter, propose decrease of the cost of diagnosis by avoiding numerous tests by selection of features which is important for prediction of disease. Applied to the task of supervised classification, the authors construct a robust learning model for disease prediction. The search for a subset of features is an NP-hard problem which can be solved by the metaheuristics. In this chapter, a wrapper approach by hybridization between Ant Colony Algorithm and Adaboost with Decision Trees to ameliorate the classification is proposed. The authors use an enhanced global pheromone updating rule. With the first experimental results, the proposed approach provides good results.

Final chapter of the book is on "Load Balancing in Cloud Computing: Challenges and Management Techniques" which is contributed by Tiwari et al. Cloud Computing has appeared as an effective alternative information technology paradigm with its on-demand resource provisioning and high reliability. This technology has the potential to offer virtualized, distributed and elastic resources as utilities to users. Cloud computing offers numerous types of computing and storage means by connecting to a vast pool of systems. However, because of its large data handling property, the major issue faced by the technology, is the load balancing problem. The load balancing is the maximum resource utilization with effective management of load imbalance. This Chapter provides information about logical and physical resources, load balancing metrics, challenges and techniques and also gives some suggestions which can be helpful for the future studies.

Muhammad Sarfraz
Kuwait University, Kuwait

Chapter 1
A Novel Hybrid Correlation Measure for Query Expansion-Based Information Retrieval

Ilyes Khennak
University of Science and Technology Houari Boumediene, Algeria

Habiba Drias
University of Science and Technology Houari Boumediene, Algeria

ABSTRACT

Query expansion (QE) is one of the most effective techniques to enhance the retrieval performance and to retrieve more relevant information. It attempts to build more useful queries by enriching the original queries with additional expansion terms that best characterize the users' information needs. In this chapter, the authors propose a new correlation measure for query expansion to evaluate the degree of similarity between the expansion term candidates and the original query terms. The proposed correlation measure is a hybrid of two correlation measures. The first one is considered as an external correlation and it is based on the term co-occurrence, and the second one is considered as an internal correlation and it is based on the term proximity. Extensive experiments have been performed on MEDLINE, a real dataset from a large online medical database. The results show the effectiveness of the proposed approach compared to prior state-of-the-art approaches.

INTRODUCTION

The large volume of textual content available on the Web is growing exponentially and the number of new websites created online is increasing rapidly. For instance, the total number of websites has grown significantly, from 900 million in 2014 to 1.6 billion in 2018. Moreover, the volume of user-created content posted on online platforms is considerably expanding, especially on social media websites. Every day, 4 million blog posts are published on the Internet and over 500 million tweets are submitted by users. The number of google search requests has also significantly increased. In 2012, Google handled more than 2 billion queries per day and this number exceeded 4 billion in 2018. In addition, the Internet

DOI: 10.4018/978-1-7998-1021-6.ch001

traffic has dramatically grown. According to the latest Cisco report, the Internet data traffic reached 1.5 ZB in 2017, and it is expected to cross 4 ZB by 2022. This explosive growth of the World Wide Web has led to the following findings:

- New terms are constantly created and generated on the Internet. According to Williams and Zobel (2005), there is one new term in every two hundreds words. Prior efforts by (Eisenstein et al., 2012; Sun, 2010) have demonstrated that this is primarily due to: neologisms, acronyms, abbreviations, emoticons, URLs and typographical errors.
- The Internet users are increasingly using these new terms in their search queries. In their study, Chen et al. (2007) stated that more than 17% of query terms are out of dictionary, 45% of them are E-speak (lol), 18% are companies and products, 16% are proper names, 15% are misspellings and foreign words (Subramaniam et al., 2009; Ahmad & Kondrak, 2005).

These new terms that the users are employing to express their needs are often ambiguous and imprecise. Hence, they negatively affect the quality of search queries and do not allow characterizing the information needs in a satisfactory manner. As a result, retrieving relevant information has become a serious and challenging issue. Many different retrieval approaches and techniques have been suggested and studied in order to overcome this shortcoming and return more relevant information. One well-known technique to fix this shortcoming and improve the retrieval performance is Query Expansion. It aims to augment the user's original query with expansion terms that best describe the actual user intent. QE is widely used in many applications including multimedia information retrieval (Wie et al., 2014), Question Answering (Park & Croft, 2015), information filtering (Leturia et al., 2013); and applied to various areas such as sport (Al Kabary & Schuldt, 2014), health (Khennak & Drias, 2017), e-commerce (Lee & Chau, 2011) and search mobile (Gao et al., 2013).

The process of generating the most relevant and related terms to be used as expansion features is the key step in query expansion. Numerous concepts such as proximity, co-occurrence, association, closeness, relatedness and relationship have been introduced and discussed in order to express the strength of correlation between an expansion term candidate and the query keywords (Carpineto & Romano, 2012).

To generate the most relevant expansion terms, we propose in this work a new robust and effective correlation measure to evaluate the relatedness between the expansion term candidates and the original query terms. The proposed correlation measure is a hybrid of two correlation measures. The first one is considered as an external correlation and it is based on the term co-occurrence, and the second one is considered as an internal correlation and it is based on the term proximity. The hybrid correlation measure gives importance to terms that frequently occur in the same context during the search process. For example, the term 'IJIRR' is often found in the same sites where the words 'Journal', 'IGI Global', and 'Retrieval' occur. The main contributions of our work are the following:

- The adoption of an external correlation measure that evaluates the co-occurrence of the expansion terms candidates with those of the query.
- The adoption of an internal correlation measure that assesses the proximity of the expansion terms candidates with those of the query.

We evaluate our proposed hybrid correlation measure using MEDLINE, a real dataset from a large online medical database. We use Rocchio and Robertson/Sparck Jones (RSJ) methods, two popular query expansion approaches, as the baseline for comparison. The rest of the chapter is organized as follows. In Section 2, we shortly review the related work. In Section 3, we present some background on query expansion. Section 4 discusses the proposed hybrid correlation measure for query expansion. Numerical results are given in Section 5 before we conclude in Section 6.

RELATED WORK

Nowadays, due to the quality of queries submitted by users to search engines which often do not characterize the information needs in a satisfactory manner, retrieving relevant information on the Internet has become a serious problem. To overcome this issue and return more relevant information, Query Expansion (QE) has been introduced. It aims to augment the users' original queries with additional expansion terms in order to enhance the retrieval effectiveness. Selecting the most appropriate and related expansion terms is a challenging task and several techniques have been proposed to address this difficulty. For instance, Pak et al. (2014) suggested a new way of using WordNet, a hand-crafted lexical resource, to select the best expansion terms. The authors used WordNet to choose the candidate expansion terms from a set of pseudo-relevant documents. Abbache et al. (2018) also explored the WordNet resource to return the appropriate expansion terms. The authors used Arabic WordNet and association rules within the Arabic language for query expansion. Colace et al. (2015) attempted to use a minimal relevance feedback to expand the initial queries with suitable terms obtained from a method for pairs of words selection based on the probabilistic topic model. Still in the same direction, Singh and Aditi (2015) introduced a hybrid method to select the expansion terms. The authors combined query term co-occurrence and query term contextual information to first select an optimal combination of query terms from a pool of terms obtained from the top retrieved feedback documents using pseudo-relevance feedback based query expansion, and then select the query context related terms using a contextual window based approach. Singh and Aditi (2017) also presented different query expansion terms selection methods. The authors combined different weights scores by using fuzzy rules to drive the weights of the expansion term candidates. Another related work was the one presented in (Lui et al., 2014). In this work, unstructured and structured data were used for enterprise search to find expansion terms that are related to the original query terms. Xu et al. (2016) investigated some learning approaches to choose and refine the expansion terms candidates. In addition, the authors used two labeling strategies and examined the usefulness of several keywords to optimize the proposed approach. A prospect-guided global query expansion strategy using word embeddings is another work that tried to select the relevant expansion terms (Fernandez-Reyes et al., 2018). In this work, the authors explored query-vocabulary semantic closeness in such a way that new expansion terms, semantically related to more relevant topics, are extracted and added in function of the whole query. The authors also included candidates pooling strategies that handle disambiguation problems without using external resources. Wang et al. (2014) sought to improve query expansion and retrieve the best expansion terms in civil aviation emergency domain ontology by considering the taxonomic and non-taxonomic relationships in the domain ontology. To calculate the semantic similarity, the authors employed the distance, the depths and the semantic sharing degree for the taxonomic relationships, and they used object properties for the non-taxonomic relationships. Zingla et al. (2018) investigated how external resources can be combined to association rules mining in order to improve expansion terms generation and selection. The authors proposed statistical, semantic and conceptual methods to generate new related terms for a given query, and introduced a new similarity measure to compute the relatedness between the original query and the expansion term candidates.

Contrary to previous works, we propose to adopt and combine two correlation measures to evaluate the expansion terms candidates. The first correlation measure is considered as an external correlation and it is based on the term co-occurrence, and the second one is considered as an internal correlation and it is based on the term proximity.

QUERY EXPANSION

The main goal of information retrieval is to find among the huge amount of data those that fulfill the user needs. Query Expansion is one of the most successful techniques for information retrieval. QE starts by running an initial search on the original query q to retrieve the pseudo-relevant documents. The pseudo-relevant documents are ranked using a document-scoring function denoted by *Score (q, d)*. One popular document-scoring function has been discussed within Okapi BM25 model and is given by Equation 1:

$$Score_{BM25}(d,q) = \sum_{t_i \in q} w_i^{BM25} \tag{1}$$

where, w_i^{BM25}, the weight of a given term t_i in a document d;

$$w_i^{BM25} = \frac{tf}{k_1\left[(1-b) + b\dfrac{dl}{avdl}\right] + tf} w_i^{RSJ} \tag{2}$$

where:

tf, is the frequency of the term t_i in a document d;
k_1, is a constant;
b, is a constant;
dl, is the document length;
avdl, is the average of document length;
w_i^{RSJ}, is the well-known Robertson/Sparck Jones weight (Robertson & Jones, 1976). It is calculated using Equation 3:

$$w_i^{RSJ} = \log\frac{(r_i + 0.5)(N - R - n_i + r_i + 0.5)}{(n_i + r_i + 0.5)(R - r_i + 0.5)} \tag{3}$$

where:

N, is the number of documents in the whole collection;

n_i, is the number of documents in the collection containing t_i;

R, is the number of documents judged relevant;

r_i, is the number of judged relevant documents containing t_i.

The RSJ weight can be used with or without relevance information. In the absence of relevance information, the weight is reduced to a form of classical *IDF*:

$$w_i^{IDF} = \log \frac{\left(N - n_i + 0.5 \right)}{\left(n_i + 0.5 \right)} \tag{4}$$

The final BM25 term-weighting function is therefore given by:

$$w_i^{BM25} = \frac{tf}{k_1 \left[\left(1 - b \right) + b \dfrac{dl}{avdl} \right] + tf} * \log \frac{N - n_i + 0.5}{n_i + 0.5} \tag{5}$$

QE then selects the suitable expansion terms from the pseudo-relevant documents and ranks them using a term-scoring function. Among the most successful term-scoring functions are Robertson/Sparck Jones term-ranking function (Equation 3) and Rocchio weight (Rocchio, 1971) given by Equation 6:

$$w_i^{Rocchio} = \sum_{d \in R} w_i^{BM25} \tag{6}$$

where, R, is a set of pseudo-relevant documents.

Finally, QE expands the original query with the top-ranked expansion terms and runs a second search with the expended query using the above document-scoring function.

TERM CO-OCCURRENCE AND TERM PROXIMITY FOR QUERY EXPANSION

The main goal of the proposed method is to return only the documents that are relevant to the given query. For this reason, we introduce the concept of term co-occurrence and term proximity during the search process. This concept is based, at first, on finding for each query term q_i the locations where it appears and then selecting, from these locations, the terms which frequently co-occur with that query term. To put it simply, we recover for each query term q_i the documents where it appears, and then assess the relevance of the terms contained in these documents with respect to the query term qi on the basis of:

- The co-occurrence, which gives value to words that appear in the largest possible number of those documents.
- The proximity, which gives value to words in which the distance separating them and the query term q_i within a document, is small.

Figure 1. The proposed approach for query expansion

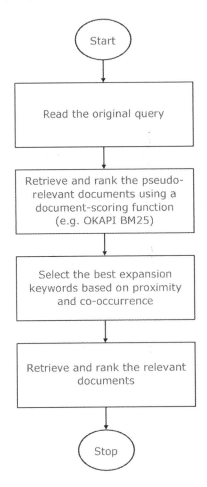

These words are then sorted on the basis of their relevance to the whole query and the top ranked ones are added to that query in order to repeat the search process. Figure 1 describes the proposed approach for query expansion.

As mentioned previously, we will find, in the first step, the terms which often appear together with the query terms. Finding these words is done by assigning more importance to words that occur in the largest number of documents where each term of the query appears. We interpret this importance via the measurement of the external correlation of each term $t_i \in V_R$ to each term $t_{j(q)}$ of the query q.

This correlation, which does not take into consideration the content of documents, computes the rate of appearance of t_i with $t_{j(q)}$ in the set of documents R. The external correlation of t_i to $t_{j(q)}$ is significant when t_i appears in the largest number of documents in which $t_{j(q)}$ occurs, and vice versa. Based on this interpretation, the external correlation *ext* of t_i to $t_{j(q)}$ is calculated using the Good Turing Discounting, as follows:

$$ext\left(t_i, t_{j_{(q)}}\right) = P\left(t_i \mid t_{j_{(q)}}\right) = \frac{1}{C\left(t_{j_{(q)}}\right)}\left[\left(C\left(t_i, t_{j_{(q)}}\right) + 1\right)\frac{N_{C+1}}{N_C}\right] \tag{7}$$

where:

$P(t_i|t_{j(q)})$, is the Good Turing probability that t_i appears with $t_{j(q)}$ in R;

$C(t_{j(q)})$, is the number of times that $T_{j(q)}[k] \neq 0$, where $k=1,...,|R|$ (i.e. the number of documents where $t_{j(q)}$ occurs in R);

$C(t_i, t_{j(q)})$, is the number of times that $(T_{j(q)}[k], T_i[k]) \neq 0$, where $k=1,...,|R|$ (i.e., the number of documents where t_i and $t_{j(q)}$ occur together in R);

N_{C+1}, is the number of pairs of terms which include $t_{j(q)}$ and occur $C+1$ time in R;

N_C, is the number of pairs of terms which include $t_{j(q)}$ and occur C time in R.

The total external correlation between a given term t_i and the query q is then estimated as follows:

$$ext\left(t_i, q\right) = \sum_{t_{j_{(q)}} \in q} ext\left(t_i, t_{j_{(q)}}\right) \tag{8}$$

The Good Turing Discounting (GTD) has been widely used for computing the probability of a complete string of words or giving probabilistic prediction of what the next word will be in a sentence. Practically, the GTD has been involved to assign a non-zero probability to sequences of N words (N-grams) with zero or low counts by looking at the number of N-grams with higher counts (Jurafsky & Martin, 2009).

Our dependence on good Turing Discounting comes to solve the problem that was encountered, in our previous works, when we applied the classical conditional probability to calculate the rate of appearance of a given term to another term. The main problem raised by the use of the conditional probability is that the words, originally with a low frequency of occurrence, were neglected and their rates of appearance with words were automatically decreased. The omission of words with a low frequency applies the omission of words which have been mentioned previously (first occurrences of rare personal names and place names, abbreviations, acronyms, etc.). For this reason, we decided to use the Good Turing Discounting to avoid dropping words by re-estimating their low-probabilities, or rather; by re-evaluating and improving their low appearance rates.

In the second step, we will find the terms which are often neighbors to the query terms. Therefore, we attribute more importance to terms having a short correlation with the query keywords. We interpret this importance via the measurement of the internal correlation between each term t_i of V_R and each term $t_{j(q)}$ of the query q. This correlation computes the correlation between t_i and $t_{j(q)}$ within a given document d_k in terms of the number of words separating them. The more t_i is close to $t_{j(q)}$, the greater is its internal correlation. We used the well-known kernel functions to measure the internal correlation:

Gaussian kernel:

$$K(i,j) = \exp\left[\frac{-(i-j)^2}{2\sigma^2}\right]$$

(9)

Triangle kernel:

$$K(i,j) = \begin{cases} 1 - \dfrac{|i-j|}{\sigma} & \textit{if } |i-j| \leq \sigma \\ 0 & \textit{otherwise} \end{cases}$$

(10)

Cosine kernel:

$$K(i,j) = \begin{cases} \dfrac{1}{2}\left[1 + \cos\left(\dfrac{|i-j|\,\pi}{\sigma}\right)\right] & \textit{if } |i-j| \leq \sigma \\ 0 & \textit{otherwise} \end{cases}$$

(11)

σ, is a parameter to be tuned.

The internal correlation *int* between t_i and $t_{j(q)}$ within a given document d_k is then calculated as follows:

$$\mathrm{int}\left(t_i, t_{j(q)}\right)_{d_k} = K(i,j)$$

(12)

where, *i* (resp. *j*), is the position of the term t_i (resp. $t_{j(q)}$) in *d*.

The terms t_i and $t_{j(q)}$ may appear more than once in a document *d*. Therefore, the internal distance between the term pair $(t_i, t_{j(q)})$ is estimated by summing all possible *int* between t_i and $t_{j(q)}$. Thus, the preceding Formula becomes:

$$\mathrm{int}\left(t_i, t_{j(q)}\right)_{d_k} = \sum_{occ(t_i, t_{j(q)})} K(i,j)$$

(13)

where, $occ(t_i, t_{j(q)})$, is the number of appearance of the term pair $(t_i, t_{j(q)})$ in the document *d*.

The average internal correlation between t_i and $t_{j(q)}$ in the whole *R* is then determined as follows:

$$\text{int}\left(t_i, t_{j_{(q)}}\right) = \frac{1}{C\left(t_{j_{(q)}}\right)} \sum_{d_k \in R} \text{int}\left(t_i, t_{j_{(q)}}\right)_{d_k} \tag{14}$$

The following Formula calculates the total internal correlation between a given term t_i and the query q:

$$\text{int}\left(t_i, q\right) = \sum_{j_{(q)} \in q} \text{int}\left(t_i, t_{j_{(q)}}\right) \tag{15}$$

Finally, in order to compute the total correlation *Dist*, the values of *ext* and *int* were normalized between 0 and 1. The overall correlation between t_i and q is obtained using the following Formula:

$$Dist(t_i, q) = \lambda ext(t_i, q) + (1 - \lambda) int(t_i, q) \tag{16}$$

where, λ, is a parameter to adjust the balance between the external and internal correlations ($\lambda \in [0,1]$).

Using Formula (17), we evaluate the relevance of each term $t \in V_R$ with respect to the query q. Then we rank the terms on the basis of their relevance and add the top ranked ones to the original query q. Finally, we retrieve the relevant documents using the above document-scoring function, presented in Section 3, as follows:

$$Score_{BM25}\left(d, q'\right) = \sum_{t_i \in q} w_i^{BM25} * \beta \tag{17}$$

where, q', is the expanded query;

$$\beta = \begin{cases} 1 & if\ t_i \in q, \\ Dist(t_i, q) & else. \end{cases}$$

EXPERIMENTS

To evaluate the effectiveness of the proposed approach, we performed a set of experiments. First, we describe the dataset, the software, and the effectiveness measures used. Then, we present the experimental results.

Dataset

The MEDLINE database was used to perform extensive experiments. The collection contains 348 566 references from MEDLINE, the on-line medical database, consisting of titles and/or abstracts from 270 medical journals over a five-year period (1987-1991). The available fields are title, abstract, MeSH in-

Table 1. Characteristics of the sub-collections used for evaluating the proposed approach

Size of the collection	(#docs)	50000	100000	150000	200000	250000	300000
	(Mb)	26.39	52.36	80.72	107.58	135.05	164.31
Size of dictionary		81937	120825	156009	184514	211504	237889

dexing terms, author, source, and publication type. Furthermore, the collection contains a set of queries, and relevance judgments.

In these experiments, the MEDLINE dataset was divided into 6 sub-collections. Each sub-collection has been represented by a set of documents, queries, and a list of relevance documents. Table 1 describes the characteristics of each sub-collection in terms of the number of documents (docs) it include, the size of the sub-collection, and the number of words in the vocabulary (dictionary).

Regarding the queries, the MEDLINE collection includes 106 queries. Each query is accompanied by a set of relevance judgments chosen from the whole collection of documents. Dividing the collection of documents into sub-collections implies the decrease in the number of relevant documents for each query. In other words, if we have n documents relevant to a given query q with respect to the entire collection, then surely we will have m documents relevant to the same query with respect to one of the sub-collections, where the value of n is certainly greater or equal to the value of m and, the probability of non-existence of any relevant document for a given query could be possible. In this case, in which the value of m is equal to 0, we have removed, for each sub-collection c, every query does not contain any relevant document in c. Table 2 shows the number of queries (*Nb Queries*) for each sub-collection, the average query length in terms of number of words (*Avr Query Len*), the average number of relevant documents (*Avr Rel Doc*).

During the indexing phase, all non-informative words such as prepositions, conjunctions, and pronouns were removed using a stop-word list. Subsequently, the most common morphological and inflectional suffixes were removed by adopting a standard stemming algorithm. Finally, the weights of the words have been computed for each document using the well-known BM25 term weighting presented above.

Software, Effectiveness Measures

All the experiments have been performed on a Sony-Vaio workstation having an Intel i3-2330M/2.20GHz processor, 4GB RAM and running Ubuntu GNU/Linux 12.04. The proposed approach has been implemented in Python. The precision and the Mean Average Precision (MAP) have been used as measures to assess the effectiveness of the systems and to compare their results obtained.

Table 2. Characteristics of the sub-collections used for evaluating the proposed approach

(#docs)	50000	100000	150000	200000	250000	300000
Nb Queries	82	91	95	97	99	101
Avr Rel Doc	4.23	7	10.94	13.78	15.5	19.24
Avr Query Len	6.79	6.12	5.68	5.74	5.62	5.51

Results

Before proceeding to compare the performance of the proposed approach with the baseline methods, we fixed the parameter σ of the internal correlation. For this aim, we considered the internal correlation as the total correlation and systematically tested a set of fixed σ values from 1 to 40 in increments of 5. Table 3 presents the precision values after retrieving 5 documents (P@5) and the Mean Average Precision (MAP) reached by the proposed approach, while using the sub-collection of 50000 documents. The number of pseudo-relevant documents (denoted by PSD) was tuned at 10, 20 and 50. Note that for all experiments, the number of expansion terms added to the initial query for the proposed method and the baseline approaches was set to 10, which is a typical choice (Carpineto & Romano, 2012).

As it may be seen from Table 3, the appropriate values for σ which bring the highest performance are 5 (10 out of 18), 10 (9 out of 18), 30 (7 out of 18) and 25 (5 out of 18). In terms of MAP, the best results are obtained for σ=30 in four cases, σ=10 in three cases, σ=5 in one case and σ=25 in one case.

In the first stage of testing, we assessed the effectiveness of our system through the use of only the external correlation, only the internal correlation, and both the external and internal correlations. In this experiment, the parameter σ was fixed to 5 and the number of pseudo-relevant documents (PSD) was set at 10. Table 4 and Table 5 present, for each sub-collection, the precision values reached by the external correlation (EXT), the internal correlation (INT), and both the external and internal correlations (EXT/INT) after retrieving 5 and 10 documents, respectively. The *Rate* in Tables 4 and 5 is the percentage of precision improvement of EXT/INT over EXT and INT.

Table 3. The best performance of the proposed approach for different σ

Kernel	PSD	σ	1	5	10	15	20	25	30	35	40
Gaussian	10	P@5	0.1560	**0.1682**	**0.1682**	0.1658	0.1658	0.1658	0.1658	0.1658	0.1658
		MAP	0.2207	0.2253	**0.2265**	0.2231	0.2230	0.2230	0.2230	0.2230	0.2230
	20	P@5	0.1609	**0.1682**	**0.1682**	**0.1682**	**0.1682**	**0.1682**	**0.1682**	**0.1682**	**0.1682**
		MAP	0.2208	0.2252	**0.2255**	0.2245	0.2245	0.2245	0.2245	0.2245	0.2245
	50	P@5	0.1609	**0.1682**	0.1658	0.1658	**0.1682**	**0.1682**	**0.1682**	**0.1682**	**0.1682**
		MAP	0.2193	**0.2241**	0.2231	0.2228	0.2235	0.2233	0.2233	0.2233	0.2233
Triable	10	P@5	0.1609	**0.1707**	0.1682	0.1634	0.1682	0.1682	0.1682	0.1682	0.1682
		MAP	0.2110	0.2245	0.2234	0.2250	0.2257	0.2258	**0.2273**	0.2271	0.2252
	20	P@5	0.1609	**0.1731**	0.1682	0.1658	0.1682	0.1682	0.1682	0.1658	0.1658
		MAP	0.2110	0.2235	0.2211	0.2234	0.2249	0.2265	**0.2274**	0.2271	0.2252
	50	P@5	0.1609	**0.1682**	**0.1682**	0.1658	**0.1682**	**0.1682**	0.1658	0.1634	0.1634
		MAP	0.2110	0.2200	0.2200	0.2235	0.2248	0.2252	**0.2259**	0.2255	0.2235
Cosine	10	P@5	0.1609	**0.1682**	**0.1682**	0.1658	**0.1682**	**0.1682**	**0.1682**	**0.1682**	0.1658
		MAP	0.2110	0.2248	0.2255	0.2249	0.2264	0.2261	**0.2278**	0.2255	0.2232
	20	P@5	0.1609	**0.1707**	**0.1707**	0.1682	0.1658	0.1658	0.1658	0.1682	0.1682
		MAP	0.2110	0.2239	0.2229	0.2251	0.2255	**0.2267**	0.2251	0.2255	0.2247
	50	P@5	0.1609	**0.1682**	**0.1682**	0.1658	0.1658	0.1658	0.1658	0.1658	0.1658
		MAP	0.2110	0.2253	**0.2265**	0.2231	0.2230	0.2230	0.2230	0.2230	0.2230

Through Table 4, we can see obviously that EXT/INT produces the highest P@5 values for all sub-collections and achieves highly significant improvement over EXT, INT(Gaussian), INT(Triangle) and INT(Cosine), e.g. on the 300000 sub-collection, there was an improvement (by EXT/INT(Triangle)) of 7.75% over EXT, 2.48% over INT(Gaussian), 4.17% over INT(Triangle) and 4.17% over INT(Cosine). Similarly, relevance precision at 10 retrieved documents improves from 0.1970 (+6.04%), 0.2009 (+3.98%), 0.2059 (+1.46%) and 0.2069 (+0.97%) to 0.2089 over EXT, INT(Gaussian), INT(Triangle) and INT(Cosine), respectively.

Table 4. Comparing the effectiveness of EXT/INT, EXT and INT in terms of precision (P@5)

#docs		EXT/INT			EXT	INT		
		Gaussian	Triangle	Cosine		Gaussian	Triangle	Cosine
100000	P@5	0.1979	0.1845	0.1846	0.1626	0.1758	0.1736	0.1692
	Rate	Gaussian			**+21.65%**	+12.51%	**+13.94%**	**+16.90%**
			Triangle		+13.47%	+4.95%	+6.28%	+9.04%
				Cosine	+13.53%	+5.01%	+6.34%	+9.10%
200000	P@5	0.2432	0.2453	0.2432	0.2164	0.2164	0.2226	0.2247
	Rate	Gaussian			+12.38%	+12.38%	+9.25%	+8.23%
			Triangle		+13.35%	**+13.35%**	+10.20%	+9.17%
				Cosine	+12.38%	+12.38%	+9.25%	+8.23%
300000	P@5	0.2435	0.2475	0.2475	0.2297	0.2415	0.2376	0.2376
	Rate	Gaussian			+6.01%	+0.83%	+2.48%	+2.48%
			Triangle		+7.75%	+2.48%	+4.17%	+4.17%
				Cosine	+7.75%	+2.48%	+4.17%	+4.17%

Table 5. Comparing the effectiveness of EXT/INT, EXT and INT terms of precision (P@10)

#docs		EXT/INT			EXT	INT		
		Gaussian	Triangle	Cosine		Gaussian	Triangle	Cosine
100000	P@10	0.1417	0.1406	0.1406	0.1296	0.1351	0.1351	0.1351
	Rate	Gaussian			**+9.34%**	+4.89%	+4.89%	+4.89%
			Triangle		+8.49%	+4.07%	+4.07%	+4.07%
				Cosine	+8.49%	+4.07%	+4.07%	+4.07%
200000	P@10	0.1979	0.1979	0.1979	0.1835	0.1824	0.1824	0.1835
	Rate	Gaussian			+7.85%	**+8.50%**	+7.41%	**+7.85%**
			Triangle		+7.85%	**+8.50%**	**+8.50%**	**+7.85%**
				Cosine	+7.85%	**+8.50%**	**+8.50%**	**+7.85%**
300000	P@10	0.2099	0.2089	0.2079	0.1970	0.2009	0.2059	0.2069
	Rate	Gaussian			+6.55%	+4.48%	+1.94%	+1.45%
			Triangle		+6.04%	+3.98%	+1.46%	+0.97%
				Cosine	+5.53%	+3.38%	+0.97%	+0.48%

Table 6. Comparing the effectiveness of EXT/INT, EXT and INT methods in terms of MAP

#docs		EXT/INT			EXT	INT		
		Gaussian	Triangle	Cosine		Gaussian	Triangle	Cosine
100000	MAP	0.1823	0.1781	0.1791	0.1658	0.1686	0.1719	0.1713
	Rate	Gaussian			+9.95%	+8.13%	+6.05%	+6.42%
			Triangle		+7.42%	+5.63%	+3.61%	+3.97%
				Cosine	+8.02%	+6.23%	+4.19%	+4.55%
200000	MAP	0.1663	0.1684	0.1686	0.1549	0.1531	0.1535	0.1537
	Rate	Gaussian			+7.36%	+8.62%	+8.34%	+8.20%
			Triangle		+8.72%	+9.99%	+3.90%	+9.56%
				Cosine	+8.84%	+10.12%	+9.84%	+9.69%
300000	MAP	0.1617	0.1607	0.1607	0.1556	0.1554	0.1526	0.1527
	Rate	Gaussian			+3.92%	+4.05%	+5.96%	+5.89%
			Triangle		+3.28%	+3.41%	+5.31%	+5.24%
				Cosine	+3.28%	+3.41%	+5.31%	+5.24%

In terms of Mean Average Precision (MAP), we observe once again that the suggested approach EXT/INT reports the best results in all the sub-collections (Table 6), e.g. on the 300000 sub-collection, EXT/INT using Gaussian function outperforms EXT, INT(Gaussian), INT(Triangle) and INT(Cosine), around 3%, 4%, 5% and 5%, respectively.

In the second set of experiments, we evaluated and compared the results of the suggested approach (EXT/INT), which use both the external and internal correlations, with those of RSJ (Robertson/Sparck Jones algorithm for Relevance Feedback) and Rocchio (Rocchio approach for Relevance Feedback); where we computed the precision values after retrieving 5 and 10 documents. In the following experiments, the parameters σ and PSD were set to 5 and 10, respectively. Figure 2 and Figure 3 show the precision values for the EXT/INT, the RSJ and the Rocchio techniques after retrieving 5 and 10 documents, respectively.

From Figure. 2, we can see an obvious superiority of the suggested approach EXT/INT compared with the Rocchio, and this superiority was more significant in comparison to the RSJ technique. It is clearly seen from Figure 2 that the proposed approach managed to improve the search results, after retrieving 5 documents, in all the sub-collections compared with the state-of-the-art methods, e.g. on the 300000 sub-collection, EXT/INT using Cosine shows greater improvement of 42.08% over RSJ and 22.59% over Rocchio. Despite the superiority shown in Figure 3, the results were not similar to those observed in Figure 2, however, the precision values of the proposed approach were the best in all the sub-collections.

Through Table 4 and Figure 2 we can conclude that the proposed method EXT/INT, compared with the rest of the search techniques, succeeded to improve the ranking of the relevant documents and made them in the first place. The precision values of the suggested system, after retrieving 5 documents, show a clear and significant superiority in front of each of EXT, INT, RSJ and Rocchio techniques, and this confirms the effectiveness of the EXT/INT approach.

In the next phase of testing, we computed the Mean Average Precision score to evaluate the retrieval performance of the EXT/INT and the Relevance Feedback methods (Figure 4). The parameters σ and

Figure 2. Comparing the performance of EXT/INT, RSJ and Rocchio methods in terms of precision (P@5)

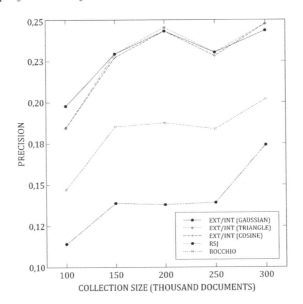

PSD were set to 5 and 10, respectively. Therefore, we used the two-tailed t-test to measure the statistical significance of differences between the MAP values.

Figure 4 shows a clear advantage of the EXT/INT approach compared to the RSJ and Rocchio approaches. The improvements over RSJ and Rocchio are statistically significant in 25 out of 30 cases ($p <$ 0.05), and 30 out of 30 improvements are positive; e.g. on the 300000 sub-collection, EXT/INT(Gaussian) outperforms RSJ by 20.31% ($p = 0.0237$) and Rocchio by 21.31% ($p = 0.0181$) while EXT/INT(Triangle) and EXT/INT(Cosine) outperform RSJ by 19.57% ($p = 0.0339$), 19.95% ($p = 0.0339$) and Rocchio by 20.56% ($p=0.0295$), 20.56% ($p=0.0295$), respectively.

In the final set of experiments, we proposed to compare the performance of EXT/INT with RSJ and Rocchio techniques while varying the values of σ and PSD. As a first step, we started by changing the value of σ from 5 to 30 and maintained the parameter PSD constant at 10 (see Figure 5). In the second step, we fixed σ at 5 and changed the value of PSD to 20 and, 50 (see Figure 6 and Figure 7). We also compared EXT/INT with RSJ and Rocchio while changing the number of expansion terms from 10 to 5 and maintained PSD and σ constant at 5 and 10, respectively (see Figure 8).

Once again, the proposed approach EXT/INT achieved a better effectiveness performance than the others, even though the number of pseudo-relevant documents PSD, the parameter σ and the number of extra terms were varied. In terms of precision, the EXT/INT results were the best among the two retrieval methods in all the sub-collections and in terms of MAP, EXT/INT performs statistically significantly better than RSJ and Rocchio in a considerable number of cases.

CONCLUSION

In this work, we propose a new robust and effective correlation measure to evaluate the relatedness between the expansion term candidates and the original query terms. The proposed correlation measure

Figure 3. Comparing the performance of EXT/INT, RSJ and Rocchio methods in terms of precision (P@10)

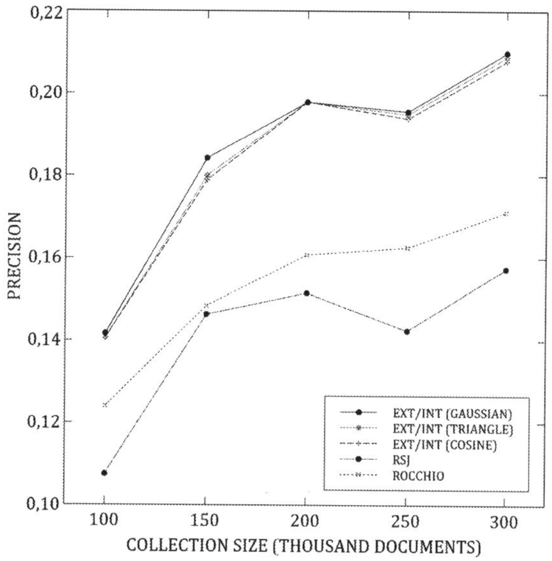

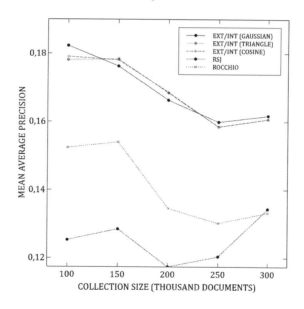

Figure 4. Mean Average Precision (MAP) results of EXT/INT, RSJ and Rocchio

is a hybrid of two correlation measures. The first correlation is considered as an external correlation. It involves the Good Turing probability to compute the term co-occurrence. The second correlation is considered as an internal correlation. It employs the well-known kernel functions to calculate the term proximity.

We thoroughly tested our approach using the MEDLINE test collection. The experimental results show that the proposed approach EXT/INT succeeds to improve the ranking of the relevant documents

Figure 5. Comparing the performance of EXT/INT, RSJ and Rocchio methods (σ=30)

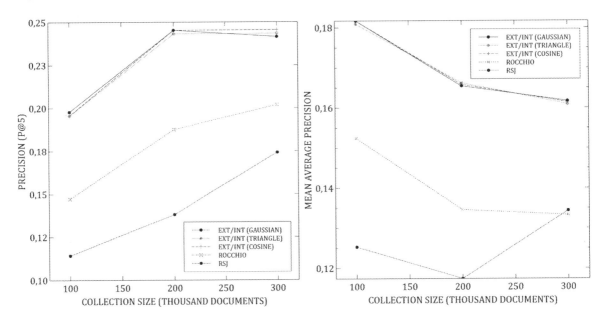

Figure 6. Precision and MAP results of EXT/INT, RSJ and Rocchio, PSD=20

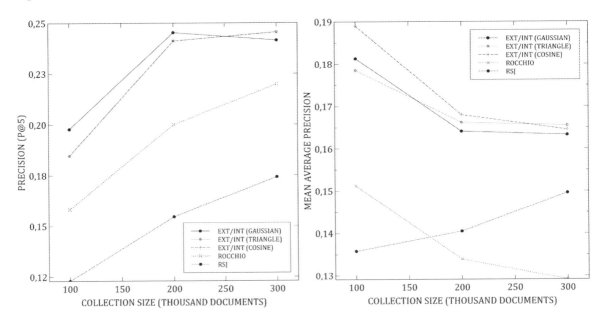

and yields a substantial enhancement in terms of precision (up to 77% over the RSJ approach, and 34% over the Rocchio method) and mean average precision (up to 45% over the RSJ approach, and 25% over the Rocchio method).

Figure 7. Precision and MAP results of EXT/INT, RSJ and Rocchio, PSD=50

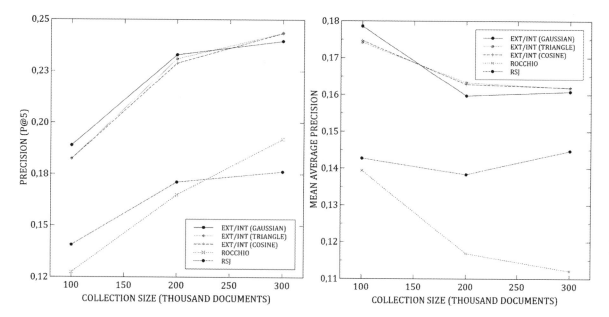

Figure 8. Comparing the performance of EXT/INT, RSJ and Rocchio

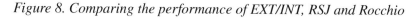
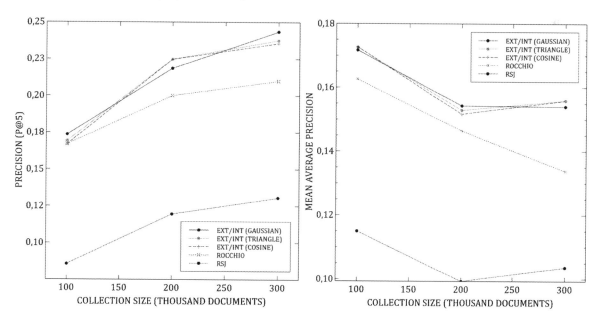

Even though the proposed method performs extremely well, there are some remaining issues that need to be investigated further. One limitation of this work is the use of a single test collection. The other one is that the semantic aspect of terms was not exploited in order to improve the retrieval effectiveness.

REFERENCES

Abbache, A., Meziane, F., Belalem, G., & Belkredim, F. Z. (2018). Arabic query expansion using Word-Net and association rules. In *Information Retrieval and Management: Concepts, Methodologies, Tools, and Applications* (pp. 1239–1254). Hershey, PA: IGI Global. doi:10.4018/978-1-5225-5191-1.ch054

Ahmad, F., & Kondrak, G. (2005). Learning a spelling error model from search query logs. In *Proceedings of the Conference on Human Language Technology and Empirical Methods in Natural Language Processing* (pp. 955-962). Stroudsburg, PA: ACL. 10.3115/1220575.1220695

Al Kabary, I., & Schuldt, H. (2014). Enhancing sketch-based sport video retrieval by suggesting relevant motion paths. In *Proceedings of the 37th international ACM SIGIR conference on Research & development in information retrieval* (pp. 1227-1230). New York: ACM. 10.1145/2600428.2609551

Carpineto, C., & Romano, G. (2012). A survey of automatic query expansion in information retrieval. *ACM Computing Surveys*, *44*(1), 1–50. doi:10.1145/2071389.2071390

Chen, Q., Li, M., & Zhou, M. (2007). Improving query spelling correction using web search results. In *Proceedings of the 2007 Joint Conference on Empirical Methods in Natural Language Processing and Computational Natural Language Learning* (pp. 181-189). Stroudsburg, PA: ACL.

Colace, F., De Santo, M., Greco, L., & Napoletano, P. (2015). Weighted word pairs for query expansion. *Information Processing & Management*, *51*(1), 179–193. doi:10.1016/j.ipm.2014.07.004

Eisenstein, J., O'Connor, B., Smith, N. A., & Xing, E. P. (2012). Mapping the geographical diffusion of new words. *Workshop on Social Network and Social Media Analysis: Methods, Models and Applications*.

Fernández-Reyes, F. C., Hermosillo-Valadez, J., & Montes-y-Gómez, M. (2018). A prospect-guided global query expansion strategy using word embeddings. *Information Processing & Management*, *54*(1), 1–13. doi:10.1016/j.ipm.2017.09.001

Gao, K., Zhang, Y., Zhang, D., & Lin, S. (2013). Accurate off-line query expansion for large-scale mobile visual search. *Signal Processing*, *93*(8), 2305–2315. doi:10.1016/j.sigpro.2012.10.011

Khennak, I., & Drias, H. (2017). Bat-Inspired Algorithm Based Query Expansion for Medical Web Information Retrieval. *Journal of Medical Systems*, *41*(2), 34. doi:10.100710916-016-0668-1 PMID:28054196

Lee, A., & Chau, M. (2011). The impact of query suggestion in e-commerce websites. In *Workshop on E-Business* (pp. 248-254). Berlin: Springer.

Leturia, I., Gurrutxaga, A., Areta, N., Alegria, I., & Ezeiza, A. (2013). Morphological query expansion and language-filtering words for improving Basque web retrieval. *Language Resources and Evaluation*, *47*(2), 425–448. doi:10.100710579-012-9208-x

Liu, X., Chen, F., Fang, H., & Wang, M. (2014). Exploiting entity relationship for query expansion in enterprise search. *Information Retrieval*, *17*(3), 265–294. doi:10.100710791-013-9237-0

Pal, D., Mitra, M., & Datta, K. (2014). Improving query expansion using WordNet. *Journal of the Association for Information Science and Technology*, *65*(12), 2469–2478. doi:10.1002/asi.23143

Park, J. H., & Croft, W. B. (2015). Using key concepts in a translation model for retrieval. In *Proceedings of the 38th International ACM SIGIR Conference on Research and Development in Information Retrieval* (pp. 927-930). New York: ACM. 10.1145/2766462.2767768

Robertson, S. E., & Jones, K. S. (1976). Relevance weighting of search terms. *Journal of the American Society for Information Science, 27*(3), 129–146. doi:10.1002/asi.4630270302

Rocchio, J. J. (1971). Relevance feedback in information retrieval. In G. Salton (Ed.), *The Smart retrieval system - experiments in automatic document processing* (pp. 313–323). Englewood Cliffs, NJ: Prentice-Hall.

Singh, J., & Sharan, A. (2015). Context window based co-occurrence approach for improving feedback based query expansion in information retrieval. *International Journal of Information Retrieval Research, 5*(4), 31–45. doi:10.4018/IJIRR.2015100103

Singh, J., & Sharan, A. (2017). A new fuzzy logic-based query expansion model for efficient information retrieval using relevance feedback approach. *Neural Computing & Applications, 28*(9), 2557–2580. doi:10.100700521-016-2207-x

Subramaniam, L. V., Roy, S., Faruquie, T. A., & Negi, S. (2009). A survey of types of text noise and techniques to handle noisy text. In *Proceedings of the 3rd Workshop on Analytics for Noisy Unstructured Text Data* (pp. 115-122). New York: ACM. 10.1145/1568296.1568315

Sun, H. M. (2010). A study of the features of internet English from the linguistic perspective. *Studies in Literature and Language, 1*(7), 98–103.

Wang, H., Fan, H., Li, J., & Wang, J. (2014). Research on the method of semantic query expansion in civil aviation emergency domain ontology. International Journal of Digital Content Technology and its Applications, 8(5), 128.

Williams, H. E., & Zobel, J. (2005). Searchable words on the web. *International Journal on Digital Libraries, 5*(2), 99–105. doi:10.100700799-003-0050-z

Xie, H., Zhang, Y., Tan, J., Guo, L., & Li, J. (2014). Contextual query expansion for image retrieval. *IEEE Transactions on Multimedia, 16*(4), 1104–1114. doi:10.1109/TMM.2014.2305909

Xu, B., Lin, H., & Lin, Y. (2016). Assessment of learning to rank methods for query expansion. *Journal of the Association for Information Science and Technology, 67*(6), 1345–1357. doi:10.1002/asi.23476

Zingla, M. A., Latiri, C., Mulhem, P., Berrut, C., & Slimani, Y. (2018). Hybrid query expansion model for text and microblog information retrieval. *Information Retrieval Journal, 21*(4), 337–367. doi:10.100710791-017-9326-6

Chapter 2
Uncertain Confidence Network–Based Collaborative Information Retrieval Relevance Feedback Algorithm

Fatiha Naouar
MARS Research Laboratory, Tunisia

Lobna Hlaoua
MARS Research Laboratory, Tunisia

Mohamed Nazih Omri
ⓘ https://orcid.org/0000-0001-7803-0179
MARS Research Laboratory, Tunisia

ABSTRACT

Collaborative retrieval allows increasing the amount of relevant information found and sharing history with others. The collaborative retrieval can reduce the retrieval time performed by the users of the same profile. This chapter proposes a new relevance feedback algorithm to collaborative information retrieval based on a confidence network, which performs propagation relevance between annotations terms. The main contribution in this work is the extraction of relevant terms to reformulate the initial user query considering the annotations as an information source. The proposed model introduces the concept of necessity that allows determining the terms that have strong association relationships estimated to the measure of a confidence. Since the user is overwhelmed by a variety of contradictory annotations, another contribution consists of determining the relevant annotations for a given evidence source. The experimental study gives very encouraging results.

DOI: 10.4018/978-1-7998-1021-6.ch002

INTRODUCTION

The optimization of retrieval time may be caused by the formulation of collaborative queries the through dialogue and the mutual consultation of queries sent and the search results received by everyone. It also enables the sharing of search history by displaying the search results put in order by relevance. One of the most popular tools for sharing results and personal judgments is the annotations. Several problems exist with respect to Collaborative Retrieval (hereafter CR). There is, in particular, the problem of the relevance of information. Indeed, a user always finds problems in meeting his/her needs in relevant information.

As in classical Information Retrieval (hereafter IR), the Collaborative Information Retrieval (hereafter CIR) is designed to return and display a set of documents to a user according to his need. On the other hand, the users of a retrieval system, are not always specialists in this field (Lin & Wang, 2006), they can make a bad choice of terms to express its information needs. A reformulation of query has been necessary, since the initial user query can return unsatisfactory results. It's a question then of amending the original user query and this happens by adding meaningful terms to improve the initial result returned. Three types of approaches use different techniques to select the terms to be added to a query. The difference between these algorithms is based on the choice of terms to be used to reformulate the query. In the first algorithm, the mechanism used allows the user to select the terms that are related to the original query terms. In the second algorithm, the re-injecting of the terms is to be selected from a terminological resource (like semantic network, thesaurus, ontology, ...). While in the third algorithm the terms are selected for a reformulation from the results of previous research (also called relevance feedback).

The first type of algorithm is based on the overall analysis of the collection of documents considered (Baeza-Yates & Ribeiro-Neto., 1999). This algorithm consists of analyzing the entire set of documents, in the collection, to extract relevant terms to add to the initial query. Two techniques are used: the similarity thesaurus and the statistical thesaurus. The most prevalent technique is based on statistical analysis of query logs (Cui, Wen, Nie & Ma, 2002). The objective is to automatically reformulate a query by adding terms of the documents that are correlated with the query terms. The correlation is based on a conditional probability. The second type of algorithm, in the literature, uses terminology resources such as the anthologies or the thesaurus containing the vocabulary to enrich queries (Abderrahim, 2013; Harb, Khaled & Nagdy, 2011). This type of algorithm uses anthologies with the equivalence relations and the subsumption (Navigli & Velardi, 2003) to find the similar terms to the original query. In (Boughammoura, Omri & Hlaoua, 2011, 2012, 2013) the authors propose a new rendering algorithm of deep Web forms which is easy to interpret by user and reflects the exact meaning of query. The final type of algorithm (Omri, 1994) is based on the principle of relevance feedback which also aims to reformulate an initial query to better reflect the contents of the collection. To do this, the user begins by submitting its initial application to the system that renders a first set of documents that the user must judge as relevant or irrelevant. The judgment of the relevance of the documents initially returned is used to select the terms to add to the original query (Lin & Wang, 2006).

In this context, the authors suggest to improve the research performance, using the relevance feedback to extend the initial query. This technique consists of extracting terms from documents deemed relevant and considered in a new extended query. This technique has been used in classical Information Retrieval (Rocchio. 1971). In their work, Singh and Sharan (2015) considered the retrieved documents, by a first search, the top ranked as relevance feedback. This is achieved by the combination of the two approaches namely, the co-occurrence of initial query terms with the terms constituting the corpus and a contextual window based approach is used to select the terms from the tops feedback documents. The relevance feedback has shown interest also, in the semi-structured and structured Information Retrieval in several works (Hlaoua, 2006; Schenkel & Thbobald, 2005).

In collaborative context, the authors propose to use the annotations as new source of information, because an annotation has a close relationship with the annotated document. It also enriches the document in question with simple terms and nearby terms to the user better that the vocabulary used by the author. However, the research work, which is based on the annotations, can give relatively relevant resulting since the annotations are diverse and can be performed by experts or non-specialist users.

Thus, the relevance feedback, using annotations in a collaborative context, allows us to solve the problems to choice the annotations to consider which carry data, and the extraction of relevant terms, that can be re-injected to expand the query. The authors have focused, in this chapter, on both problems.

To treat annotations, they suggest an annotations' filtering model to determine the relevant annotations and classifying them by grouping the coherent annotations in the same class. The problem of classifying them can be addressed by analyzing the semantic relations between the annotations.

The annotations that are then filtered and classified will considered then as a new source of information for the relevance feedback. They proposed an algorithm based on the confidence for the extraction of relevant terms.

In the next section, the authors present the related works developed to improve the collaborative retrieval. Then, the authors describe their annotation treatment methods for filtering and classification in Section 3. In Section 4, the authors propose and discuss the method of relevance feedback based on a propagation of confidence for the extraction of terms. And in section 5, the authors detail the experimental study and the authors discuss the obtained results. Finally, in Section 6, the authors conclude and propose prospects of their work.

Background

Several research works have been performed to improve the collaborative retrieval systems in the aim of improving the collaborative retrieval, while other several algorithms were proposed and which were based on the context while others were based on the user profile.

Several algorithms have been adopted to improve the retrieval systems, to improve the performance of collaborative retrieval. The authors found systems that have tried to improve the collaboration between the members of the same group during the retrieval process by concentrating on support to the collaboration in the process, while others have tried to maintain the collaboration support when formulating queries by users (Morris & Horvitz, 2007). Other works have tried to create the systems that can support the interactive information and this with introducing new functionalities and supports based both on the Web and on the mobile systems (Shah, Marchionini & Kelly, 2009). These systems should collect useful behavioral data during users' information retrieval process.

In the literature, several algorithms have been based on the context to improve the performances of collaborative retrieval, while others are based on the user's profile.

The context was considered in the different phases of research. It should be mentioned, for example, those who have tried to consider the current search session to help the user to formulate his query or by consider the context in the search process using relevance feedback technique (Lin & Wang, 2006). Other works have tried to consider the context in interactions with the system by identifying the concepts introduced in a query (Lopes, 2013) or by exploitation of the specific area information using the context-based ontology (Mata & Claramunt, 2011; Daoud & Huang 2013). The evaluation of the integration of the context in the retrieval process is considered a major problem. Several works assert that the absence of the user in the evaluation process is one of the problem, while others tried to question the relevance judgments that depend on the state of mind of the user as well as the context and consequently they are not stable and vary in the time (Bouramoul, Kholladi & Doan, 2011; Tamine, Boughanem & Daoud, 2010), and they found that certain criteria are scalable and does not really reflect the context of a user.

Several other works were based on the user profiles to improve collaborative retrieval: the authors find the works of Naderi, Rumpler and Pinon (2007) which considered that the need for a user does not only depend of the query but also on their profile, as its construction and evolution are the problems that has been solved in several researches (Achemoukh & Ahmed-Ouamer, 2012). Several other works have tried to improve the search for users operating a well-defined language. There may be mentioned, for example among the work done to improve the retrieval of the Arabic documents that of Safi (2014) who tried to suggest a method which is based both an ontology and user's profile to provide custom results.

There are several other works in the literature, who tried to solve the problem of the initial query which may be incorrectly typed by the user. The authors found the work of Razan Taher (2004) which proposed a support system that allows the user to reformulate his query basing himself on the document and "feedback" of the collaborative group. In her work, the author has tried to present all the queries and results of the group to construct a query from the queries of others. This model is based on two assumptions. The first hypothesis is to consider that the group members have the same research topic, while the second hypothesis consider the behavior of users: In her work, the author considered that each user must provide an opinion on other users as well as on the documents found. The results found are very dependent on the views of members of the group. Lioma, Moens and Azzopardi (2008) tried to enrich the initial query by adding the terms from the tags extracted from an external source of the document which is the collaborative annotation system online Del.icio.us. For a given query, the Del. icio.us system suggests the most relevant tags. The author used the top n relevant tags returned by the system, and tested her algorithm with 36 queries, but the results obtained did not give any improvement: no significant difference in performance between the initial queries and the extended queries. Naouar, Hlaoua and Omri (2013a) tried to improve the initial user query by the relevance feedback technique. Their algorithm consists in adding the relevant terms co-occurrence based extracts from semi-structured documents. This algorithm has given best results for the top 20 documents returned by the system.

It should be noted that the problem is always a data extraction problem, which has been developed in several works. Also, it can be mentioned the work of Omri (2004; 2012) which is based on flexible systems of the knowledge extraction and is capable of dealing with the vagueness and uncertainty of the extraction process. Other researchers have tried to present the extraction models through integrating statistics and linguistics knowledge (Fkih & Omri, 2012). While other works represent the extraction of information as a technique based on a semantic analysis of a text in the form of ontology or on the detection of opinion by using the scoring extraction technique (Chahal, Singh, & Kumar, 2017; Boudia, Hamou, & Amine, 2016).

In this chapter, the authors propose a new propagation algorithm that reflects the semantic relationships between the terms, to extract the relevant terms of the new source of information which represent a valid annotations for the relevance feedback.

ANNOTATION'S TREATMENT

The electronic documents can be annotated in the same way as the paper documents. The activity of electronic annotation allows users of the same group to act together and this is by critics and taking notes. According to the source of the information used (Mokhtari & Dieng-Kuntz, 2008), the annotation can be done by different ways by the contents of the document or from a source, external to the document. However, the annotation reflects the subjectivity of different people. While annotating a document, users may deviate from the original object while others can express their subjective opinion. Several works have been performed to validate the annotations: the authors can mention the work of Cabanac which tried to evaluate the relevance of an annotation based on opinions expressed in a debate that is based on the concept of "social validation" (Cabanac, 2008). To validate his work, he tried to compare its results with the perceptions of 173 people. So validation always depends on the opinions of the individual who took part in son of the discussion.

Other research work has tried to valid the annotations by the filtering, to extract those which are relevant. the authors can mention the works of Naouar, Hlaoua & Omri (2013b) who considered that an annotation can have a degree of relevance if it brings information to the annotated object. It's considered relevant if it is linked semantically to the original object or other annotations with a non-zero degree of relevance. The author use a probability model based on the conditional probability in which an annotation is considered a probabilistic event. To validate her work, the author considered a set of annotation which can be, not only a commentary on the original document which may be a media object, but also a reaction to previous comments. The semantic relationship translated in a similarity. Their algorithm has shown its interest for top 5 documents returned by the system. In this article the authors opted for this filtering system

Despite the filtering these annotations are always heterogeneous and their number is still high (can reach thousands). The coherent annotations can be grouped in the same class and therefore the extraction of the terms to re-inject can be performed from the annotation classes. The annotations classification method is detailed in the next section.

Classification Mechanism

To classify the relevant annotations, the authors consider that an annotation class can contain the annotations that have strong semantic relationships: more the annotations are coherent more they are considered semantically linked. Several steps are performed for the classification. Initially, the annotations are considered independent. Secondly, a comparison in pairs is performed for these annotations. And in recent times, the authors group the semantically related annotations in the same class. The classes obtained in the previous step will be aggregated according to their semantic relationships two by two.

The authors consider that an annotation class consists of a set of terms $T = \{t_1, t_2, ..., t_n\}$. To give an idea of the representativeness of a term ti of an annotation class, the authors calculate the combination of the factors tf*icf. The term frequencies tf of an annotation class allows determining how much a term is comprehensive while the inverse frequency icf determines how much a term is specific to this class. For each term ti of an annotation class, the authors calculated its number of occurrences in his annotation class and the size of the annotation class (eq. 1).

$$tf\left(t_i, Ca_j\right) = \frac{\sum_{j=1..n} Occ\left(t_i, Ca_j\right)}{size\left(Ca_j\right)} \tag{1}$$

with t_i represents a term of an annotation class and Ca_j represents an annotation class. The value of *icf* for a term t_i in all annotation classes *CA*, is given by the following equation (eq. 2):

$$icf\left(t_i, CA\right) = \log \frac{|CA|}{\left|\left\{ca_j \in CA : t_i \in Ca_i\right\}\right|} \tag{2}$$

with |*CA*| is the cardinality of all classes in the annotation collection and |{$ca_j \in CA : t_i \in Ca_i$}| is the cardinality of the set of annotation classes where the term t_i appears (that is to say $tf(t_i, Ca_j) \neq 0$).

The calculation of *tf * icf* is given by the following equation (eq. 3):

$$tf*icf = tf(t_i, Ca_j)*icf(t_i, CA) \tag{3}$$

After calculating the factor of *tf*icf* for each term t_i of an annotation class Ca_j, the authors propose to move to the grouping of these classes. The grouping of annotation classes is based on the semantic relation between them. In their work, and the authors consider that two annotations are semantically linked if they have a number of common terms higher than a threshold. The algorithm, the classification of annotations, is described below.

Algorithm 1: Classification Annotations' Algorithm

```
Begin Classification
Input:
   N Annotations
Output:
   Annotation Classes  // different classes of annotations
Treatment:
for i from 1 to N-1 do
    for j from i+1 to N do
          for k who browse the terms do
              if t_k ∈ a_i = t_k ∈ a_j then
              if (tf * icf_i (t_k) > threshold) and   (tf * icf_j (t_k) > threshold)
then
                  Ca_1=a_i∪a_j
              Endif
              Endif
          Endfor
      Endfor
Endfor
End Classification
```

After calculating the factor of **tf*icf** for each term **t**$_i$ of an annotation class **Ca**$_j$, the authors move to the grouping of these classes. The grouping of annotation classes is based on the semantic relation between them. In their work, the authors consider that two annotations are semantically linked if they have a number of common terms higher than a threshold. The algorithm the classification of annotations is described below.

After the classification phase, the authors obtain a set of relevant annotations classes that will be the input of their extraction algorithm of relevant terms, which will be detailed in the next sections.

RE-INJECTION OF RELEVANCE BASED ON CONFIDENCE

Motivation

One of the most techniques used in several researches is the relevance feedback. The main object in this paragraph is to show how the authors can extract relevant terms to improve initial user query. For this reason, the authors considered the filtered and classified annotations as a source of information for the reformulation of initial query.

In this chapter, the authors have distinguished two types of terms' membership: those that appear in the title of the document and others in the descriptive part. Intuitively, the authors can see that the terms belonging to the title may be more significant that the terms belonging to the body of the text. In this context, the authors have considered the measure of the possibility theory that is based on the necessity and the possibility. A term is considered necessary to be re-injected if it appears in the title of a document, while it is considered possible to be re-injected if it appears only in the body of a document. This idea was developed in (Naouar, Hlaoua & Omri, 2012) and showed an improvement for the 20 top documents.

To improve the possibilistic algorithm and be examining of the terms of the annotation classes; the authors noticed that many terms semantically related to annotation classes: the term has the high value of necessity and the terms constituting the annotation class. Their proposed model extract the relevant terms of the annotations classes, instead of basing ourselves only on the calculation of the terms frequencies. The authors suggest exploiting the association relationship between these terms. The authors also brought to search the terms that are semantically related with the terms that have the high value of necessity and consider relevant. In the following, the authors propose to exploit the notion of confidence in order to express the semantic relationship between terms.

Proposed Possibilistic Model

By examining the annotations after treatment, the authors can distinguish the terms that appear in the document title. This is why the authors thought to discriminate this appearance type by considering the measure' found in possibility theory. The authors used a model based on a possibilistic network allowing introducing the different relations of dependency detailed in the works of (Naouar, Hlaoua & Omri, 2013a, 2015). In their works, the authors base the necessity of a term by the following definition: A term of the annotation class is considered necessarily to extract if it appears frequently in the titles of the documents. To give meaning of representativeness of a term of an annotation class of a relevant document, the authors used the combination of factors **tf*ief**. Term frequencies of a given document are interesting to measure how an element is comprehensive so that the inverse frequency to measure how a term is specific to the collection.

In their work, the authors have calculated the necessity of a term of an annotation class by the following equation (eq. 4):

$$N(t) = \frac{\sum_{i=1..n} tf\left(t, e_i\right) * ief\left(t, e_i, E_i\right)}{\sum_{i=1..n} tf\left(e_i\right)} \tag{4}$$

with *N(t)* represents the necessity value of the term *t* of an annotation class and the factor *tf*ief* is performed using the equation (eq. 5):

$$tf\text{*}ief(t, e_i, E_i) = tf(t, e_i)\text{*}ief(t, E_i) \tag{5}$$

with *tf (t, e_i)* is given by the following equation (eq. 6):

$$tf\left(t, e_i\right) = \frac{\sum_{i=1..n} Occ\left(t, e_i\right)}{size\left(e_i\right)} \tag{6}$$

with *Occ (t, e_i)* is the occurrence of a term *t* of an annotation class in the element *e_i* and *e_i* represents an element *e_i = {title}*. While the calculation of the value *ief* of the term *t* for all elements *E_i* of the entire collection is made by the equation (eq. 7):

$$ief\left(t_1, E_i\right) = \log \frac{\left|E_i\right|}{1 + \left|\left\{e_i \in E_i : t_1 \in e_i\right\}\right|} \tag{7}$$

The extraction of the terms in the possibility theory has shown improvement for the top 5 documents while the top 10 and the top 20 documents did not improve. To improve the possibilistic algorithm for the top 10 and the top 20 documents returned by the system, and examining the terms of annotation classes, it should be noted that there are relationships between terms constituting the annotation classes, terms belonging title of the document and the terms constituting the initial query of the user. In their work, to extract relevant terms of the classes' annotations instead of relying solely on calculations of the frequency of terms, the authors propose to exploit the association relationship between terms.

Notion of Confidence

The analysis of the extracted terms based on the necessity has shown that these terms can belong to one or more annotations and one or more annotation classes. In addition and by hypothesis, two terms that appear together in the same annotation class can be linked semantically. The semantic relationship between terms is translated by notion of confidence.

The confidence between a term t_i belonging to an annotation class and a term $tNec_j$ necessity-based extract is noted $Conf\,(t_{i\_\to}\,tNec_j)$ allows measuring the conditional probability of t_i knowing $tNec_j$. The calculating of the confidence value between two terms is given by the next equation (eq. 8):

$$Conf\left(t_i \to tNec_j\right) = \frac{Sup\left(t_i \to tNec_j\right)}{\left|tNec_j\right|} \in \left[0,1\right] \tag{8}$$

with $|\,tNec_j\,|$ is the number of annotation class containing the term $tNec_j$, and $Sup\,(t_{i\_\to}\,tNec_j)$ is the degree of support. The rule is considered complete when the confidence value is equal to 1. The support is given by the following equation (eq. 9):

$$Sup(t_i \to tNec_j) = |t_i \wedge tNec_j| \tag{9}$$

with $|\,a\,|$ is the number of the annotation class containing the term a. It is the probability of appearance of all matching the annotation class $t_i \wedge tNec_j$.

Extraction Based on Propagation's Confidence

Their goal is to select the terms semantically related to a relevant term extracted according to the measure of necessity. Consequently, the authors are brought back to propagate the degree of necessity in all terms constituting the annotation classes. The authors then consider that an annotation class Ca_l consists of a set of terms $Ca_l = \{t_1, t_2, ..., t_j\}$. The term $tNec_j$ is considered to be the term most necessary extracted of their possibilistic algorithm (Naouar, Hlaoua & Omri, 2012). For the term extracted by necessity, it will determine its association relationships with all the terms of the annotation class Ca_l. The term t_i that has a strong association relationship with the term $tNec_j$ is considered relevant. An association between two terms t_i and $tNec_j$ is denoted by $t_{i\_\to}\,tNec_j$. This notation means that if $tNec_j$ appears then t_i also appears in the same annotation class (Naouar, Hlaoua & Omri, 2017). The association between terms resulted in confidence and is calculated by the formula (14). The Figure 1 shows a propagation of confidence.

The propagation of confidence between the terms allows constructing a network which the nodes represent the terms and arcs represent relationships between these terms. In their case, the arcs connecting the two terms are weighted by the degree of confidence. In addition, the use of confidence takes into account the terms that do not have a high frequency in an annotation class but that may be, considered relevant. That is to say, in their work, the authors consider relevant the terms, which appear together in an annotation class: the term of the highest degree of necessity and a term belonging to the annotation class although its frequency of co-occurrence may not be high. In this instance, the authors can consider that the terms are semantically related.

The construction of the network takes in input the term extracted by the necessity and by the annotation classes. The association relationships between the terms are determined by the confidence value given in formula (8) between the term most necessary and other terms constituting each annotation class. The authors start with the hypothesis that a term of an annotation class that has strong association relationships with the most necessary term can be considered relevant for the re-injection. An alternative is to

Figure 1 Confidence Propagation

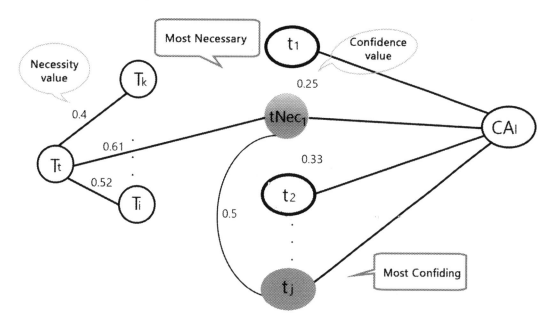

exploit the association relationships between terms by relations of co-occurrence may penalize the terms that do not have a high frequency but which may be relevant (Figure 1).

Then, there is a difference in the importance of the terms for each document and instead of reformulating the initial query of the user with a simple addition of the extracted terms; the authors thought to weigh the terms and this by, therefore, performing a weighted reformulation.

Weighted Reformulation

The rewriting of the query can be done by adding the terms in a simple manner or a weighted manner. To highlight the terms that are representative of the relevant documents, the authors tried to reformulate the original query of the user by re-injecting the relevant terms extracted from valid documents in a weighted manner.

The term weighting is a statistical measure which the principle is based on the hypothesis Luhn (1958): «when an author writes a text, he repeats certain terms to develop an aspect of the subject ». Therefore more works are proposed for the measurement of "important." Among these works are those who are interested in calculating the weight of the terms in an automatic way. A good weight for a term must meet two important factors:

- Completeness: that is to say, the description of the document as complete
- Specificity: that is to say, a better differentiation to distinguish better documents.

Since the scores of the necessity and of the confidence do not reflect the importance of the term, the authors used *tf-idf* for weighting (Robertson & Walker, 1997). The *tf-idf* method takes into account the specificity of a term for a document. It is considered the one of the methods that can satisfy the two aspects. This method is formed by the combination of two main factors: a local weighting factor (*tf*), which determines the local representation of a term in the document, and the second factor of overall weighting (*idf*), which measures the overall representativeness of the term vis-à-vis the collection of documents.

The *tf-idf* measure is given by the next equation (eq. 10):

$$tf - idf(t,d,D) = tf(t,d)*idf(t,D) \tag{10}$$

Since a query is made up of one or more terms. For each query term *t*, the authors can calculate the *tf(t, d)* frequency of occurrence of the term *t* in document *d*. Therefore, *idf(t, D)* represents the frequency documentary for *N* documents constituent the collection are given by the next equation (eq. 11):

$$idf\left(t, D\right) = \log \frac{N}{1 + \left|\left\{d \in D : t \in d\right\}\right|} \tag{11}$$

with *t* represents a term of document *d* and *d* represents the document of the collection *D*.

The inverse document frequency which means that a term is considered relevant for a query is a term that appears in a minimum number of documents in the collection. In this way, it can be concluded that this term is specific to those documents.

EXPERIMENTAL STUDY AND RESULTS' ANALYSIS

In their experimental study, the authors evaluate the different aspects: initially, the authors start with the treatment of annotations. Then the authors will consider these annotations as a source of information to extract the relevant terms using the confidence propagation algorithm. The authors will test their algorithms with the long queries.

Motivation

To proceed to the experimentation, it should be noted that the authors have considered the following assessment environment:

- **A system of collaborative retrieval:** The authors have implemented basic system retrieval. This system uses a collection inspired from the popular and social system "YouTube" and which can provide services through collaborative annotation for multimedia resources.
- **A collection of document:** This is a collection of "YouTube". It will be built by the documents returned by the system itself and that will be indexed for the extraction of the information resources already described in the previous sections.
- A set of 10 queries in various fields and the judgment was performed by students and researchers. For each query typed, the authors consider the annotations of the n top relevant documents returned by the system.

To evaluate their model, the authors used the precision rate for the top 5, 10 and 20 documents using the residual relevance (Chang, Cirillo & Razon, 1971). The use of the residual method can demonstrate the real impact of relevance feedback contrary to the method of "Freezing" which is based on the ranks of the documents in the list of results (Ruthven & Lalmas, 2003). In the residual evaluation, the documents used for the judgment of relevance are removed from the collection. For each query, the number of documents considered is marked until the first relevant document is judged. In what follows, the corresponding test results are based on the residual value.

To evaluate the effectiveness of their algorithm, the authors calculated the improvement rates TA for different query given by the next equation (eq. 12):

$$TA = \frac{newprecision - oldprecision}{oldprecision} \tag{12}$$

TA(5) represents the rate of improvement, to show the importance of the relevance feedback of the top five documents and TA (10) and TA (20) respectively to show the performance of the top 10 and top 20 documents found. The new precision and the old precision are respectively the results of the search after the relevance feedback and the basic results, in the same residual collection.

Impact of the Propagation of Confidence

In this section, the authors study the impact of the criterion of propagation of confidence to extract the weighted terms from the annotation classes filtered according to the equation (10) to be re-injected into the original query. The authors calculated the degree of necessity for each term of an annotations class. Then, the authors determined the weighting values terms having the highest necessity scores.

The propagation of confidence can be determined from a term extracted by the necessity and with a non-zero weight, the term with a strong association relationship of each annotation class. The propagation of confidence can translate semantics between terms. The terms with strong semantic relations, which do not appear already in the initial query will be re-injected to reformulate the initial query of the user. The reformulation is carried out by calculating the weight of all the query terms: the terms of the original query user and the re-injected terms. The table 1 presents the results compared to the basic version.

Table 1. Precision based on necessity and propagation of confidence

Precision and % of Improvement	Number of Documents		
	5	10	20
Base Precision	0.28	0.24	0.22
Inject 1 Term according to Necessity (% improvement)	0.38 (35.71%)	0.34 (41.66%)	0.31 (40.9%)
Inject 2 Terms according to Necessity (% improvement)	0.31 (10.71%)	0.34 (41.66%)	0.32 (45.45%)
Propagation of Confidence (2 Terms) (% improvement)	0.46 (65%)	0.39 (62.5%)	0.34 (54.5%)

Table 2. Recall rate of Confidence Propagation

Recall Rate and % of Improvement	Number of Documents		
	5	10	20
Initial Recall Rate	0.07	0.11	0.16
Recall Rate of Propagation of Confidence (% improvement)	0.16 (129%)	0.23 (109%)	0.30 (87.5%)

Table 3. F-measure of Confidence Propagation

F-Measure and % of Improvement	Number of Documents		
	5	10	20
Base F-Mesure	0.11	0.15	0.19
F-Measure of Propagation of Confidence	0.24	0.30	0.32
(%improvement)	(118%)	(100%)	(68%)

According to Table 1, it should be noted that the obtained *precision* using relevance feedback by propagation of confidence has improved compared to the initial query especially in the top five documents returned. It was able to achieve an average of 0.46 compared to 0.28 using the original query.

The propagation of confidence gave better precision than the addition of a single term. The authors also note that the improvement rate could reach 65% for the top 5 documents and 62.5% for the top 10 documents. The re-injection of the terms based on necessity has improved the initial query but the weighted feedback based on confidence has given a better precision. This may be explained by the fact that the terms extracted by the necessity are all terms of the titles which usually consist of a reduced number of terms. These cannot represent all the terms that may be relevant to the query. What has been solved (see Table 2) by the terms which are linked semantically to them, extracted according to the measure of confidence. To evaluate the performance of their model, the authors have tried to represent in the following table recall rate.

According to Table 2, the authors can see that the recall rate has improved from the initial query compared to the reformulated query. The reformulation performed with the extracts terms to base on the propagation of confidence has an improvement rate equal to 129% for the top 5 documents. Although the *Recall* showed good improvement for the top 20 documents returned by a search and could reach a value of 0.3, while the rate of improvement has not exceeded the 87.5% since the initial recall is high. These notes are confirmed in the table of *F-measure* case. Table 3 presents the *F-measure* of propagation of confidence.

The study of the performance of this propagation according to the *F-measure* could reach a rate equal to 118% for the top 5 documents and 100% for the top 10 documents, as a results returned by the system. This improvement proves the effectiveness of propagation.

Study of the Term Weighting

In this section, the authors will study the impact of term weighting for the rewording of the initial user query. The authors started on the re-injecting of most confident terms by a simple addition to the original

Table 4. Precision of the weighted and the un-weighted reformulation

Precision and % of Improvement	Number of Documents		
	5	10	20
Base Precision	0.28	0.24	0.22
Precision of the Un-Weighted Reformulation	0.37	0.31	0.25
(% improvement)	(32.14%)	(29.16%)	(13.63%)
Precision of the Weighted Reformulation	0.46	0.39	0.34
(% improvement)	(65%)	(62.5%)	(54.5%)

query. Then, the authors calculated the weighting of the original query terms and the terms re-injected. Those had a zero weight will not be rewritten during the reformulation (see Table 4).

From Table 4, it should be noted that the un-weighted reformulation with propagation of confidence could improve initial precision; it could reach a value of 32.14% for the top 5 documents. The weighting of the terms of the initial query and the terms to re-inject and that are extracted on the basis of confidence gave better improvement which is equal to 65% for the top 5 documents and 62.5% for the top 10 documents compared to a rate that has not exceeded 13% for tops the 20 documents for the unweighted reformulation. The authors consider the relevance feedback based on confidence propagation with weighted terms in the rest of their experiments.

Feedback Variation's Study of Several Terms

Although the authors found an improvement with the addition of two terms, and the authors have tried to reformulate the initial query by adding several terms extracted by propagation of confidence. The calculation of the average rate of precision of the reformulation of the query is shown in Table 5.

From Table 5, it is found out that the addition of one, two or three terms improves the initial results. But the best improvement for the top 5, 10 and 20 documents is achieved with the addition of two terms. The accuracy rate could reach a maximum value equal to 0.46 for the top 5 documents returned by the system while it is equal to 0.39 for top 10 and 0.34 for the top 20 documents. The adding of 4 or 5 terms has given a precision of 0.20 for the top 5 documents while the initial precision is 0.28. That can be explained by the fact that the addition of several terms can divert the original user's needs.

In the rest of experiments, the authors consider the relevance feedback based on confidence propagation by adding 2 relevant terms.

So far, the authors have considered in their work, the short queries that is to say, which are composed by keywords and that their number does not exceed three terms. The authors examine the contribution of their algorithm in the case of long queries. In the next section, the authors will study the impact of the variation of the query length.

Study of the Query Length

The authors consider that a long query contains a description of the user's need. The authors then tried to make retrieval by typing a query consisting of twenty terms. The re-injection is made according to the algorithm of the propagation of confidence. The table below summarizes the results found.

Table 5. Average precision by adding many terms

Precision and % of Improvement		Number of Documents		
		5	10	20
Average Initial Precision		0.28	0.24	0.22
Average Precision after Reformulation	with one term	0.30	0.33	0.32
	% improvement	7.14	37.5	45.45
	with 2 terms	0.46	0.39	0.34
	% improvement	65	62.5	54.5
	with 3 terms	0.32	0.33	0.30
	% improvement	14.28	37.5	36.36
	with 4 terms	0.20	0.30	0.30
	% improvement	-	25	36.36
	with 5 terms	0.20	0.26	0.23
	% improvement	-	8.33	4.54

Table 6. Average precision for a long query vs. a short query

Precision and % of Improvement		Number of Documents		
		5	10	20
Short Query	Average Initial Precision	0.28	0.24	0.22
	Average Precision	0.46	0.39	0.34
	% improvement	65	62.5	54.5
Long Query	Average Initial Precision	0.24	0.17	0.14
	Average Precision	0.29	0.26	0.22
	% improvement	20.83	52.94	57.14

From Table 6, it should be mentioned that their algorithm could improve the outcome of an initial long query containing a description of the need for a user for top 5, 10 and 20 documents. The rate of improvement could reach a value of 53% for the top 10 documents and 57% for the top 20 documents while the rate of improvement could not exceed 21% for the top 5 documents but which always remains less than the rate of improvement of the short query that is equal to 65%. This is explained by the use of several terms to describe better the need of the user which can divert the sense of user query.

Impact of Annotations Treatment

The authors will study, in this section, the interest of annotations treatment and the authors will consider the different types of annotations for the reformulation of the initial query. This reformulation will be performed using the unfiltered annotations initially, then the filtered annotations, then the unfiltered classified annotations and finally the filtered and classified annotations. In table 7, show the results of

Table 7. Average precision with and without treatment annotations

Precision and % of Improvement		Number of Documents		
		5	10	20
Base Precision		0.28	0.24	0.22
Annotations without Classification	Unfiltered (%improvement)	0.27 (-)	0.23 (-)	0.28 (27.27%)
	Filtered (%improvement)	0.30 (7.14%)	0.25 (4.16%)	0.29 (31.81%)
Annotations Classified	Validated (%improvement)	0.48 (71%)	0.42 (75%)	0.36 (64%)
	Unfiltered (%improvement)	0.29 (3.57%)	0.24 (-)	0.23 (4.54%)
	Filtered (%improvement)	0.46 (65%)	0.39 (62.5%)	0.34 (54.5%)

the reformulation terms extracted according to the propagation confidence algorithm compared to the basic version.

From Table 7, the authors can see that the classification and the filtering processes are essential to improve the initial query of the user. Indeed, the classification of filtered annotations has given better results than the unfiltered annotations. The classified and filtered annotations were able to achieve a rate of improvement equal to 65% for the top 5 documents returned by the system, compared to a negative rate for the unfiltered annotations. The classification of unfiltered (gross) annotations gave a slight improvement compared to the original query, it gave an accuracy rate equal to 0.29 compared to the initial accuracy which is 0.28 that is to say, with an improvement rate equal to 3.57%.

The authors also note that the filtered annotations showed its interest by improving the precision rate of the initial query of the user. Even the filtering of unclassified annotations improves initial accuracy which became 0.30 compared to 0.28 with an improvement rate equal to 7.14%. The authors achieved a rate equal to 65% using annotations filtered while the use of annotations validated by the expert was able to achieve a rate of improvement equal to 71% for the top 5 documents and 75% for the top 10 documents returned by the system, which proves the importance of filtering. These results show that filtering and classified annotation is essential to consider them as source of information in the relevance feedback.

Blind Reformulation

The blind relevance feedback consists in the re-injecting, in an automatic manner, the relevant terms extracted from the documents considered relevant without the user intervention. To deepen their study, the authors tested their algorithm by considering the top four documents returned by the system for an initial user searches. From these documents, the authors will filter the annotations in an automatic way, classify and re-inject the most relevant terms extracts by propagation of confidence. The results are shown in Table 8.

Although the reformulation is blind, the authors observed a still improvement in the precision compared to the accuracy of the original user query. This precision could reach a value of 0.35 with respect

Table 8. Improvement rate of blind reformulation by propagating confidence

Precision and % of Improvement	Number of Documents		
	5	10	20
Base Precision	0.28	0.24	0.22
Reformulation Blind with Filtered Annotations (%improvement)	0.38 (35.71%)	0.33 (37.5%)	0.26 (18.18%)

to the initial one equal to 0.28 for the top 5 documents. The improvement rate reaches its maximum for the top 10 documents with a value 37.5% in the terms of extraction with propagation of confidence.

CONCLUSION

In this chapter, the authors have proposed an information retrieval model based on confidence's network. It should be mentioned that the originality of their model appears in two main contributions. The first contribution is the extraction of relevant terms to reformulate the initial user query considering the annotations as an information source. The second contribution is the introduction of the concept of necessity and the principal of relevance feedback in a collaborative setting. It also should be noted that the authors have considered the annotations of documents resulting from the initial user query and deemed relevant as a source of information. In the proposed model, when a term of an annotation appears in the title of a relevant document, it can be considered as necessarily relevant. The authors have used a probabilistic model for the filtration processes and a hierarchical clustering for the classification processes. An algorithm for the propagation of confidence has been developed to extract new re-injected terms. Experiments the authors conduct have shown that their proposed model has improved the initial user query with a rate of improvement that could reach a value of 65% for the top 5 documents, 62.5% for the top 10 documents and 54.5% for the top 20 documents returned.

As a future work, the authors will focus on improving the performance of their model, essentially the precision measure. After the processing of the classification annotations that is performed in a first time in a static manner the new annotations may be added to these classes. The authors will try to improve the classification which can be done in a second step with a dynamic manner when adding a new annotation.

REFERENCES

Abderrahim, M. A. (2013). Utilisation des ressources externes pour la reformulation des requêtes dans un système de recherche d'information. The PBML 99: The Prague Bulletinof Mathematical Linguistics, 87-99. doi:10.2478/pralin-2013-0006

Achemoukh, F., & Ahmed-Ouamer, R. (2012). Modélisation d'évolution de profil utilisateur en recherche d'information personnalisée. CORIA 2012, 83-97.

Boudia, M. A., Hamou, R. M., & Amine, A. (2016). A New Approach Based on the Detection of Opinion by SentiWordNet for Automatic Text Summaries by Extraction. *International Journal of Information Retrieval Research, 6*(3), 19–36. doi:10.4018/IJIRR.2016070102

Boughammoura, R., & Omri, M. N. (2011). SeMQI: A New Model for Semantic Interpretation of Query Interfaces. *Proceedings of NGNS.*

Boughammoura, R., Omri, M. N., & Hlaoua, L. (2012). VIQI: A New Approach for Visual Interpretation of Deep Web Query Interfaces. *Proceedings ICITeS.* 10.1109/ICITeS.2012.6216656

Boughammoura, R., Omri, M. N., & Hlaoua, L. (2013). Information Retrieval from Deep Web based on Visuel Query Interpretation *International Journal of Information Retrieval Research, 2*(4), 45–59. doi:10.4018/ijirr.2012100104

Bouramoul, A., Kholladi, M.-K., & Doan, B.-L. (2011, May). Using Context to Improve the Evaluation of Information Retrieval Systems. *International Journal of Database Management Systems, 3*(2), 22–39. doi:10.5121/ijdms.2011.3202

Cabanac, G. (2008). Annotation collective dans le contexte RI: définition d'une plate-forme pour expérimenter la validation sociale. In *Conférence en Recherche d'Information et Applications* (pp. 385–392). CORIA.

Chahal, P., Singh, M., & Kumar, S. (2017). Semantic Analysis Based Approach for Relevant Text Extraction Using Ontology. *International Journal of Information Retrieval Research, 7*(4), 19–36. doi:10.4018/IJIRR.2017100102

Chang, Y. K., Cirillo, C., & Razon, J. (1971). Evaluation of feedback retrieval using modified freezing, residual collection and test and control groups. In The SMART retrieval system- experiments in automatic document processing (pp. 355-370). Academic Press.

Chebil, W., Soualmia, L. F., Omri, M. N., & Darmoni, S. J. (2015). Biomedical Concepts Extraction Based on Possibilistic Network and Vector Model. *Artificial Intelligence in Medicine, 9105*, 227–231.

Daoud, M., & Huang, J. X. (2013). Modeling geographic, temporal, and proximity contexts for improving geotemporal search. *Journal of the American Society for Information Science and Technology, 34*(1), 190–212. doi:10.1002/asi.22648

Fkih, F., & Omri, M. N. (2012). Complex Terminology Extraction Model from Unstructured Web Text Based Linguistic and Statistical Knowledge. *International Journal of Information Retrieval Research, 2*(3), 1–18. doi:10.4018/ijirr.2012070101

Garrouch, K., Omri, M. N., & Kouzana, A. (2012). A New Information Retrieval Model Based on Possibilistic Bayesian Networks. *Proceedings ICCRK'12*, 9105, 1-7.

Hlaoua, L. (2006). *Reformulation de requêtes par structure en RI dans les documents XML.* Lyon: CORIA.

Lin, H., Wang, L., & Chen, S.-M. (2006). Query expansion for document retrieval based on fuzzy rules and user relevance feedback techniques. *Expert Systems with Applications, 31*(2), 397–405. doi:10.1016/j. eswa.2005.09.078

Lioma, C., Moens, M. F., & Azzopardi, L. (2008). Collaborative annotation for pseudo relevance feedback. In *ECIR workshop on exploiting semantic annotation in information retrieval*. ESAIR.

Lopes, C. T. (2013). *Context-Based Health Information Retrieval* (PhD dissertation). University of Porto. Retrieved from http://www.carlalopes.com/pubs/lopes_PhD_2013.pdf

Luhn, H. (1958). The automatic creation of literature abstracts. IBM Journal of Research and Development, 2(2), 159–165.

Mata, F., & Claramunt, C. (2011). GeoST: Geographic, thematic and term-poral information retrieval from heterogeneous web data sources. In *Proceedings of the 10th International Conference on Web and Wireless Geographical Information Systems (W2GIS'11)*, (pp. 5–20). Heidelberg, Germany: Springer.

Mokhtari, N., & Dieng-Kuntz, R. (2008). Extraction et exploitation des annotations contextuelles. In Proceedings of Extraction et gestion des connaissances (EGC'2008). Academic Press.

Morris, M. R., & Horvitz, E. (2007). Search Together: An interface for collaborative Web Search. *Proceedings of the 20th annual ACM symposium on User interface software and technology.*

Naderi, H., Rumpler, B., & Pinon, J. M. (2007). An Efficient Collaborative Information Retrieval System by Incorporating the User Profile. In *Adaptive Multimedia Retrieval* (Vol. 4398, pp. 247–257). User, Context, and Feedback Lecture Notes in Computer Science. doi:10.1007/978-3-540-71545-0_19

Naouar, F., Hlaoua, L., & Omri, M. N. (2012). Possibilistic Model for Relevance Feedback in Collaborative Information Retrieval. *International Journal of Web Applications, IJWA, 4*(2), 78–86.

Naouar, F., Hlaoua, L., & Omri, M. N. (2013a). Relevance Feedback for Collaborative Retrieval Based on Semantic Annotations. In *The International Conference on Information and Knowledge Engineering IKE'13*, (pp.54-60). Las Vegas, NV: Academic Press.

Naouar, F., Hlaoua, L., & Omri, M. N. (2013b). Relevance Feedback in Collaborative Information Retrieval based on Validated Annotation. *International Conference on Reasoning and Optimization in Information Systems ROIS'2013.*

Naouar, F., Hlaoua, L., & Omri, M. N. (2015). Collaborative Information Retrieval Model Based on Fuzzy Confidence Network. Journal of Intelligent and Fuzzy Systems.

Naouar, F., Hlaoua, L., & Omri, M. N. (2017). Information retrieval model using uncertain confidence's network. International Journal of Information Retrieval Research, 7(2), 34-50. doi:10.4018/IJIRR.2017040103

Omri, M. N. (1994). *Système interactif flou d'aide à l'utilisation de dispositifs techniques: SIFADE* (PhD thesis). l'université Pierre et Marie Curie, Paris, France.

Omri, M. N. (2004). Pertinent Knowledge Extraction from a Semantic Network: Application of Fuzzy Sets Theory. *International Journal of Artificial Intelligence Tools, 13*(3), 705–719. doi:10.1142/S0218213004001752

Omri, M. N. (2012). Effects of Terms Recognition Mistakes on Requests Processing for Interactive Information Retrieval. *International Journal of Information Retrieval Research, 2*(3), 19–35. doi:10.4018/ijirr.2012070102

Robertson, S. E., & Walker, S. (1997). On relevance weights with little relevance information. In *20th annual international ACM SIGIR conference on Research and development in information retrieval*, (pp. 16–24). ACM Press. 10.1145/258525.258529

Rocchio, J. (1971). Relevance feedback in information retrieval. In The SMART retrieval system-experiments in automatic document processing. Prentice Hall Inc.

Ruthven, I., & Lalmas, M. (2003). A survey on the use of relevance feedback for information access systems. *The Knowledge Engineering Review, 18*(2), 95–145. doi:10.1017/S0269888903000638

Safi, H. (2014). AXON: Un Système de RI Personnalisée dans des Textes Arabes basée sur le profil utilisateur et l'expansion de requêtes. *Proceedings of CORIA 2014.*

Schenkel, R., & Thbobald, M. (2005). Relevance Feedback for Structural Query Expansion. In INEX 2005 Workshop Pre-Proceedings (pp. 260-272). Academic Press.

Shah, C., Marchionini, G., & Kelly, D. (2009). Learning Design Principles for a Collaborative Information Seeking System. In *Proceedings of ACM SIGCHI Conference 2009*. Boston, MA: ACM. 10.1145/1520340.1520496

Singh, J., & Sharan, A. (2015). Information retrieval. Context Window Based Co-occurrence Approach for Improving Feedback Based Query Expansion in Information Retrieval. International Journal of Information Retrieval Research, 5(4), 31-45.

Taher, R. (2004). Soutien Personnalisé pour la Recherche d'Information Collaborative. In *2ème Congrès MAJECSTIC 2004*. Manifestation de JEunes Chercheurs Sciences et Technologies de l'Information et de la Communication.

Tamine, L., Boughanem, M., & Daoud, M. (2010). Evaluation of contextual information retrieval effectiveness: Overview of issues and research. *Journal of Knowledge and Information Systems, 24*(1), 1–34. doi:10.100710115-009-0231-1

Chapter 3
Enhancing Information Retrieval System Using Change-Prone Classes

Deepa Bura
Manav Rachna International Institute of Research and Studies, India

Amit Choudhary
Maharaja Surajmal Institute, India

ABSTRACT

In today's competitive world, each company is required to change software to meet changing customer requirements. At the same time, an efficient information retrieval system is required as changes made to software in different versions can lead to complicated retrieval systems. This research aims to find the association between changes and object-oriented metrics using different versions of open source software. Earlier researchers have used various techniques such as statistical methods for the prediction of change-prone classes. This research uses execution time, frequency, run time information, popularity, and class dependency in prediction of change-prone classes. For evaluating the performance of the prediction model, sensitivity, specificity, and ROC curve are used. Higher values of AUC indicate the prediction model gives accurate results. Results are validated in two phases: Experimental Analysis I validates results using OpenClinic software and OpenHospital software and Experimental Analysis II validates result using Neuroph 2.9.2 and Neuroph 2.6.

INTRODUCTION

The unending growing complexity and dependency has led to a rise in demand of high quality software that can be maintained at cheaper costs. Finding software change proneness is a significant and essential activity for improving software feature and reducing maintenance effort formerly the software is installed in real world. Koru & Liu (2007) proved change prone classes as a significant peripheral quality attribute that signifies degree of alterations in a class through various versions of software. Software industry is expanding manifolds day by day. Software changes to incorporate new features or to remove errors.

DOI: 10.4018/978-1-7998-1021-6.ch003

This rapidly changing software demand has resulted in significant increase of effort from development to testing phase in software life cycle. Developing and maintaining software requires resources such as development time, cost to build and effort required. But all these resources are limited. Research has also been carried out to find the association between fault prone classes and object oriented metrics. Weak classes of any software can be predicted using these quality attributes. Changes if predicted during earlier stages of life cycle, can help a developer in efficiently allocating project's resources by properly allocating the appropriate resources to weaker change prone class, so that such type of classes can be maintained properly and tested rigorously. Predicting such changes can be useful as such evaluations can be utilized to forecast changes from one release to next.

Maintenance phase is considered as one of the costly and significant phases of software. Malhotra & Khanna (2013) identified maintenance cost incurs 40-70% of entire cost of software. Estimation of change in classes i.e. probability with which class will modify or not needs to be evaluated as it can help in reducing maintenance cost and testing. As the software evolves it demands more rigorous testing so that good quality software can be developed with less changes and defects. By focusing on weak change prone classes utilization of resources can be done in a better way. Detection of such classes earlier in life cycle model of software can reduce maintenance costs as because if an error is detected early in a product, it would require lesser amount of resources to correct that error. Else in a later stage the cost of correcting an error increases exponentially in every unnoticed phase. Quality problems related to design can be identified in software before implementing codes, if developers are able to identify change prone classes early in life cycle of the software. Similarly, existing design can be customized or alternate designs can be selected easily. These types of prediction models give high return on investment. As a result, change proneness prediction model contributes in improving quality of the software and reduces development cost also. Thus change prediction model serves to deliver high quality software at optimal costs, as lesser changes and faults are carried forward in later stages of software life cycle.

Various object oriented metrics are used throughout the software process. It is not possible to use a single metric to quantify various aspects of OO application. Various different metrics are required to completely analyse software. To predict change prone classes, various researchers have used various object oriented metrics like size, cohesion, coupling, inheritance, etc. This research summarizes different object oriented features which can be utilized to predict amount of change in classes. This will benefit researchers to get through various metrics elaborated here. In addition to that, it will help the researchers to predict more parameters for estimating changes in a class.

Researchers and Practitioners have used various Object-Oriented metrics throughout the software process. But it is not feasible to use a single metric for quantifying various aspects of Object-Oriented application. Several different metrics and methods are needed for completely analyzing the software. Things that need to be considered before developing an efficient change proneness prediction model: (1) it is required to review the effectiveness of several methods as various methods may give different outcomes with different types of data sets. (2) Secondly it becomes essential to test whether the prediction model provides good results on another data set or not.

This study aims to build an efficient change prone prediction model that will predict change prone classes. The study includes the following objectives:

1. It aims to explore the association amongst different Object-Oriented metrics and change prone classes.
2. To propose some new dynamic metrics that can help in predicting degree of change in class.

RELATED WORK

Change proneness gives the degree of change across various versions of software. These change prone prediction model can help developers in efficient resource allocation, developing improved quality software and reduced maintenance costs. In the last two decades' researchers and practitioners have made a lot of effort for finding the association amongst change prone classes and object oriented metrics. Research gives a strong correlation amongst object oriented features and change prone class.

Godara and Singh (2015) proposed a model in which dynamic features were used to evaluate the frequency of change in a particular class. Further to minimize the rules and to improve the accuracy, Artificial Bee Colony (ABC) algorithm was used. Using ABC algorithm most significant rules ere extracted to define change prone classes of a software. Catolina et al. (2018) stated that number of developers working on a project also affects change proneness feature of a class. Results concluded that considering this feature improves effectiveness of the change prone model. Malhotra and Khanna (2018) analyzed evolution metrics if considered along with object oriented metrics results in better prediction of change prone classes.

Bansal and Jajoria (2019) conducted various experiments using meta heuristic algorithms on intra and cross projects. Research predicted that hybrid algorithms give better accuracy. Bansal et al. (2019) compared six machine learning algorithms and stated that resampling leads to more accurate model.

Godara and Singh (2017) explored various types of dependencies in a software. Research stated that if such dependencies can be predicted earlier in software development life cycle using UML 2.0 class diagrams it would result in a better-quality product and would minimize testing and maintenance efforts.

Bura et al. (2017) studied various metrics used for finding change prone classes and evaluated all the metrics on two open source software OpenClininc and OpenHospital. Researchers investigated that if object-oriented features are used for change proneness prediction model it would give better results. Previous researchers used static object-oriented metrics for prediction of change prone classes. But they failed to incorporate dynamic metrics for prediction of degree of change proneness of any class. Our research tries to incorporate dynamic metrics for predicting change prone classes. Lu et al. (2012) investigated various object-oriented metrics for predicting change proneness of a class. Overall, Researchers concluded that object-oriented features can predict degree of change in a class. All these researchers used existing static object-oriented metrics for prediction of change prone classes.

Han et al (2008) calculated how one class depends on other using behavioral dependency. They measured change proneness in terms of behavioral dependency. If BDM (Behavior Dependency Measurement) of a class is higher than other, it is more likely to change. Using UML2.0 (Unified Modeling Language 2.0) Sequence diagrams and class diagrams they evaluated the feature of behavioral dependency. Their research proved behavioral dependency can be effectively used for finding possibility of change in a class. However, their research ignored other factors which affects change proneness of a class.

Lu et al (2012) used AUC technique (the area under relative operating characteristic) for evaluating predictive effectiveness of OO metrics. The steps followed were: (1) Compute Area under a relative characteristic and corresponding variance for each object oriented metrics. (2) For computing the average AUC random effect model is employed. (3) Sensitivity analysis is performed for investigating whether the result of AUC technique is applicable vigorously to the data selection. Results show that size metrics can moderately differentiate between a likely to change and non-likely to change class whereas cohesion and coupling metrics have low predictive capability of finding change prone classes. Inheritance feature have very reduced predicting capability as compared to size, cohesion and coupling metrics. Their research work just considered three metrics size, cohesion and coupling for finding change prone classes. However, other factors were ignored in the research. Elish and Zouri (2014) constructed logistic regression models for finding change-prone classes. Research analyzed statistical correlation between change prone classes and coupling metrics. The results show that a prediction model made with coupling feature gives more accurate results than a model built with cohesion feature. Wherein, a prediction model made with import coupling metrics is more accurate than a model built with export coupling metrics. Research mainly focussed on two attributes i.e. coupling and cohesion. Their research just determined which one is better attribute for finding change proneness of a class. In this research we have incorporated dependency feature for finding the association between the classes and other factors such as frequency and Implementation Period are also considered.

Romano and Pinzger (2011) empirically studied the orrelation between object oriented features and changes in interfaces of source code. They evaluated ten Java open-source systems for predicting the results. Furthermore, they evaluated the metrics to find degree of change in Java interfaces. Results revealed strongest association between cohesion metric of external interface and changes in source code.

Zhou and Leung (2009) based on Eclipse analyzed 1) Effect of class size (whichever metrics of size is taken) on change proneness. 2) Their research analyzed size metrics lead to an overestimation of association between object oriented features and change proneness. Zhu et al (2013) validated Pareto's law. Using classification methods, they identified change prone classes. They used open source software product, Datacrow for static metrics collection and change in class. Pareto's Law states that 80% of changes in software can be found in 20% of the classes. Experimental results show that results can be used for finding change prone classes and for enhancing developer's efficiency. Researchers tried to find out the relation amongst object oriented features and change in interface of source code. But they didn't analyze other factors which contribute in affecting change proneness of a class.

Cetolino and Ferrucci (2019) conducted a detailed study to check whether ensemble techniques can lead to improved prediction models.

Khomh et al (2009) tested the assumption i.e. if a class with code smell is more change prone than the classes without code smell. They analyzed various versions of Azerus (9 releases) Eclipse (13 releases), in which they found 29 code smells. Their research studied relationship between code smell and change proneness. Their results revealed classes have a high probability of change with code smells. Eski and Buzluca (2011) studied association of object oriented features and change proneness. Experimental outcomes of the research indicated that the portions of the software which have a low level quality, change often during the software life cycle development process. Janes et al (2006) used arithmetical models for exploring the relationship between OO features and defect prone classes. The results of the models were evaluated via correlations, dispersion coefficients and Alberg diagrams. Abdi et al (2009) used probabilistic model using Bayesian nets to predict change impact in object-oriented systems. By assigning probabilities to network nodes a model was built. For studying the relation of software attributes and impact of change, data of a real system was used. By executing various scenarios, research analyzed coupling as a good predictor of change. Researchers used various complex technologies and models for prediction of change prone classes. All these models required a lot of time for evaluation of change prone classes. Compared to this our prediction model is simpler and requires less time for prediction.

Wilkie and Kitchenham (2000) determined number of classes involved in a change-ripple. Research also analyzed the effect of CBO values and public function. Results show that high CBO values and high public function count values exhibit more ripple effects. Classes with large public and private member functions participate more often in change ripples. Bacchelli et al (2010) used the tool infusion, to extract FAMIX-compliant object-oriented models. Using this model, they computed a catalog of object oriented features proposed by Chidamber and Kemerer. Code development was analyzed using change metrics. For using the change metrics in the experiments, source code was linked with entities, i.e., classes. Bergenti and Poggi (2000) developed an approach wherein, UML diagrams were analyzed to suggest changes to the software design which would cause design patterns to occur. Their research included automated finding of design patterns. Input to the tool used was UML design (class and collaboration) diagrams in XMI (XML Metadata Interchange) format. Researcher's analyzed association amongst object-oriented metrics and change prone classes. But, outcomes for software in real world was not presented in their research.

Malhotra and Khanna (2018) proposed to use metrics based on evolution along with metrics evaluated from object- oriented concepts. Finding change prone classes based upon these two factors would lead to improved results. The study was analyzed using two android software Contacts & Gallery2. Khiaty et al. (2017) proposed to use group based method, evolution metrics and object-oriented metrics to find change prone classes. The research suggested that an improvement of 10% increases in accuracy using above mentioned methods.

Godara et al. (2018) used machine learning techniques to evaluate the performance of change prediction model. Various dynamic measures were evaluated to find the change prone classes. Proposed model was evaluated on open source software to check the accuracy of the model.

Kyriakakis et al. (2019) defines the uses of PHP, author states that various flexible program can be made using dynamic features of PHP. And it provides several patterns, programs built using such patterns provide additional benefit that these are less prone to changes.

Overall, all the previous research is focused mainly on application of static object-oriented attributes. However, dynamic features are ignored. If dynamic features are used in the change prediction model it can lead to more efficient model. Our research tries to fill all the above mentioned gaps, and incorporates both static and dynamic features (class dependency and frequency) for prediction of change prone classes in an object oriented software. Our proposed prediction method is simpler and can be applied in real world for building efficient object oriented software. Further, it can be used for effectively allocating the manpower resources such that change prone classes are more focused and can lead to reduction in maintenance and testing efforts.

RELATIONSHIP BETWEEN CHANGE PRONENESS AND OBJECT ORIENTED METRICS

This section, presents association between object oriented features and change prone classes. To explore this relationship dependent and independent variables are defined in this study.

Independent Variables

Various aspects of a software process can be enumerated using object oriented metrics. Malhotra and Chug (2013) stated a single metric is not sufficient to study all the aspects of software. A number of metrics or their combination is required to completely understand the software. Various object oriented metrics (i.e. independent variables) are summarized here in Table 1.

Table 1. Object Oriented metrics for change proneness prediction

S.No	Metrics	Definition	Dimension
1.	LOC (Line of code) • No: of Lines • SLOC (Source line of code) • BLOC (Blank line of code) • Comment line • LDC (Lines with Declarative Code) • LEC(Lines with Executable Code) • Statement Count	• count of all lines • count of lines with source code • count of blank lines • count of lines with Comment • count of lines with declarative source code • count of lines that will be executed • count of total declarative and executable code	Size
2.	Methods • No: of Methods • No: of local methods • No: of private methods • No: of public methods • No: of instance method	• count of methods in a class • count of methods not inherited • count of local/not inherited methods • count of public methods • object created using class. It contains instance method	Size
3.	No: of children	count of immediate subclasses	Inheritance
4.	No: of attributes per class	count of total no: of variables of a class	Size
5.	No: of instance variable	count of variables contained by object	Inheritance
6.	Response for class	It shows interaction of class methods with other methods	Coupling
7.	Coupling between objects	Represents the no: of other types of classes a class is coupled to	Coupling
8.	DIP(Depth of Inheritance)	Count of nodes from parent node to root node.	Inheritance
9.	Lack of Cohesion	Percentage of methods in the class using a particular data field.	Cohesion
10.	WMC(Weighted methods per class)	Count of complexities of all methods.	Size
11.	Interface ■ No: of methods ■ Arguments(i) ■ No: of instance method ■ APP(i)	■ count of methods declared in interface. ■ count of arguments of declared methods in interface(i) ■ No: of instance method ■ Measure of mean size of method declared. App(i)=Arguments/No: of methods(i)	Size
12.	Coupling between Methods (CBM)	It is a measure of new/redefined methods to which all the inherited methods are coupled.	Coupling
13.	Number of Object/Memory Allocation (NOMA)	It is a measure of the total number of statements that allocate new objects or memories in a class.	Size
14.	Average Method Complexity(AMC)	It is average method size of each class. It does not count virtual and inherited methods.	Size

Various characteristics of software that are included in Table 1 comprises of coupling, inheritance, size, cohesion, etc. For calculating all these metrics Understand for Java (UFJ) software is used.

Apart from all these metrics other metrics such as Implementation Period for class, class dependency, log information, frequency and popularity are also proposed in this research for finding change prone classes.

Dependent Variables

With the increase in utility of software, software requires many modifications and upgradations. Finding change prone classes lead to better enhancements in any software with a minimal cost. This research aims to explore the association amongst different object oriented features and change prone attributes. Possibility of occurrence of change in software is mentioned as change proneness. Change can be in relation to addition, deletion or modification of source line of code (SLOC). Change proneness is used as dependent variable in this study.

EMPIRICAL DATA COLLECTION

This section explains the data collection methods and sources that are used in this study. Two open source software (developed using Java language) from warehouse (www.sourceforge.net) are analyzed. Changes in software are analyzed by calculating the number of changes in different versions of same software.

Firstly, Open clinic software is analyzed, which is open source incorporating management of hospital enclosing management of organization, financial, medical lab etc. The two stable versions of open clinic software analyzed in this study are v3 and v4. Version 3 was released on September 17, 2010 and consists of 237 classes and version 4 was released on May 28, 2011 and consists of 254 classes. Another software that is analyzed is open hospital software, which supports management and hospital activities. Its two stable versions that were evaluated are v1.7.2 and v1.7.3. Version 1.7.2 was released on May 21, 2013 and consists of 349 classes and version 1.7.3 was released on September 13, 2014 and consists of 363 classes. Table 2 exhibits the details of software used in this study such as various version, language used, total LOC, total no. of common classes, total classes in which change encountered, and the classes without change.

Table 2 exhibits the details of software used in this study such as various version, language used, total LOC, total no. of common classes, total classes in which change encountered, and the classes without change.

Object oriented metrics were collected between different versions of software using following steps:

Object Oriented Metrics Collection

With the help of http://sourceforge.net source code is collected for both versions of software. All the object oriented metrics stated above in table I are collected using Understand for Java(UFJ)tool for previous version of software (Open Clinic Software v3, Open Hospital Software1.7.2). It is static code analysis tool. As the research is predicting change in object oriented classes, accordingly metrics for only these

Table 2. Data set used

Name	Version1	Version2	P/L used	Total LOC	Total classes	Classes with change	Classes without change
Open Clinic Software	3	4	Java	44,211	248	107	141
Open Hospital Software	1.7.2	1.7.3	Java	59,575	356	20	336

classes are considered. In this research, metrics for classes are generated using UFJ tool, although metrics for methods and files can also be generated with the help of this tool. As we are predicting change prone classes we have taken metrics for classes only.

Common Classes' Collection

Here, common classes from both versions (previous and new) are collected. Changes in these classes were taken into consideration for both the versions of the software. Similar approach is used by (Zhou and Leung, 2009) also.

Classes' Comparison

After step 2, common classes that were collected are compared line by line using DiffMerge Software. It has been developed by a software company named SourceGear. By comparing, each class is categorized as a change prone class and non-change prone class. Change in a class is considered if:

- There is addition, deletion, or modification in SLOC of class in the newer version of software.
- Addition, deletion or modification in comment is not considered as change.
- Addition or deletion of blank line does not affect change.
- Reordering of lines does not affect the change.
- Change in class definition affects the change.

Data Point Collection

Step 3 and step 1 were used to generate data points. In Open Clinic Software 248 classes are present in both the versions. Out of total, 107 classes exhibited change (which constitutes 43% of total classes) and 141 classes did not change. In Open Hospital Software, 152 classes exhibited change (which constitutes almost 42% of total classes) and 204 classes did not change.

Using source code of both the versions obtained from http://sourceforge.net_data statistics for both the OpenClinic software and OpenHospital software are analyzed as shown in Table 3 and Table 4.

Using various statistics given in Table 3 and Table 4 data set characteristics for OpenClinic software and OpenHospital software were analyzed. The statistics evaluated in this study include minimum, maximum, mean, median, and standard deviation for every object oriented metrics. All these statistics are related to metrics present in classes. Minimum values relate to the class having minimum value of a particular metrics. And maximum relates to the class having maximum value of a particular metrics. Observations show software systems that have less number of children (NOC) and least value of inheritance results in low values of NOC metric and DIT metric. For example, mean value for NOC metric for (OpenClinic Software is 0.49 and OpenHospital software is 0.43) and the DIT metric is (OpenClinic, 3.03 and OpenHospital, 2.01). LCOM measure is high for the software systems. It counts for method invocation within a class. Its higher value suggests larger number of methods are invoked in a class. Similar approach is followed in Briand et al. (2000) and Cartwright & Shepperd (2000).

Apart from these metrics we propose some other metrics such as Implementation Period, run time information (i.e. log information), class dependency, frequency and popularity are also proposed in this research work, which can be utilized effectively in predicting change prone classes.

Table 3. Statistics for OpenClinic software

Metrics	Min.	Max.	Mean	Mid.	SD
NL	4	2032	233.97	52	2007.54
SLOC	4	4928	227.3	110	310.5
BLOC	0	178	23.32	7	232.7
LC	0	257	28.81	4	257.5
LDC	2	245	25.73	9	249.6
LEC	0	989	82.72	18	632.79
SC	2	1,109	110.38	28	931.91
NOM	0	18	.87	0	16.62
NLM	0	75	14.21	3	117.23
NPRM	0	12	0.68	0	15.9
NPM	0	62	10.9	3	99.97
NIM	0	68	11.89	3	105.78
NOC	0	10	0.49	0	15.59
NOA	0	22	1.98	1	21.48
NIV	0	115	8.25	2	71.09
RFC	0	117	23.2	5	185.68
CBO	0	27	6.82	2	57.8
DIT	1	4	3.03	2	30.03
LCOM	0	102	89.9	49.8	728.23
WMC	0	155	25.69	6	211.65
CBM	0	19	4.8	2	48.9

Table 4. Statistics for OpenHospital software

Metrics	Min.	Max.	Mean	Mid.	SD
NL	2	2050	203.97	52	2027.54
SLOC	4	6759	177.5	98	564.3
BLOC	0	213	33.12	8	256.7
LC	0	263	32.11	6	265.5
LDC	1	273	35.73	9	252.6
LEC	0	1081	87.12	34	752.79
SC	1	1,217	119.88	56	987.91
NOM	0	54	.67	0	19.82
NLM	0	85	11.61	4	127.53
NPRM	0	22	0.78	0	18.8
NPM	0	69	8.5	3	102.80
NIM	0	69	11.99	3	106.18
NOC	0	7	0.43	0	12.09
NOA	0	42	0.88	1	18.28
NIV	0	119	8.25	2	72.10
RFC	2	186	17.4	3	179.08
CBO	0	20	5.02	1	43.8
DIT	1	3	2.01	2	50.03
LCOM	0	100	79.3	51.2	778.23
WMC	1	215	15.69	5	232.65
CBM	0	2	5.8	2	54.9

- **Implementation Period:** Implementation Period of a class is directly related to size of the class. The research proposes to use this feature for predicting change prone classes.

For calculating the Implementation Period, Eclipse Test and Performance Tools Platform (TPTP) profiling tool is used. Research uses Eclipse SDK version 3.6.2. Size can be estimated from the Implementation

Table 5. Implementation Period

Classes	Implementation Period
a11	0.008
a12	0.001
a13	0.001
a20	0.0
Eight	0.001
Fifth	0.01

Period of product, it can be in relation to classes, methods etc. Using TPTP the Implementation Period can be generated, it creates an XML report of the time. TPTP gives three types of Implementation Period:

Base Time: It is the total time taken by methods to execute. Implementation Period of other methods called from this method is excluded from base time.

$$T_{bt} = T_{me} - T_{oe} \tag{1}$$

where, T_{bt} =Implementation Period of message in seconds and T_{oe} = time taken by other methods to execute

Average base time: It is the average base time needed for execution of method once. It is denoted as T_{abt}.

Cumulative base time: It is the time required by methods to execute. However, it also takes into account Implementation Period of methods that are called from this method.

$$T_{cbt} = T_{me} - T_{oe} \tag{2}$$

Calls: It can be defined as the count of times a method is invoked.

The Implementation Period analysis tool records all data that is related to the count of method calls and their Implementation Period. The gathered data can be viewed in several different ways:

Execution Statistics: These statistics provide information about the Implementation Period of each method that has been called as well as the number of calls. Additionally, it also shows the method invocation details, i.e. which method is invoked by other methods and how often it is invoked.

Execution Flow: It visualize the thread based execution flow of the observed application. This view contains a time scale diagram.

UML Interactions: This view shows an UML based view of the execution flow and method invocations. The UML diagram can either be based on class or thread interactions.

Implementation Period for some of the classes is given in Table 5, evaluated using eclipse TPTP tool. Higher value of Implementation Period indicates higher probability of change proneness of a class.

Log Information

Software metrics can be categorized as static and dynamic. Metrics which are applied to source code are static metrics and metrics which are obtained during run time are dynamic metrics. Earlier Researchers and Practitioners have focused significantly on static metrics; however dynamic metrics have been ignored up to a significant level. But this metrics needs more concentration as it gives the actual information because it is collected during run time. In this research we emphasize on the concept whether a method which is executed imports or exports other object's method.

Table 6. Log information

Classes	Log information
a11	3
a12	5
a13	7
a20	5
Eight	3
Fifth	11

At runtime, within considered scope we can count the total number of messages which are sent and received by objects. For evaluating log information we consider which methods are executed during runtime and the count of times each method is run. Table 6 gives log information for our application.

Class Dependency

Class Dependency can be used as one of the significant attributes for predicting the change proneness in software. If a class is affected by change, it will affect another class also. This can be evaluated by finding dependencies between classes. UML2.0 class diagrams (CD) and sequence diagrams (SD) are used for evaluating class dependency. Similar approach has been used in research by Han et al. (2008).

For measuring the class dependency from the source code, UML class diagrams and sequence diagrams are generated from the code. Class dependency can be measured using the below stated approach:

- Build separate object dependency model
- Build complete system dependency model
- Create Class Route table
- Find weighted sum of routes
- Evaluate the Dependency for each class

Build Separate Object Dependency Model

Using SD and CD of Unified Modeling Language 2.0, separate Object Dependency model can be constructed.

For a SD, an Object Dependency model consists of 2-tuple (O,M), where,

O- denotes every object in SD.

M- denotes message passed amongst objects.

Message $m \in M$ consists of below mentioned attributes:

$m_D \in O$ - Message dispatched by source object

$m_A \in O$ - Message arrived at Receiver object where $m_D \neq m_A$

m_T - Message title

$m_p \in M$ - Parent message if present where, $m_p \neq M$. If parent message is not applicable, then it is the originating message and is represented as "-"

$m_{LR} \in O$- Likelihood rate of execution of message in SD such that $0 \leq m_{LR} \leq 1$.

$m_{PR} \in O$- Projected rate of execution of message in SD such that $0 \leq m_{PR} \leq 1$.

Table 7. Class Dependency values

Classes	Class Dependency	
a11	2.690476	
a12	0.896825	
a13	2.690476	
a20	0.309523	
Eight	0.246031	
Fifth	0.198412	

Build Complete System Dependency Model

For finding the class dependency for the complete system, dependency values of objects are combined into a single system dependency model.

Create Class Route Table (CRT)

For creating the class route table, the paths between source and destination object are traversed. These paths become input to CRT. Route is evaluated from the traversed path of incoming message of destination to outgoing message of source. Messages encountered during traversal are added to CRT. In case there is a direct dependency between source and destination, at that time the title of message incoming to destination is same as the message departing from source. In other words, in direct class dependency only a single message is counted in CRT. However, in case of indirect dependency outgoing message of source can be traversed with the help of parent message from the destination to source traversed in backward direction.

Find Weighted Amount of Routes

Weighted amount of routes for every pair of source class C_S and destination class C_D can be evaluated from CRT using below mentioned equation (3).

$$Weighted\,amount\,of\,routes(C_S, C_D) = \sum \frac{1}{N} \times F_{LR} \times F_{PR} \qquad (3)$$

where,

N - count of messages in CRT
F_{LR} - Likelihood rate of execution of message in CRT
F_{PR} - Projected rate of execution of first message in CRT

Calculate Class Dependency

The value of class dependency for any class, for instance C_i can be evaluated by summing the pair of corresponding classes (C_i, C_j) as shown in equation 4.

$$CD(C_i) = \sum_{1 \leq i,j \leq n} Weighted \quad sum \quad of \, Routes(C_i, C_j) \qquad (4)$$

Table 7 shows class dependency values of some of the classes using above method. Higher values of dependency indicate higher probability of changes in a class.

Frequency

For evaluating the frequency feature, frequent item set mining method is used in this research. Frequency can be defined as the number of times a method is called by another method. A software consists of *n* number of functions, which can be called by other functions. Since a class has many methods, it is likely to happen some methods are frequently called by others, while others are not called. Because of this frequency attribute can be used as one of the main attribute for predicting change prone classes. For finding this attribute of how frequently a method is called, rules for method calls are generated.

In data mining, frequent sets play a vital role. It can be used to find patterns from databases such as association rules. The most important problem that can be tackled using frequent item set is the mining of association rules. Various item sets, and their characteristics can be identified using frequent item set mining. In data mining, transaction can be defined as set of instances, wherein each class is referred to as item in each method call. In this research, calling of methods by various classes is referred to as instance. And every class is referred to as item.

Frequent item set mining algorithm finds common classes for a method called. Classes which have minimum support are selected. Minimum support states the minimum no: of intervals the calling of method occurs in the common set of classes. Further classes are categorized as { 1-term grouping, 2-term grouping… (n-1)-term grouping} based on method call. For example, if classes are {m, n, o}, then 1-term groupings are {m}, {n}, {o} and the 2-term groupings is {m, n}, {n, o}, {m, o} obtained from common set. Similarly, based upon the size of the classes set, the groupings are used accordingly by frequent item set mining algorithm. Table 8 shows rules generated using frequent item set mining algorithm.

Association rules are generated after finding frequent item sets. Association rules are conditional statements such as if/then statements which can be used to uncover relationships between disparate data. Data found in item is known as antecedent. Item found in combination with antecedent is known as consequent. For identifying significant relationships association rules are created using if/ then patterns. Support can be defined as number of times an item appears in database. Confidence can be defined as count of times if/then statements have been found to be true.

After the identification of a set of frequent item sets, association rules are produced. Association rules are conditional statements such as if/then statements which can be used to uncover relationships between disparate data and information repository. An association rule consists of two parts, i.e. Antecedent and

Table 8. Rules generated for the method calls using frequent item set mining algorithm.

Classes	Two Length Combination	Two length Rule above threshold value	Three length rule above threshold value
al12 al11 al13 thirddisp print1 fourthdisplay	[al12, al11] [al12, al13] [al11, al13] [al12, print1] [al12, fourthdisplay] [al11, thirddisp] [thirddisp, print1] [thirddisp, fourthdisplay]	[al12, al11] [al12, al13] [al11, al13] [thirddisp, print1] [thirddisp, fourthdisplay]	[al12, al11, al13] [al12, al13, al11] [al11, al13, al12]

Figure 1. Flowchart for ABC Algorithm

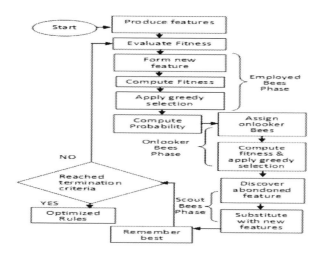

Table 9. Optimized Rules using ABC

Optimized Rules
[thirddisp, print1]
[print1, thirddisp]
[thirddisp, fourthdisplay]
[fourthdisplay, thirddisp]
[a112, a111, a113]
[a111, a113, a112]
[a113, a112, a111]
[a112, a113, a111]
[a113, a111, a112]

consequent. Data found in item is known as antecedent. Item found in combination with antecedent is known as consequent. For identifying significant relationships association rules are created using if/ then patterns. Support can be defined number of times an item appears in database. Confidence can be defined as number of times if/then statements have been found to be true.

Till now all the change prediction models have considered the metrics explained in Table 1. This chapter contributes some more attributes (time, class dependency, frequency) which can be used to predict change prone classes. However, in order to develop an effective prediction model, there is a need to minimize the dimensions of input set. This was done by finding a subset of independent variables that were significant in predicting the dependent variable and change prone classes. Artificial Bee Colony algorithm (ABC) as shown in Figure1 is used for reducing the number of input variables.

Table 9 gives a set of optimized rules which have been generated using ABC algorithm. Using these optimized rules, frequency of how many times a method is called is evaluated. Higher value of frequency attributes indicates higher chances of change to occur. Frequency, is:

Table 10. Frequency

Classes	Frequency
a11	7.631578
a12	5.000000
a13	7.631578
a20	2.631578
Eight	0.315789
Fifth	0.105263

$$F = \frac{No : of \; times \; method \, occurs \; in \; input}{Number \; of \; values} \tag{5}$$

Using the above equation 5, values of frequency attribute can be obtained which was optimized using ABC algorithm. Table 10 gives the generated values for this metric.

Popularity

This metrics is obtained from the frequency metrics, it indicates how popular a method is in terms of calling and being called. It can be evaluated with the help of equation 6.

$$Popularity = F_1 + F_2 \tag{6}$$

where,

$$F_2 = \frac{\left(M_1\right) \cdot \left(M_2\right)}{Total \; Number \; of \; methods}$$

M_1- count of intervals a method is called be various methods
M_2- count of intervals a method calls various methods

EXPERIMENTAL FRAMEWORK

In this section firstly we describe the values obtained for various metrics and secondly we briefly describe the methods and techniques used for evaluating our change prediction model.

For effectively predicting change prone class, apart from existing change object oriented features other features such as Implementation Period, class dependency and frequency are also evaluated in this chapter.

For calculating the Implementation Period, Eclipse TPTP tool is used wherein, Eclipse SDK version 3.6.2 is used. Values generated for methods is given in Figure 2.

Figure 2. Implementation Period generated using Eclipse TPTP profile tool

Package	<	Base Time (seconds)	Average Base Time (seconds)	Cumulative Time (seco...	Calls
▲ ⊕ code	◇	9.990104	0.014933	10.189101	669
▷ ⊙ Newfirst	◇	6.091768	3.045884	6.091768	2
▷ ⊙ OBDM	◇	2.239859	0.003441	2.393795	651
▷ ⊙ ExeTime	◇	1.088570	1.088570	1.088570	1
▷ ⊙ First	◇	0.349820	0.058303	10.189101	6
▷ ⊙ Table	◇	0.153935	0.051312	0.153935	3
▷ ⊙ Frequent	◇	0.033917	0.011306	6.125685	3
▷ ⊙ Findifvalue	◇	0.032234	0.010745	0.032234	3
▲ ⊕ Test	◇	0.198998	0.000287	10.142756	694
▷ ⊙ Fourth	◇	0.041822	0.001307	0.048686	32
▷ ⊙ Third	◇	0.039354	0.004919	0.046445	8
▷ ⊙ First1	◇	0.030868	0.003087	10.142756	10
▷ ⊙ Second	◇	0.021149	0.021149	0.169005	1
▷ ⊙ a17	◇	0.011022	0.003674	0.013611	3
▷ ⊙ a16	◇	0.010882	0.003627	0.024553	3
▷ ⊙ Writer	◇	0.010811	0.000031	0.010811	347
▷ ⊙ a14	◇	0.006255	0.002085	0.034157	3
▷ ⊙ a13	◇	0.005041	0.001680	0.039251	3
▷ ⊙ a12	◇	0.003724	0.001241	0.043021	3

Figure 3. Dependency values generated using Sequence and class diagrams

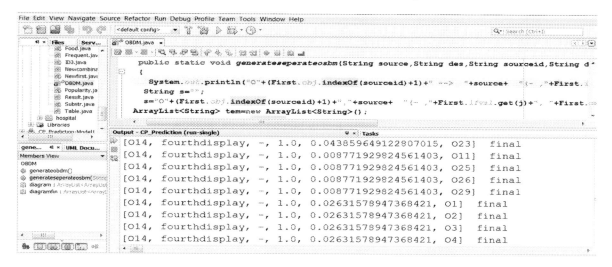

Using UML2.0 sequence and class diagrams, class dependency values are generated as shown in Figure 3. Dependency indicates if a class is affected by change how it will affect other class.

Count of times how frequently a method is called by other method is defined as frequency. Frequency values are generated as shown in Figure 4.

For evaluating and comparing the proposed change prediction model we have used the multivariate logistic regression method.

Statistical Logistic Regression Method

This method is used when combination of independent variables contributes in prediction of dependent variable. Complete description is given by Hosmer & Lemeshow (2004) Menard (2002). Logistic re-

Figure 4. Frequency values evaluated using optimized rules

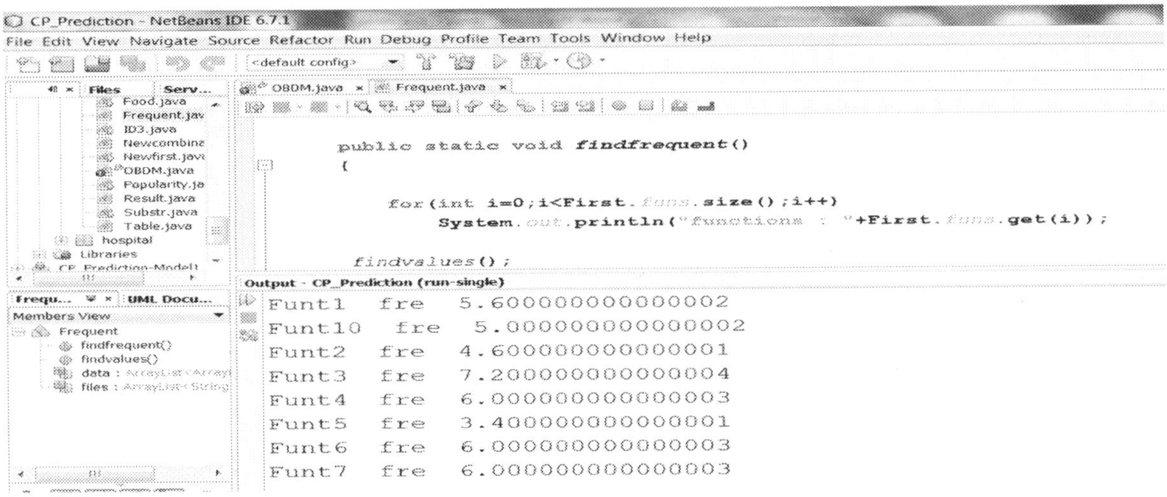

gression analysis is classified into: univariate and multivariate logistic regression analysis. Univariate predicts association amongst the two variables i.e. dependent and independent and discovers the importance of their relationship. Conversely, multivariate regression is used for building prediction model for the identification of change prone class. This type of analysis results in finding important metrics. For identifying significant metrics two types of selection methods are used:(i) Forward selection: In this type of selection, a single metric is analyzed at every step. (ii) Backward selection: In this type all the metrics are taken initially and eliminated one after the other till stopping condition is not met.

Mathematically it can be expressed as:

$$prob\left(X_1, X_2, X_3, \ldots\ldots X_N\right) = \frac{exp^{f(x)}}{1 + exp^{f(x)}} \tag{7}$$

where,

$$f\left(x\right) = C_0 + C_1 X_1 + C_2 X_2 + \ldots + C_N X_N$$

where the variable X denotes the independent variables and prob is the probability of change proneness of a class.

Odds ratio (OR): It defines the ratio of the likelihood that the event will be caused to the probability event will not be caused. Event here refers to the occurrence of change in the latest version Hosmer & Lemeshow (2004). It is represented by exp (C_i).

Maximum Likelihood Estimation: Statistical method predicts model's coefficients. It predicts the coefficients which support the possibility functions and contribute in making the log value as high as possible. Larger value indicates the improved effect of the independent variable on the expected result variable.

Statistical significance(Sig.): All (C_i) i.e. coefficients have significant level. Higher value of this attribute indicates, independent metrics have lesser impact in estimating change prone classes. We have considered threshold value of 0.7.

Model Development Procedures

For data classification, implementation of Artificial Bee Colony algorithm was done using Java language with WEKA tool and LibSVM. We have used WEKA tool for the validation of our prediction model. This tool is used with association rules, machine learning techniques, classification and for preprocessing of data.

For evaluating the classification process's precision and correctness, we have used a tenfold cross validation. Here we have divided the data set into 10 equally partitions (folds), wherein one partition is consumed for testing part and rest all others are used for training purposes. The process was repeated 10 times, such that every time one of the part became test data. Average of 10 results produced an accuracy of estimation.

For evaluating the performance of the prediction model we have used following methods:

1. **Sensitivity & Specificity:** For characterizing the accuracy of the prediction model we have used sensitivity and specificity. Sensitivity is defined as the accuracy by which the percentage of classes are correctly identified to be change prone class amongst all the classes which are actually change prone. And specificity is defined as the accuracy by which the percentage of non-change prone classes are correctly identified.
2. **Receiver Operating Characteristics (ROC) Curve:** It is an essential tool for analytic test evaluation. Here sensitivity i.e. (true positive rate) is plotted against specificity i.e. (false positive rate) at different cut off points. Accuracy of prediction model is achieved by selecting cut off point that has higher sensitivity and specificity as suggested by Emam et al. (1999)

RESULT ANALYSIS

This section shows validation results for our model using Open Clinic Software and Open Hospital Software. Using tenfold cross validation, we have illustrated the results. The results can be compared with other prediction models developed using various techniques given by Malhotra and Jangra (2015) which reveals the proposed model gives better results.

Table 11 and Table 12 shows results for statistics obtained from OpenClinic Software and OpenHospital software using LR multivariate technique. We have obtained the statistics B(coefficient), SE (Standard error), Sig. (Significance) and OR (Odds ratio) for our metrics which are B.D. (Behavioral Dependency), Freq.(Frequency), Pop.(Popularity), Exec. Time(Implementation Period), T.E.(Log information) using LR multivariate technique. Values of B, SE, Sig. and OR indicates behavioral dependency and frequency have a significant effect in predicting change.

Table 13 and Table 14 shows validation results obtained using LR technique and our proposed model which is based on ID3 and ABC (Artificial Bee Colony Algorithm). Values of specificity (69.7) and sensitivity (70.7) for LR technique of OpenClinic software has AUC (0.750) which is less than AUC (0.925) obtained by our prediction model. Similarly, AUC obtained for OpenHospital Software using

Table 11. Statistics for LR multivariate analysis of OpenClinic software

Metrics	B	SE	Sig.	OR
B.D.	0.021	0.21	0.001	1.212
Freq.	0.351	0.25	0.000	1.311
Pop.	0.121	0.11	0.003	0.501
Exec. Time	0.011	0.05	0.025	0.312
T.E.	0.001	0.15	0.031	0.112

Table 12. Statistics for LR multivariate analysis of OpenHospital software

Metrics	B	SE	Sig.	OR
B.D.	0.052	0.31	0.000	1.321
Freq.	0.231	0.021	0.000	1.512
Pop.	0.122	0.032	0.000	1.311
Exec. Time	0.001	0.254	0.010	0.517
T.E.	-0.02	0.212	0.010	0.252

Table 13. Validation results for OpenClinic software

Method	Specificity	Sensitivity	Cut Off Point	AUC
LR	69.7	70.7	0.012	0.750
proposed model	80.2	82.4	0.545	0.925

Table 14. Validation results for OpenHospital software

Method	Specificity	Sensitivity	Cut Off Point	AUC
LR	68.2	68.2	0.245	0.725
proposed model	79.8	81.2	0.564	0.915

LR method is 0.725 and AUC obtained by our prediction model is 0.915. The above values indicate that proposed prediction model gives better values as compared to LR multivariate technique.

EXPERIMENTAL ANALYSIS II

This section shows the Experimental Analysis using the proposed approach. Open source software Neuroph2.9.2 and Neuroph2.6 is used to find the accuracy of change prediction model. K-Means clustering,

K-Means Clustering

K-Means clustering is applied for clustering data sets. The data set is split into k disjoint clusters, where the value of k is constant. The algorithm has two steps. In the first step, k centroids are defined one for each cluster. And in the second step, the data points are linked to the nearest centroid.

K-Means Clustering for Neuroph2.9.2 and Neuroph2.6

The process of k-Means clustering system applied to dataset of Neuroph2.9.2 and Neuroph2.6 is given as follows: SimpleKMeans is performed with initial value set as 0, maximum candidates is 100 and number of iterations considered as 2. Sum of squared errors within cluster is 0.0. Neuroph2.9.2 and Neuroph2.6

Table 15. Clustering output of Neuroph software

Attribute	full data	cluster 0	cluster 1
	2	1	1
Software	Neuroph2.9.2	Neuroph2.6	Neuroph2.6
CBO	281.5	366	197
NOCH	104	114	94
NOA	3431	4928	1934
NIV	264.5	341	188
DIT	16	17	15
NOMMIN	1	1	1
NOMMAX	84.5	97	72
NIM	1652.5	2148	1157
NLM	2777	3818	1736
RFC	434.5	559	310
NOSM	171.5	233	110
NPRM	112	167	57
NPROM	63.5	69	58
NPM	1305.5	1679	932
LCOM	50.5	91	10
NC	276.5	366	187
NLSC	31862.5	42295	21430
NOI	1987.5	2540	1435
NCM	2083	2864	1302
RCM	16	17	15
NMI	2083	2864	1302
NIMI	175.5	236	115
NEMI	1477	1912	1042
NCCM	129	175	83
NCMI	85.5	116	55
NCI	385.5	480	291
NOC	213.5	266	161
TI	2083	2864	1302
ITI	175.5	236	115
ETI	1477	1912	1042

are selected as two clusters wherein, number of instances is 2 and number of attributes considered are 30 Object-Oriented metrics (CBO, NOCH, NOA, NIV, DIT, NOMMIN, NOMMAX, NIM, NLM, RFC, NOSM, NPRM, NPROM, NPM, LCOM, NC, NLSC, NOI, NCM, RCM, NMI, NIMI, NEMI, NCCM, NCMI, NCI, NOC, TI, ITI, ETI). Test mode is evaluation on training data and clustering model is full training set.

Cluster 0: Neuroph2.9.2 366, 114, 4928, 341, 17, 1, 97, 2148, 3818, 559, 233, 167, 69, 1679, 91, 366, 42295, 2540, 2864, 17, 2864, 236, 1912, 175, 116, 480, 266, 2864, 236, 1912

Cluster 1: Neuroph2.6 197, 94, 1934, 188, 15, 1, 72, 1157, 1736, 310, 110, 57, 58, 932, 10, 187, 21430, 1435, 1302, 15, 1302, 115, 1042, 83, 55, 291, 161, 1302, 115, 1042

The missing values in the data set are globally replaced with Mean/mode. Final cluster centroids output is given in table.

The values of metrics of two versions of Neuroph software is given in Table 15. The mean of cluster 1 and 0 for all metrics are provided. For example, after clustering the mean of the value for NOC metric is 213.5 ((266+ 161)/2).

Naïve Bayes

This is a well-established Bayesian method that is mainly expressed for executing classification tasks. When the independent variables are assumed as statistically independent, Naïve Bayes model provides more effective classification tools which are easy for usage and interpretation. Naïve Bayes is mostly suitable for large number of independent variables. Due to these reasons, Naïve Bayes performs better than other sophisticated classification techniques. Results of Naïve Bayes classification for all the three software's is evaluated in this section.

Naïve Bayes Classifier Output for Neuroph2.6 and Neuroph2.9.2

The proposed system used Naïve Bayes classifier with the number of Instances equal to 2 and the attributes considered as 30.

The Mean, standard deviation, weight sum and precision of 30 attributes of Neuroph2.6 and Neuroph2.9.2 are given in Table 16. Confusion Matrix is given as follows:

a b is classified as
1 0 | a = Neuroph2.6
0 1 | b = Neuroph2.9.2
Following values are obtained from the confusion matrix:

TP is 1, TN is 1, FP is 0 and FN is 0.

After clustering, classification is done for evaluating the data sets. Here the Naïve Bayesian classifier is applied for classification of software chosen as data sets. The metrics after classification procedure is given in Table 17 for the two versions of Neuroph software. The TP Rate, FP rate, precision, recall F-measure, MCC, ROC area and PRC area are found to be 1,0, 1,1, 1,1 for Neuroph software.

Table 16. Naïve Bayes classifier for Neuroph2.6 and Neuroph2.9.2

Metrics	Mean		Standard Deviation		Weighted Sum		Precision	
Software	Neuroph 2.6	Neuroph 2.9.2	Neuroph 2.6	Neuroph 2.9.2	Neuroph 2.6	Neuroph 2.9.2	Neuroph 2.6	Neuroph 2.9.2
CBO	169	338	28.1667	28.1667	1	1	169	169
NOCH	100	120	3.3333	3.3333	1	1	20	20
NOA	2994	5988	499	499	1	1	2994	2994
NIV	153	306	25.5	25.5	1	1	153	153
DIT	16	16	0.3333	0.3333	1	1	2	2
NOMMIN	1	1	0.0017	0.0017	1	1	0.01	0.01
NOMMAX	75	100	4.1667	4.1667	1	1	25	25
NIM	991	1982	165.1667	165.1667	1	1	991	991
NLM	2082	4164	347	347	1	1	2082	2082
RFC	249	498	41.5	41.5	1	1	249	249
NOSM	123	246	20.5	20.5	1	1	123	123
NPRM	110	220	18.3333	18.3333	1	1	110	110
NPROM	55	66	1.8333	1.8333	1	1	11	11
NPM	747	1494	124.5	124.5	1	1	747	747
LCOM	0	81	13.5	13.5	1	1	81	81
NC	179	358	29.8333	29.8333	1	1	179	179
NLSC	20865	41730	3477.5	3477.5	1	1	20865	20865
NOI	1105	2210	184.1667	184.1667	1	1	1105	1105
NCM	1562	3124	260.3333	260.3333	1	1	1562	1562
RCM	16	16	0.3333	0.3333	1	1	2	2
NMI	1562	3124	260.3333	260.3333	1	1	1562	1562
NIMI	121	242	20.1667	20.1667	1	1	121	121
NEMI	870	1740	145	145	1	1	870	870
NCCM	92	184	15.3333	15.3333	1	1	92	92
NCMI	61	122	10.1667	10.1667	1	1	61	61
NCI	378	567	31.5	31.5	1	1	189	189
NOC	210	315	17.5	17.5	1	1	105	105
TI	1562	3124	260.3333	260.3333	1	1	1562	1562
ITI	121	242	20.1667	20.1667	1	1	121	121
ETI	870	1740	145	145	1	1	870	870

Sensitivity = TP/(TP+FN) = 1/(1+0) = 1

Specificity = TN/(TN+FP) = 1/(1+0) = 1

Accuracy = (TP+TN)/(TP+TN+FP+FN) = (1+1)/(1+1+0+0) = 1

Precision = TP/TP+FP = 1/(1+0) = 1

Recall = TP/(TP+FN) = 1/(1+0) =1

Table 17. Naïve Bayes classifier output for Neuroph2.6 and Neuroph2.9.2

		Value	Percentage
Correctly Classified Instances		2	100%
Incorrectly Classified Instances		0	0%
Kappa statistic		1	
Mean absolute error		0	
Root Mean squared error		0	
Relative absolute error			0.00%
Root relative squared error			0.00%
Total Number of Instances		2	

TP Rate	FP Rate	Precision	Recall	F-Measure	MCC	ROC Area	Area class
1	0	1	1	1	1	1	Neuroph2.6
1	0	1	1	1	1	1	Neuroph2.9.2

F-Measure = 2*precision*recall/(precision+recall) = 2*1*1/(1+1) = 1.

From the above results, it is found that the sensitivity, specificity, recall, precision, accuracy and F-Measure of classification process are found to be 1 which reveals the accuracy of the proposed system.

Logistic Regression Analysis

Logistic regression processes the relationship between the dependent variable and independent variables by approximating likelihoods by a logistic function, which is the accumulative logistic distribution. Logistic regression is a special type of the general linear model and thus equivalent to linear regression.

Logistic regression is evaluated for all the Object-Oriented metrics to predict the accuracy of their values in two versions of software.

Logistic Regression Value for Neuroph2.6 and Neuroph2.9.2

The Logistic regression value for Neuroph2.6 and Neuroph2.9.2 is given in Table 18.

The instances taken hereare the two versions Neuroph 2.6 and Neuroph 2.9.2. From the Table 19, the correctly classified instances are 2 which implies that the classification is performed correctly. The values of incorrect classified instances, mean absolute error, Root Mean squared error are zero. The Relative absolute error and Root relative squared error are found to be 0.001%. The TP Rate, FP Rate, Precision, Recall, F-Measure, MCC, ROC Area are 1, 0, 1, 1, 1, 1 and 1. The weighted average of TP Rate, FP Rate, Precision, Recall, F-Measure, MCC, and ROC Area are 1, 0, 1, 1, 1, 1 and 1. Values obtained of TP Rate, FP Rate, Precision, Recall, F-Measure, MCC, and ROC Area for all the three open source software shows the accuracy of proposed model in terms of Object- Oriented metrics, as all the above used metrics has been evaluated using code analyzer and trace events feature of prediction model

Table 18. Logistic regression output for Neuroph2.6 and Neuroph2.9.2

Parameter	Even ratios	Odd ratios
CBO	0.9941	-0.0059
NOCH	0.9512	-0.05
NOA	0.9997	-0.0003
NIV	0.9935	-0.0065
DIT	0.6065	-0.5
NOMMAX	0.9608	-0.04
NIM	0.999	-0.001
NLM	0.9995	-0.0005
RFC	0.996	-0.004
NOSM	0.9919	-0.0081
NPRM	0.9131	-0.0091
NPROM	0.9987	-0.0909
NPM	0.9877	-0.0013
LCOM	0.9944	-0.0123
NC	1	-0.0056
NLSC	0.9991	0
NOI	0.9994	-0.0009
NCM	0.6065	-0.0006
RCM	0.9994	-0.5
NMI	0.9918	-0.0006
NIMI	0.9989	-0.0083
NEMI	0.9892	-0.0011
NCCM	0.9837	-0.0109
NCMI	0.9947	-0.0164
NCI	0.9905	-0.0053
NOC	0.9994	-0.0095
TI	0.9918	-0.0006
ITI	0.9989	-0.0083
ETI	0.9989	-0.0011
Intercept		66.4671

Change Prone Prediction of Neuroph Software

The change prone class, its execution time, frequency and popularity of two different versions of Neuroph are given in Table 20.

Total number of classes in Neuroph 2.9.2 and Neuroph 2.6 software are 366 and 187. Using the behavioral dependency approach number of classes that are predicted to be behaviorally dependent are 35. After evaluating dependent class, execution time and frequency of each dependent class is evaluated

Table 19. Logistic regression value for Neuroph2.6 and Neuroph2.9.2

					Value			Percentage
Correctly Classified Instances					2			100%
Incorrectly Classified Instances					0			0%
Kappa statistic					1			
Mean absolute error					0			
Root Mean squared error					0			
Relative absolute error								0.001%
Root relative squared error								0.001%
Total Number of Instances								2
	TP Rate	FP Rate	Precision	Recall	F-Measure	MCC	ROC Area	Area class
Weighted average	1	0	1	1	1	1	1	Neuroph2.6
	1	0	1	1	1	1	1	Neuroph2.9.2
	1	0	1	1	1	1	1	

as depicted in Table 20. Further, popularity feature is evaluated which specifies the degree of change proneness of a class.

From the above table, the frequency, execution time and popularity of each dependent class of Neuroph software are obtained. Depending on popularity rank, the change proneness is predicted. For example, the class NeuralNetwork exhibit *slow* execution time and frequency of the methods called in class is 15. So, NeuralNetwork is ranked with popularity 1. It indicates the most sensitive class which is to be given more attention in next release of software. Thus, such type of information is significant to software developers as the NC metrics is significantly reduced to behavioral dependent classes and popularity values provides the rank to change prone classes.

CONCLUSION AND FUTURE WORK

The chapter examines association amongst change prone classes and object oriented features. In addition to existing object oriented attributes the research proposes some new attributes such as Implementation Period of class, run time information of methods, frequency of method call, class dependency and popularity. Higher values of proposed metrics indicate higher is the probability of a class to be changed. For calculating the Implementation Period, Eclipse TPTP profiling tool is used, wherein Eclipse SDK version 3.6.2 is used. Runtime information of methods is used to evaluate the values of log information which is a dynamic metric and gives the accurate values of imported and exported methods. For evaluating the frequency attribute, frequent item set mining algorithm is used. For finding this feature of how frequently a method is called, rules for method calls are generated using association rules. For effectively building the prediction model, dimensions of the input set are reduced using, Artificial Bee Colony algorithm (ABC), which optimizes the rules for finding change prone classes. Further, using source code of Open Hospital application values for proposed metrics were generated. Research evaluated higher values of proposed metrics indicates, higher probability of degree of change prone class. The

Table 20. Change prone prediction of Neuroph software

S.No	Change prone class	Execution time	Frequency	Popularity
1	BackPropagation	Faster	2	7
2	BenchmarkTask	Faster	1	8
3	Connection	Faster	1	8
4	DelayedNeuron	Faster	1	8
5	Hashtable	Faster	1	8
6	ImageRecognitionHelper	Faster	1	8
7	InputFunction	Faster	1	8
8	InputStreamAdapter	Faster	2	7
9	IterativeLearning	Faster	2	7
10	LMS	Faster	3	6
11	Layer	Faster	2	7
12	LearningRule	Faster	3	6
13	MomentumBackpropagation	Faster	1	8
14	NeuralNetwork	Slow	15	1
15	Neuron	Faster	5	5
16	NeurophException	Faster	3	6
17	Observable	Faster	2	7
18	OutputStreamAdapter	Faster	2	7
19	PerceptronLearning	Faster	1	8
20	PluginBase	Faster	3	6
21	Properties	Faster	1	8
22	RangeRandomizer	Faster	1	8
23	RuntimeException	Faster	1	8
24	SigmoidDeltaRule	Faster	1	8
25	SummingFunction	Medium	8	3
26	SupervisedLearning	Faster	3	6
27	TrainingElement	Faster	1	8
28	TrainingElement	Faster	1	8
29	TrainingSetImport	Faster	1	8
30	TransferFunction	Medium	10	2
31	UnsupervisedHebbianLearning	Medium	6	4
32	UnsupervisedLearning	Faster	2	7
33	Weight	Faster	1	8
34	WeightsFunction	Faster	2	7
35	WeightsRandomizer	Faster	3	6

results were validated using various versions of open source software. For evaluating the performance of the prediction model we used Sensitivity, Specificity and ROC Curve. Higher values of AUC indicate the prediction model gives significant accurate results. And the proposed metrics contribute to predict accurate change prone classes.

For effectively evaluating change proneness in object oriented software, following future directions can be utilized by practitioners and researchers in their research work and studies. As the research is focused on real life software, the usage of commercial data should be increased up to a considerable extent so that real time results can be obtained more effectively. For validating the results, inter project validation can be used in which training set of one project can be used for testing in other similar projects. This would lead to better planning of scarce resources and would help in generating a good quality software. Several studies in literature have used machine learning technique, more machine learning methods can be used for analyzing the performance of change prediction model. A limited work is done using threshold methodology of metrics, the work can be extended by identifying threshold values of all the metrics for change proneness prediction.

REFERENCES

Abdi, M. K., Lounis, H., & Sahraoui, H. (2009, July). Predicting change impact in object-oriented applications with bayesian networks. In *Computer Software and Applications Conference, 2009. COMPSAC'09. 33rd Annual IEEE International* (Vol. 1, pp. 234-239). IEEE. 10.1109/COMPSAC.2009.38

Al-Khiaty, M., Abdel-Aal, R., & Elish, M. O. (2017). Abductive network ensembles for improved prediction of future change-prone classes in object-oriented software. *The International Arab Journal of Information Technology*, *14*(6), 803–811.

Bacchelli, A., D'Ambros, M., & Lanza, M. (2010). Are popular classes more defect prone? In *Fundamental Approaches to Software Engineering* (pp. 59–73). Springer Berlin Heidelberg. doi:10.1007/978-3-642-12029-9_5

Bansal, A., & Jajoria, S. (2019). Cross-Project Change Prediction Using Meta-Heuristic Techniques. *International Journal of Applied Metaheuristic Computing*, *10*(1), 43–61. doi:10.4018/IJAMC.2019010103

Bansal, A., Modi, K., & Jain, R. (2019). Analysis of the Performance of Learners for Change Prediction Using Imbalanced Data. In *Applications of Artificial Intelligence Techniques in Engineering* (pp. 345–359). Singapore: Springer. doi:10.1007/978-981-13-1819-1_33

Bergenti, F., & Poggi, A. (2000, July). Improving UML designs using automatic design pattern detection. In *12th International Conference on Software Engineering and Knowledge Engineering (SEKE)* (pp. 336-343). Academic Press.

Bura, D., Choudhary, A., & Singh, R. K. (2017). A Novel UML Based Approach for Early Detection of Change Prone Classes. *International Journal of Open Source Software and Processes*, *8*(3), 1–23. doi:10.4018/IJOSSP.2017070101

Catolino, G., & Ferrucci, F. (n.d.). An extensive evaluation of ensemble techniques for software change prediction. Journal of Software: Evolution and Process, e2156.

Catolino, G., Palomba, F., De Lucia, A., Ferrucci, F., & Zaidman, A. (2018). Enhancing change prediction models using developer-related factors. *Journal of Systems and Software, 143,* 14–28. doi:10.1016/j.jss.2018.05.003

Elish, M. O., & Al-Zouri, A. A. (2014, January). Effectiveness of Coupling Metrics in Identifying Change-Prone Object-Oriented Classes. In *Proceedings of the International Conference on Software Engineering Research and Practice (SERP)* (p. 1). The Steering Committee of The World Congress in Computer Science, Computer Engineering and Applied Computing (WorldComp).

Emam, K., Benlarbi, S., Goel, N., & Rai, S. (1999). *A validation of object-oriented metrics.* Technical Report ERB-1063, National Research Council of Canada.

Eski, S., & Buzluca, F. (2011, March). An empirical study on object-oriented metrics and software evolution in order to reduce testing costs by predicting change-prone classes. In *Software Testing, Verification and Validation Workshops (ICSTW), 2011 IEEE Fourth International Conference on* (pp. 566-571). IEEE. 10.1109/ICSTW.2011.43

Godara, D., Choudhary, A., & Singh, R. K. (2018). Predicting Change Prone Classes in Open Source Software. *International Journal of Information Retrieval Research, 8*(4), 1–23. doi:10.4018/IJIRR.2018100101

Godara, D., & Singh, R. K. (2015). Enhancing Frequency Based Change Proneness Prediction Method Using Artificial Bee Colony Algorithm. In *Advances in Intelligent Informatics* (pp. 535–543). Cham: Springer. doi:10.1007/978-3-319-11218-3_48

Godara, D., & Singh, R. K. (2017). Exploring the relationships between design measures and change proneness in object-oriented systems. *International Journal of Software Engineering, Technology and Applications, 2*(1), 64–80.

Han, A. R., Jeon, S. U., Bae, D. H., & Hong, J. E. (2008, July). Behavioral dependency measurement for change-proneness prediction in UML 2.0 design models. In Computer Software and Applications, 2008. COMPSAC'08. 32nd Annual IEEE International (pp. 76-83). IEEE.

Hosmer, D. W. Jr, & Lemeshow, S. (2004). *Applied logistic regression.* John Wiley & Sons.

Janes, A., Scotto, M., Pedrycz, W., Russo, B., Stefanovic, M., & Succi, G. (2006). Identification of defect-prone classes in telecommunication software systems using design metrics. *Information Sciences, 176*(24), 3711–3734. doi:10.1016/j.ins.2005.12.002

Khomh, F., Penta, M. D., & Gueheneuc, Y. G. (2009, October). An exploratory study of the impact of code smells on software change-proneness. In *Reverse Engineering, 2009. WCRE'09. 16th Working Conference on* (pp. 75-84). IEEE. 10.1109/WCRE.2009.28

Koru, A. G., & Liu, H. (2007). Identifying and characterizing change-prone classes in two large-scale open-source products. *Journal of Systems and Software, 80*(1), 63–73. doi:10.1016/j.jss.2006.05.017

Kyriakakis, P., Chatzigeorgiou, A., Ampatzoglou, A., & Xinogalos, S. (2019). Exploring the frequency and change proneness of dynamic feature pattern instances in PHP applications. *Science of Computer Programming, 171,* 1–20. doi:10.1016/j.scico.2018.10.004

Lu, H., Zhou, Y., Xu, B., Leung, H., & Chen, L. (2012). The ability of object-oriented metrics to predict change-proneness: A meta-analysis. *Empirical Software Engineering, 17*(3), 200–242. doi:10.100710664-011-9170-z

Malhotra, R., & Chug, A. (2013). An empirical study to redefine the relationship between software design metrics and maintainability in high data intensive applications. In *Proceedings of the World Congress on Engineering and Computer Science (Vol. 1)*. Academic Press.

Malhotra, R., & Jangra, R. (2015). Prediction & Assessment of Change Prone Classes Using Statistical & Machine Learning Techniques. Journal of Information Processing Systems, 1-26.

Malhotra, R., & Khanna, M. (2013). Investigation of relationship between object-oriented metrics and change proneness. *International Journal of Machine Learning and Cybernetics, 4*(4), 273–286. doi:10.100713042-012-0095-7

Malhotra, R., & Khanna, M. (2018). Prediction of change prone classes using evolution-based and object-oriented metrics. *Journal of Intelligent & Fuzzy Systems, 34*(3), 1755–1766. doi:10.3233/JIFS-169468

Menard, S. (2002). *Applied logistic regression analysis* (Vol. 106). Sage. doi:10.4135/9781412983433

Pritam, N., Khari, M., Kumar, R., Jha, S., Priyadarshini, I., Abdel-Basset, M., & Long, H. V. (2019). Assessment of Code Smell for Predicting Class Change Proneness using Machine Learning. *IEEE Access: Practical Innovations, Open Solutions, 7*, 37414–37425. doi:10.1109/ACCESS.2019.2905133

Romano, D., & Pinzger, M. (2011, September). Using source code metrics to predict change-prone java interfaces. In *Software Maintenance (ICSM), 2011 27th IEEE International Conference on* (pp. 303-312). IEEE. 10.1109/ICSM.2011.6080797

Wilkie, F. G., & Kitchenham, B. A. (2000). Coupling measures and change ripples in C++ application software. *Journal of Systems and Software, 52*(2), 157–164. doi:10.1016/S0164-1212(99)00142-9

Zhou, Y., Leung, H., & Xu, B. (2009). Examining the potentially confounding effect of class size on the associations between object-oriented metrics and change-proneness. *Software Engineering. IEEE Transactions on, 35*(5), 607–623.

Zhu, X., Song, Q., & Sun, Z. (2013). Automated identification of change-prone classes in open source software projects. *Journal of Software, 8*(2), 361–366. doi:10.4304/jsw.8.2.361-366

Chapter 4
Search for Information in Text Files

Mouhcine El Hassani
Sultan Moulay Slimane University, Morocco

Noureddine Falih
Sultan Moulay Slimane University, Morocco

Belaid Bouikhalene
Sultan Moulay Slimane University, Morocco

ABSTRACT

As information becomes increasingly abundant and accessible on the web, researchers do not have a need to go to excavate books in the libraries. These require a knowledge extraction system from the text (KEST). The goal of authors in this chapter is to identify the needs of a person to do a search in a text, which can be unstructured, and retrieve the terms of information related to the subject of research then structure them into classes of useful information. These may subsequently identify the general architecture of an information retrieval system from text documents in order to develop it and finally identify the parameters to evaluate its performance and the results retrieved.

INTRODUCTION

Currently, the new information and communication technologies (NICT) have a very important role in the life of humanity, resulting in a considerable amount of information, available in digital form, such as books published on the Internet, electronic journals, information disseminated in social networks like Facebook, Twitter and many others. It is essential to extract those that are relevant and reliable. Therefore, it seems necessary to advocate a credible and efficient system that processes all textual information, in order to deduce structured and useful knowledge.

The basis of textual inquiry is to organize information into word classes and entities, while fixing the associations between these classes and the mutual interactions of their objects.

DOI: 10.4018/978-1-7998-1021-6.ch004

As a result, all new found information would enrich a structured database represented in tables that represent each type of data.

PRINCIPLE OF TEXT MINING

Several technical definitions of text mining can be found on the Internet and in textbooks, like that of Un Yong Nahm and all. in "Text Mining with Information Extraction" (Un Yong Nahm and Raymond J, 2002), but the best known is the entire process of looking for patterns related to artificial intelligence that aims to identify association rules from unstructured text. Many methods are based on sorting, grouping (from SQL queries: Structured Query Language) words, and counting the number of repeated words to identify their importance.

To fully understand the principle of finding information, the user expresses his needs in different forms, either a query composed by independent keywords or linked by logical operators such as AND, OR, NO ..., some research applications of information uses them to view indexes of databases containing web pages or collected files.

In general, a text mining process takes place in four steps:

- We begin by preparing the data for processing, transforming the raw data from one form to another in order to submit them to appropriate operations.
- The second is the search for frequent patterns in the extracted text and extraction association rules.
- The third step is to present data in visual form using graphs or diagrams. A data processing tool such as 2D or 3D visualization software would be needed to recognize relevant and useful information.
- In the fourth phase, both cleaning and optimization operations are applied to reduce the size of the found information.

However, Data processing techniques do not only depend on these four steps but also on the location of the used information and, particular, the used algorithms and methods.

Information Extraction Method

Extracting information is the first and most important step in preprocessing the text. During extraction, we try to find a structured text in natural language (Yong U., 2004). The Advanced Defense Research Projects Agency (DARPA) has funded a series of specific annual conferences, called "Message Understanding Conferences" (MUCs) (Lehnert et al., 1991), in which researchers focus on unstructured text extraction methods. For each (MUC), participants received sample messages and instructions on the type of information to be extracted, and developed a system to process these messages. The performance of participant's system was assessed against their competitors.

A template defining a list of sites and substrings extracted from the document will be used to present and structure the extracted data. In general, the information to be extracted is defined by a model representing a list of boxes to fill, although they are sometimes represented by annotations in the file. Vacuum loads can be a group of specified values or strings instantly retrieved from the document.

Figure 1. Example template representing a text for a job offer

Announcement: Need, Web Developer
Location: Rabat. Morocco
This person is responsible for designing and implementing the ABC Server web interface components and general background development tasks.

A successful candidate must have experience that includes:
• One or more of the following: Solaris, Linux, Windows / NT.
• Programming in C/ C++, Java.
• Access to the database and integration: Oracle, ODBC
• CGI and scripting: one or more of JavaScript.
• Perl, PHP, ASP
• Exposure to the following is a plus: JDBC, Front Page and / or Copper Fusion.
 2 years experience (or equivalent) is required
Completed template
• Ref: \ Web Developer "
• Location: Rabat. Morocco
\ Languages: \ C/ C++ ". \ Java". \ JavaScript ". \ Perl". \ PHP ". \ ASP"

In the example, shown in Figure 1, we give a text representation for the preprocessing and related constraints.

The Figure 1 presents a simple document model of an information extraction operation obtained from a social network, which publishes job offers. The text contains only sectors loaded by strings extracted directly from the document. Sectors can have multiple boxes to load and that represent advertising activities as programming languages) development environment, applications and domains...

Text mining may yield interesting and important inputs for predictive modeling and can provide insightful recommendation for decision makers. Practical applications has been shown in analyzing hotel reviews, banner pages of courses, conference advertisements, job offers, job advertisements, company newspapers, and many more. Furthermore, the extraction of knowledge starting from text is still an adequate method to automate the update of the static and dynamic webpages.

Technics of the artificial intelligence using automatic learning were presented to extract information from files and texts documents in order to easily generate databases starting from information, making the text more accessible online. For example, the information extracted from the working stations on the Web can be used to build a consultable database, for the inventory of computer equipment, in order to clearly define its needs.

Information is useful only if it meets the needs of the users, for this, an information retrieval system should first recover the files and documents responding to customer requests, then index and organize them before storing and publishing them.

The Figure 2 represents the general architecture of the information retrieval process.

A user sends a request to the recovery system, that it consults the previously indexed documents and classifies them according to the relevance score meeting the needs of the client, and then returns the set of results. The user writes simple sentences, these depend on the language and his style, the word order of the text expressions influences the quality of the results obtained, a recovered document does not necessarily have to contain all the terms of the query. Another type of queries called proximity queries,

Figure 2. General Architecture of the Information Retrieval Process

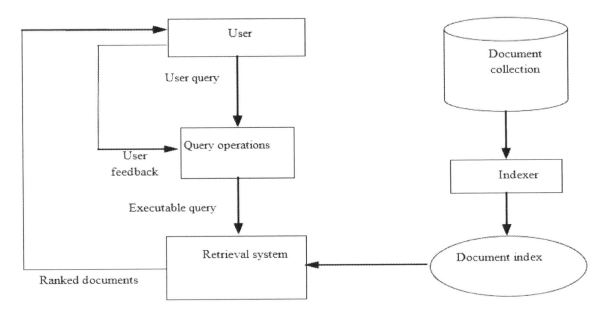

the system calculates the proximity (distance) of the terms that make up the queries and classifies the pages and documents found, taking into account this proximity factor and the order of the terms. The user can set this order in advance. Other searched expressions can be enclosed in two quotation marks, thus forcing the search engine to retrieve the complete document and return the results or URL links of similar pages.

SCHEMATIC DIAGRAM OF TEXT EXTRACTION (TEXT MINING)

Approximate exploration of information assumes that the "keep" information is already in a local database. However, in many applications, digital information is only available as free natural language files, but not in well-organized databases. Because information retrieval addresses the difficulty of transforming a set of text files into a more structured database, the extracted data generated by a Text Mining module can facilitate the KDD (Knowledge Discovery in Databases) process. Artificial intelligence uses KDD for further use of knowledge extraction from data, as shown in Figure 3. Extracting information plays an obvious role in text mining.

Admittedly, the construction of a Text Mining system is a difficult operation; however, there were new significant improvements in the processes use of machine learning giving help to automate the realization of Text Mining systems.

By manually handling a small number of documents with the goal of extracting data, Text Mining systems can be useful, for long text, for building a database. Nevertheless, the exactitude of the current Text Mining systems is limited and, consequently, a database deduced automatically will comprise surely a significant number of faults. However, the question that might interest us is whether the knowledge acquired from this database is clearly less credible than in the case of a cleaner database. This article

Figure 3. Schema of text mining process

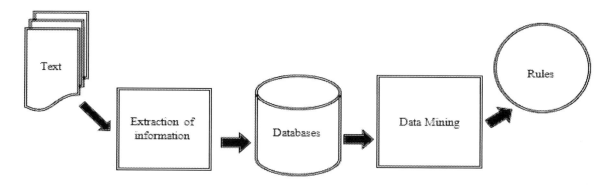

presents examples showing that noticed rules, starting from an automatically retrieved database, are an inaccuracy close to that discovered from a manually constructed database.

PROCESS OF EXTRACTING INFORMATION

Several originators set out the process of extraction of information in stages of distinct granularity, using specific systems of extraction created for this purpose. The analysis of the various approaches, used for information extraction, helps to identify six main stages of this process:

- Pretreatment.
- The discovery of the proper names.
- Syntactic analysis.
- The extraction of the events and the relations.
- Resolution of the anaphora (the anaphora (female substantive) is a stylistic device which consists in beginning worms, sentences, sets of sentences or worms by the same word or the same syntagm).
- Production of operating results.

Pretreatment

In this stage, we divide the document text into several portions that constitute phases, segments, empty zones, etc. This operation can be carried out by various components related to the programming language, like the string Tokenizer of java, the splitters, the segmenters, etc. Note that the tokenization consists of dividing the text into several Tokenas delimited by a character or spaces preset in advance. This technic is effective for most of texts written by using various languages, except for Chinese, Japanese, and other specific languages.

The phase, following the treatment is the lexical and morphological analysis of the text. It consists in locating the words and sentences representing the exceptions and ambiguities, and then specialized dictionaries of several languages are used to resolve these constraints. These dictionaries can gather the names of countries, cities of the scientific terms, etc. A simple example consists to progressively locate the words of a text editor, like Word, with the seizure, and to give suggestions of the faults made during the seizure. Users can always introduce new terms and enrich the dictionary.

The Discovery of Proper Names

It is one of the most significant tasks in the information extraction process. It makes it possible to locate all classes and entities representing the proper names, such as people, companies, monuments, countries. This information can be easily identified, since they are written in the form of text and even by the availability of the tools of control of the programming languages "the regular expressions of java".

Syntactic Analysis

During this stage, a syntactic analysis of the sentences in the documents is carried out. After having identified the basic entities and classes in the preceding phase, sentences are analyzed to identify the group of names of some of these entities and groups of verbs. In this stage of analysis, the work is prepared for the next stage of extraction of the events and the relationships in which they collaborate. The groups of nouns and verbs are used like sections to start to work at the stage of correspondence of reason. The identification of these groups is performed by the application of a set of especially built regular expressions. However, the complete analysis is not an easy task; it thus requires expensive calculations, which, slow down all the process of information extraction. Since we deal with such a difficult problem, the complete analysis is likely to introduce errors. On the other hand, sometimes, the total syntactic analysis is not necessary. Thus, information retrieval research groups tend to use what is called the partial or surface analysis instead of integrality. By using only local information, they observed that the not very deep analysis creates partial syntactic fragments, which overlap only with higher degree of confidence. Following the application of the partial syntactic analysis, they performed better than sites, which tried to create complete syntactic structures (Ralph G., 1997).

Extraction of Events and Relationships

This process is carried out by the creation and the application of extraction rules, which specify different reasons. The text is adjusted with these reasons and, if a correspondence is found, the element of the text is labeled and extracted afterwards. The formalism of this writing differs from a system of extraction of information to another (Alexandre S., 2004).

Resolution of the Ankaphora

Any class given in a text can be revoked on several occasions and each time that could be returned differently. In order to recognize all the manners used to give a name to this entity, one carries out a documented resolution of reference. There are several types of correlation, but the best current types are the proper names and the pronominal nomenclature, when a name is replaced in the first case by a pronoun and by another name or a noun phrase in the second (Ronen F., 2007).

Production of Operating Results

This phase contains the modification of the structures, which were arisen during preceding operations in the models of exit according to formats specified by a process. It can include different operations of standardization for the dates, the hour, the currencies, etc. For example, a method of district for the percentages can be carried out and the number of surface 60.96 will be fully converted 61.

Because a particular process of information extraction cannot have all the possible components, all the operations should not obligatorily be completed in just one extraction of information. According to Appelt and Israel in MUC-5 1993, there are several factors affecting the choice of the system components, such as:

- The language: as previously said for the text processing in the case of Chinese or Japanese. These languages do not comprise clear words and limits of sentences. Texts in German language contain words of difficult morphological structures; witch requires a comparison to English documents in such cases.
- The kind of text and properties: in the transcriptions of abstract speeches, for example, misspellings can occur in addition to the implicit limits of the sentence. If the information must be extracted from these texts, these questions must be taken into account and be addressed when designing system by adding the corresponding modules.
- The process of extraction: for the recognition of the names, the modules of analysis and resolution of anaphora cannot be necessary.

EVALUATION OF THE EXTRACTION OF INFORMATION

By considering the text entry or a block of texts, the awaited exit of a system of extraction of information can be defined in a precise way. To facilitate the evaluation of various systems and approaches of the extraction of information, «the IR research community» in this respect adopted the parameters of precision and recall. They measure the system effectiveness from the point of view of the user, i.e. the extent to which the system produces all the suitable output (recall) and only the suitable exit (precision). Thus, the recall and the precision can be regarded respectively as the measurement of exhaustiveness and exactitude. To define them in a formal way, this one allots to # key the total number of slots, which must be filled according to an annotated corpus of reference, representing a degree of reliability or a Gold Standard, and # correct (# incorrect) the number of slots correctly filled (incorrectly) the answer of the system. A slit known as is filled correctly if it is not aligned with a slit in the Gold Standard (slit parasitic) or if an invalid value were allotted to it. Then, the precision and the recall can be defined as follows:

$$Precision = \frac{\# \, correct}{\# \, correct + \# \, incorrect}$$

$$recall = \frac{\# \, correct}{\# \, key}$$

In order to obtain a finer image of the performance of information extraction system, the precision and the recall are often measured separately for each type of site.

Measurement *F* is used as balanced harmonic mean of precision and recall, it is defined as follows:

$$F = \frac{\left(\beta^2 + 1\right) * Precision * recall}{\left(\beta^2 * Precision\right) + recall}$$

In the definition above, β is a nonnegative value, used to adjust their relative weighting (When $\beta^2=1.0$ the recall and the precision are considered to have the same weight, for lower values of β more weight is given to the precision).

Other parameters are also used in the literature, such as the error rate of slit, SER (Thierry P., 2013) (Gokhan et al, 2011), which is given by:

$$SER = \frac{\# incorrect + \# missing}{\# key}$$

where *#missing* indicates the number of sites in the reference, which are not aligned with any site in the system response. It reflects the relationship between the total number of erroneous slot and the total number of slots in the reference. According to particular cases, unquestionable needs standard for errors (ex: the parasitic slits) can be balanced in order to consider them more or less significant than others.

CONCLUSION

In this chapter, it is shown that text-mining systems can be developed rapidly and evaluated easily on existing Information Extraction (IE) corpora by using existing information extraction and data mining technology (Liu A.et al., 2011). General steps are presented for better information extraction performance, shedding light on key elements that should be considered when extracting data information, particularly from unstructured texts (Garcia E., 2016). Also, Factors, such as accuracy, recall, F-measurement and the error rate of the slot, are used to better improve the evaluation in the extraction of information.

REFERENCES

Alexandre, S. (2004). *Textual Information Extraction Using Structure Induction*. LIRIS-CNRS.

Feldman, R. (2007). *The Text Mining Handbook Advanced Approaches in Analyzing Unstructured Data*. Cambridge University Press.

Garcia, E. (2016). *The Extended Boolean Model*. Retrieved from www.minerazzi.com

Gokhan, T., & Renato, D. (2011). *Spoken Language Understanding: Systems for Extracting Semantic Information from speech*. John Wiley & Sons, Ltd.

Grishman, R. (1997). Information Extraction: Techniques and Challenges. *Computer Science, 1299*, 10–27.

Lehnert, W., Cardie, C., Fisher, D., Riloff, E., & Williams, R. (1991). Description of the CIRCUS, System as Used for MUC-3. In *Proceedings of Third Message Understanding Conference (MUC-3)* (pp. 223-233). University of Massachusetts.

Liu, A. U., & Bing, P. (2011). *Information Retrieval and Web Search. In Web Data Mining* (pp. 211–268). Springer-Verlag Berlin Heidelberg.

Nahm. (2004). *Doctoral Dissertation: Text mining with information extraction.* University of Texas at Austin.

Thierry, P., Horacio, S., Jakub, P., & Roman, Y. (2013). *Multi-source. In Multilingual Information Extraction and Summarization. Theory and Applications of Natural Language Processing* (pp. 27–28). Springer Publishing Company.

Yong Nahm, U., & Raymond, J. (2002). *Text Mining with Information Extraction. In Mooney Department of Computer Sciences* (p. 2). Austin, TX: University of Texas.

Chapter 5
An Approach of Documents Indexing Using Summarization

Rida Khalloufi
Sultan Moulay Slimane University, Morocco

Rachid El Ayachi
Sultan Moulay Slimane University, Morocco

Mohamed Biniz
Sultan Moulay Slimane University, Morocco

Mohamed Fakir
Sultan Moulay Slimane University, Morocco

Muhammad Sarfraz
https://orcid.org/0000-0003-3196-9132
Kuwait University, Kuwait

ABSTRACT

Document indexing is an active domain, which is interesting a lot of researchers. Generally, it is used in the information retrieval systems. Document indexing encompasses a set of approaches that can be applied to index a document using a corpus. This treatment has several advantages, like accelerating the research process, finding the pertinent contains related to a query, reducing storage space, etc. The use of the entire document in the indexing process affects several parameters, such as indexing time, research time, storage space of treatment, etc. The focus of this chapter is to improve all parameters (cited above) related to the indexing process by proposing a new indexing approach. The goal of proposed approach is to use a summarization to minimize the size of documents without affecting the meaning.

DOI: 10.4018/978-1-7998-1021-6.ch005

INTRODUCTION

There is an enormous amount of textual material, and it is growing every moment and time. Think of the internet comprised of web pages, news articles, status updates, blogs and so much more. The data is unstructured and the best that we can do to navigate it is to use search and skim the results.

There is a great need to reduce much of the text data to shorter and focused summaries that capture the salient details. So, we can navigate it more effectively as well as check whether the larger documents contain the information that we are looking for. We cannot possibly create summaries of all of the text manually; there is a great need for automatic methods.

They are many reasons why we need automatic text summarization tools. Here are some of them:

- Summaries reduce reading time.
- When researching documents, summaries make the selection process easier.
- Automatic summarization improves the effectiveness of indexing.
- Automatic summarization algorithms are less biased than human summarizes.
- Personalized summaries are useful in question-answering systems as they provide personalized information.
- Using automatic or semi-automatic summarization systems enable abstract commercial services to increase the number of texts, they are able to process (Torres & Juan, 2014).

The rest of the chapter is organized as follows. Section 2 gives a description of the automatic text summarization. Section 3 is dedicated to present the principal of indexing document and its steps. Section 4 proposes a new approach of indexing based on summarization to reduce the size of the document preserving the meaning. Section 5 is devoted to the experimental results obtained and criteria used in evaluation. Finally, the conclusion is given in Section 6.

AUTOMATIC TEXT SUMMARIZATION

Automatic text summarization is the process of creating a short and coherent version of a longer document. We are generally good at this type of task as it involves first understanding the meaning of the source document and then distilling the meaning and capturing salient details in the new description. As such, the goal of automatically creating summaries of text is to have the resulting summaries as good as those written by humans.

It is not enough to just generate words and phrases that capture the gist of the source document. The summary should be accurate and should read fluently as a new standalone document. The different dimensions of text summarization can be generally categorized based on its input type (single or multi document), purpose (generic, domain specific, or query-based) and output type (extractive or abstractive) (Kumar, Goh, Basiron, Choon, & Suppiah, 2016).

There are two main approaches to summarize text documents: Extractive Methods and Abstractive Methods. Extractive text summarization (Gupta & Lehal, 2010) involves the selection of phrases and sentences from the source document to make up the new summary. Techniques involve ranking the relevance of phrases in order to choose only those most relevant to the meaning of the source.

Abstractive text summarization (Kasture, Yargal, Nityan, Kulkarni, & Mathur, 2014) involves generating entirely new phrases and sentences to capture the meaning of the source document. This is a more challenging approach but is also the approach ultimately used by humans. Classical methods operate by selecting and compressing contents from the source document.

Classically, most successful text summarization methods are extractive because it is an easier approach. But, abstractive approaches hold the hope of more general solutions to the problem (Nallapati, Zhou, santos, Gulcehre, & Xiang, 2016).

Extractive Methods

The key concept of extractive summarization is to identify and extract important document sentences and put them together as a summary. That is, the generated summary is a collection of original sentences. There are several approaches to sentence extraction. But the following subsections will describe a single example, namely, frequency-based approach.

Frequency Based Approach

Frequency Based Approach assumes that important words in document will be repeated many times compared to the other words in the document. Thus, Luhn (Luhn, 1958) proposed to indicate the importance of sentences in the document by using word frequency. Since then, many of the summarization systems use frequency-based approaches in their sentence extraction process. Two techniques that use frequency as a basic form of measure in text summarization are: word probability and term frequency-inverse document frequency.

Word Probability

It was assumed that one of the simplest ways of using frequency is by taking the raw frequency of a word i.e., by simply counting each word occurrence in the document. However, this measure can be greatly influenced by the document length. One way to make adjustment for the document length is by computing the word probability (Sripada & Jagarlamudi, 2009). The probability f(w) of a word w is given by Equation 1.

$$f\left(w\right) = \frac{n\left(w\right)}{N} \tag{1}$$

where

- $n(w)$ = The frequency count of the word w in the document,
- N = The total number of words in the document.

The findings from the analysis carried by on human-written summaries indicate that people tend to use word frequency to determine the key topics of a document. SumBasic (Vanderwende, Suzuki, Brockett, & Nenkova, 2007) is an example of summarization system that exploits word probability to create summaries. The SumBasic system first computes the word probability (as given in Equation 1) from the input document. Then for each sentence, it computes the sentence weight as a function of word probability as follows:

$$weight\left(s_j\right) = \frac{\sum_{w \in s_j} f\left(w\right)}{\left|\left\{w \middle| w \in s_j\right\}\right|} \tag{2}$$

Based on the sentence weight, it then picks the best scoring sentences.

Term Frequency–Inverse Document Frequency

Term frequency-inverse document frequency (*tf-idf*) has been traditionally used in information retrieval (IR) to deal with frequent occurring terms or words in a corpus consisting related documents (Seki, 2002). Its purpose was to address the following question: Are all content words that frequently appear in documents are equally important? For instance, a collection of news articles reporting on earthquake disaster will obviously contain the word 'earthquake' in all documents. Thus, the idea of *tf-idf* is to reduce the weight of frequent occurring words by comparing its proportional frequency in the document collection. This property has made the expression *tf-idf* to be one of the universally used terminologies in extractive summarization. Here, the term frequency (*tf*) is defined as:

$$tf_{i,j} = \frac{n_{i,j}}{\sum n_j} \tag{3}$$

where $n_{i,j}$ represents the frequency count of the word i in document j. Each word is then divided or normalized by the total number of the words in document j. This term weight computation is similar to the word probability computation given in Equation 1. Next, the inverse document frequency (*idf*) of a word i is computed as follows:

$$idf_i = \log \frac{|D|}{\left\{d \middle| t_i \hat{I} D\right\}} \tag{4}$$

where, the total number of documents in the corpus is divided by the number of documents that contain the word i. Based on Equations 3 and 4, the expression *tfidf* of word i in document j is computed as follows:

$$tfidf = tf_{i,j} * idf_i \tag{5}$$

Figure 1. Different steps in the indexing process

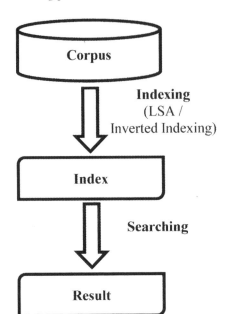

DOCUMENT INDEXING

The principle of documents indexing is illustrated in Figure 1. This figure shows the different steps adopted in indexing process.

In Figure 1, an inverted index is an index into a set of documents of the words in the documents. The index is accessed by some search method. Each index entry gives the word and a list of documents, possibly with locations within the documents, where the word occurs. The inverted index data structure is a central component of a typical search engine indexing algorithms. A goal of a search engine implementation is to optimize the speed of the query: find the documents where word X occurs. Once a forward index is developed, which stores lists of words per document, it is next inverted to develop an inverted index. Querying the forward index would require sequential iteration through each document and to each word to verify a matching document. The time, memory, and processing resources to perform such a query are not always technically realistic. Instead of listing the words per document in the forward index, the inverted index data structure is developed, which lists the documents per word. With the inverted index created, the query can now be resolved by jumping to the word ID (via random access) in the inverted index. Random access is generally regarded as being faster than sequential access.

The use of the entire document in indexing process has some inconvenience. It is because the documents, which have large sizes, consume more time, more memory and more resources. This has motivated the authors to propose the new indexing approach based on summarization I the following section.

Figure 2. Indexing process using summarization

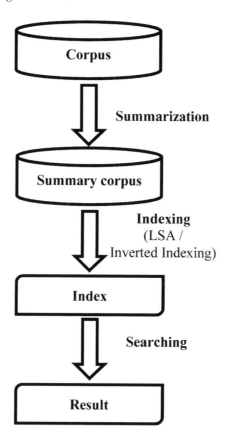

SUMMARIZATION AND INDEXING

In this work, we summarize the corpus using Frequency-based Approach, in order to get a corpus with fewer number of words and low size (summary index). The next step is indexing the last corpus to get an Index using (Inverted indexing). Finally, we have an index, which can be used for searching a query to get the result as described in Figure 2.

EXPERIMENTAL RESULTS

This section is meant for the experimental study done in the proposed model of work shown in Figure 2.

Evaluation Criteria

Many different measures for evaluating the performance of IR systems have been proposed. The measures require a collection of documents and a query. All common measures described here assume a ground truth notion of relevancy: every document is known to be either relevant or non-relevant to a particular query. In practice queries may be ill-posed and there may be different shades of relevancy.

Precision

Precision (Biniz & El Ayachi, 2018) is the ability to retrieve top-ranked documents that are mostly relevant. Precision, denoted by P, is the fraction of the documents retrieved that are relevant to the user's information need, it is defined as follows:

$$P = \frac{Nb\, relevant\, documents\, retrieved}{Total\, Nb\, of\, retrieved\, doucments} \qquad (6)$$

Recall

Recall (Biniz, El ayachi, & Fakir, 2017) is the ability of the search to find all of the relevant items in the corpus. The fraction of the documents that are relevant to the query that are successfully retrieved. Recall R is defined as follows:

$$R = \frac{Nb\, relevant\, documents\, retrieved}{Total\, Nb\, of\, relevant\, doucments} \qquad (7)$$

EXPERIMENTAL STUDIES

In this section, we present some experimental studies and a comparison between the two IR systems (Indexing Normal Corpus and Indexing Summarized Corpus). The corpus contains 5,686,428 words selected from 895 journal articles published by Elsevier in 2011–2018 (Kwary, 2017). The corpus is classified into four subject areas: Health sciences, life sciences, Physical Sciences, and Social Sciences. It follows the classifications of Scopus, which is the largest abstract and citation database of peer- reviewed scientific journals, books and conference proceedings.

Table 1 shows results obtained by comparing the two process of indexation presented in this chapter. The criteria used in this study are: Number of treated documents in one hour, Time of search and Average document size. The results figuring in the table justify that the use of summarization in indexing process is better and superior.

Table 1. Comparison of indexing normal corpus and indexing summarized Corpus

	Corpus	Sum Corpus
How fast does it index (Number of documents/hour)	40871 Doc/h	73800Doc/h
How fast does it search (Latency)	2316ms	1308ms
Average document size (words)	6353	600

Table 2. Example of searching results

Example of query	Corpus	Summarized corpus
The clinical response to treatment	Doc 98 Doc 2 Doc 110 Doc 79	Doc 2 Doc 110 Doc 79 Doc 117
Paths to a malaria vaccine illuminated by parasite genomics	Doc 272 Doc 129 Doc 215 Doc 202 Doc 47 Doc 240 Doc 211	Doc 272 Doc 129 Doc 215 Doc 202 Doc 305 Doc 211 Doc 129

Table 3. Precision and Recall results

	Normal Corpus	Summarized Corpus
Precision	0.84	0.81
Recall	0.62	0.61

Example of Searching Results (Corpus/SumCorpus)

Table 2 illustrates two examples of searching query, the results given for each example are shown in this table. Generally, the results shown in the table prove the similarity of relevant research.

Evaluation of the Two Systems

Precision and recall measures of the two systems are calculated and cited in Table 3. The results found are slightly different, which shows similarity in relevance.

CONCLUSION

In this work, an approach for indexing is proposed and presented. It allows to build an index of document. This approach is based on summarization to reduce the size of document. According to experimental results, we note that indexing of Summarized Corpus results gives results similar to indexing of a normal Corpus. Therefore, we can think to build new systems based on summary corpus to win time and size.

REFERENCES

Biniz, M., & El Ayachi, R. (2018). Optimizing Ontology Alignments by Using Neural NSGA-II. *Journal of Electronic Commerce in Organizations*, 16(1), 29–42. doi:10.4018/JECO.2018010103

Biniz, M., El Ayachi, R., & Fakir, M. (2017). Ontology Matching Using BabelNet Dictionary and Word Sense Disambiguation Algorithms. *Indonesian Journal of Electrical Engineering and Computer Science, 5*(1), 196–205. doi:10.11591/ijeecs.v5.i1.pp196-205

Gupta, D. B., & Lehal, G. S. (2010). A Survey of Text Summarization Extractive Techniques. doi:10.4304/jetwi.2.3.258-268

Kasture, N. R., Yargal, N., Nityan, N., Kulkarni, N., & Mathur, V. (2014). A Survey on Methods of Abstractive Text Summarization. *International Journal for Research in Emerging Science and Technology, 1*(6).

Kumar, Y. J., Goh, O. S., Basiron, H., Choon, N. H., & Suppiah, P. C. (2016). A Review on Automatic Text Summarization Approaches. *Journal of Computational Science, 12*(4), 178–190. doi:10.3844/jcssp.2016.178.190

Kwary, D. A. (2017). A corpus and a concordancer of academic journal articles. *Data in Brief, 16,* 94–100. doi:10.1016/j.dib.2017.11.023 PubMed

Luhn, H. P. (1958). The Automatic Creation of Literature Abstracts. *IBM Journal of Research and Development, 2*(2), 159–165. doi:10.1147/rd.22.0159

Nallapati, R., Zhou, B., Santos, C. N., Gulcehre, C., & Xiang, B. (2016). Abstractive Text Summarization Using Sequence-to-Sequence RNNs and Beyond. ArXiv:1602.06023 [Cs]

Seki, Y. (2002). *Sentence Extraction by tf/idf and Position Weighting from Newspaper Articles.* Academic Press.

Sripada, S., & Jagarlamudi, J. (2009). Summarization Approaches Based on Document Probability Distributions. *Proceedings of the 23rd Pacific Asia Conference on Language, Information and Computation,* 521–529.

Torres, M., & Juan, M. (2014). Automatic Text Summarization. doi:10.1002/9781119004752.fmatter

Vanderwende, L., Suzuki, H., Brockett, C., & Nenkova, A. (2007). Beyond SumBasic: Task-focused summarization with sentence simplification and lexical expansion. *Information Processing & Management, 43*(6), 1606–1618. doi:10.1016/j.ipm.2007.01.023

Chapter 6
Building Text Summary Generation System Using Universal Networking Language, Rhetorical Structure Theory, Sangatis and Sutra:
Summary Generation Using Discourse Structures

Subalalitha C. N.
SRM Institute of Science and Technology, India

ABSTRACT

This chapter discusses how text summaries could be generated by using a high-level semantic representation. The semantic representation is built using the discourse structure which is comprised of three text representation techniques, namely, universal networking language (UNL), rhetorical structure theory (RST), and Saṅgatis. Sangati is an ancient concept that is used in Sanskrit language literature to capture coherence. This discourse structure is indexed using a concept called sūtra which has been used in both Tamil language and Sanskrit literatures. The chapter mainly focusses on how summary could be generated by using this unique discourse structure and the indexing technique concept, sūtra. Forum for information retreival (FIRE) corpus has been used to test the system and a performance comparison has been done with the one of the state-of-art summary generation systems that is built on discourse structure.

DOI: 10.4018/978-1-7998-1021-6.ch006

INTRODUCTION

The usage of mobile phones for accessing the information on the web demands for re-representation of the information suiting the size of the mobile. Generating gist of stories be it daily news, movie reviews have been trending to save the time of the web users these days. Summary generation systems play a vital role behind these innovations in shortening the content of the web pages and feeding the crisp version to the user without compromising on the core content quality. Semantic representation of the text becomes quintessential in order to capture the essence of the text to produce a quality summary (Balaji et al., 2016). Discourse structure is one of the highest level semantic structures that can capture coherence hidden in the text by linking the text fragments with semantic relations (Asher et al., 2011). This chapter discusses about a summary generation system built using a discourse structure that is in turn built using the discourse parser which uses three different semantic structures namely, Universal Networking Language (UNL), Rhetorical Structure Theory (RST) and saṅgatis (Subalalitha and Ranjani Parthasarathi, 2017).

The discourse parser can find the semantic relations between various levels of texts namely, clauses, sentences and paragraphs. Indexing the discourse structure created by the discourse parser plays a vital role in inheriting the semantics captured by the discourse structure. The indexing is done by using a concept called sūtra which has been used in ancient Indian literatures to express the description of text in a crisp manner (Subalalitha and Ranjani Parthasarathi, 2014). The characteristics of sūtras have many similarities with the discourse relations identified by the discourse parser. Therefore, the semantic fragments containing the discourse relations retain the semantics even in the indices as well.

The indices built by the sūtras can be used by various NLP applications namely, summary generation system, Question Answering QA) system and Information Retrieval (IR) system. This chapter focusses on how these semantic indices can be used for building summary generation systems. A summary is a crisp representation of a large text. A summary could represent a single document or many documents. Many summaries from a single document is also possible when a document contains multiple topics. This chapter focusses on how summaries can be built using the discourse structure.

The rest of the chapter is organized as follows. Section 2 gives the foundation of the semantic structures namely, UNL, RST, saṅgatis and sūtra. Section 3 describes the existing works on summary generation systems. Section 4 illustrates the working of the discourse structure-based summary generation system. Section 5 gives the details of evaluation and section 6 gives the conclusion.

BACKGROUND

Universal Networking Language

The UNL expresses information and knowledge present in an NL text in the form of a semantic network which is represented as a directed graph (Uchida et al., 1999). The UNL graph is composed of Universal Words (UWs) and UNL relations. The UWs indicate the conceptual representation of an NL word and they constitute the UNL vocabulary which in turn consists of components such as head word, semantic constraints and UNL attributes. The head word represents the concept of an NL word in English and the semantic constraint. A headword of a UW is an English expression, a word, a compound word, a phase or a sentence in English. The semantic constraint restricts the interpretation of a UW to a specific

Figure 1. UNL graph for Example 1

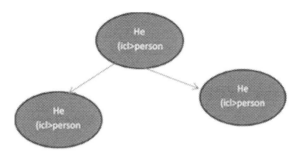

concept and the UNL attributes are normally used to represent information conveyed by natural language grammatical categories, such as tense, mood, aspect, number, etc. In order to identify these components, resources such as UNL Knowledge Base (UNL KB) and UW dictionary are mainly required. Figure 1 shows the example of UNL graph representation for an English sentence given in Example 1.

Example 1: He won the race

Rhetorical Structure Theory (RST)

RST is a descriptive theory for organizing an NL text.

(Mann & Thompson 1988). The key idea was to use discourse relations to facilitate the organization. Discourse relations connect the coherent text fragments of a text document. The smallest text fragment is called as an Elementary Discourse Unit (EDU). A clause or a sentence is chosen as an EDU in RST. Text fragments beyond clauses and sentences, which may comprise many EDUs are called Complex Discourse Units (CDUs)

(Asher et al., 2011). Text fragments are divided into two categories, namely, the nucleus and the satellite. The nucleus represents the salient part of the text, while the satellite represents the additional information about the nucleus. The relation denotes discourse relations which define a particular kind of link that can hold between two non-overlapping text fragments, namely, the nucleus and the satellite. There are multi nuclear discourse relations that link two nuclei instead of a nucleus and a satellite.

The discourse relations are organized into three categories, namely, subject matter relations, presentational relations and multi nuclear relations. In subject matter relations, a satellite is a question, a request, or a problem posed by the reader that is satisfied or solved by the nucleus. In presentational relations, a satellite intends to increase the reader's inclination in accepting the facts stated in the nucleus. A multi nuclear relation connects two nuclei instead of connecting a nucleus and a satellite. *Elaboration, Evaluation, Interpretation, Means, Cause, Result, Otherwise, Purpose, Solutionhood, Condition, Unconditional* and *Unless* are subject matter relations. *Antithesis, Background, Concession, Enablement, Evidence, Justify, Motivation, Preparation, Restatement* and *Summary* are presentational relations. *Conjunction, Disjunction, Contrast, Joint, List, Multi Nuclear Restatement* and *Sequence* are multi nuclear relations.

An example is illustrated in Figure 2. The Nucleus- DiscourseRelation-Satellite structure is denoted as NRS sequence in this chapter.

Figure 2. Nucleus- Discourse Relation-Satellite for Example 2

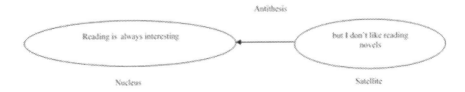

Example 2: Reading is always interesting but I don't like reading novels.

Saṅgatis

Sanskrit literature has many nuggets that could be applied to modern linguistic applications. One such nugget is the concept of saṅgati. saṅgatis induce the desire to know what is being said next in a text; or, expositions of Vedic texts are organized in the form of sūtrās (statements), adhikaraṇā (sub topic), pāda (section), adhyāya(chapter) and śāstrās (whole content). sūtrās express content in crisp, short statements; adhikaraṇā is the organization of a set of related sūtras on a sub-topic. A set of adhikaraṇās forms a pāda, and a set of pādas forms an adhyāya. sūtrās being cryptic in nature, need to be explained.

The explanation is normally organized at the level of *adhikaraṇā*. An *adhikaraṇā* is said to have five components, namely, the subject of discussion, doubt/ambiguity in understanding the subject, *saṅgati* indicating coherence/continuity for this discussion, the opponent's view and the proponent's (proposed) view. Of these, *saṅgati* is explained at various levels. At the sūtra level, in terms of how this sūtra is related to the previous sūtra; at the *adhikaraṇā* level as to how this sūtra is relevant to the *adhikaraṇā*, at the *pāda* level as to how it is relevant to that *pāda,* and so on. Similarly, *saṅgati* is discussed between *adhikaraṇās*, and between *pādas* as well. There are many types of saṅgati relations that have been used in the expository text of the śāstrās. A partial list of *saṅgati*s considered, their equivalent meaning in English, and the type of texts linked by *saṅgati*s are listed in Table 1 (Srivenkatesha Subba Yajva Shastri, 1934).

It can be observed that similar to RST relations, saṅgatis also link two different text units. This chapter makes use of the terms, nucleus and satellites, to denote and distinguish the text units, that convey the salient information and the additional information respectively, as was done in RST. Example 3 shows the usage of *ātidesîka* sangati.

Table 1. Definition of saṅgatis

S. No	*saṅgati*	**English Meaning**	**Texts Linked by** *saṅgati*	
			Text₁	**Text₂**
1	*Upodghāta*	Introduction	Introduction of a scenario	Explanation of the Scenario
2	*apavāda*	Exception	A scenario	An Exceptional scenario
3	*ākṣepa*	Objection	A scenario	An objection for the scenario
4	*ātidesîka*	Transference	Scenario₁	Scenario₂ inherited from scenario₁
6	*pratyudaharaṇa*	Counter-Example	A scenario	Counter Example of the scenario

Figure 3. Usage of ātideśîka Saṅgati

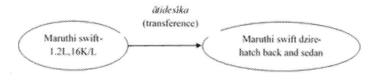

Example 3: Maruti Swift has a 1.2L engine, and provides 16K/L mileage. Dzire is a Maruti Swift with a hatch-back, and is a sedan.

It can be observed that the *ātideśîka* saṅgati illustrates the inheritance of the properties of the car brand, Maruthi Swift in the car brand, Maruthi Swift Dezire. The text that contains the information inherited from some other text becomes the nucleus, and the other becomes the satellite.

sūtra: An Overview

sūtras have been used in the ancient Tamil and Sanskrit literatures to describe a large content in a crisp manner. In Tamil literature, sūtras have been used in a grammar master piece called, Nanool to define the grammar rules, whereas, in Sanskrit literature, sūtra has been used in various shaastras like, Nyaya, Vedanta and grammar(Pavananthi Munivar, 1991).

The definition of the *sūtra* as per *Nannool* is given below in Tamil followed by the English transliteration and its meaning in English.

Definition of sūtra
சில் வகை எழுத்தில் பல்வகைப் பொருளை
செவ்வ நாடியிர் செறித்தினிது விளக்கித்
திட்ப நுட்பஞ் சிறந்தன சூத்திரம்
English Transliteration
Cil vakai eḻuttil palvakaip poruḷai
cevva nāṭiyir cerittiṇitu viḷakkit
tiṭpa nuṭpañ cirantaṇa cūttiram
Gloss: The speciality of the sūtras is to coherently convey the semantics precisely, accurately, and with certainty, using a few words.

As per Sanskrit Literature the definition of *sūtra* is transliterated in English as follows.

alpākṣaram asandigdham sāravad viśvatomukham astobham anavadyam ca sūtram sūtravido viduḥ.

The meaning of the above definition is, "Of minimal syllabary, unambiguous, pithy, comprehensive, continuous, and without flaw: who knows the *sūtra* knows it to be thus."

As per Sanskrit literature, *sūtra* is an aphorism (or line, rule, formula) or a collection of aphorisms in the form of a manual or, more broadly, a text in Hinduism or Buddhism. Literally, it means a thread or line that holds things together and is derived from the verbal root *siv-*, meaning, *"to sew"*.

It can be observed that the *sutras* have been used by both the literatures to express the content of a coherent text in a concise manner. The first line in the definition of the *sutras* as per *Nanool*, "Cil vakai eluttil palvakaip porulai" (representing multiple semantics in a few words) denotes the characteristic of a text index. An efficient text index should be the representative of a sentence, paragraph, or document from which it is extracted. Furthermore, sutras express continuity between the texts they represent. Hence, inspired by these qualities of sutras, it has been used for indexing the discourse structures.

How are sutras and Discourse Structures Linked?

It was observed that the characteristics of sutras when they are linked to other sutras have similarities with RST and saṅgati. Also, saṅgatis have been used in sutra based texts in Sanskrit literature. This has been motivation behind identifying a crisp sutra like representation for UNL-RST- saṅgati discourse structure.

The Nannool defines the characteristics of a sutra as follows (Pavananthi Munivar 1991).

ஆற்றல்ʼʻஎழுக் கரிமா நேʼʻக்கʼ தவளைப்
பாய்த்தʼ பருந்தின் வீழ் வண்ண சூத்திர நிலை

Transiliteration of the Text

Ārroluk karimā nōkku tavalaip
Pāyttu paruntin vīl vaṇṇa cūttira nilai

Meaning of the Text

"sutras have the characteristics of a river's flow, lion's vision, frog's jump and eagle's flight".

The river flow characteristic represents a string of sutras that are linked and interpreted in one direction. The lion has the ability to look forward and turn backward. This characteristic represents sutras that are linked with the previous and next sutras. Frogs jump covering a considerable amount of space on the ground. This characteristic represents sutras that are connected with sutras that are not adjacent to them. Eagles fly high in the sky; when they see a prey, they reach the ground, pick it up and continue to fly in the same direction as they did before. This characteristic represents the sutras that deviate from the topic of focus and return to the topic of focus. A pictorial representation of these four characteristics is given in Figure 4.

Literature Survey

This chapter discusses about the works related to the indexing mechanism suitable for discourse structures and about the state of the art summary generation systems.

IR systems have used RST for indexing the documents by using the discourse relation between the text segments (Sahib & Ali shah 2006). Both of these discourse parsers have used cue phrases as signals find the discourse relations between the clauses. In both of these techniques, the discourse structures are indexed as the triplet, <RelationName, Nucleus, Satellite> and a weight is given to each triplet based on its frequency, and the number of important words present.

A query focussed summary generation system based on RST has been developed by Bosma (2004). A QA system is essential for the summary generation system to locate a node from the discourse structure

Figure 4. sūtra Characteristics

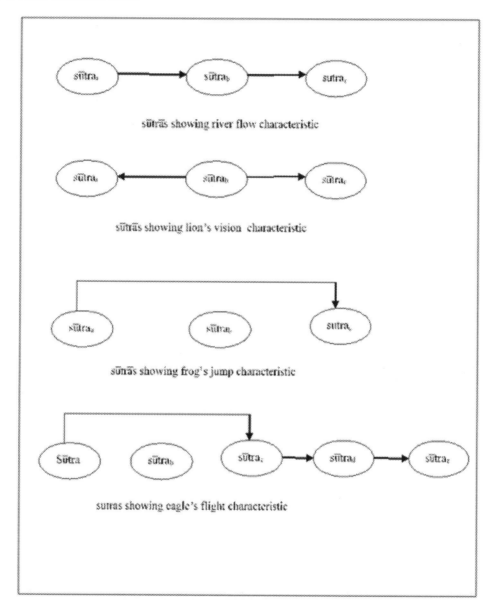

that is relevant to the query. The summary generation system will append the nodes that are related to this node in the discourse structure, based on some weight factors to form a summary.

Durrett et al (2016) have presented a single-document summarization that combines compression and anaphoricity constraints. The summary is generated based on a rich set of sparse features whose weights are learned on a large corpus. Compression rules have been used to delete part of text in sentences. ROUGE scores have been used to test the system.

Wang and Ling (2016) have proposed a abstractive summary generation system for opinionated text using an attention-based neural network model. and fluent summaries. An importance-based sampling method is to extract the important part of the text. Human Judgement has been used as the metrics for evaluation.

Cohan, A. and Goharian (2017), Citation-context has been used to generate summaries using discourse models. ROUGE scores has been used to evaluate the summary using on TAC2014 scientific summarization dataset.

Abstractive summaries have been generated using Abstract Meaning Representation(AMR) which is represented in the form of a semantic graph (Liu et al., 2017). This source graph is reduced to a summary graph. The framework is data-driven and can work for any domain.

Abstractive summaries has been proposed by Balaji et al (2016) using a semi-supervised bootstrapping approach for the identification of important components for abstractive summarization. The summary is generated by perceiving the input texts as graphs. A modified spreading activation algorithm forms the summary by identifying the important sub graphs that are inturn decided based on the connectivity. ROUGE scores have been used for evaluation

This chapter discusses about a unique summary generation system which is different from the existing systems by the following facts

1. Discourse structure construction by UNL, RST and sangatis
2. Indexing the discourse structure by sutras .

UNL is good at representing the semantics between the words, whereas, RST is good at representing the semantics between the clauses and sentences and sangatis are good at capturing the semantics between the paragraphs. This creates a semantically well-coupled discourse structure. The characteristics of sutras goes well with the discourse structures which aid in inheriting the semantics while indexing the discourse structures.

The next section discusses about the summary generation system which is built using these four unique semantic structures.

Working of the Summary Geration System

Figure 5 show the architecture of the summary generation system. The input documents are fed into the UNL-RST-Sangati discourse parser. The parser tags the discourse relations between the text fragments in a bottom up tree like fashion (Navaneetha Krishnan and Parthasarathi, 2015).

Discourse Structure Construction

The tree construction is a bottom-up approach wherein, the leaves are formed first, and then united to form a tree using the UNL-RST-sangati discourse parser (Subalalitha and Ranjani Parthasaarthi, 2012). A leaf node represents a clause or a sentence, whereas, non-leaf nodes are the nuclei that are popped up from the leaf nodes. The non-leaf nodes may either represent a sentence or a group of sentences. The nuclei from the leaf level are popped up to the immediate next level of the tree which forms the first level of the tree. The NRS sequences are formed at each level of the tree and different sets of features are used forming NRS sequences between the leaf nodes and non-leaf nodes of the tree. This procedure is repeated until the tree is left with one node (i.e) the root of the tree.

Figure 5. Summary Generation Architechture

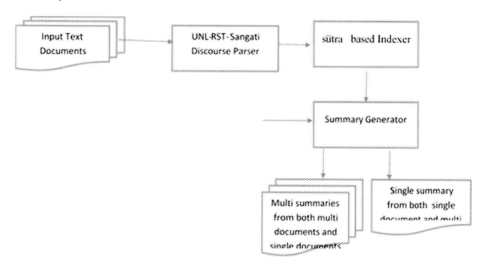

Table 2 shows the subset of leaf node features when a leaf node is a clause or a sentence (i.e) Type 1 features to identify sangatis. **Table 3** shows the subset of features to form NRS sequences when a non-leaf node is a sub tree (i.e) Type 2 features to identify sangatis. These features are chosen by analysing the corpus of 600 Tamil tourism documents.

These paragraph level trees are united to form a document level RS-Saṅgati tree using document level feature sets.

Table 2. Features for identifying saṅgatis (Type 1)

saṅgati	**Rules**
upajīvya	Presence of *Elaboration* and *Means* or Re-instate discourse relations in the satellite UNL graph along with UNL concept or semantic constraint similarity between the nucleus and satellite UNL graphs.
uttāna	Presence of *Contrast* and *Antithesis* discourse relations in NRS sequence along with UNL concept or semantic constraint similarity.
ātideśika	UNL graph similarity in terms of concepts, except the main subject concept between the nuclei UNL graphs.

Table 3. Features for Non-Leaf Nodes(Type 2)

saṅgati /RST discourse relation and the sub tree containing it	**saṅgati /RST discourse relation and the sub tree containing it**	**Nucleus**	**Satellite**	**saṅgati**
apavāda & Tsubedu1	ākṣepa & Tsubedu2	Tsubedu1 and Tsubedu2	NIL	uttāna
dṛṣṭanta & Tsubedu1	Sequence & Tsubedu2	Tsubedu1 and Tsubedu2	NIL	uttāna
upodghāta & Tsubedu1	Elaboration & Tsubedu2	Tsubedu1	Tsubedu2	viśeṣa
Sequence & Tsubedu1	List & Tsubedu2	Tsubedu1 and Tsubedu2	NIL	prāsaṅgika

Figure 6. Discourse Structure for Example 4

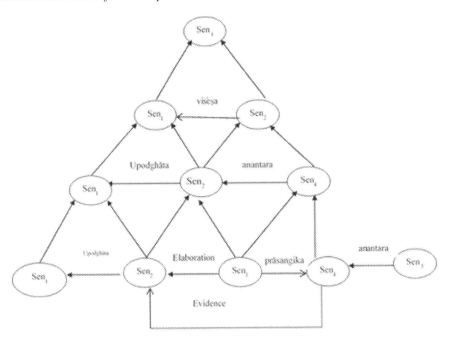

Example 4 shows the Tamil text taken from the corpus, its transliteration along with the gloss, and the discourse structure for the text. Figure 6 shows the UNL-RS-saṅgati tree for the example text.

Example 4: திருநெல்வேலி மாவட்டம் திருநெல்வேலி நகரை தலைமையகமாக கொ·ரண்டு இயங்குகிறது (Sen₁). இந்தியாவின் பழமையான நகரங்களில் திருநெல்வேலியும் ஒன்றாகும் (Sen₂). 3000 ஆண்டு பழமையான திருநெல்வேலி நகரம் தாமிரபரணி ஆற்றின் கரையில் அமைந்துள்ளது. (Sen₃). திருநெல்வேலி பழமையான நகரம் என்பதற்கு அரிச்ச நல்லூர் பகுதியில் தொ·ரல் பொ·ரருள் ஆராய்ச்சியாளர்கள் கண்டுபிடித்த முதுமக்கள் தாழி சிறந்த சான்றாகும் (Sen₄). இவற்றை ஆராய்ந்த தொ·ரல் பொ·ரருள் ஆராய்ச்சியாளர்கள் திருநெல்வேலி நகரம் 2800 ஆண்டு பழமையானது என உறுதியளித்தனர் (Sen₅).

English Transliteration: Tirunelvēli māvaṭṭam tirunelvēli nakarai talaimaiyakamāka koṇṭu iyaṅkukiṟatu(Sen₁). Intiyāviṉ paḻamaiyāṉa nakaraṅkaḷil tirunelvēliyum oṉṟākum (Sen₂). 3000Āṇṭu paḻamaiyāṉa tirunelvēlinakaram tāmiraparaṇi'āṟṟiṉ karaiyilamaintuḷḷatu.(Sen₃). Tirunelvēli paḻamaiyāṉa nakaram eṉpataṟku' ariccanallūr pakuthiyil tolporuḷ ārāycciyāḷarkaḷ kaṇṭupiṭitta mutumakkaḷ tāḷi ciṟantacāṉṟākum(Sen₄). Ivaṟṟai' ārāynta tolporuḷ ārāycciyāḷarkaḷ tirunelvēlinakaram 2800 āṇṭu paḻamaiyāṉatu 'eṉa' uṟutiyaḷittaṉar. (Sen₅)

English Translation: Tirunelveli city is the headquarters of Tirunelveli district (Sen₁). Tirunelveli city is one of the oldest cities in India (Sen₂). 3000 years' old Tirunelveli city is located on the river banks of Thamirabarani river (Sen₃). The discovery of an urn by researchers near Arichanallur area is evidence to show, that Tirunelveli is an ancient city (Sen₄). . After investigating, archaeologists confirmed that Tirunelveli is a 2800 year old city (Sen₅).

Figure 7. Architecture of sūtra Based Indexer

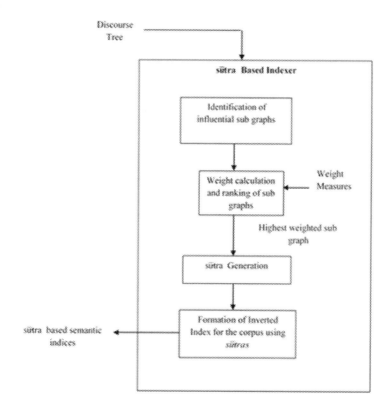

Sutra Based Text Representation and Indexing

Figure 7 shows the architecture of the sūtra based text identifier which identifies the NRS sequences matching the characteristics of sūtra . The input to the the sūtra -based indexer is a discourse structure which is built using the RST and *saṅgati* . The discourse structure needs to be represented as a tree, wherein each discourse tree represents a $CDU_{paragraph.}$ The sūtra generation involves analysis of the sub graphs present in the discourse tree and selection of the most influential sub graph. As per the proposed approach, a sūtra comprises of a set of noun concepts and a set of RST relations and saṅgatis which are associated with the noun concepts. The details of each of these steps are given below.

sūtra Generation

sūtra Generation is done through the following steps.

(a) Identification of all possible sub graphs that are connected directly to the root of the RS-saṅgati tree at each level, that lies between the root and the leaf of the tree.
(b) Weighting the sub graphs based on the following factors.
   ◦ The level at which the sub graphs are present. Leaf nodes are treated as $level_0$ and the number goes up as we go up the tree.
   ◦ The presence of influential discourse relations and saṅgatis in the sub graphs

Table 4. Influence scores for the Example 4

Discourse Relations/ saṅgatis	Influence Score
viśeṣa	0.015
Upodghāta	0.005
Elaboration	0.2
prāsangika	0.075
Anantara	0.125

(c)   Generation of a sūtra from the highest weighted sub graph.

The sub graphs denote the NRS sequences of the UNL-RS-saṅgati tree. The sūtra generation aims at focussing on the influential sub graphs. The supposition is that the influential sub graphs are the ones which are coherently linked with the most influential node of the UNL-RS-saṅgati tree, which is the root of the tree. Hence, the sub graphs that are directly connected to the root node are extracted from each level for sūtra generation. The leaf level is omitted for this analysis.

The notion behind considering the level factor to assign weights to the sub graphs to form the sūtra is that, each level of the UNL-RS-saṅgati tree is constructed by popping it up from the level below. Consequently, the importance of the NRS sequences or the sub graphs increases as the level increases in the UNL-RS-saṅgati tree. Hence, a sub graph is ranked based on the level at which it is present. The weight factor is normalised by considering the number of levels present in the UNL-RS-saṅgati tree. The number of levels present in the UNL-RS-saṅgati tree depends on the size of the CDU for which the tree is constructed, and hence, the normalization is done by dividing the level of the tree by the number of levels present in the UNL-RS-saṅgati tree.

The influential discourse relations or saṅgatis refer to the ones that are specific to the domain, and are presumed to link important parts of the text. Furthermore, the queries posed by the user may be biased towards the domain, and hence, the sūtra which represents a document as an index needs to consider the domain specific discourse relations and saṅgatis. The influence score is assigned to each discourse relation and saṅgati, by calculating the probabilities of its occurrence in the corpora of 1000 Tamil language tourism domain specific text documents. For each sub graph, the normalized influence weight is calculated by adding the influence scores of the relations present in that sub graph, and dividing it by the number of relations in the sub graph.

The influence score of the discourse relations and the saṅgatis present in the discourse structure shown in Figure 6, is shown in Table 4.

It can be observed that the sub graphs from Figure 6, namely, Sen_1-Sen_2 (SubG1), Sen_2-Sen_4 (SubG2) and Sen_1-Sen_2- Sen_4 (SubG3), are identified from the level 1_1 and the sub graph, Sen_1-Sen_2 (SubG4) is identified from level 1_2 of the RS-saṅgati tree. It should be noted that the sub graphs, Sen_1-Sen_2 extracted twice at different levels, as the saṅgatis linking the nodes, Sen_1 and Sen_2 are different at these levels. Table 5 shows the weights assigned to these sub graphs.

The Total weight is calculated as the weighted sum of the two weight factors, level-based weight and influence weight, as shown in Equation 1.

Total weight= α×(Level-based weight)+ (1-α) ×(Influence weight)   (1)

Table 5. Weight Calculation

Weight Factors	SubG1	SubG2	SubG3	SubG4
Level Based weights	0.5	0.5	0.5	0.75
Influence weight	0.005	0.125	0.065	0.015
Total Weight	0.2525	0.3125	0.2812	0.3835

Figure 8. Formation of Sutra for a Single Text Document

CDU
CDU
CDU
Sūtra Generator
Sūtra for CDU
Sūtra for CDU
Sūtra for CDU

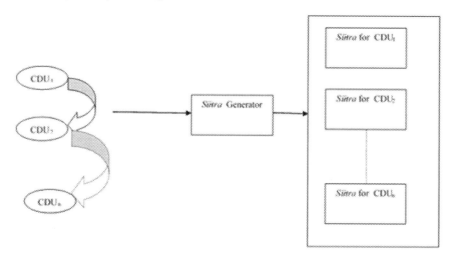

It can be observed that the sub graphs at the highest level of the tree will tend to get the highest score. To normalise this, the *Level based weight* is multiplied by a factor, "α", and the *Influence weight* is multiplied by a factor, "(1-α)". Currently, the value of "α" is set as 0.5. By analysing the weight values, the value of "α" can be changed depending on the requirement. In this example, the sub graph SubG4 gets the higher score and is chosen for sūtra generation.

The *sūtra* for a CDU comprises a set of noun concepts, set of discourse relations and saṅgatis chosen from the top weighted sub graph. Since nouns convey the essence of a text, the noun concepts are chosen to represent the CDU. The set of discourse relations and saṅgatis which are present in the top weighted sub graph are chosen to form a *sūtra* along with the noun concepts. Also, the discourse relations/saṅgatis that link the top weighted sub graph with the rest of the sub graphs present in the CDU, are also added to

Figure 9. sūtra for the discourse tree

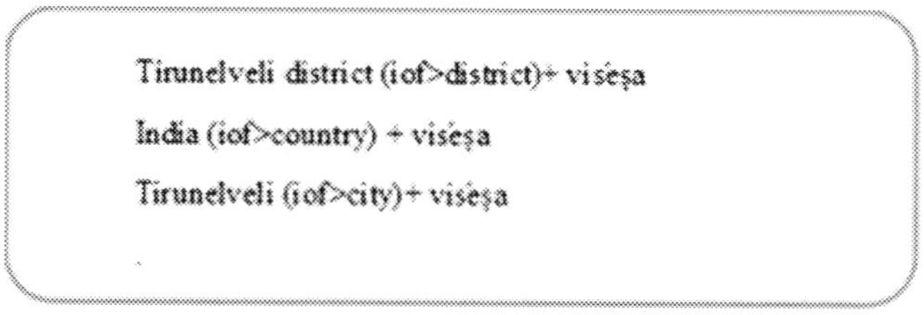

Tirunelveli district (iof>district)+ viśeṣa
India (iof>country) + viśeṣa
Tirunelveli (iof>city)+ viśeṣa

Figure 10. Representation of the sūtra as an Inverted Index

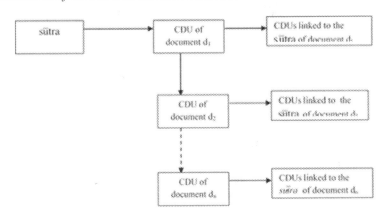

the sūtra . Figure 8 shows the *sūtra* generation for a single text document, and Figure 9 shows the sūtra for the discourse tree shown in Figure 6.

It can be observed that the text given in Example 4 expresses the specialities of Tirunelveli, and it is captured by the sūtra through the noun concepts and the associated saṅgati, namely, viśeṣa. This sūtra can be used as the semantic index to the CDU in NLP applications, such as the IR system, summary generation or QA systems. On the NLP application front, given a query, "Specialities of Tirunelveli" or "Specialities of India", the document containing the text will be retrieved by mapping the cue word, "speciality" with the saṅgati, "viśeṣa," along with the query words "Tirunelveli or India".

sūtra as Index

For a given document, the sūtras are constructed for each $CDU_{paragraph.}$ Figure 10 shows the inverted index representation of the sūtra. Each *sūtra* identified for a $CDU_{paragraph}$ is stored along with the $CDUs_{paragraph}$ that are linked to it at the document level RS tree. This unique quality of the sūtra aids in retaining the coherence of the discourse structure in the index too. Each *sūtra* is tagged with its respective CDU identifiers and the document identifier.

The sutra based text representation is tested using summary generation mechanism which has been described in the next section.

Summary Generation System

Since the noun concepts that constitute the sūtra are UWs, the nouns present in the NL query are converted to UWs. If the cue phrases are explicit in the query, then they are mapped with the discourse relations and saṅgatis; else, a default domain dependent discourse relation or saṅgati is used for the CDU retrieval. Then, these sets of discourse relations and saṅgatis and the noun concepts present in the query are matched with the sūtra index and the associated CDUs are retrieved to form a summary. As discussed previously, the sūtra based indexer stores each CDU, along with the CDUs that are semantically related through the discourse relations in the same document. Let the main CDU be denoted as CDU_{main} and the related CDUs as $CDU_{linked.}$ Then the summary is comprised of $CDUs_{main}$ and $CDUs_{linked}$. Since the sūtra indexer stores each index as an inverted index, a multi document summary can also be generated.

Since the summary is built on top of the UNL-RST-saṅgati framework, the summary is a graph that comprises the components of this framework such as, UNL relations, discourse relations and saṅgatis. The NL summary can be obtained by removing the discourse relations and saṅgatis leaving behind only the nuclei and satellites. The nucleus and satellites are, in turn, UNL graphs which can be deconverted by a deconverter framework which is out of the scope of this chapter.

The summary generation algorithm is as follows.

Summary Generation Algorithm

Given an NL query, the sūtra based summary generator matches the query concepts with the sūtra based indices and the summary is generated using any of the following cases.

Case 1: If the query contains cue phrases, then it is mapped with the respective RST based discourse relations/saṅgatis and used along with the UWs present in the query, to retrieve $CDUs_{main}$ and $CDUs_{linked}$. The sūtras of the $CDUs_{linked}$ and the UWs present in the query are matched. The $CDUs_{linked}$ that match with the query and the $CDUs_{main}$ form the summary graph.

Case 2: If the query does not contain cue phrases, then the semantic constraint of the last UW is checked. If it contains "iof", then the UWs present in the query along with the default RST based discourse relation, "Elaboration" and the "prasangika" saṅgati are used to retrieve the $CDUs_{main}$ and $CDUs_{linked}$. Again the $CDUs_{linked}$ are included in the summary, based on the query-sūtra relevance.

Case 3: If step 1 is false and if the last UW of the query does not contain, "iof", then the $CDUs_{main}$ and $CDUs_{linked}$ are retrieved using the UWs and the default RST based discourse relation and saṅgati . The $CDUs_{linked}$ are included in the summary, if their sūtra contains the UWs whose semantic constraint contains, "iof" and the last NL word of the query.

This summary generation algorithm leans towards generating summaries for the tourism domain specific documents. Each case of the algorithm is explained below with an example.

Explanation with Examples

Case 1: For the queries containing the cue phrases, the cue phrases are mapped to a discourse relation or a saṅgati, and the relevant CDUs are retrieved. Consider the query given in Example 5

Example 5
Query: ஆழியாறு அணையின் சிறப்பு
Transliteration: Āḻiyāṟu' aṇaiyin ciṟappu
Translation: Speciality of Aazhiyaaru Dam.

The cue phrase, "சிறப்பு (speciality)" can be mapped with the saṅgati, "*viśeṣa*" and can be used along with the UWs present in the query for retrieving the CDUs, thereby forming a summary.

Case 2: The presence of "iof" in the last UW of the query denotes that the query is specific about an instance which may denote a city, river, etc. Consider the query given in Example 6. The last UW of the query is, "Manakulavinayagar temple (iof> temple)", which is an instance of the super class,

"Temple". The CDUs whose sūtrās contain the UWs along with the default RST based discourse relation and saṅgati will yield a relevant summary.

Example 6

Query: புதுவையில் உள்ள மணக்குள விநாயகர் ஆலயம்

Transliteration: Putuvaiyil uḷḷa maṇakkuḷavināyakar ālayam

Translation: Manakulavinayagar temple at Pondichery.

Case 3: The last case deals with the queries whose last UW does not contain, "iof". This denotes the scenario in which the query demands a summary of a specific instance or instances, not mentioned but implied in the query. Consider Example 7

Example 7

Query: "தமிழ் நாட்டின் கோ·ரவில் நகரம்" .

English Transliteration: Tamiḻnāṭṭin kōvil nakaram

English Translation: Temple city of Tamil Nadu

The summary is expected to contain information about the city, "காஞ்சிபுரம்" (Kanchipuram), which is the Temple city of Tamil Nadu, and is not present in the query.

The sūtra based summary generator first retrieves the CDUs whose sūtrās contain the noun concepts, Tamil Nadu (iof>state) and (Temple City). Since there is no cue phrase present in the query, the default discourse relation, "Elaboration" and the saṅgati, "prasangika" are used along with the noun concepts for the CDU retrieval. All the CDUs$_{main}$ are included in the summary. Since the term, "Kanchipuram" is not present in the query, it may or may not be present in the CDUs$_{main.}$ Since the CDU$_{main}$ is the nucleus and CDUs$_{linked}$ that are linked to it are satellites, the intuition is that the CDUs$_{linked}$ may contain the elaborated content of CDUs$_{main..}$ Hence, there is a chance of the presence of the term "Kanchipuram" in any of the sūtras of the CDUs$_{linked.}$ This is checked by searching for a noun concept with a semantic constraint "iof>city", which denotes an instance of a city in the sūtras of CDUs$_{linked}$. The semantic constraint, "iof>city " is chosen by finding the instance of (iof) the last NL word of the query. Here, the last UW is, கோ·ரவில்நகரம்"(Temple City) and the last NL word is நகரம்"(city) and so the semantic constraint, "iof>city" is used for searching the UW in the sūtra of the CDUs$_{linked}$ along with the other UWs, and the default RST based discourse relation and saṅgati identified from the query. The CDUs$_{linked}$ that satisfy this condition and the CDUs$_{main}$ together form the summary. It can be observed that the sūtrās of the CDUs$_{main}$ and CDUs$_{linked}$ aid in picking up the closely relevant summary, even if the query contains insufficient details

It can be observed that the above queries demand a summary, which should contain information about various places like, temples, tourist spots and rivers, whereas, the summary for the query, Temple city of Tamil Nadu" should deal only with a single place. The proposed sūtra based summary generation mechanism generates summaries for both the cases, as the sūtra based indexer is capable of retrieving different CDUs that are semantically woven together based on some common criteria. In other words, the coherence captured in the RST-saṅgati discourse structure is retained in its indices too. Hence, the two qualities of sutra namely, crispness and continuity are captured by the proposed approach that the text given in Example 4 expresses the specialities of Tirunelveli, and it is captured by the sūtra through the noun concepts and the associated saṅgati, namely, viśeṣa. This sūtra can be used as the semantic index to the CDU in NLP applications, such as the IR system, summary generation or QA systems. On the NLP application front, given a query, "Specialities of Tirunelveli" or "Specialities of India", the document containing the text will be retrieved by mapping the cue word, "speciality" with the sangati, "viśeṣa," along with the query words "Tirunelveli or India".

Evaluation

The evaluation focusses sūtra based query focussed summary generation mechanism.

The summary generation system which uses sūtra as an index has been evaluated, using the Forum for Information Retrieval Evaluation (FIRE) guidelines (FIRE, 2010). The FIRE evaluation task comprises 2, 00,000 documents, a set of 15 queries and a narration that states the necessary information to be present in each document retrieved by the IR system. The proposed summary generation approach uses these set of documents for constructing the summary generation system. The queries are used to generate the summaries, and the quality of the summaries is analysed manually by comparing it with the "narration" criteria given for each query in the FIRE task.

A comparison has also been made with the existing RST based summary generation proposed by Bosma (2004) by constructing a summary generation system that follows the ideas of Bosma (2004) using the FIRE data. The summaries are evaluated through human judgement by three people who are experts in this domain. The summaries are assigned scores 1, 2 and 3 which indicate low, medium and high query-summary relevance respectively. The sūtra based summary generator has achieved an average score of 2.3 and the summary generation system proposed by Bosma (2004) has achieved an average score of 1.75.

The summary generation mechanism proposed by Bosma (2004) generates a query-focussed summary using the RST based discourse structure which is represented as a graph. Given a query, a QA system locates an answer sentence which is represented as a node in the discourse graph. Using the answer sentence or node as the entry point, a summary is generated by appending the nodes that are semantically closer to the answer node in the discourse structure. This is measured by using certain weight measures. The query processing and the query-index match done by the QA system, have not been discussed by Bosma (2004). The weights of each node or vertex (represented by an EDU) and an edge (represented by a discourse relation) are determined as shown in Equations 2 and 3.

$$weight(edge) = a + b *(1/sentences(satellite(r))) \tag{2}$$

where, e is the edge that was created for the discourse relation r, where $satellite(r)$ is the satellite of r, and $sentences(s)$ is defined as the number of sentences of a span s, a is the basic weight, and b is a constant factor of the 'satellite size' component of the edge weight;

$$weight(vertex) = c *(1/words(s)) \tag{3}$$

where, v is the vertex that was created for the sentence s, where, $words(s)$ is the number of words in s, and c is a constant.

It can be observed that the vertices and the edges that are appended to the node pointed by the query to form a summary do not have any direct link with the query, and there may be possibilities where the summary could deviate from the query. Consider the query and the summary output of both the sūtra based summary generation mechanism, and Bosma's approach shown in Example 8.

Note: Though the output summary is not deconverted, the NL sentences corresponding to the retrieved summary are shown here, for better understanding.

Example 8

Query:"ஸ்டீவ் இர்வின் மரணம்"

Transliteration: Sṭīv irviṉ maraṇam

Translation: Death of Steve Irvin

sūtra based summary

திகிலை ஏற்படுத்தும் முதலைகளை கொஞ்சி குழாவும் அவருடைய காட்சிகளை சிறு குழந்தைகள் மட்டுமின்றி தொலைக்காட்சியில் அனைவரின் கவனத்தையும் ஈர்த்த ஆஸ்திரேலியாவை சேர்ந்த ஸ்டீவ் இர்வின் இன்று (03.09.2006) தண்ணீரில் ஆபத்தான விலங்கினங்கள் பற்றிய ஒரு டாகுமெண்டரி எடுக்கும்பொழுது ஸ்ட்ரிங்க்ரேஸ் எனப்படும் ஒருவகை மீனினத்தின் தாக்குதலுக்கு உள்ளாகி இறந்தார்.*(CDU id 365;Document id 271)*

தனது நெஞ்சில் பாய்ந்த மீனின் விஷ வாலை வெளியே இழுத்துவிட்டுத் தான் நீருக்குள் மயக்கமாகி பிணமாகியுள்ளார் குரோகோடைல் ஹன்டர் ஸ்டீவ் இர்வின்.**(CDU id: 768; Document id- 151)**

English Transliteration

Tikilai ēṟpaṭuttum mutalaikaḷai koñci kuḷāvum avaruṭaiya kāṭcikaḷai ciṟu kuḷantaikaḷ maṭṭumiṉṟi tolaikkāṭciyil aṉaivariṉ kavaṉattaiyum īrtta āstirēliyāvai cērnta sṭīv irviṉ iṉṟu (03.09.2006) Taṇṇīril āpattāṉa vilaṅkiṉaṅkaḷ paṟṟiya oru ṭākumeṇṭari eṭukkumpoḻutu sṭriṅk rēs eṉappaṭum oruvakai mīṉiṉattiṉ tākkutalukku uḷḷāki iṟantār

Taṉatu neñcil pāynta mīṉiṉ viṣa vālai veḷiyē iḻuttuviṭṭut tāṉ nīrukkuḷ mayakkamākipiṇamākiyuḷḷār kurōkōṭail haṉṭar sṭīv irviṉ

English Translation

Steve Irwin, an Australian who attracted not only kids but everybody on TV through his brave gestures by playing with crocodiles dies today on 3.9.2006. While shooting a documentary on a dangerous fish variety named, string rays, he died due to the attack of the fish.

The crocodile hunter steve Irwin pulled out the poisonous tail of the fish which tried to attack him ;became unconscious and then he died.

Bosma's Approach

Table 8 Performance of Sutra Based Query Focussed Summary Generation System.

Avg_Score_RST-Sangati Sutra	Avg_Score_RST-Sutra	Avg_Score_RST-Sangati Sutra_dominat set of relations	Avg_Score_Bosma
2.3	1.9	2.1	1.75

செப்டம்பர் 4, 2006 இல் தண்ணீரில் ஆபத்தான விலங்கினங்கள் பற்றிய ஒரு விளக்கப் படம் எடுக்கும் பொழுது பெருந்திருக்கை (*stingray*) என்றும் அட்டவண்ணைத்திருக்கை என்றும் சொல்லப்படும் ஒரு கொட்டும் திருக்கை மீன் எனப்படும் ஒருவகை நீர்வாழ் இனத்தின் தாக்குதலுக்கு உள்ளாகி இறந்தார். (**EDU id:341; Document id- 456**)

அவருடைய மனைவியும் முதலைகளை பராமரிப்பவர். ஸ்டீவ் இர்வினுடைய தந்தையும் தாயும் கற்றுக்கொடுத்ததுதான் இந்த முதலை விளையாட்டும் பராமரிப்பும். (**EDU id:343; Document id- 456**)

Transliteration

Ceptampar 4, 2006 il taṇṇīril āpattāṉa vilaṅkiṉaṅkaḷ paṟṟiya oru viḷakkap paṭam eṭukkumpoḻutu peruntirukkai (stingray) eṉṟumaṭṭavaṇṇait tirukkai eṉṟum collappaṭum oru koṭṭumtirukkaimīṉ eṉappaṭum oruvakai nīrvāḻ iṉattiṉ tākkutalukku uḷḷāki iṟantār.

Avaruṭaiya maṉaiviyum mutalaikaḷai parāmarippavar. Sṭīv irviṉuṭaiya tantaiyum tāyum kaṟṟukkoṭuttatutāṉ inta mutalai viḷaiyāṭṭum parāmarippum.

English Translation

On September 4, 2006, while taking a documentary about dangerours species, he died due to the attack of a fish variety called, string rays.

His wife also takes care of crocodiles. Irwin's father and mother taught him about taking care of crocodiles.

It can be observed that both the CDUs retrieved by the sutra based summary generation approach are related to the query, whereas in Bosma's approach, the second EDU is related to the person, "Steve Irwin" specified in the query, but not completely related to the entire query. While looking from the query focussed summary generation perspective, the proposed approach generates a summary by retrieving the texts through the index from different documents that are completely related to the query. In Bosma's approach, the summary is generated by retrieving a text through the index and adding the texts that are related to the text which may or may not be related to the query. This leads to deviations in the sentences constituting the summary generated by Bosma's approach. The other reasons for better performance by the sutra based summary generation mechanism, are the use of sangatis and retrieval of CDUs for summary generation rather than EDUs . Bosma's approach indexes EDUs while the proposed approach uses CDUs which has more context coverage when compared to that of a EDU pertinent to the query.

In order to analyse the influence of sangatis in the sutra construction, a performance comparison was done between the sutra generated by using RST alone. Also, it was observed that a particular set of discourse relations and sangatis dominated in the sutra construction. In order to bring out the influence of such discourse relations and sangatis, the sutra constructed using only them and summary was generated. Table 8 shows the average scores of the summary generator that uses sutra based RST, RST+sangatis and dominat set of discourse relations and sangatis.

Following are the descriptions of the notations used in the table.

Average Score of Summary Generated by RST-sangati discourse Parser= Avg_Score_RST-Sangati sutra
Average Score of Summary Generated by RST discourse Parser based sutra-=Avg_Score_RST-Sutra

The difference in scores achieved by RST-sangati and RST sutra involve two reasons. The first main reason is the sutra representation which aids in picking up relevant CDUs for summary. The second reason is the use of sangatis in RST-sangati which has lesser influence when compared to that of the sutra influence. This is mainly due to the corpus used which had more RST based discourse relations than sangatis. The usage of narrative kind of texts where presence of sangatis will be more will help showing a huge difference between RST-sangati and RST sutras. The score shown by the sutra generated by using fixed set of RST based discourse relations and sangatis indicate that the corpus used predominantly contains these fixed set.

CONCLUSION AND FUTURE WORK

In this chapter, we have discussed a query focussed summary generation mechanism in which the input documents are represented by a discourse structure. The discourse structure is constructed using three types of text representation techniques namely, UNL, RST and sàngatis using UNL-RST- sàngatis discourse parser which constructs discourse structure at paragraph and document levels. The discourse structure is constructed in the form of a tree. Furthermore, the summary generation system makes use of a concept called sutra for indexing the discourse structure. Both sutras and sangatis are have been used in ancient Tamil and Sanskrit liteatures.

The UNL-RST-saṅgati discourse parser constructs a primitive discourse model, using UNL and RST features and saṅgatis. Improving the feature set and corpus will eventually improve the efficiency. A learning paradigm also needs to be incorporated in the UNL-RST-saṅgati discourse parser, in order to make use of all possible features present in the corpus for the discourse parsing task. This UNL-RS-saṅgati tree has been used as the base for deriving a sūtra for the NL documents. sūtra based concise representation has been used as an indexer and tested on summary generation system. A performance comparison has been done with one of the existing RST based summary generation systems. Generating cross lingual and multi lingual summary generation is possible with the discussed approach. The sūtra representation is obtained using only two factors, which need to be enhanced. The factor, "α" needs to examined by setting different values to it.

The overhead involved in the discussed approach is the requirement of a UNL framework, as the UNL-RST-saṅgati discourse parser requires the input text documents to be enconverted to UNL. Since the output of the sūtra based summary generator is a language independent UNL-RST-saṅgati graph, the NL summary can be decoded to any target language by using an appropriate UNL deconverter and RS-saṅgati decoders. Though the discussed approach does not involve the generation of cross lingual and multi lingual summaries, the current sūtra based summary generator can be extended to generate such summaries in the future. Apart from the summary generation system, the sūtra based concise representation is also suitable for IR and QA systems.

REFERENCES

Asher, N., Venant, A., Muller, P., & Afantenos, S. (2011). Complex discourse units and their semantics. *Nation (New York, N.Y.)*, *2*(3), 7.

Balaji, J., Geetha, T. V., & Parthasarathi, R. (2016). Abstractive summarization: A hybrid approach for the compression of semantic graphs. *International Journal on Semantic Web and Information Systems*, *12*(2), 76–99. doi:10.4018/IJSWIS.2016040104

Bosma, W. (2005). Query-based summarization using rhetorical structure theory. *LOT Occasional Series*, *4*, 29–44.

Cohan, A., & Goharian, N. (2017). *Scientific article summarization using citation-context and article's discourse structure.* arXiv preprint arXiv:1704.06619

Durrett, G., Berg-Kirkpatrick, T., & Klein, D. (2016). *Learning-based single-document summarization with compression and anaphoricity constraints.* arXiv preprint arXiv:1603.08887

Liu, F., Flanigan, J., Thomson, S., Sadeh, N., & Smith, N. A. (2018). *Toward abstractive summarization using semantic representations.* arXiv preprint arXiv:1805.10399

Mann, W. C., & Thompson, S. A. (1988). Rhetorical structure theory: Toward a functional theory of text organization. *Text-Interdisciplinary Journal for the Study of Discourse*, *8*(3), 243–281. doi:10.1515/text.1.1988.8.3.243

Munivar, P. (1991). *Nannool Kandikaiyurai-Ezhuthathikaram.* Chennai, India: Mullai Nilayam.

Navaneethakrishnan, S. C., & Parthasarathi, R. (2015). Building a Language-Independent Discourse Parser using Universal Networking Language. *Computational Intelligence*, *31*(4), 593–618. doi:10.1111/coin.12037

Shoaih, M., & Shah, A. A. (2006). *A new indexing technique for information retrieval systems using rhetorical structure theory.* RST.

Srivenkatesha Subba Yajva Shastri. (1934). *Bhatta Deepika with Bhatta Chintamani Commentary by Vancheshwara.* Chennai: Madras Law Journal Press.

Subalalith1a, C. N., & Parthasarathi, R. (2017). Query Focused Summary Generation System using Unique Discourse Structure. International Journal of Information Retrieval Research, 7(1), 49-69.

Subalalitha, C. N., & Parthasarathi, R. (2012). An approach to discourse parsing using sangati and rhetorical structure theory. In *Proceedings of the Workshop on Machine Translation and Parsing in Indian Languages* (pp. 73-82). Academic Press.

Subalalitha, C. N., & Ranjani, P. (2013). A Unique Indexing Technique for Indexing Discourse Structures. *Journal of Intelligent Systems.*, *23*(3), 231–243.

Subalalitha, C. N., & Ranjani, P. (2014). A Unique Indexing Technique for Discourse Structures. *Journal of Intelligent Systems*, *23*(3), 231–243. doi:10.1515/jisys-2013-0034

Uchida, H., Zhu, M., & Della Senta, T. (1999). *A gift for a millennium*. Tokyo: IAS/UNU.

Wang, L., & Ling, W. (2016). *Neural network-based abstract generation for opinions and argu1ments*. arXiv preprint arXiv:1606.02785

Chapter 7
Automatic Ontology Construction:
Ontology From Plain Text Using Conceptualization and Semantic Roles

Amita Arora
J. C. Bose University of Science and Technology, India

ABSTRACT

World wide web has information resources even on unthinkable subjects. This information may be available instantly to anyone having Internet connection. This web is growing exponentially, and it is becoming difficult to locate useful information in such a sheer volume of information. Semantic web extends the current web by emphasizing on interoperable ontologies which are capable of processing high quality information so that the agents placed on top of semantic web can automate the work or curate the content for the user. In this chapter, an extensive research in the area of ontology construction is presented, and after having a critical look over the work done in this field and considering the limitation of each, it has been observed that constructing ontology automatically is a challenging task as this task faces difficulties due to unstructured text and ambiguities in English text. In this work an ontology generation technique is devised covering all important aspects missing in the existing works giving better performance as compared to another system.

INTRODUCTION

Semantic web is a major evolution in connecting information for effective information retrieval. The goal of semantic web is to make the web understandable by both human and machine. This task is done by using ontologies as it is the better way to represent knowledge (A. Zouaq, 2011). In other words, constructing ontologies aim at capturing domain knowledge that gives a commonly agreed understanding of a domain, which may be reused, shared among applications and groups.

DOI: 10.4018/978-1-7998-1021-6.ch007

In this chapter, a new approach to build ontology automatically is proposed, based on extracting semantic roles present in the given sentences of a given text along with usual concepts and their relationships. The extracted information about different roles, concepts and relationships among the concepts from different sentences in the document are then merged to construct ontology for whole document. The proposed approach is implemented and the performance of the proposed technique is evaluated. Experiments show the ontology thus created captures most of the information given in the document. The present proposal may be important to understand the document as we have both syntactic and semantic information about a sentence or a text.

In general, process of building ontology adopts following steps. Firstly the concepts are extracted then underlying semantic relations (hierarchical or non-hierarchical) among these concepts are extracted and then these relations and concepts are connected using suitable criteria. However, the work done till now in automated creation of ontologies from plain text mostly capture only hierarchal relationships such as *car-(is-a)-vehicle* or *steering-(part-of)-car* but non-hierarchical relations such as performed, begin etc as in *Ghulam_Ali-(performed_at)-concert* or *music_festival-(begins)-tomorrow* are not captured accurately by the existing approaches (Sourish Dasgupta, 11 Feb 2018) (Gillam, 2005). But the present approach uses semantic roles along with other components such as concepts and their relationships. The ontologies corresponding to each sentence in the given text is constructed and these ontologies are then merged by aligning the concepts in them to create a bigger ontology for complete document. More precisely, the semantic similarity technique is used to match and merge these structures related to semantic roles in addition to matching of relations and concepts. In particular, a set of ontology merging rules are designed and later used to merge the structures in the two different ontologies. The multiword concepts are also taken into account while identifying concepts and semantic roles. This way the limitations of the previous contributions are removed as those works were focusing mostly on single word concepts and taxonomical i.e. hierarchical relations.

ONTOLOGY DEVELOPMENT METHODS

To reduce the high cost of building ontologies manually, automatic construction of ontology has been the focus of recent research. (Fekade Getahun, 2017) (Abeer Al-Arfaj, 2015) (Gillani Andleeb, 2015)

A detailed description of methodologies and approaches to address this activity is given as follows:

Ontology from Unstructured Text

Constructing ontology from unstructured text is the process of identifying concepts, relations among these concepts and properties of concepts from textual information and using them to construct and maintain ontology.

Few approaches by some researchers attempt to build ontology from unstructured text manually, semi-automatically or automatically by employing different ideas. We describe here some of the approaches as follows:

Statistical Techniques and Hearst's Patterns

Khurshid Ahmad et al. (Gillam, 2005) have worked on unstructured text to construct ontology which makes automatic identification of keywords used as concepts using statistical techniques and then using Hearst's patterns (Hearst, 1992) to enhance the ontology. In this work domain expertise is needed to provide evidences.

Supervised Approach

A supervised approach to automatic Ontology Population is given by Hristo Tanev et al. (Hristo Tanev Tanev, 2008). They have populated ontology of Named Entities in which geographical locations and person names are used as two high level categories and each category has ten sub-classes. Unknown named Entities from the test set are classified using this model. As no annotated corpus is used in the learning process, this approach is weakly supervised.

Concept-Relation-Concept Tuple-Based Ontology Learning

Abbreviated as CRCTOL (Tan, January 2010) is an approach devised by Tan et al. for constructing ontologies from domain-specific documents. For performing ontology learning tasks it uses linguistics and statistics-based techniques. For part of speech tagging and other syntactic information Stanford's part-of-speech tagger is used along with the Berkeley Parser. Nouns and noun phrases are extracted in the form of multi-word terms using some predefined rules. Terms are identified whether they belong to specific domain using a manually built domain lexicon. To find is-a relations lexico-syntactic patterns are used.

Unsupervised Learning

Drymonas et al. (Drymonas1, 2010) from the Technical University of Crete designed OntoGain system for the unsupervised learning of ontologies from unstructured text in medical and computer science domains. OntoGain also uses linguistics and statistics-based techniques for acquisition of ontology. It uses The OpenNLP suite of tools and the WordNet Java Library for preprocessing of text such as tokenization, lemmatization, pos tagging, and parsing. To build a hierarchy agglomerative clustering and Formal Concept Analysis is implemented. For this initially each term is considered to be a cluster and these clusters are merged at each step based on the similarity measure. Association rule mining is used to extract the non- taxonomic relations.

Document Based Ontology

Jizheng Wan et al. (Jizheng Wan, 2011) have proposed the concept of Document based Ontology (DbO) for constructing ontology from unstructured text which gives importance only to the properties of a document ignoring their context. The concept structure and entity instances are taken care of in this work. Statistical techniques such as Latent Semantic Analysis and Markov Model are used for detecting synonyms and to predict next word.

Re-Engineering and Reusing Resources

Mari Carmen et al. (Mari Carmen Sua´rez-Figueroa, 2012) suggests multiple ways of building ontology instead of giving any one methodology for different situations by re-engineering and reusing knowledge resources

Glossary Based Approach

GOSPL (Christophe Debruyne, 2013) given by Christophe Debruyne has aimed at building hybrid ontology where concepts are defined both formally and informally. This methodology provides collaboration between the ontology engineers and domain experts and uses Glossary as a special linguistic resource. The concept of "sameness" is explored in detail according to which different terms from different communities referring to same concept do not imply to be synonyms.Fact modelling by applying the principle of separation in conceptualization is used which is an interpretation process called reasoning. The approach provides only the setting in which ontologies can be built but they have not given the method how community can use it.

Probabilistic Modelling

Hoifung Poon and Pedro Domingos (Domingos, 2014) have given an approach that overcomes the problem of inducing ontology from individual words by focusing on phrasal verbs etc. This approach is different from existing approaches as the ontology is induced probabilistic modelling to reduce uncertainty and noise. Also knowledge extraction and ontology population go hand in hand. Unsupervised Markov logic Network is used in this approach to form hierarchical clustering from logical expressions having is-a relations among them. The *is-a* relation among relation cluster can be found among relation clusters but it fails to do same for entity clusters. Active voice is well handled here but they are not able to handle passive voice. Moreover semantic relations are not extracted nor can this approach scale up to large corpora.

Naive Bayes Classification

G. Suresh Kumar (G. Suresh kumar, 2015) has proposed an approach to extract concepts and relations for a question answering system in which domain attributes and associations are extracted from relevant documents. A binary decision tree-based rule engine is proposed giving output as a triplet of candidate keyword, predicate and associated object. The relation between the concepts is through the relation predicted by classifier. Lexico-syntactic probability and lexico-semantic probability are used here. But only pre-classified classes of relations can be there.

Julia Hoxha et al. (Julia Hoxha, 2010) also use Naive Bayes Classification for constructing ontology. The classifier is used for categorizing text to determine the label of document. SVM is used to cluster similar documents. In this method summarization is performed to shorten the text. Taxonomical relations such as synonyms, hypernyms and hyponyms are extracted here. Hearst's patterns are used for extracting hierarchies from text. At first candidate classes are extracted and then other hypernym, synonyms are extracted and represented in the form of taxonomy.

Machine Reading and Lexico Semantic Method

Bothma (Bothma, 2010) gives a semi-automated approach for learning ontologies from Swedish text. Machine reading, statistical and lexico- semantic methods are used to extract concepts, a few taxonomic and a pre-defined set of non-taxonomic relations. This approach is also error prone as noun phrases are not taken into account to be extracted as concepts. Also no consideration is given to attributes of concepts.

Rapid Prototyping

UPON-Lite (MISSIKOFF, 2016) by Missikoff et al. is an automatic ontology development methodology that insists there should be no intermediation of ontology engineers in the process of building ontology. The methodology which is user centric is based on an incremental process that constructs rapid prototypes of trial ontologies. Researchers suggest the use of supporting tools like gloss extractors and ontology editing tool like Protégé for producing OWL ontology.

Hierarchical Semi-Supervised Classification

Bhawna Dalvi (Bhavana Dalvi, 2016) have proposed a hierarchical semi-supervised classification approach completes the incomplete class hierarchies by adding new instances to the existing ones or by discovering new classes and extending the existing ontology by placing them at appropriate places in the ontology using. This approach can be used for document classification task and entity classification into class hierarchy of a knowledge base also but is not applied to class-hierarchies that are non-tree structured.

Statistical, Machine-Learning, and Custom Pattern-Based Method

Open Calais (Marius-Gabriel, 2016) by Marius-Gabriel system by Thomson Reuter's which is linked to a market leading ontology extracting entities (persons, events, places), relationships etc and gives results in *rdf* format. The semantic content of users' input files is analyzed using a combination of statistical, machine-learning, and custom pattern-based methods. It also maps the metadata-tags to Thomson Reuters unique Ids supporting disambiguation and linking of data across all the documents being processed by it.

Topic Modelling Algorithm

Monika et al. (Monika Rani, 2017) explores topic modelling algorithms such as LSI & SVD and Map Reduce LDA (Mr. LDA) for learning Ontology. The study and experimental result give enough proof of the effectiveness of using Mr. LDA topic modelling for learning ontology. Experimental results in the paper demonstrate the effectiveness of the proposed system in term of building richer topic-specific knowledge and semantic retrieval. Terminology ontology building is a preliminary step for semantic-based query (Topics and Words Detection) optimization for knowledge management. Their method is scalable but requires human intervention.

User Centric Approach

A methodology is proposed by Kenneth et al. (Kenneth Clarkson, 2018) that performs user-centric ontology population that needs human intervention at each step as the user is required to assist in developing, linking and maintaining the conceptualization of that domain, making the use of some already available ontology. Three main steps are followed where the first one is to select the relevant ontologies, then aligning the concepts with the same of the target ontology using a new hierarchical classification approach and after that user is assisted to develop, replace or enhance their initial ontology by creating, splitting or merging the concepts or adding new instances to existing concepts by extracting new facts from unstructured data.

LexOnt (K. Arabshian, 2012) by K. Arabshian is a system that also constructs the ontology semi-automatically including user at each step. It uses Wikipedia, WordNet and Programmable Web directory of services. It also uses existing ontology to extract relevant terms. LexOnt constructs the ontology in iterations, by interacting with the user. The user has the ability to choose, add terms to the ontology and rank those terms. It is a plug-in tab for the Protégé ontology editor. The system accepts unstructured text as input and *interacts with the user to facilitate the ontology creation process.*

Morpho Syntactic analysis

Sourish Dasgupta and Jens Lehman (Sourish Dasgupta, 2018)build initial ontology using the fundamental knowledge about the target domain. A corpus of text relating to that domain is analyzed syntactically and semantically to perform semantic enrichment. Morpho-syntactic analysis of the text is done to extract concepts for building ontology.

Concepts Maps

OntoCmaps (A. Zouaq, 2011) by A. Zouaq is a domain independent ontology learning tool. It extracts deep semantic representations from corpora. It generates conceptual representations which are in the form of concept maps. This tool relies on the inner structure of graphs to extract the important elements that are identified as the important concepts. *This system is not able to capture non-hierarchical relationships.*

PROBLEM DEFINITION

Following are few important challenges as observed in the process of learning ontology which are faced by researchers given as:

- **Unstructured Texts:** There is an open challenge according to S. Gillani Andleeb (Gillani Andleeb, 2015) to learn an effective personalised ontology from the critical information. This information may be scattered amongst various kinds of documents originating from various sources such as emails and web pages or user's local information repository that does not have meta data. For this reason, the results for discovery of relations between concepts are also not satisfactory (Maimon, 2015).

- **Ambiguity in English text/Multiple senses of a Word:** As there may be multiple senses of word each of these having a different meaning based on the context of the word's usage in a sentence, it has to be resolved. Producing inconsistent or duplicate entries and dealing with these inconsistencies is quite challenging. (Abeer Al-Arfaj, 2015)

Due to above inherent problems the ontology techniques earlier proposed have some deficiencies stated as follows:

1. **Lack of Fully Automatic Techniques for Ontology Development:** Due to unstructuredness and ambiguity in texts, there are very less standard tools for developing ontology as explained by (Bothma, 2010) (Gillam, 2005). Existing techniques use supervised learning which require large amount of data for training.
2. **Ignoring Other Useful Information from the Texts:** Existing techniques typically consider word frequencies, co-occurrence statistics, and syntactic patterns such as Hearst patterns (Stephen Roller, July 15 - 20, 2018.) and cover only those terms or sentences, (by ignoring others) that satisfy these constraints. The ignored text may also contain useful information such as non-taxonomical relations (relations other than *is-a*, *has-a* or *part-of* etc.) or data properties. In general, the information in a text has multiple layers such as semantic roles denoting the context of a concept and semantic relations. Ideally all levels of information should be used to construct the ontology for a given text.

After having a critical look over the work done in this field and considering the limitation of each, it has been observed that constructing ontology automatically is a challenging and important task. The work done till now in automated engineering of ontologies capture only taxonomical relationships such as is-a, part of etc.

Moreover only limited language constructs such as nouns are considered as the building blocks for ontologies ignoring other constituents (such as verbs and adverbs) of a language in the given text. Also larger texts and compound or complex sentence structure in the text imposes difficulty in exploring the semantic content of the text and constructing ontology. In this work an ontology generation technique will be devised covering all important aspects missing in the existing works. Particularly semantic roles along with the other constituents such as nouns, verbs etc. will be used to build ontology without limitation of its size.

BASIC APPROACH

The proposed technique takes unstructured text as input, applies natural language processing techniques to identify the concepts, roles etc. and utilises a new algorithms to merge them into an ontology. Therefore following textual components are playing key roles to design the present ontological framework.

1. **Semantic Roles:** Semantic roles information along with other information such as concept and relations to generate ontology. Semantic roles are representations that express the abstract role that arguments of a predicate (usually expressed by verb in the sentence) can take in the event (Martin, 2015) (Janowicz, 2005). For example a concept can be an *agent* or *accompanier* or a *location* in a sentence. Attaching these semantic roles with each constituent not only help to merge sub-ontologies

(ontologies created for each sentence in the given document) but also contribute to deeper text understanding in the form of final ontology.

2. **Concepts:** All concepts instead of just key concepts (frequently used concepts) are identified and used.
3. **Non-Taxonomical Relationships:** Non-Taxonomical Relationships among concepts instead of just taxonomical relationships are used.

All these constituents will be identified and used in the sequence as is given in the architecture of the system in the following section.

ARCHITECTURE OF PROPOSED SYSTEM

In order to realize the basic approach or model computationally, following is the proposed architecture of the system as shown in Figure1.

1. **Natural Language Processor:** In this system the input text documents are first processed by a natural language processor which uses Stanford dependency parser (Marneffe, 2015) that performs the tokenization at sentence level and dependency parsing. This component also performs name entity recognition tagging and anaphora resolution and transforms.
2. **Information Extractor:** These sentences are transformed into tagged structures that are used by the Information Extractor module. This module extracts the required information i.e. concepts, relations, properties and semantic roles of concepts.
3. **Sub-Ontology Constructor:** The information i.e. concepts, relations, properties and semantic roles of concepts extracted in above module is used in constructing intermediate structures or sub-ontologies for each sentence.
4. **Sub-Ontology Merger:** These sub-ontologies are further required to be merged to form the complete ontology of the document. In our proposed ontology mapping and merging scheme, process of merging takes into consideration not only the shared concepts and similar relations but also the semantic roles each concept is playing in a sentence. A set of rules is used which is designed specifically for this purpose.
5. **Ontology Representer:** This module takes the bigger ontology, generated as result of above step, as input and represents it both graphically and as an *rdf* document.

The following section focuses on the detailed design of the proposed system and also includes the data design and algorithm design of each module.

DETAILED DESIGN OF THE SYSTEM

In this section, detailed design of the components of the proposed system is given by using the following subsection. It may be noted that in the process of designing a component following two issues are taken in to account.

Figure 1. Architecture of the Proposed System

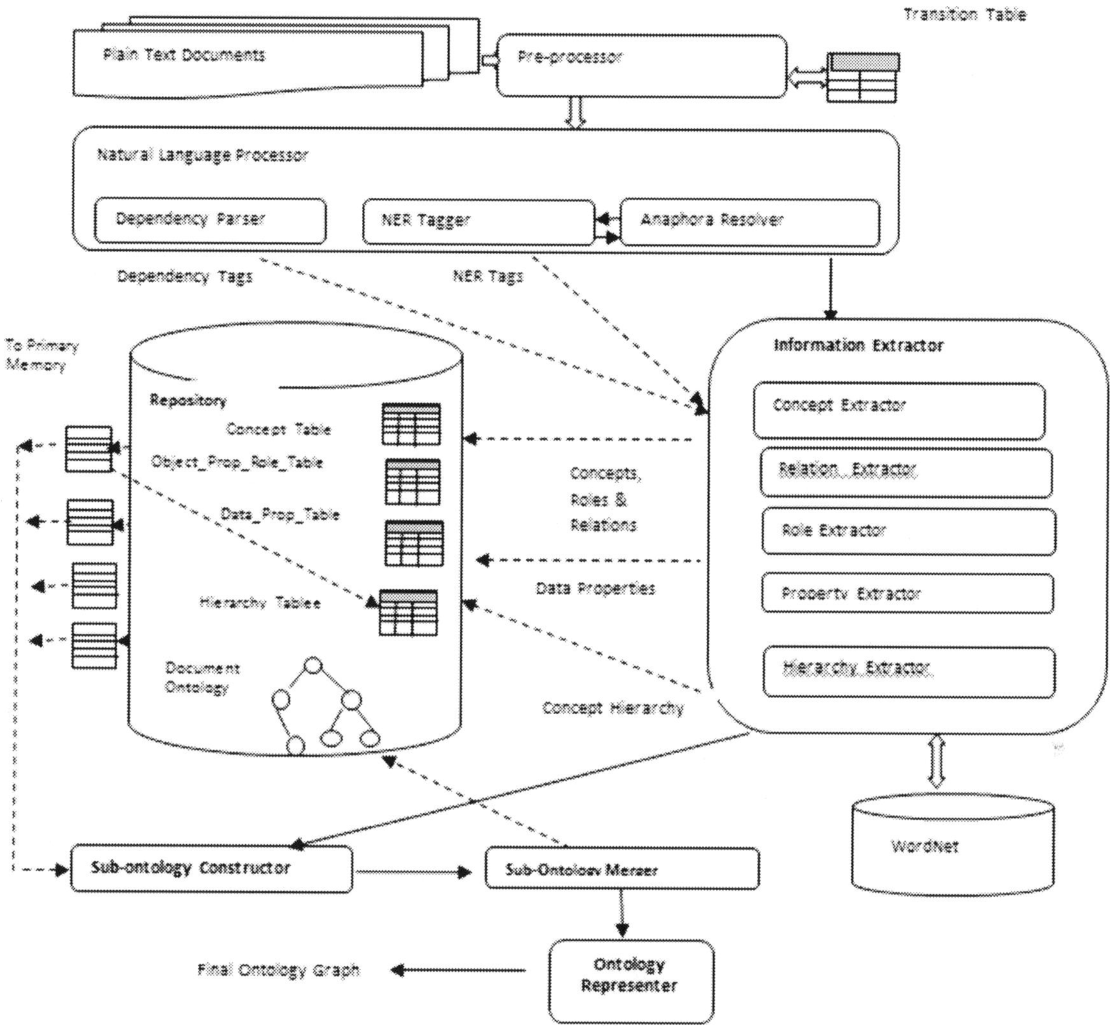

1. **Input Data or Information Required and its Representation**: In the process of designing a component, first the data or information required is identified and then that data or information is represented using a suitable scheme by providing the format or structure of the data, storage of data and its utilization wherever required.

2. **The Algorithm**: For each component their respective algorithms are given to express the way of utilizing structure of the data or information to achieve a particular intermediate (or final) result.

In the coming subsections, we will give detailed design of each component of the system considering above two issues.

Pre-Processor

The text documents being processed for constructing ontology may contain words, phrases or sentences which are redundant and unnecessary e.g. the phrases like "*as a matter of fact*", "*in all honesty*", "*considering*" and many more do not contribute towards meaningful information of the text and may be processed to be removed from this document. The sentences being followed phrases like "namely", "specifically", "thus", "to put it another way" etc. just contain the redundant information and may be removed. To perform this task, different kind of transition words or phrases are first identified and then treated according to their type. The pre-processor takes the unstructured text as input and searches in the text for the transition words or phrases already stored in the dictionary. If a match is found in the text, it removes the transition word, or the transition phrase or the text following that word or phrase is removed. Action to be taken is decided according to the type of transition word or phrase e.g. for words like *such as, for instance* etc. which are Introductory type transition phrases, these words along with the text following these words is un-necessary and can be removed from the text without harming or distorting the information to be conveyed by the text.

Data Design for Pre-Processor

Since the present work is dealing with text written in English language, therefore, many types of transition words or phrases, found in the documents written using English language, are identified to take the appropriate action as stated below. These transition words are given in Table 1. The table also describes the type of these phrases or words and defines the action which can be taken if such types of transition words or phrases are identified by the pre-processor module.

Data Storage: This table is stored in secondary memory and is brought to primary memory as the first step of removing these un-necessary words.

After deleting these transition words, the document is free from complex sentence structures.

Data Utilization: These simple sentences are given as input to natural language processor so that the necessary information can be extracted as illustrated in the next section.

Algorithm Design for Pre-Processor

The algorithm for pre-processing of text documents is shown in Figure 2.

The algorithm takes the text document as the input and begins by processing each sentence of the text document to check whether any of the phrases kept in Table have any occurrence in the sentence in step 1. If yes then step 2 finds the type of the phrase by looking into the table and takes the appropriate action like deleting the phrase or deleting the consequent sentence in step 3. The output of this algorithm is the pre-processed text document that is free from the un-necessary or redundant words or phrases.

Natural Language Processor

This section describes the processing of natural language processor which analyzes input sentences from plain text documents syntactically and annotates the document with linguistic features that are needed by Information Extractor module. This module is having following components:

Table 1. Transition Words Action Table

Transition word/ phrase type	Example words	Action Taken
Addition	indeed, further, as well (as this), either (neither), not only (this) but also (that) as well, also, moreover, what is more, as a matter of fact, in all honesty, and, furthermore, in addition (to this), besides (this), to tell the truth, or, in fact, actually, to say nothing of, etc.	Transition word/phrase removed
Introduction	such as, as, particularly, including, as an illustration, for example, like, in particular, for one thing, to illustrate, for instance, especially, notably, by way of example, etc.	Transition word/phrase removed. Also the text following the transition word/phrase in the sentence is removed.
Reference	speaking about (this), considering (this), regarding (this), with regards to (this), as for (this), concerning (this), the fact that, on the subject of (this),	Transition word/phrase removed
Similarity	similarly, in the same way, by the same token, in a like manner, equally, likewise, etc	Transition word/phrase removed
Clarification	that is (to say), namely, specifically, thus, (to) put (it) another way, in other words,	Transition word/phrase removed. Also the text following the transition word/phrase in the sentence is removed.
Conflict	but, by way of contrast, while, on the other hand, however, (and) yet, whereas, though (final position), in contrast, when in fact, conversely, etc.	Transition word/phrase removed
Emphasis	even more, above all, indeed, more importantly, Besides, etc.	Transition word/phrase removed
Result	as a result (of this), consequently, hence, for this reason, thus, because (of this), in consequence, so that, accordingly, as a consequence, so much (so) that, so, therefore, etc.	Transition word/phrase removed
Purpose	for the purpose of, in the hope that, for fear that, so that, with this intention, to the end that, in order to, Lest, with this in mind, in order that, so as to, so, etc.	Transition word/phrase removed
Consequence	under those circumstances, then, in that case, if not, that being the case, if so, otherwise	Transition word/phrase removed
Sequential Transition	in the (first, second, etc.) place, initially, to start with, first of all, thirdly, (&c.), to begin with, at first, for a start, secondly, etc.	Transition word/phrase removed
Continuation	subsequently, previously, eventually, next, before (this), afterwards, after (this), then, etc.	Transition word/phrase removed
Conclusion	to conclude (with), as a final point, eventually, at last, last but not least, in the end, finally, lastly, etc.	Transition word/phrase removed
Degression	to change the topic, incidentally, by the way, etc.	Transition word/phrase removed
Resumption	to get back to the point, to resume, anyhow, anyway, at any rate, to return to the subject, etc.	Transition word/phrase removed
Concession	but even so, nevertheless, even though, on the other hand, admittedly, however, nonetheless, despite (this), notwithstanding (this), Albeit (and) still, although, in spite of (this), regardless (of this), (and) yet, though, granted (this), be that as it may, etc.	Transition word/phrase removed
Summation	as was previously stated, so, consequently, in summary, all in all, to make a long story short, thus, as I have said, to sum up, overall, as has been mentioned, then, to summarize, to be brief, briefly, given these points, in all, on the whole, therefore, as has been noted, hence, in conclusion, in a word, to put it briefly, in sum, altogether, in short, etc.	Transition word/phrase removed

Figure 2. Algorithm for Pre-processor

```
Algorithm pre_processor()

Input: text document, dictionary of transition words ,Table 3.1

Output: pre-processed text document

Begin

        for each sentence of the text document
    1.  if any of the phrase from dictionary of transition words  is present in the
        sentence
    2.  find the type of the phrase
    3.  take action according to the Table 3.1
    end for
```

a) Anaphora Resolution
b) Dependency Parser
c) NER Tagging

These components are described as follows:

Anaphora Resolver

For extracting the correct information from text it is necessary to replace the pronouns in a sentence to its mention as a noun in some previous sentence. This process called anaphora or co-reference resolution is performed here using Java RAP tool (Qiu, Kan & Chua, 2004) which takes plain text as input and gives output in the form of plain text with in-place substitution of anaphora with its antecedent.

Data Design for Anaphora Resolver

We get the anaphora resolved sentences as output of this tool. The details for data design for anaphora resolver is as follows:

Output Data Format: As an example for the following sentence

"An Air India flight to HongKong was brought down at Kolkata late last night after some passengers complained of smoke in the cabin. The flight with passengers landed at the Kolkata airport. Under those circumstances, they were accommodated in nearby hotels."

'they' will be replaced by "*passengers*" as

Figure 3. Algorithm for Anaphora Resolver

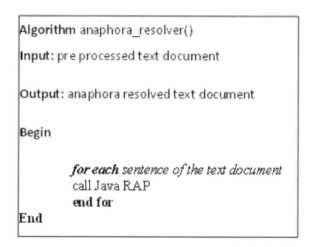

"*An Air India flight to HongKong was brought down at Kolkata late last night after some passengers complained of smoke in the cabin. The flight with passengers landed at the Kolkata airport. Under those circumstances, passengers were accommodated in nearby hotels.*"

Data Storage: The anaphora resolved sentences are stored in *String* in primary memory.
Data Utilization: These anaphora resolved sentences are used by dependency parser module.

Algorithm Design for Anaphora Resolver

The algorithm for anaphora resolver is shown in Figure 3 as follows:

As shown in algorithm anaphora_resolver, we pass the preprocessed text document as input to the Java RAP tool. The tool processes it and gives the anaphora resolved text document as output.

Dependency Parser

Documents as plain text are given to Stanford dependency parser [dep] (Marneffe, 2015) which provides the result in the form of a part of speech tagged sentences of each document along with the dependencies

Figure 4. Stanford Dependency Parser Output

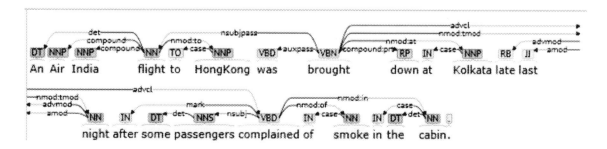

among the constituents of each sentence. In this dependency graph vertices are the words in a sentence and an edge exists between each word and its syntactic head. The graph forms a tree rooted at the main verb. The edges are labelled with dependency types. These dependencies are utilized to find the concepts, relations and properties of concepts from the text.

The Stanford dependency tagging for the first sentence will be given as in the Figure 4.

Data Design for Dependency Parser

The details for data design for dependency parser is as follows:

Data Structure Used: Since the Stanford Dependency Parser is used to parse the sentences, we are not explicitly keeping the grammar rules used for parsing. However, 52 grammatical relations which Stanford parser utilises in its final representation are identified and taken in to account while finding concepts etc. in the next phase. All 52 relations used are given in Table 2.

Output Data Format: The sentence when parsed through the dependency parser has following format as shown in Figure 5. Here all the words numbered and are given dependency tags in pairs.

Output Data Storage: This tagged structure of the sentence is kept into primary memory in a *String* type data after removing the brackets, hyphens and numeric values provided by the tagger.

Data Utilization This data is utilized by Information Extractor module.

Algorithm for Dependency Parser

The algorithm for dependency parser is shown in Figure 6.

The algorithm takes the anaphora resolved pre-processed text document as the input to the Stanford Dependency Parser which parses the text and provides dependency tags to each word of each sentence of the document.

Table 2. Stanford Dependency Relations

Sr. No.	Dependency Relation	Definition
1	root	Root
2	dep	Dependent
3	aux	Auxiliary
4	Auxpass	passive auxiliary
5	cop	Copula
6	arg	Argument
7	agent	Agent
8	comp	Complement
9	acomp	adjectival complement
10	ccomp	clausal complement with internal subject
11	xcomp	clausal complement with external subject
12	obj	Object
13	Dobj	direct object

continued on following page

Table 2. Continued

Sr. No.	Dependency Relation	Definition
14	iobj	indirect object
15	Pobj	object of preposition
16	Subj	Subject
17	nsubj	nominal subject
18	nsubjpass	passive nominal subject
19	csubj	clausal subject
20	csubjpass	passive clausal subject
21	cc	Coordination
22	conj	Conjunct
23	expl	expletive (expletive "there")
24	mod	Modifier
25	amod	adjectival modifier
26	appos	appositional modifier
27	advcl	adverbial clause modifier
28	det	Determiner
29	predet	Predeterminer
30	preconj	Preconjunct
31	vmod	reduced, non-finite verbal modifier
32	mwe	multi-word expression modifier
33	mark	marker (word introducing an advcl or ccomp
34	advmod	adverbial modifier
35	neg	negation modifier
36	rcmod	relative clause modifier
37	quantmod	quantifier modifier
38	nn	noun compound modifier
39	npadvmod	noun phrase adverbial modifier
40	tmod	temporal modifier
41	num	numeric modifier
42	number	element of compound number
43	prep	prepositional modifier
44	poss	possession modifier
45	possessive	possessive modifier ('s)
46	prt	phrasal verb particle
47	parataxis	parataxis
48	goeswith	goeswith
49	punct	punct
50	ref	ref
51	sdep	sdep
52	xsubj	xsubj

Figure 5. Dependency Tagged Sentence

root (ROOT-0 , brought-8) det (flight-4 , An-1) compound (flight-4 , Air-2)
compound (flight-4 , India-3) nsubjpass (brought-8 , flight-4) case (HongKong-6
, to-5) nmod:to (flight-4 , HongKong-6) auxpass (brought-8 , was-7)
compound:prt (rought-8 , down-9) case (Kolkata-11 , at-10) nmod:at (brought-8 ,
Kolkata-11) advmod (night-14 , late-12) amod (night-14 , last-13) nmod:tmod (
brought-8 , ight-14) mark (complained-18 , after-15) det (passengers-17 , some-16
) nsubj (omplained-18 , passengers-17) advcl (brought-8 , complained-18) case (
smoke- 0 , of-19) nmod:of (complained-18 , smoke-20) case (cabin-23 , in-21)det (
cabin-23 , the-22) nmod:in (complained-18 , cabin-23

Figure 6. Algorithm for Dependency Parser

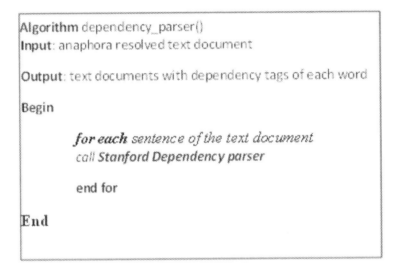

NER Tagging

The nouns in the sentence are named entities. A noun in a sentence can refer to some person, location, organization or time. A natural language processing tool SENNA (Ronan Collobert, 2011) is utilized here. SENNA is used in our work to provide NER tags to the nouns of the sentence.

Data Design for NER Tagger

The details for data design for NER Tagger is as follows:

Data Structure Used: SENNA has dictionary of 130 thousand words which is used to map every word to a vector of 50 floating numbers. SENNA also keeps Gazetteer list and uppercase information as mentioned earlier in Chapter 2. SENNA provides the following tags that can be extracted by it as shown in Table 3.

Table 3. NER Tags

NER Tag
Person
Location
Organization
Time

Figure 7. NER Tagging of Sentence (Pictorial Representation)

Figure 8. NER Tagged Sentence

An	B-ORG
Air	I-ORG
India	E-ORG
Flight	O
To	O
HongKong	S-LOC
was	O
brought	O
down	O
at	O
Kolkata	S-LOC
late	S- TIME
last	S- TIME
night	S- TIME
after	O
some	O
passengers	O
complained	O
of	O
smoke	O
in	O
the	O
cabin	O

Output Data Format: For the sentences of the example given above the following will be the NER tagged sentence shown pictorially in Figure 7.

S-PER, S-LOC, S-ORG and S-TIME tags may be given to the entities, B-NP,I-NP and E-NP specify the beginning, intermediate and end of the named entity.

We get the sentences along with their tags associated with each word as shown in the Figure 8.

This structure of sentences shows the respective named entity tagged for individual words such as S-LOC for location, ORG for organisation; S-TIME for time and O stands for others.

Data Storage The named entity tagged sentences are stored in a *String* in primary memory

Data Utilization: These tagged sentences can be used further by information extractor module.

Algorithm Design for NER Tagger

The algorithm for NER tagger shown in Figure 9.

The algorithm starts with passing the pre-processed document to SENNA which performs the tagging for each sentence of the document and gives the name entity tagged sentences of the document as output which are used by Information Extractor module as an input for further processing.

Information Extractor

The Information Extractor is designed here for extracting information from sentence structures. The information extracted is generally concepts, their semantic roles in the sentence, properties and relations. It takes the co-reference resolved sentences having dependency tags and NER tags attached to them.

Concept, Relation and Role Extractor

These are the concepts participating directly in a relation given by the verb in the sentence and concepts which are not directly related to the verb. Concepts may be existing in the text in the form of a single word or a multi word i.e. a single noun may be there representing the concept or a noun phrase is used

Figure 9. Algorithm for NER Tagger

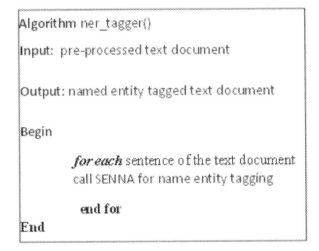

Table 4. Dependency Tags, Concepts, Possible Roles and Relations

Dependency Tag	Concept	NER tag	Role	Relation
Nsubj Nsubjpass	actor concept	None Person Organization Location	Agent agent organization location	Verb
Rcmod Vmod	actor concept	None	Agent	Verb
Dobj pobj iobj xcomp agent	acted upon concept	None	Theme	Verb
Tmod	acted upon concept	Time	Temporal	Verb
Prep_ X X=with X=to X=in X=at X=after X=on	acted upon concept/indirect concept	none none location none location time none location time none	accompanier location theme location temporal theme location temporal theme	
Poss	actor concept acted upon concept	None None	Agent Possession	Has

in the sentence for a concept. Stanford parser takes into account of these multi word concepts very efficiently but to give these concepts a proper representation, these are combined to form a multiword concept. We analysed the dependency tags along with NER tags from SENNA and established whether the concept is performing an action or an action is being acted upon that concept. We further assigned semantic roles to these concepts depending upon whether they are actors or acted upon concepts and their NER tags e.g. a word is having dependency tag as *nsubj* and is having named entity tag as *Person*. This word will be framed as *actor concept* and the semantic role of this *actor concept* will be established as *agent*. If the dependency tag for a word is *Tmod* and the name entity tag is *Time* the concept will be having type *acted upon* and the semantic role *Temporal*. Table 4 shows the possible types of concepts and possible roles according to the NER and dependency tags.

Data Design for Concept_Relation_Role Extractor

The information thus extracted using Table 4 by this module needs to be stored in tables in a database. Following tables are created for this module:

Concept Table

The concept table contains the all the concepts extracted from all the documents with their respective document_id, sentence_ id and concept_ id assigned to each concept. This table is filled by the concept_extractor module and is stored in secondary memory.

Data Format: The metadata for concept table in Java DB (Derby) database is as shown in Table 5.

The metadata for Concept Table contains Document identification number Doc_id, Sentence identification number sentence_id, Concept identification number Concept_id and the name of the concept Concept_name.

Data Storage: All these fields are stored as having *VARCHAR* as their datatype.

Data Utilization: Concept table is utilized by Property_extractor and Hierarchy_extractor modules by bringing it into primary memory.

Object Property Table

This table contains the extracted actor concepts denoting the subjects, Acted upon concepts denoting the objects, their semantic roles in the sentence and the relation between the subject and the object denoted by relation_name.

Data Format: The metadata for Object_Property_Table in Java DB is shown in Table 6.

The metadata for Object Property Table contains Document identification number Doc_id, Sentence identification number sentence_id, Relation identification number, Actor Concept identification number Actor_concept_id, the semantic role of actor concept, Acted upon Concept identification number

Table 5. Metadata for Concept Table

Field Name	Data Type
Doc_id	VARCHAR
Sentence_id	VARCHAR
Concept_id	VARCHAR
Concept_Name	VARCHAR

Table 6. Metadata for Object_Property_Table

Field Name	Data Type
Doc_id	VARCHAR
Sentence_id	VARCHAR
Rel_id	VARCHAR
Actor_concept_id	VARCHAR
Ac_has_role	VARCHAR
Relation_Name	VARCHAR
Acted_upon_concept	VARCHAR
Au_has_role	VARCHAR

Acted_upon_concept_id, the semantic role of acted upon concept, and the name of the object proper-tyrelation _name.

Data Storage: All these fields are stored as having *VARCHAR* as their datatype.

Data Utilization: This table is filled by object_property module and is stored in secondary memory. This table is drawn into primary memory so that it can be used by ontology_matcher_merger module.

Algorithm Design for Concept_Relation_Role_Extractor()

Concept extraction, relation extraction and role extraction go hand in hand. The concepts on which the action is being done and concepts doing action are captured along with the action i.e. the relation among these concepts and are stored in tables having concepts and relation associated with them. The algorithm for extracting concepts, their semantic role in the sentence and relations among the concepts takes the sentence token list, dependency tags and name entity tags from the output the natural language processing module. It also uses Table 4 which maps the concepts to their semantic roles according to their dependency tag and name entity tag. The algorithm is given in Figure 10.

Here in this algorithm, the output of natural language processing module i.e. the sentence token list which is dependency parser tagged and the name entity tags from SENNA are given as input. Depending upon the dependency tags and name entity tags, concepts are extracted in step 1.The concepts are

Figure 10. Algorithm for Concepts, Roles and Relation Extractor

```
Algorithm concept_relation_role_extractor()
Input: sentence token list, dependency tags, name entity tags from SENNA
Output: actor concepts, acted upon concepts, roles, relations
Begin
 for each token in the sentence list
  1. analyze the dependency tag and name entity tag for possible concepts, relations and role
  //refer columns Dependency tag and Concept from Table 3.4
  a) extract actor concepts
  b) extract acted upon concepts
  c) extract concepts not directly related to verb
                            //refer columns NER tag and Role from Table 3.4
  d) extract roles
                            //refer column Relation from Table 3.4
  e) extract relations
                            //refer column Dependency tag from Table 3.4
  2. analyze the dependency tag for "nn" or "nnp"
                            // multiword concepts representation
     a) concatenate the concepts using "_"
     b) store all concepts in concept_table
  3. store concepts, roles, relations in Object_Prop_Role_ Table
 end for
End
```

generalized as actor concepts or acted upon concepts in step 1.a and step1.b and provided their semantic roles according to their tags and Table 4 in step 1.e. The algorithm also looks for the multiword concepts and extracts and stores them by adjoining them with an underscore in step 2. Object properties (relations among these concepts) are also extracted by this algorithm in step 1.e. The concepts along with their semantic roles and the relations between them are stored in Object_Prop_Role_Table in step 3.

Property Extractor

The properties of the concepts participating in ontology may have some property associated with them given by the sentence. These properties are those that modify the concept in some manner .e.g. in the following sentence:

"This is a red book".

red which is an adjective in the sentence becomes data property for the concept *book* in the ontology. These properties are extracted by processing the dependency parsed structure of the sentence.

Data Design for Property Extractor

These extracted properties are stored along with their concepts in a table in the database.
   Data Format: We use data property table that contains the properties of the extracted concepts. The metadata for Data_Property table in Java DB is given as follows in Table 7.
   The metadata for Data_Property Table contains the Document identification number Doc_id, Sentence identification number Sentence_id, Concept identification number Concept_id and a property field has_prop to show the data property associated with the concept.
   Data Storage: This table is stored in secondary memory.
   Data Utilization: This table is brought into primary memory to be used by Ontology Generator.

Algorithm Design for Property_Extractor

The properties that modify concepts in some manner are called data properties and are extracted from text according to their dependency tags given as input along with the sentence token list. The algorithm for extracting properties is given in Figure 11.
   In this algorithm, the output of natural language processing module is given as input which is sentence token list along with their dependency tags. In step 1 and step 2.a, this algorithm analyses the tokens of

Table 7. Metadata for Data_Property Table

Field Name	Data type
Doc_id	VARCHAR
Sentence_id	VARCHAR
Concept_id	VARCHAR
Has_prop	VARCHAR

Figure 11. Algorithm for Property Extractor

```
Algorithm property_extractor()

Input: sentence tokens list with dependency tags next to each token in the list

Output: concepts properties

Begin

    1. for each token in the sentence list
    2. for each concept from concept_ list
       a) analyze the dependency tag "amod" for extracting properties of concepts
       b) store the concept properties in data_prop_table
       end for

    end for
```

each sentence having '*amod*' dependency tag which identify the adjective associated with the concept determining its data property. These data properties are stored in a Data_Property Table along with their associated concept in step 2.b.

Hierarchy Extractor

From the list of concepts extracted in Concept_Table hierarchy of concepts is extracted. All the concepts from Concept_Table are brought to a concept list in primary memory. The concepts are syntactically matched to determine whether some concept matches partially with some other multiword concept (compound nouns). If a concept matches with head noun of the compound noun, it is added to the hierarchy table with relation "has_a". Otherwise if a concept matches with other part of compound noun which is not head noun, it is added to hierarchy table with relation "has_ instance".

Data Design for Hierarchy Extractor

Hierarchy table is generated if concepts are related to each other with part-whole relation or is-a relation. This table captures the possible taxonomical relations among concepts.

Data Format: The metadata for Hierarchy_Table is shown in Table 8.

The metadata of this table contains the document identification number Doc_id, Hierarchy identification number H_id, name of the sub concept sub_concept and the name of super concept super_concept.

Data Storage: This table is generated by Hierarchy_extractor module using the concept table and is stored in secondary memory.

Data Utilization: This table is utilized by ontology_matcher_merger by bringing it into primary memory so that concepts having a hierarchy in the form of sub concepts and super concepts can be merged.

Table 8. Metadata for Hierarchy Table

Field Name	Data type
Doc_id	VARCHAR
H_id	VARCHAR
Sub_concept	VARCHAR
Super_concept	VARCHAR

Algorithm for Hierarchy Extractor

There may be a possibility that some concepts extracted from text possess a hierarchical relation to some other concepts. This relation can be an *is-a* relation or *has-instance* relation. The hierarchy extractor algorithm takes the concept list and finds the super concepts and their sub concepts and establishes the proper relation between them. The algorithm is given as in Figure 12.

The algorithm takes the list of concepts which include single word and multiword concepts and generalises them into a hierarchy if exist. The single word concept may be subsumed by some other multiword concept. The single word concept may be same as the head noun of the multiword concept or as the other part of the multiword concepts. This algorithm stores both of these concepts by establishing has_instance or has_a relation between them in hierarchy_Table.

Figure 12. Algorithm for Hierarchy Extractor

```
Algorithm hierarchy_extractor()
Input:  concept_list from concept_Table
Output: super_concept, sub_concept
 Begin
    1. for each concept from concept_list
        compare concept with each multi word concept syntactically  for partial matching
        a)  If concept matches with head noun of multi word concept
                super_concept = concept
                Relation = "has_a"
                sub_concept= multiword concept
        b)  If concept matches with other part of multi word concept except head noun
                super_concept = concept
                Relation = "has_instance"
                sub_concept= multiword concept
    2.  store in Hierarchy_Table
        end for
 End
```

Sub-Ontology Generator

For each sentence a sub-ontology is created using Jena API comprising of concepts along with their semantic roles, data properties, relations as their object properties, and hierarchy if exists. These sub-ontologies are shown graphically by using the GraphViz tool (Emden Gansner, 2006).

Data Design for Sub-Ontology Generator

The contents of Object_Property_Role_Table, Properties_Table and Hierarchy_Table are brought into lists in the primary memory. These lists are used to create sub-ontology for each sentence using Jena API.

Data Format and Storage: The sub-ontologies are stored in *rdf* structures in the memory.

Data Utilization: These sub-ontologies are used further by sub-ontology merger to construct the final ontology.

Sub-Ontology Merger

The sub-ontologies thus created for each sentence are merged to form a single ontology. This process starts with merging the very first ontology with a NULL ontology. For merging ontologies relations and concepts of different ontologies are matched for their syntactic and semantic similarity using WordNet (T. Pedersen, 2004) and the Hierarchy_Table. The semantic roles of concept nodes are also used in the matching process. These are also matched for similarity wherever there are similar concepts..

This module considers all cases where relation or concept nodes of an ontology may or may not be matching to concept or relation node of other ontology. Also there may be dissimilarity in matching concept nodes.

Data Design for Sub-Ontology Merger

To tackle these cases we have purposed some rules here that are stored in primary memory according to which nodes in sub-ontology are merged with their corresponding semantic similar nodes of other ontologies.

Data Structure Used: Following rules are designed in our work which are being applied in the algorithm for merging sub-ontologies

Rule 1: Relations in both sub ontologies are semantically same. Also their respective concepts and the roles of concepts in these relations are matching semantically. In addition to this hierarchies of concepts are taken into consideration for merging the concepts as shown in Figure 13.

Figure 13. Rule 1

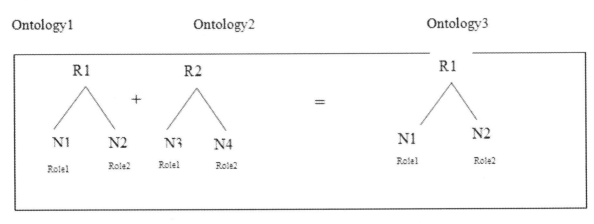

Rule 2: The dangling non-matching concept node in sub-ontology. In this case relations R1 of Ontology1 and R2 of Ontology2 are semantically similar and their related concept nodes i.e. N1 is semantically matched with N3 and N2 is semantically matched with N4. Here N5 is a non matched concept, which will be aligned as shown in Figure 14.

Figure 14. Rule 2

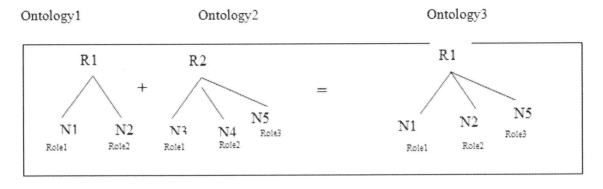

Rule 3: Some concept nodes are semantically matching, but corresponding relation is semantically dissimilar in both sub-ontologies. In this case relations R1 of ontology1 and R2 of ontology2 do not match while the concept N1 and N3 are similar. These will be aligned as shown in Figure 15.

Figure 15. Rule 3

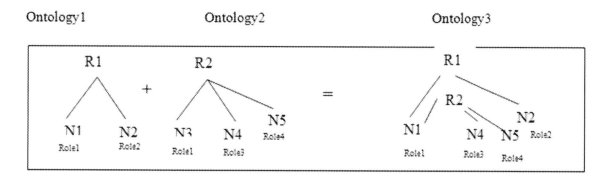

Rule 4: Concept nodes are matching semantically excluding their semantic roles and their corresponding relations are also semantically dissimilar in both ontologies. The matching concepts are merged to be a single concept keeping their respective semantic roles in each sentence intact. In this case relations R1 of ontology1 and R2 of ontology2 do not match while the concept N1 and N3 are semantically similar having roles Role1 and Role3 respectively. These will be aligned as shown in Figure 16

Figure 16. Rule 4

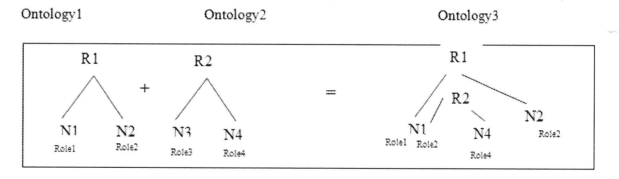

Data Utilization: These rules are used by ontology matcher merger to construct the final ontology.

Algorithm for Ontology Matcher Merger

In the process of ontology construction here sub ontologies are created for each sentence after extracting the concepts, their semantic roles and establishing the correct hierarchy among them and extracting their object and data properties. These sub-ontologies are matched and merged to form the whole ontology. Some rules have been crafted for the purpose of matching and merging these sub-ontologies which are utilized by the ontology_matcher_merger algorithm which takes two different sentence sub-ontologies as input, uses WordNet in the process of matching and merges the ontologies according to these rules

Figure 17. Algorithm for Ontology Matcher Merger

```
Algorithm ontology_matcher_merger()

Input: Ontology O1, Ontology O2, WordNet

Output: Merged ontology O3

Begin

1. Check if O1 is NULL then assign O3 = O2;

2. Analyze relation in both ontologies for equality

a) analyze actor concepts and acted upon concepts of both ontologies for equality
// Rule 1 (Figure 3.13)

b) analyze actor concepts role and acted upon concepts role of both ontologies for equality

3. integrate the two ontologies by merging the sub-ontologies where the matching is found
   and store in O3.

4. align the non-matching dangling concepts // Rule 2 (Figure 3.14)

5. align non matching relations pairs with non-matching concepts    // Rule 3 (Figure 3.15)

6. align non matching relations pairs with matching concepts      // Rule 4 (Figure 3.16)

End
```

to produce a merged ontology. The algorithm for matching and merging ontologies is given as follows in Figure 17.

This algorithm applies the devised rules by us for merging the ontologies in a manner such that all the concept pairs, relation pairs are aligned while integrating these ontologies. In step 1, there is a check to ascertain that any of the ontologies to be merged are not null otherwise the merged ontology will be the not null ontology itself. Then in step 2 and 3, the relation pairs from both ontologies are analysed to find the matching concept pairs or matching relation names. The rule devised are applied here in step 4, 5 and 6 to integrate these ontologies and assure that all the matching concept pairs or matching relation pairs are merged well and the non-matching relations or non-matching concepts are aligned well in the integrated ontology.

Ontology Representer

The sentence ontologies are merged in the ontology matcher merger and regenerated to form complete text document ontology using Jena API. The merged final ontology can be converted into dot file which is further shown graphically by GraphViz tool (Emden Gansner, 2006).

Data Design for Ontology Representer

The document ontologies are stored in secondary memory in .rdf or .owl form.

The above described algorithms of different modules are used by ontology generator algorithm. This algorithm takes plain text documents as input. The process for generating complete ontology from a set of documents is given in the algorithm as shown in Figure 18.

Algorithm Design of Ontology_ Generator

This algorithm generates the overall ontology for a given text document by calling the methods defined for the all the modules of the system as shown in Figure 18. The algorithm takes the unstructured text document as input and processes it sequentially through these methods and gives a final ontology of that text document.

The algorithm first starts with processing each sentence of each document. Each sentence is preprocessed by the module pre_processer to remove transition words or phrases and then anaphora_resolver() is called in step 2 which resolves the coreferences. Dependency tagging is carried out in step 3 followed by named entity recognition in step 4. After performing all the natural language processing on the document, this is passed for further processing to the Information Extractor. In step 5 concepts, relations and semantic roles are extracted by calling concept_relation_role_extractor().

In step 6 data properties of the concepts are extracted by calling property_extractor. In step 7 hierarchies are established by calling hierarchy_extractor(). Step 8 generates the sentence ontologies. In step 9, these ontologies are merged to form the final ontology by calling ontology_matcher_merger(). Step 10 generates and shows the final ontology using Jena API and also shows the ontology graphically through GraphViz tool.

Figure 18. Algorithm for Ontology Generator

```
Algorithm Ontology_ Generator
Software Tools Used: Stanford Dependency Parser, Senna, JavaRAP,
Input: A set of text documents, WordNet
Output: Ontology of documents
Begin
for each document
    for each sentence
    1.  pre_processor();
    2.  anaphora_resolver();
                                        //output is pronouns resolved to their
                                                            noun mentions
    3.  dependency_parser();
                                    //output is part of speech tagged sentences along with
                                                            //their dependencies
    4.  ner_tagger();
                                    // output is named entity tagged nouns
    5.  concept_relation_role_extractor();
                                    //output is concept, roles, object properties
    6.  property_extractor();          //output is data properties of concepts
    7.  hierarchy_extractor();         // output is hierarchies of concepts if exist
    8.  Generate sentence ontologies using Jena API for ontology
                                    // generate sentence  ontologies
    end for
    9.  ontology_matcher_merger();  // match and merge ontologies to generate full
        ontology
    10. Generate the ontology in .rdf format using Jena API and GraphViz
end for
End
```

WORKING OF SYSTEM THROUGH EXAMPLE

The process of constructing ontology takes place in two steps. First step is to form the sub-ontological structures from the sentences of the document and in second step the full document ontology is built using the previously formed sentence sub-ontologies. It is assumed here that the inputs are correct.

For a sample text document having following three sentences:

Sentence1: *An Air India flight to HongKong was brought down at Kolkata late last night after some passengers complained of smoke in the cabin.*
Sentence 2: *The flight with passengers landed at the Kolkata airport.*
Sentence 3: *Under those circumstances, Passengers were accommodated in nearby hotels*

After processing the sentences from all the extractors except following tables are obtained. The Concept_Table contains the concepts retrieved from all sentences in all documents as shown in Table 9.

Table 10 contains the object properties i.e. relations among the concepts and role each concept is playing. As mentioned above some concepts are directly related to the verb in the sentence. These concepts are stored in table with the relation name.

Other concepts which are not directly related to the verb directly are stored without relation name and their relation is identified by the name of label and role each concept is playing in relation with the other concept.

Table 11 stores the data properties of the concepts extracted from each sentence in the document by the property extractor module.

Hierarchy extractor module finds the hierarchy among the concepts from the Concept_ Table and stores in Hierarhcy_Table as shown in Table 12.

For each of these three sentences, ontologies are generated in the first step (Figure 19, Figure 20).

Table 9. Concept_Table

Doc_id	Sentence_id	Concept_id	Concept_Name
D0	S0	Cid0	Air_India_Flight
D0	S0	Cid1	HongKong
D0	S0	Cid2	Kolkata
D0	S0	Cid3	Passengers
D0	S0	Cid4	Smoke
D0	S0	Cid5	Cabin
D0	S1	Cid6	Flight
D0	S1	Cid7	Passengers
D0	S1	Cid8	Kolkata_airport
D0	S2	Cid9	Passengers
D0	S2	Cid10	Night
D0	S2	Cid11	Hotels

Table 10. Object_Property_Role_Table

Doc_id	Sentence_id	Rel_id	Actor_concept_id	Ac_has_role	Relation_Name	Acted_upon_concept_id	Au_has_role
D0	S0	Rel_id0	Cid0	Agent	Brought_down	Cid2	Location
D0	S0	Rel_id1	Cid3	Agent	Complained	Cid4	Theme
D0	S1	Rel_id2	Cid6	Agent	Landed	Cid8	Location
D0	S2	Rel_id3	Cid9	Agent	Accommodated	Cid11	Theme
D0	S0	Rel_id0	Cid10	Temporal	Brought_down	Cid0	Agent
D0	S0	Rel_id1	Cid5	Location	Complained	Cid3	Agent
D0	S0	Rel_id4	Cid1	Location	To	Cid0	Agent
D0	S1	Rel_id5	Cid7	Accompanier	With	Cid7	Agent

Table 11. Property_Table

Doc_id	Sentence_id	Prop_id	Concept_id	Has_prop
D0	S1	Pid0	Night	Last
D0	S2	Pid1	Hotels	Nearby

Table 12. Hierarchy_Table

Doc_id	H_id	Sub_concept	Super_concept
D0	H_id1	Air_india_flight	Flight
D0	H_id2	Kolkata_airport	Kolkata

Figure 19. Sentence Sub-ontologies

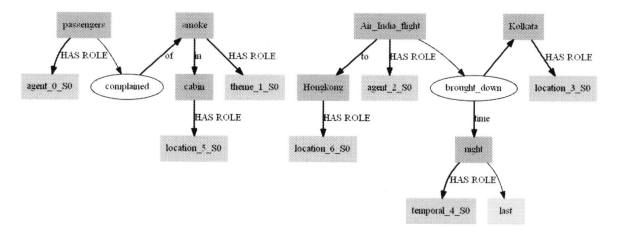

Figure 20. Sentence Sub-ontologies

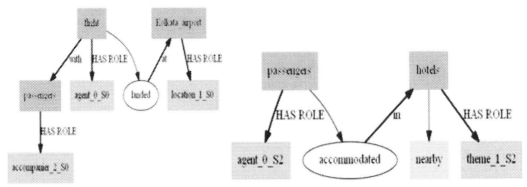

Table 13. Base Forms of Relational Words

Relation Name	Possible base form of the word in WordNet
brought down	lower, take down, let down, get down, bring down: move something or somebody to a lower position, overthrow, subvert, overturn, cause the downfall of, impose something unpleasant, **land**, put down, cause to come to the ground, reduce, cut down, cut back, trim, trim down, trim back, cut, cut down on; make a reduction in
Landed	set down: reach or come to rest, put down, bring down: cause to come to the ground, **bring down**, bring into a different state, bring ashore, deliver (a blow), set ashore, shore: arrive on shore, shoot down, land: shoot at and force to come down, landed: owning or consisting of land or real estate
Accommodate	suit, fit: be agreeable or acceptable to, adapt, make fit for, or change to suit a new purpose, provide with something desired or needed, hold, admit: have room for; hold without crowding, lodge, accommodate: provide housing for, oblige, accommodate: provide a service or favour for someone, reconcile, conciliate: make (one thing) compatible with (another)
Complain	kick, plain, sound off, quetch, kvetch: express complaints, discontent, displeasure, or unhappiness, make a formal accusation; bring a formal charge

Here in the Figure 20, green boxes show the concepts, ellipses show the object properties, yellow boxes show the data properties and the pink boxes show the roles of the concepts. The second step here is to apply ontology matching and merging algorithm on these ontologies. Here relations (object properties) as shown by the ellipses in the sentence ontologies are considered at first. All possible base forms from WordNet (T. Pedersen, 2004) are taken for each relation and used for matching similarity. Table 13 shows the possible base forms of the relations identified in the document.

There can be different cases while applying the ontology_matcher_merger algorithm. Each case is considered separately and the purposed rules are applied to match and merge different constituents of the ontology.

Case 1: Applying the Rule 1(Figure 13)

Each base form of the word or phrase representing the relation in one sentence is matched with -the all possible base forms of the relations in other sentences for applying the Rule 1. As evident from the above table the relations *brought_down* and *landed* match as the relation *brought_down* has base form *land* and also *landed* has base form *bring down* so *borught-down* in ontology1 replaces *landed* in the merged ontology. *Air_india_flight* and *Flight* are matched using hierarchy_Table and their respective

Figure 21. Similarity Matching in Case 1

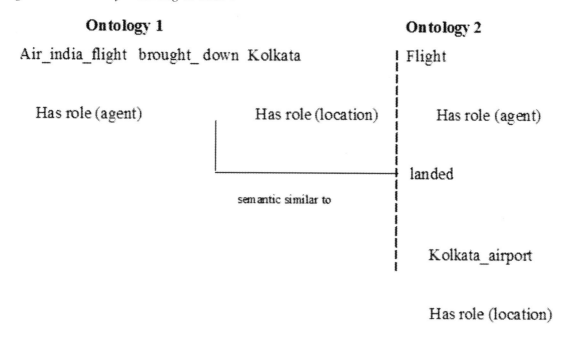

roles are also matched. In the similar manner *Kolkata* and *Kolkata_airport* are matched using Hierarchy_Table and by matching their respective semantic roles as shown in Figure 21.

Case 2 *HongKong* is a dangling non matching concept in Ontology1 and is merged with Ontology2 according to Rule2 (Figure 14).

Case 3 The concept "*passengers*" has role "*agent*" in first ontology and is in relation with "*complained*" while in second ontology it's role is "*accompanier_with*" with no matching relation in Ontology2. In the merged ontology there is just one node for "*passengers*" and has three roles *agent_s0*, *accompanier_with_s1*, and *agent_s2* which is obtained by applying Rule4 (Figure 16) again while merging this with Ontology3.

The *rdf* file generated corresponding to this sample document is shown in Figure 22.

The final ontology can be shown graphically using GraphViz in which the dot file is generated first as shown in Figure 23.

This dot file is then converted by the GraphViz software to a graph depicting the final merged ontology as shown in Figure 24.

In the merged ontology redundant concepts are represented by a single node having multiple edges. Hence the merged concepts of the documents are represented in the ontology with the roles they are playing in each sentence.

Figure 22. .rdf File of Sample Document

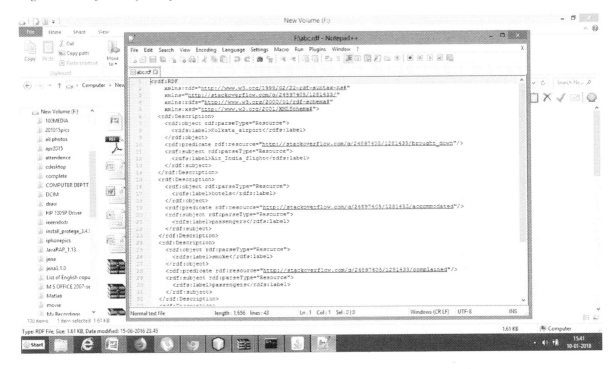

IMPLEMENTATION DETAILS

We have implemented our work on Intel Core i3 with 4GB RAM using Windows 7 Operating System. We have used NetBeans 8.0.2 which is using Apache Derby as relational database which is bundled with NetBeans 8.0.2. Apache Derby is based on Java, JDBC and SQL standards. We have used Stanford Dependency Parser for annotating the sentences of text documents. The corpus on which Stanford Dependency Parser has been trained by (Marie-Catherine de Marneffe, 2013) contains about 250,000 words of unedited web text. SENNA tool is used here for name entity tagging. We have used JavaRAP tool for anaphora resolution. WordNet (University, 2010) is used here for finding synonyms for matching and merging the concepts. GraphViz tool is used for showing the ontology pictorially. We have used Jena API to construct and store our ontology in the form of *.rdf* files.

Dataset-A set of 50 random news articles in English language has been taken for experimentation. These news articles are assumed to be grammatically correct. The dataset is shown in Appendix

As it is not convenient to show the ontologies for each news article in the set, implementation of a few news articles is displayed as follows:

Document1: *Prime minister Narendra Modi will leave for the Belgium capital tomorrow night. He will attend the Nuclear Security Summit in Washington and visit Saudi Arabia. Prime minister will take part in the long-pending Summit for the first time.*

The final ontology will be shown graphically in the Figure 25.

Automatic Ontology Construction

Figure 23. dot File for sample document

```
digraph mygraph{
  complained ->brought_down
  { ranksep=1.2 rankdir=LR complained brought_down }
  brought_down ->accommodated
  {.ranksep=1.2 rankdir=LR brought_down accommodated }
  passengers ->complained
  passengers [shape=box,style=filled,color=Green];
  passengers -> agent_0 [style=bold,label="HAS ROLE"];
  agent_0 [shape=box,style=filled,color=Pink];
  complained ->cabin
  {.rank= same rankdir=TB passengers cabin }
  cabin [shape=box,style=filled,color=Green];
  cabin -> location_0 [style=bold , label="HAS ROLE"];
  location_0 [shape=box, style=filled , color=Pink];
  hotels ->nearby
  nearby [shape=box,style=filled,color=Yellow];
  Air_India_flight ->brought_down
  Air_India_flight [shape=box,style=filled,color=Green];
  Air_India_flight -> agent_1 [style=bold,label="HAS ROLE"];
  agent_1 [shape=box,style=filled,color=Pink];
  brought_down ->Kolkata_airport
  {.rank= same rankdir=TB Air_India_flight Kolkata_airport }
  Kolkata_airport [shape=box,style=filled,color=Green];
  Kolkata_airport -> location_1 [style=bold , label="HAS ROLE"];
  location_1 [shape=box, style=filled , color=Pink];
  agent_2 [shape=box,style=filled,color=Pink];
  brought_down ->Kolkata_airport
  {.rank= same rankdir=TB Air_India_flight Kolkata_airport }
  location_2 [shape=box, style=filled , color=Pink];
  Passengers ->accommodated
  Passengers -> agent_3 [style=bold,label="HAS ROLE"];
  agent_3 [shape=box,style=filled,color=Pink];
  accommodated ->hotels
  {.rank= same rankdir=TB Passengers hotels }
  hotels [shape=box,style=filled,color=Green];
  hotels -> location_3 [style=bold , label="HAS ROLE"];
  location_3 [shape=box, style=filled , color=Pink];
  eight [shape=box,style=filled,color=Green];
  eight ->brought_down[style=bold,label="time"];
  eight ->temporal_0[style=bold,label="HAS ROLE"];
  temporal_0 [shape=box,style=filled,color=Pink];
  eight ->last
  last [shape=box,style=filled,color=Yellow];
  Hongkong [shape=box,style=filled,color=Green];
  Hongkong ->Air_India_flight[style=bold,label="to"];
  Hongkong ->location_1[style=bold,label="HAS ROLE"];
  location_1 [shape=box,style=filled,color=Pink];
  passengers [shape=box,style=filled,color=Green];
  passengers ->Air_India_flight[style=bold,label="with"];
  passengers ->accompanier_2[style=bold,label="HAS ROLE"];
  accompanier_2 [shape=box,style=filled,color=Pink];
}
```

Figure 25. Ontology of Document 1

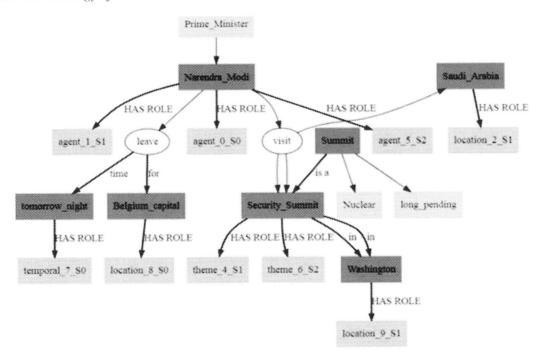

Document 2: *Sania Mirza was born in Mumbai and settled at Hydrabad. She began playing tennis at early age. She became a great tennis player and she defeated top player Nadia.*

The ontology for Document 2 will be shown graphically in the Figure 26

Document 3: *"The Mayor and water supply officials of Mangaluru City Corporation have been claiming that there is enough water at a vented dam at Shambhoor, on the upstream of the Thumbe dam. They are exposed as a reality check on Sunday revealed that the dam of a hydro power project at Shambhoor is empty". The ontology will be shown graphically in the Figure 27*

PERFORMANCE EVALUATION

The set of 50 news articles taken for experimentation is used also as test data set for performance analysis. We have compared our system with Open Calais (Marius-Gabriel, 2016) system by Thomson Reuter's which is linked to a market leading ontology extracting entities (persons, events, places), relationships etc and gives results in *rdf* format.

As shown in the Table 14, our system has scored similar precision as the other system. But our system outscores in recall and F-measures to Open Calais system in extracting the correct entities and relations.

The evaluation results indicate that our system provides good results in constructing ontology. The reason for the better performance of our system is its ability to extract all the non-taxonomical relation

Figure 26. Ontology of Document 2

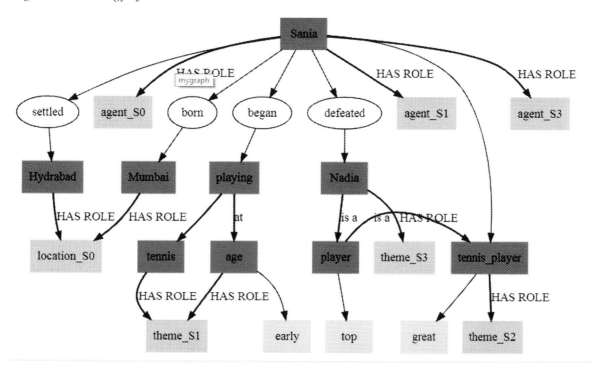

Figure 27. Ontology of Document 3

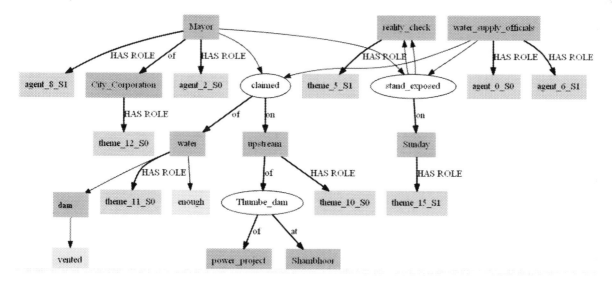

as compared to the other system which works on a specified set of taxonomical and non-taxonomical relations.

The reason for low recall in extracting relations in our system is that while pre-processing we remove some transition words(Table 3) to reduce the complexity of sentence e.g. *as was previously stated,*

Table 14. Result Comparison

System	Precision			Recall			F-measure		
	Concept	Relation	Data Properties	Concept	Relation	Data Properties	Concept	Relation	Data Properties
Open-Calais	100%	100%	100%	56%	25%	69.20%	71.79	40.4	81.79
Proposed System	100%	97.10%	100%	87.28%	82%	86.80%	93.2	88.9	92.9

Figure 28. Performance Analysis of Proposed System and Open Calais System

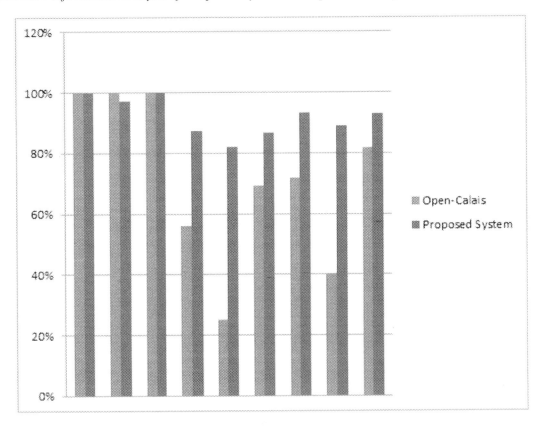

speaking about, that being the case, to summarize etc. The verbs in these transition words are not taken as relations in the ontology. Moreover the system is dependent on the accuracy of the parser used for extracting dependency. Stanford dependency parser has an F-score of 85.78 (Jonathan K. Kummerfeld, 12–14 July 2012) for attaching noun phrase, modifier, clause etc.

We can show the performance analysis of our system and Open Calias graphically as shown in Figure 28.

As stated earlier our system extracts all the concepts not only the key concepts as are drawn from the text by the other system.

To improve the results with extracted relations, other ontologies or a thesaurus besides WordNet can be used for semantic similarity matching to avoid wrong matching of relations and concepts.

CONCLUSION

Ontologies have become a powerful tool for text understanding. In this chapter a novel scheme for building ontologies from unstructured text is proposed based on considering semantic roles. Matching the semantic roles of concepts gives an additional feature for efficient merging of sub-ontologies leading to efficient construction of final ontology for better and more correct understanding of text. The rules required for various modules are designed and represented and the approach has been implemented using Java technology. The performance of the system is evaluated by looking coverage of concepts and relationships in the final ontology. The experiment shows that the ontology of the documents obtained by this scheme covers 93.2% concepts and 90.10% relationships present in the document in the given set of documents.

REFERENCES

Abeer Al-Arfaj, A. A.-S. (2015). Ontology Construction from Text: Challenges and Trends. *International Journal of Artificial Intelligence and Expert Systems*, *6*(2).

Abinaya, C. &. (2013). Semi-Automatic Ontology Merging of Domain Specific Ontologies. International Journal of Science and Research.

Alani, H. (2006). Position Paper: Ontology Construction from Online Ontologies. *WWW2006*.

Andreia, D. P. N., & Parente de Oliveira, J. M. (2012). Simple Method for Ontology Automatic Extraction from Documents. *International Journal of Advanced Computer Science and Applications*, *3*(12). doi:10.14569/IJACSA.2012.031206

Arabshian, K., P. D. (2012). LexOnt: A Semi-Automatic Ontology Creation Tool for Programmable Web. In *AAAI Spring Symposium: Intelligent Web Services Meet Social Computing*, (pp. 2-8). AAAI.

Bhavana Dalvi, A. M. (2016). Hierarchical Semi-supervised Classification with Incomplete Class Hierarchies. In WSDM'16. San Francisco, CA: ACM.

Bothma, J. D. (2010). Ontology learning from Swedish text. *International Conference on Computer Science and Education*.

Bumans, G. (2010). *Mapping between Relational Databases and OWL Ontologies: An Example. In Computer Science and Information Technologies, Scientific Papers* (Vol. 756). University of Latvia.

Christophe Debruyne, T.-K. T. (2013). Grounding Ontologies with Social Processes and Natural Language. *Journal on Data Semantics*, *2*(2-3), 89–118. doi:10.100713740-013-0023-3

Domingos, H. P. (2014). *Unsupervised Ontology Induction from Text*. Academic Press.

Drymonas, K. Z. (2010). Unsupervised Ontology Acquisition from Plain Texts: The OntoGain System. *LNCS*, *6177*, 277–287.

Emden Gansner, E. K. (2006). *Drawing graphs with dot*. Academic Press.

Fekade Getahun, K. W. (2017). Integrated Ontology Learner: Towards Generic Semantic Annotation Framework. In *MEDES'17*. Bangkok, Thailand: ACM.

Gillam, K. A. (2005). *Automatic Ontology Extraction from Unstructured Texts*. On the Move to Meaningful Internet.

Gillani Andleeb, S. (2015). *From text mining to knowledge mining: An integrated framework of concept extraction and categorization for domain ontology*. Budapesti Corvinus Egyetem.

Hearst, M. A. (1992). Automatic Acquisition of Hypernyms from Large Text Corpora. Proc. of Collins.

Hristo Tanev Tanev, B. M. (2008). *Weakly Supervised Approaches for Ontology Population*. Academic Press.

Janowicz, K. (2005). Extending Semantic Similarity Measurement with Thematic Roles GeoS'05. In *Proceedings of the First international conference on GeoSpatial Semantics* (pp. 137-152). Springer-Verlag Berlin Heidelberg. 10.1007/11586180_10

Julia Hoxha, A. S. (2010). An Approach to Formal and Semantic Representation of Logistics Services. In *Proceedings of the ECAI'10 Workshop on Artificial Intelligence and Logistics*, (pp. 73-78). Academic Press.

Kenneth Clarkson, A. L. (2018). User-Centric Ontology Population. *ESWC-Conferences*.

Kgotatso Desmond Mogotlane, J. V.-D. (2016). Automatic Conversion of Relational Databases into Ontologies: A Comparative Analysis of Protégé Plug-ins Performances. *International Journal of Web and Semantic Technology*.

Kummerfeld, D. H. (2012). Parser Showdown at the Wall Street Corral: An Empirical Investigation of Error Types in Parser Output. In *Proceedings of the 2012 Joint Conference on Empirical Methods in Natural Language Processing and Computational Natural Language Learning*, (pp. 1048–1059). Jeju Island, South Korea: Academic Press.

Li, J. H. (2013). *An Entropy-Based Weighted Concept Lattice for Merging Multi-Source Geo-Ontologies*. doi:10.3390/e15062303

Maimon, O. (2015). Ontology Learning from Text: Why the Ontology Learning Layer Cake is not Viable. *International Journal of Signs and Semiotic Systems*, 4(2), 1–14. doi:10.4018/IJSSS.2015070101

Mari Carmen Sua'rez-Figueroa, A. G.-P.-L. (2012). *The NeOn Methodology for Ontology. In Ontology Engineering in a Networked World*. Springer-Verlag Berlin Heidelberg. doi:10.1007/978-3-642-24794-1

Marie-Catherine de Marneffe, M. C. (2013). *More constructions, more genres: Extending Stanford Dependencies*. Academic Press.

Marius-Gabriel. (2016). *Semantically Enriching Content Using OpenCalais*. Thomsan Reuters.

Marneffe, M. (2015). *Stanford dependency parser*. Retrieved from nlp.stanford.edu/software/stanford-dependencies

Martin, D. J. (2015). *Speech and Language Processing*. Copyright.

Missikoff, A. D. (2016). A Lightweight Methodology for Rapid Ontology Engineering. *ACM, 59*(3), 79-86.

Monika Rani, A. K. (2017). *Ontology Learning Based on Topic Modeling*. Semi-Automatic Terminology.

Pedersen, T. S. P. (2004). WordNet: Similarity - Measuring the Relatedness of Concepts. In Human Language Technology Conference of the North American Chapter of the Association for Computational Linguistics Demonstrations (pp. 38-41). Boston: Academic Press.

Princeton University, . (2010). *About WordNet*. Princeton University.

Ronan Collobert, P. K. (2011). Natural Language Processing (Almost) from Scratch. *Journal of Machine Learning Research, 12*, 2461–2505.

Sourish Dasgupta, A. P. (2018). *Formal Ontology Learning from English IS-A Sentences*. arXiv:1802.03701v1 [cs.AI]

Stephen Roller, D. K. (2018). Hearst Patterns Revisited:Automatic Hypernym Detection from Large Text Corpora. In *Proceedings of the 56th Annual Meeting of the Association for Computational Linguistics (Short Papers)* (pp. 358–363). Melbourne, Australia: Academic Press.

Suresh Kumar, G. Z. (2015). Concept relation extraction using Naıve Bayes classifier for ontology-based question answering systems. Journal of King Saud University – Computer and Information Sciences, 13–24.

Tan, X. J.-H. (2010, January). CRCTOL: A semantic-based domain ontology learning system. *Journal of the American Society for Information Science and Technology, 61*(1), 150–168. doi:10.1002/asi.21231

Wan, J. B. (2011). *A New Semantic Model for Domain-Ontology Learning*. Springer-Verlag Berlin Heidelberg.

Zouaq, A., Gasevic, D., & Hatala, M. (2011). Towards open ontology learning and filtering. *Information Systems, 36*(7), 1064–1081. doi:10.1016/j.is.2011.03.005

Chapter 8
Emotion Analysis of Different Age Groups From Voice Using Machine Learning Approach

Mihir Narayan Mohanty
Siksha 'O' Anusandhan (Deemed), India

ABSTRACT

Emotion detection from voice is a complex task, whereas from the facial expression it is easy. In this chapter, an attempt is taken to detect the emotion through machine using neural network-based models and compared. As no complete database is available for different age groups, a small database is generated. To know the emotion of different age groups substantially, three groups have been generated with each group of 20 subjects. The efficient prosodic features are considered initially. Further, the combination of those features are taken. Each set of features are fed to the models for classification and detection. Angry, happy, and sad are the three emotions verified for different group of persons. It is found that the classifier provides 96% of accuracy. In earlier work, cluster-based techniques with simple features pitch, speech rate, and log energy were verified. As an extension, the combination of features along with machine learning model is verified in this work.

INTRODUCTION

Speech is a linguistic act is to convey information. Human thoughts and ideas include both implicit and explicit information during conversations. Intentions, emotions and cognitive states are unusually significantly convey at the time of interaction. Considerable information on their moods, mental states, environmental and demographical information can be extracted and fed as inputs for behavioral studies. This information can be used to understand their need, preferences, desires and intentions for planning human resources. Some of the emotions mostly used in literatures are: anger, disgust, happy, sad, fear, bore and neutral (Loizou, 2007) (Zeng, Raisman, and Huang, 2009) (Ramakrishnan, 2012) (Ververidis, and Kotropoulos, 2006) (Schuller, et. al., 2007). Three primary factors that tend to drive this field are: emotional speech database, feature extraction and classification methods and are discussed in this chapter.

DOI: 10.4018/978-1-7998-1021-6.ch008

Database collection of unambiguous emotional speech utterances play a major role to authenticate research direction in this field. Database selected for detection of speech emotion must take into account: type of speaker, language used, gender, age, real or acted utterances, balanced or unbalanced voices and so on. Reliability of emotional database tends to remain a challenge in terms of detection authenticity. However, generation and use of standard database have smoothened the complexity of research by clarifying the taxonomy of speech emotions. A review on emotional speech databases with informations on number of subjects (male, female), age of speaker, duration of utterances, categories of emotions, language, purpose of collection, size, type of utterances involved (natural, acted, elicited and simulated) and their availability has been presented in (Palo, et. al., 2015). However, most emtional speech database reviewed by these authors are not open to public access. This database is of regional Indian language (oriya) that has been recorded in suitable circumstances.

Emotional speech features can be broadly segregated into acoustic (prosodic and spectral), linguistic, contextual, nonlinear, statistical, and hybrid features etc (Wu, Falk, and Chan, 2011) (Lee, Narayanan, and Pieraccini, 2001) (Chandrasekar, Chapaneri, and Jayaswal, 2014). Literatures have reported efficient characterization of emotional speech samples by removing redudant features using feature reduction and selection techniques (Vogt and Andre, 2006) (Seehapoch, T., & Wongthanavasu, 2013). Different feature reduction techniques as Principal Component Analysis (PCA), Greedy Feature Selection (GFS), Sequential Floating Forward Selection (SFFS) and Sequential Floating Backward Selection (SFBS), Forward Selection (FS) along with PCA, elastic net, fast Correlation-based filter have been attempted. These feature reduction and selection algorithms have their own limitations. For example, in recognize different emotional classes PCA uses transformed set of original features and does not take into account its subsets. Thus it is suitable for unsupervised learning techniques.

Research in emotion recognition from speech signal gradually progressed by different researchers is discussed in this section. Approach of non-grid motion estimation for yawn detection in human drivers was discussed by Mohanty, Mishra, and Routray (2009). Recognition of negative and non-negative emotions from call center speech were highlighted by combining both acoustic and language features (Lee and Narayananm, 2005). They introduced an information-theoretic notion of *emotional salience* to collect emotion information at the language level. Emotion classification of 36.4% for females and 40.7% for males using linear discriminant classifier (LDC) could be achieved by them with combination of all emotions, rather than using only acoustic parameters. Short-term features related to the emotional content of speech using a corpus of 64 data collections are discussed for emotion classification (Fragopanagos and Taylor, 2005). The concept of basic emotions and their universality, 'primary' vs. 'secondary' emotions, evolutionarily hard-wired vs. socially learned emotions have provided a different frame work in defining and grouping emotional classes (Makhoul, 1975). A review on linear speech prediction was done by the authors and also different algorithm for LP analysis of speech was analyzed (Ram, Palo and Mohanty, 2013) (Quatieri, 1996). Spectral features such as Mel-frequency cepstral coefficient (MFCC) takes into human hearing and auditory mechanism has been mostly used features for speech emotion detection (Samal, Parida, Satpathy and Mohanty, 2014) (Mohanty and Chandra, 2014). As a variant of LPC, Linear Prediction Cepstral Coefficient (LPCC) uses more robust cepstral domain in characterizing emotional speech utterances. The effectiveness of LPCC has been explored in classifying student speech emotions using Neural Network classifier (Hermansk, 1990). Perceptual Linear Prediction features of speech signals have suitably proved their superiority over LPC features as they use equal loudness and power law characteristics of human systemsin representing speech emotions (Farrell, Mammone, and Assleh, 1994). LPC, LPCC, MFCC and PLP as features of children speech emotion with multilayer perceptron classifier (MLP) have been a major source of comparison of these frequency domain features in terms of their robustness (Sivanandam and Deepa, 2011). Neural networks have been effective in classifying speech and emotional speech recognition effectively. Use of different neural network classifiers as MLP, RBFN, Support vector machine (SVM) and other learning methods etc. have been extensively used in different fields of pattern recognition including speech and emotional speech recognition (Javidi and Roshan, 2013) (Haykin, 2005) (Reynolds and Rose, 1995) (Sant'Ana, Coelho, and Alcaim, 2006) (Zão, Cavalcante, and Coelho, 2014) (El Ayadi, Kamel, and Karray, 2011) (Davis and Mermelstein, 1980) (Xiang and Berger, 2003) (Palo, et. al, 2015). The concept of Soft Computing, Artificial neural network, various supervisory learning methods, Fuzzy logic and complete experimental procedure for MLP are few pattern recognition mechanisms useful in this field .Algorithms like Least Mean Square (LMS), Back Propagation (BP) and their application in NN emphasized in literatures can provide some insights of their usefulness for speech and emotion detection (Sivanandam and Deepa, 2011) (Haykin, 2005). D.A.Reynolds *et.al* introduced Gaussian mixture model (GMM) and evaluated itfor text-independent speaker identification (Reynolds and Rose, 1995). They claimed that Gaussian components representing some general speaker-dependent spectral shapes to model arbitrary densities. For the evaluation of the proposed model a database with 49 speaker conversation is considered. The database contains both clean and telephonic speech. For a five second test length signal the percentage of correct identification was more than 90% for different variant of GMM.*pH* time-frequency vocal source feature closely related to the excitation source (Quatieri, 1996). Use of this feature for emotional speech recognition has been explored effectively (Zão, Cavalcante, Coelho, 2014). A binary acousticmask which used GMMfor masking purpose for better multi-style emotion recognition has been used by the authors for classifying few basic speech emotions. In their work, Berlin Database of Emotional Speech (EMO-DB) and Speech under Simulated and Actual Stress (SUSAS) databases were used. Different types of emotion data is taken from EMO-DB and stress condition speech was taken from SUSAS. A simple classifier *M_dim_fBm*for the speaker identification and verification tasks based on the multidimensional fBm (*fractional Brownian motion*) model was proposed by them. They claimed the superior performance of the *M_dim_fBm*classifier over conventional classifiers using Hurst features to aggregate new information on the speaker identity. M. El Ayadi *et al.* discussed important issues in design of an emotional speech database, reviewed feature extraction methods, and addressed classification techniques with concluding remarks on performance and limitations of current speech emotion recognition systems (El Ayadi, Kamel, and Karray, 2011). S.B. Davis *et.al* summarized parametric representations of a speech signal by dividing the parameters based on the Fourier spectrum and linear prediction spectrum (Davis and Mermelstein, 1980). MFCC, LFCC (linear-frequency cepstrum coefficients) comprised the first group and LPC, LPCC were put in second group. For each parameter word templates were generated using an efficient dynamic method. They computed a set of ten MFCC coefficients every 6" 4 ms and compared with other parameter sets. They claimed the superiority of MFCC over other feature as itrepresents the perceptually relevant aspects of the short-term speech in better way.A comprehensive review onGMM-based speaker verification systems and an integrated system as structural Gaussian mixture models (SGMMs) with neural network to achieve both computational efficiency and high accuracy in text-independent speaker verification is emphasized in (Xiang and Berger, 2003). Time frequency features along with LPC and vector quantization using MLP classifier is another development in the field of children speech emotion recognition (Palo, et.al., 2015).

The success of any speech emotion recognition (SER) system is largely dominated by: number of emotional states, database, and feature selection and classification scheme used. In the last decades and so researcher have focused by and large in these areas of SER system. Speaker's age, gender, speaking style, language can greatly influence the acoustic and prosodic features of speech 9 (Bosch, 2003). Existing efforts in this field have focused on the recognition of a subset of basic emotions from speech signals, e.g., "Relief" detection, "Stress" detection (Mohanty and Jena, 2011) (Ai, Litman, Forbes-Riley, Rotaru andd Purandare, 2006) (Devillers, and Vidrascu, 2006), and detection of irritation and resignation (Laukka, Neiberg, Forsell, Karlsson, and Elenius, 2011), "Emotional" and "Neutral", "Anger" and "Neutral" (Huber, Batliner, Buckow, No¨th, Warnke, Niemann, 2000), "Negative" and "Non-negative" (Litman and Forbes-Riley, 2006) (Lee and Narayanan, 2003). However, some authors have been dealt with certain application- dependent affective states, e.g., "Annoyed" and "Frustrated" detection (Ang, Dhillon, Krupski, Shriberg, Stolcke, 2002), detecting "Certainty" (Liscombe, Hirschberg, Venditti, 2005).

Around the mid-1980s first investigation of speech emotion recognition by a machine using statistical properties of certain acoustic features have been investigated (Tolkmitt and Scherer, 1986). Harmony features based on the psychoacoustic harmony perception known from music theory for emotion recognition have been proposed by B. Yang et.al. (2010) . Mel-frequency cepstral coefficients (MFCCs) statistical features over three phoneme types (stressed vowels, unstressed vowels, and consonants) were computed by the authors Bitouk et al. (2010). Emotional speech recognition using modulation spectral features (MSFs) were proposed, where an auditory filter-bank and a modulation filter-bank for speech analysis (Lee, Narayanan, and Pieraccini, 2001). They claimed the robustness of MSFs over short-term spectral representations such as perceptual linear prediction (PLP) coefficients and MFCCs. Polzehl et al. (2011), used both linguistic and acoustic features in their work. Statistics of pitch, loudness, and MFCCs have been used by them in acoustic and linguistic modelling. The exploration of probabilistic and entropy-based models of words and phrases, e.g., term frequency (TF), term frequency-inverse document frequency (TF-IDF), bag-of-words (BOW) and the self-referential information (SRI) were done. He et al. (2011), have proposed empirical model decomposition (EMD) that uses the speech into intrinsic mode functions (IMF) to calculate the average entropy for the IMF channels. He also proposed a method to calculate the average spectral energy in the sub-bands of speech spectrograms for stress and emotion classification.

One of the most important steps in SER system is the classification state to predict correct class. Most of emotional models of speech in 1990s used extensively classifiers as linear discriminate classification (LDC) and maximum likelihood Bayes (MLB) (Dellaert, Polzin, and Weibel, 1996). Researcher, in recent years has begun working with artificial neural networks (ANNs), Multilayer perceptron network, Radial basis function network (RBFN), decision trees, K-nearest neighbor (KNN) variants of support vector machines (SVMs), Bayesian networks GMMs, hidden Markov models (HMMs), and hybrid or ensemble methods have been the topics of discussion for emotion recognition. Albornoz et al. (2011), tested and compared GMM, HMM, and MLP for emotion classification.

Automatic recognition of different types of emotion from human speech is a challenging task for researchers. Mostly this job is measured under diffrent acoustic conditions. Concept of negative and non-negative emotions was used by Lee *et al.*. Both acoustic and language features was considered in their work (Lee, Narayanan, and Pieraccini, 2001). Authors in Ververidis and Kotropolos (2004) extracted 87 statistic features from energy, spectral features, and pitch from Danish emotional speech database. Four different emotions happy, anger, sorrow, and surprise was classified by Cheng *et.al.* They have taken time, amplitude pitch, and formant features for classification of speech for four types of class (Cheng et al., 2009). For the classification of emotional speech from German database 1586 acoustic, and 24 linguistic features were extracted by Schuller *et al.* Short-term statistics, auto regressive, wavelet, and spectral moment features were provided by the authors in Ntalampiral et al. (2012). FFT and statistical features were also considered for the feature extraction in a study (Hayes, 1996). Beside these techniques a lot of works were done by different researchers for the analysis of different types of emotion from speech Ntalampiras et al., 2012; Hayes, 1996; Mohanty, Routray & Kabisatpathy, 2010). Still there is scope for analyzing the emotions for different regional language speech.

Classification schemes as Hidden Markov Model (HMM), Gaussian Mixture Model (GMM), Neural network as RBFN, Support Vector Machine (SVM), Probabilistic Neural Networks (PNN), MLP, Classification Tree (CT), K-nearest neighbour (KNN) have been applied in the field of emotional speech recognitions (Kolodyazhniy, Kreibig, Gross, Roth, and Wilhelm, 2011) (Fulmare, Chakrabarti, and Yadav, 2013) (Mohanty and Routray, 2014) (Palo and Mohanty, 2016). The proven accuracy of neural network classifiers like RBFN and MLP in classifying human speech emotions effectively has provided significant insight on their superiority as compared to others (Li and Zhao, 1998) (Nwe, Foo, and De Silva, 20003) (Ali, Zehra, and Arif, 2013) (Lee, and Narayanan, 2003).

However, VQ as a feature reduction technique has been found little presence in these literatures baring a few (Li and Zhao, 1998). To exploit the capability of removing redundant features using VQ with acoustic features has been one area of focus in this chapter. We have aimed to explore the effectiveness of NN classifiers as MLP and RBFN using a proposed derived reduced feature set with application of VQ. Also the recognition accuracy of VQ classifier is compared with NN classifiers using different extracted feature sets.

The proposed algorithm used for extraction of emotional speech features has been described in section 2. The classification schemes, database selection have also been discussed in this section. The complete experimental set up has been explained in section 3. An overview of results and associated discussions have been summarized in Section 4. Finally section 5 concludes the work based on cues from simulated experiments.

METHODOLOGY

As described in previous section, many methods are already used. However still there is scope to work in this area. The common prosodic features and its statistical parameters have been shown considerable performance (Ram, Palo, and Mohanty, 2013). As the novelty of this work, the combination these prosodic features are considered carefully in this work. The block diagram of the work procedure is given in Figure 1.

The emotional speech databases used for research purposes have been generalized into three broad categories. These categories are natural, induced and simulated. Features extracted from natural and spontaneous emotion can faithfully represent the states with greater ecological validity.

EMOTIONAL SPEECH DATABASE

Regional Odia Language Database Generation

Most of the databases of different emotional speech are not freely accessible so that we have produced our own database in an Indian language (oriya) for this purpose. Recording of emotional speech utterances of two male and two female professionals for angry, sad and happy emotions have been carried out

Figure 1. Experimental setup for Proposed Method

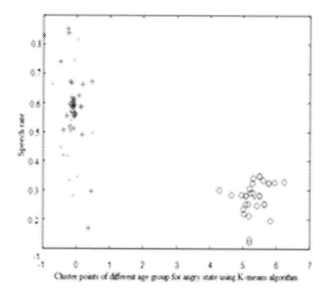

under noise free environment. Different amount of utterances of each emotion with different sentence and duration between 4 to 15 seconds have been generated. Sampling frequency of 16 kHz with 16 bits has been used to record the database. Twenty utterances of each emotion have been chosen for our purpose. A total of sixty utterances have been used to extract the proposed features and simulation of the classifiers.

Features Extraction

Selecting a suitable feature extraction technique that represent a particular speech emotion against all odds and biases, independent of computing platform is essential for any emotion recognition system. While choosing the features following points were taken care of: region of analysis, feature types, and feature that depends on language, age, gender and speaking style. Segmented features based on framing and windowing are called local features. They take care of the statistical dependency of the whole sentence and its limitations. Statistical features are the type of Global features generally extracted from whole utterances. Global features have higher classification accuracy, lower classification time. Cross validation and feature selection algorithms can be applied to Global features with lower execution time than local features. However Global features are suitable to distinguish high arousal against low arousal emotions (Nwe, et, al., 2003). Further the feature size is less compared to local features hence may not be suitable for our chosen SVM classifier.

Speaker emotion state, variation, anxiety, enthusiasm, choice of grammar or vocabulary can be best described by the prosodic features. It depends on rhythm, stress and inflection of speech and can be used as a vital source of knowledge by researchers of speech emotion recognition. Prosody feature such as fundamental frequency, pitch, formant, speaking rate, energy etc. can be used to deliver added sense to natural spoken word to provide emotion of speaker. Pitch, speaking rate, log energy with their different combination are used in this experiment for classification of angry emotions against neutral utterances using SVM.

Pitch

The fundamental frequency (F0), often referred to as the pitch, is one of the most important features for determining emotion in speech (Ali, Zehra and Arif, 2013). Pitch varies with age and is gender dependent which the recognition system must adhere to prevent misclassification. Autocorrelation Function (ACF) is applied for pitch estimation for our purpose.

Energy

Energy or intensity often indicates the volume of the speech. Therefore, it is a natural source of valuable speech emotion information. Mathematically it can be calculated by taking the sum of the absolute values for each data frame. Since human hears a sound in logarithmic scale, log energy features are extracted to better represent the emotional speech.

$$e(n) = \sum_{i=1}^{w} |x_i(n)|^2 \tag{1}$$

Log Energy

Volume of the speech can be specified by Engergy. The quality of the voice is naturally lift with major increase in amplitude when people get excited or agitated. Speech signal are low amplitude or energy for sad or bore emotion. Log energy is an important feature for emotional speech analysis. The log energy can be found for a signal $x_k(n)$ using the relation:

$$.e_{log}(n) = 10 log \sum_{k=1}^{w} |x_k(n)|^2 x_k(n) \tag{2}$$

where, w is the analyzing window.

Speech Rate

Speaking rate like rhythm involves the counting of some pattern per second. Individual, psychological and physiological, cultural, linguistic, demographic profiles of speech signal influence the speaking rate. As it is speaker and language dependent, thus suitable for our chosen database to classify angry against neutral emotion. As the database recorded have different speakers with variation in age, gender and language we expect this feature relevant in classifying above two classes of utterances. The mean speaking rate for an utterance, number of vowel segment $N_V(x)$ and duration of utterance $D(u)$ is defined as

$$SR(x) = \frac{N_V(x)}{D(u)} \tag{3}$$

Feature Combination

The basic prosodic features log energy, pitch and speech rate are combined iteratively. From this four combined features as pitch-log energy, pitch-speech rate, speech rate-log energy and pitch-speech rate-log energy have been derived. These feature combinations have been used as input vectors to SVM classifier. Experimental results show an improvement in performance of the classifier with combined features.

Clustering Technique

As in Palo, et. al. (2015), two types of clustering techniques as K-means and FCM are verified for comparison. The purpose of the work is to differentiate speaker's emotion of various types of speech. Consider there are '*P*' numbers of features include all types of emotion. By applying clustering technique, features are separated into *L* clusters each having a cluster center C_l, *l*=1,2,...,*L*. Every cluster center is linked with the consequent class. By taking the help of squared error function, the cluster can be formed by minimizing the objective function *b*. Best convergence of '*b*' will ensure sufficient clustering of the preferred emotion. Objective function can be found by:

$$b = \sum_{l=1}^{L}\sum_{p=1}^{P} s_p^{(l)} - C_l^2 \qquad (4)$$

where, ‖ ‖ is norm representing the distance between C_l and the data point $s_p^{(l)}$. K-means clustering has been performed using following steps

1. The centroid is selected from each *L* feature points, select the centroid.
2. Obtain *L* cluster by iteratively repeating the procedure. In the process, allot all the source data point to the respective nearest centroid.

The centroids are revised by calculating the cluster centers iteratively, until further distinction in cluster center is cleared.

FCM Clustering

In earlier work emotion has been detected from the speech signal using fuzzy based technique (Smruti, Sahoo, Dash, & Mohanty, 2015). Authors have used both prosodic and linear features for building the fuzzy models for recognition of different speech emotion. They have considered the adult speech data base and feature hybridization was used for getting better result. Also the fuzzy based classifier is used for the classification of different types of emotional speech. FCM was used by the authors for the clustering the emotion of the people with different age group (Palo, Mohanty, & Chandra, 2018). Every feature value can be related with a number of cluster in this technique.

Classifier Design

Selection of suitable classifier to classify the extracted features into different human emotion is a complex task. The selection becomes further difficult since prior knowledge about the characteristics of the features. Different researchers reported varied classification accuracy with different classifiers (Lee and Narayanan, 2003) (Smruti, Sahoo, Dash, and Mohanty, 2015) (Palo and Mohanty, 2017) (Javidi and Fazlizadeh, 2013) (Palo, Mohanty, and Chandra, 2015).

To classify the extracted features into different human emotions, we need to select a classifier that can properly model the data and achieve better classification accuracy. 12 MFCCs, log energy (LE), the first three formant frequencies and pitch and its variants to classify happiness, anger, and neutral emotional states with MLP, GMM and C5.0. They reported MLP classifier performs better than other two with an average accuracy of 68.3%. Using pH time frequency feature and LP_VQC feature with MLP classifier average classification accuracy of 69.5% and 77.8% were achieved in (Palo and Mohanty, 2016) and above 80% using MFCC features. Ease of implementation with well defined training algorithm once the network parameters are specified are the key advantages that make MLP superior to other ANNs. Hence it is mostly used standard ANN classifier by the researchers of emotional speech recognition (Palo, et. al., 2015) (Palo, et. al., 2018). An attempt has been taken to explore the superiority of this classifier with pitch, log energy, speech rate and different combination of these features for speech emotion detection. The model is choosen as Support Vector Machine (SVM) for detection and classification.

Neural Network

There have been a number of classifiers used for recognition of emotion in speech signals. Each have their advantages and limitation. So the choice is not unanimous and based on conditions of input features. MLP and HMM are most commonly used classifier for emotions in speech signal. They are relatively simple, accurate and easy to implement. HMM is suitable for statistical sequential features like GMM and VQ. The classification performance of HMM is not so satisfactory, though it has dynamic time wrapping capability (Joshi and Zalte, 2013). GMM is a statistical model that can perform well for the classification of different emotions from speech signal. This method can be chosen for speech emotion recognition that include several global features. It is quite difficult for the involvement of large amount of data. Temporal structure cannot be formed due to assumption that all feature vectors are independent in this. The computation time and complexity increases due to elimination of redundant data in this approach. Requirement of separate training and testing algorithm is another constraint. It follows a probability approach and more suitable for spectral feature. It is well known method for emotion speech classification using density estimation and clustering. For non-linear mapping ANN founds to be most effective. Their recognition accuracy out perform conventional HMM and GMM for reduced feature sets. They are having good processing quality and simplified model for a small set of features. It is found that a 64 codebook VQ method gives equivalent performance with a one hidden layer MLP using 128 hidden nodes. There are three basic ANN classifiers found in this field as MLP, RBFN and recurrent neural network. MLP and RBFN classifiers has been used in this work and compared with statistical based VQ classifier. RBFN are faster in training than MLP. Its performance is better than both MLP and VQ. Out of all these classifiers statistical classifiers as HMM, GMM and VQ follow probabilities for state transitions. Contrarily, ANNs use connections of weights and biases. Further HMM are serial structured whereas ANNs are basically parallel. Since speech frequencies occur in parallel, ANN has more advantages and can converge to an optimal solution. Hence ANN approach suits us.

Multilayer Perceptron

A multilayer perceptron (MLP) (Haykin, 2005), uses error back propagation as the learning method in classifying different class hence suitable for pattern recognition. It is a multi-layer, feed forward network that utilizes a supervised learning technique. This algorithm is performed in two steps for training MLP network: a forward step and a backward step. The computational units are engaged in propagating the signal from input to output in forward training step for pattern recognition. In backward propagation steps the synaptic weights are updated according to an error correction and minimization rule for filling the gap between training and testing samples. Thus the forward pass phase computes the function signal while the backward phase computes the error signal.

MLP structure consists of input layer, hidden layer and output layer with index variables *i, j* and *k* respectively as in Figure2. The basic features of these layers are: there is no connection within a layer, no direct connection between input and output layer, fully connected between layers, numbers of output units need not equal number of input units and there can be one or more hidden layers. First layer draws linear boundaries, second layer combines the boundaries and the third layer generates arbitrarily complex boundaries. The input signal is propagated to hidden layer through a weight layer W and from hidden layer to output with a weight vector V.

The input vector is propagated through a weight layer *V*.

The output $g_j(t)$ at j^{th} hidden layer is given by

$$g_j\left(t\right) = \sum_i x_i\left(t\right)W_{ji} + b_j \tag{5}$$

where x_i is the input value at i^{th} node, φ is the activation function and g_j is output of jth hidden node before activation. The output of jth hidden node after activation is

$$n_j\left(t\right) = \varphi\Big(g_j\left(t\right)\Big) \tag{6}$$

b_j and b_k are the respective bias vectors of the corresponding nodes.

The output O_k of of kth output node is computed as,

$$O_k\left(t\right) = \varphi\Big(g_k\left(t\right)\Big) \tag{7}$$

where,

$$g_k\left(t\right) = \sum_j n_j\left(t\right)V_{kj} + b_k \tag{8}$$

synaptic weight correction in MLP network is proportional to the negative gradient of the cost function with respect to that synaptic weight and is given as,

$$" V = -\alpha \frac{\partial \xi}{\partial V}$$

(9)

where, α is the back propagation algorithm learning rate parameter.

RBFN classifier found to be more effective than MLP classifier (Kolodyazniy et al., 2011). As compare to MLP, it can replicate any nonlinear function by a single hidden layer using Gaussian activation function. It is faster to train, computationally simpler and more efficient in a given scenario (Haykin, 2005). In RBFN there are the same three layer structure like MLP. Input layer, hidden layer, and output layer are three main component of RBFN structure. In this neural network model all the features are represented in a N dimensional space by using radius and center point. Any shape or function can be modified by using the radial units of the hidden layer. It is needed to take more number of hidden layers than the number of radial units for forming a basis for pattern recognition. Figure 2 for a basic RBFNN is shown below.

The Gaussian activation function used in RBFN is given by:

$$G_j\left(X\right) = exp\left[-\left(X - \mu_j\right)^T \sum_j^{-1}((X - \mu_j)\right]$$

(10)

Figure 2. Radial Basis Function Network

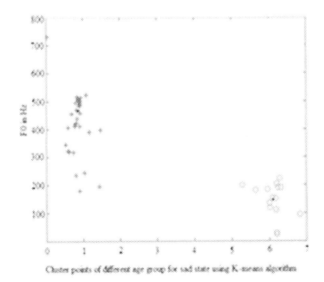

Cluster points of different age group for sad state using K-means algorithm

Support Vector Classification

Support Vector Machine is a dominant and proficient neural network based classifier. It is basically a binary classifier and It has the ability to deal with high diemnsional input data feature with theoretical bounds on the generalization error. SVM based classifiers have not many parameters for tuning and it is very simple for the implementation. The trained SVM is defined only by the most support vectors. It is explained as follows:

Consider T_N be set of N labeled data points in an M-dimensional hyperspace:

$$T_N = [(\mathbf{x}_1, d_1), \cdots, (\mathbf{x}_N, d_N)] \in (\mathbf{X} \times \mathbf{D})^N \tag{11}$$

in which $\mathbf{x}_i \in \mathbf{X}$, where $\mathbf{X}$ is the input space and $d_i \in \mathbf{D}$, $\mathbf{D} = \{-1, +1\}$ is the label space.

The problem is formulated to design a function ψ such that $\psi : \mathbf{X} \rightarrow \mathbf{D}$ predicts d from the input $\mathbf{x}$.

However, '$\mathbf{X}$' can be transformed into an equal or higher dimensional feature space for making it linearly separable (Cover's Theorem) (Nwe, et. al., 2003). Now the problem of finding a *nonlinear* decision boundary in $\mathbf{X}$ has been transformed into a problem of finding the optimal *hyperplane* for separating the two classes.

The hyperplane in transformed domain is said as the feature space and can be parameterized by $(\mathbf{w}, b)$ pair as:

$$\sum_{j=1}^{P} w_j \phi_j(\mathbf{x}) + b = 0 \tag{12}$$

The mapping $\phi(\cdot)$ need not be computed explicitly; instead, an inner product kernel of the form

$$\langle \phi(\mathbf{x}_i), \phi(\mathbf{x}_j) \rangle = K(\mathbf{x}_i, \mathbf{x}_j) \tag{13}$$

Figure 3. Support vector machine

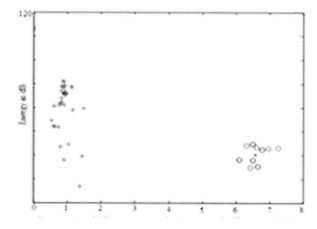

can be used for finding the optimal hyper planes.

Gaussian RBF kernels is used as the kernel function as given in [24]. The patterns in the input space even after transformation are not perfectly separable with linear functions (hyperplanes).

For a training set T_N, the optimal values of the weight vector $\mathbf{w}$ and bias b must be choosen in such a manner that, they satisfy the constraint

$$d_i\left(\mathbf{w}^{\mathrm{T}}\mathbf{x_i} + b\right) \geq 1 - \zeta_i, \ \text{for} \ i = 1, 2, \cdots, N \tag{14}$$

$\zeta_i \geq 0$, for all i, and such that the weight vector $\mathbf{w}$ and the slack variables ζ_i minimize the cost functional

$$\Phi\left(\mathbf{w}, \P\right) = \frac{1}{2}\mathbf{w}^{\mathrm{T}}\mathbf{w} + C\sum_{i=1}^{N}\zeta_i \tag{15}$$

where, C is user-specified positive parameter.

The decision function in the feature space as:

$$y\left(\mathbf{x}\right) = \sum_{i=1}^{N}\alpha_i d_i K\left(\mathbf{x_i}, \mathbf{x}\right) + b \tag{16}$$

where, $K(\mathbf{x_i}, \mathbf{x})$ represents the kernel [21-22].

The final classification can be obtained through,

if y(**x**)>0 **x** is in class 1
if y(**x**)<0 **x** is in class 2

Results and Discussion

Clustering of the angry emotion based on three age groups as 10-20 years, 21-50 years and 51-70 years. K-means clustering algorithm has been used for this purpose bcause this is one of the popular clustering technique suitable for data clustering. Figure 4 shows the K-means clustering foe angry speech. From this figure it can be observed that cluster for 10-20 and 21-50 years people are more closure as compared to other age group.

Figure 5 displays the comparison using K-means clustering with F0 features of sad emotion. Speech of age 51-70 years people is compared with 21-50 years. For these two age grooup a cluster with widely separated for these two classes using sad emotional state.

A comparison of children and an adult group between 21 to 50 years of age using log energy features has been done in Figure 6 for bore emotion. From this figure it can be energy for children speech is more as comapre to adults. Then the cluster can separated widely for any emotional state.

Prosodic features as pitch, log energy and their feature combination were extracted for angry and neutral utterances of the prepared databases. To evaluate the performance of learning classifiers the experimental frame work is divided into two phases for speech emotion. In first phase basic acoustic pitch, log energy, and speech rate features of neutal and angry utterance have been used as input vectors to

Figure 4. K-means clustering of angry speech emotion for different age groups using speech rate

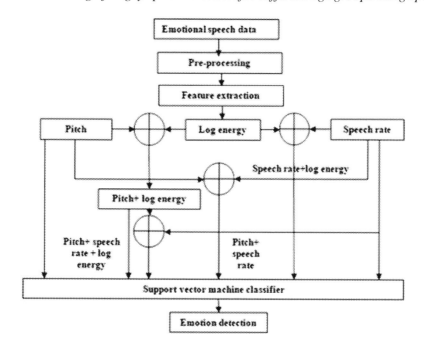

Figure 5. K-means clustering of sad speech emotion for different age groups using F0 features

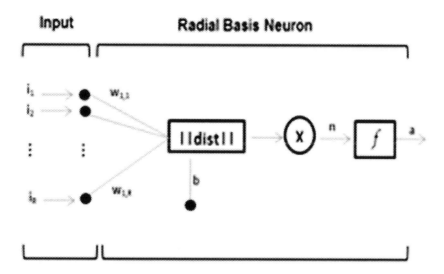

SVM classifier. Table 1 provides the corresponding recognition accuracy and mean square error (MSE) with the learned classifier. In second phase the combination features have been used for classification. A classification accuracy 62.8% using pitch+intensity+formant, 47.7% with intensity+formant, 54.5% with pitch+formant and 62.12% using intensity+formant were reported (Palo, et. al., 2018).

Figure 6. K-means clustering of sad speech emotion for different age groups using F0 features

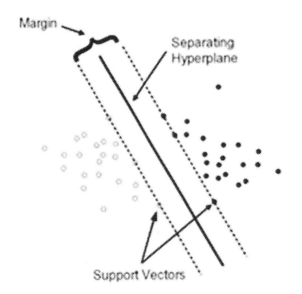

Table 2 provides the comparative analysis in terms of percentage classification accuracy and MSE of four combined prosodic features (pitch and log energy, pitch and speech rate, speech rate and log energy and pitch and speech rate and log energy) for neutral and angry emotions.

It indicates the increase in energy and frequency component when people get angry. This is proved to be correct irrespective of gender, age and language of speaker type as evident from our database. Hence it can be a good measure to detect other speech emotions as well. Both angry and neutral features are fed as input to the SVM classifier for training purposes. Ninety percentages of data were used for training and rest was used for testing the above classifier.

The comparison of classifier performance using SVM in Table 5 and 6 indicates its ability to classify these emotions with a high degree of accuracy. Percentage classification accuracy increased by a significant account when different feature combinations of prosodic features were used. As shown in Table 1, pitch is having the lowest classification accuracy among all basic prosodic features used here. Speech rate gives the highest classification percentage with the said classifier. Thus people speak faster when in angry then normal voice. It has the better performance as compared to the earliest work (Palo, eet. al., 2018) as presented in Table 1.

Combined features used in above classifier demonstrated the superiority of among other combinations. Different classification percentage with MSE using combined feature with above classifier is shown in Table 2. Increase in accuracy and reduction in MSE of combined features compared to basic prosodic features prove their robustness in classifying angry emotions. A 0.324 MSE for speech rate indicates its superiority over other basic prosodic features used. Similarly pitch+log energy+speech rate as combined feature surpasses all other features so far used in our experiment. Performance of MLP classifier is presented in Table 2 and 3. Table 4 shows the performance of the RBFN classifier.

Table 1. Comparison of Features Based on Different Age Group (Palo, et. al., 2018)

Features	Child			Adult		
	Angry	Sad	Bore	Angry	Sad	Bore
Pitch (mean)	643.5	204.2	127.9	350.7	155.3	109.3
Pitch (max)	844	255	175	667	183	231
Pitch (min)	495	162	89	120	126	61
Speech rate(mean)	0.34	0.17	0.19	0.54	0.28	0.23
Speech rate(max)	0.58	0.24	0.36	0.86	0.36	0.27
Speech rate(min)	0.20	0.14	0.13	0.37	0.24	0.19
Log energy(mean)	32.1	24.6	28.8	18.5	13.9	15.2
Log energy(max)	36.1	29.3	31.7	25.9	16.8	20.2
Log energy(min)	17.8	18.5	24.9	12.7	10.2	10.5

Table 2. Accuracy using MLP and Mean square error with different prosodic features

Acoustic features	Pitch	Log energy	Speech rate
Accuracy	52%	59.3%	65.7%
MSE	0.771	0.418	0.324

Table 3. Accuracy using MLP and Mean square error with combined features

Hybrid features	Log energy+speech rate	Pitch+speech rate	Log energy+pitch	Log energy +pitch+speech rate
Accuracy	74.2%	78%	78.3%	87.7%
MSE	0.192	0.124	0.159	0.025

Table 4. Accuracy with RBFN Classifier

Features	Angry	Sad	Happy	Average Accuracy (%)
Log energy+speech rate	75.64%	69.77%	74.15%	72.65%
Pitch+speeh rate	62.59%	63.80%	66.79%	65.14%
Log energy+pitch	70.15%	65.30%	68.34%	67.22%
Log energy +pitch+speech rate	72.60%	65.02%	71.14%	68.78%

Table 5. SVM percentage recognition and Mean square error with different basic features for angry utterances (Palo, eet. al., 2018)

Acoustic features	Pitch	Log energy	Speech rate
Accuracy	60%	68.3%	76.7%
MSE	0.771	0.418	0.324

Table 6. SVM percentage recognition and Mean square error with different combined features for angry

Combined features	Log energy+speech rate	Pitch+speech rate	Log energy+pitch	Log energy +pitch+speech rate
Accuracy	89.7%	91%	94.3%	96.7%
MSE	0.194	0.124	0.159	0.025

CONCLUSION

Desire for interacting with machines makes speech emotion and its detection a vital component for different users. However, speech is associated with inherent variability due to growing physiological and auditory mechanism. Research involving speech has been a motivation factor for this experiment and can be applied in many fields. Additionally, the detection system becomes a far reach due to difficulties encountered in collecting adequate spontaneous children speech emotional utterances exhibited in real-world environment. The database collected may be extended that can provide a desired platform for further study in future. Though, the database is in its primitive stage, the combinational effect shows better effect. Further the combination may be chosen carefully for even better performance and kept for future work of the related researchers.

REFERENCES

Ai, H., Litman, D. J., Forbes-Riley, K., Rotaru, M., Tetreault, J., & Purandare, A. (2006). Using system and user performance features to improve emotion detection in spoken tutoring systems. Proceedings of Interspeech, 797–800.

Albornoz, E. M., Milone, D. H., & Rufiner, H. L. (2011). Spoken emotion recognition using hierarchical classifiers. *Computer Speech & Language*, *25*(3), 556–570. doi:10.1016/j.csl.2010.10.001

Ali, S. A., Zehra, S., & Arif, A. (2013). Performance evaluation of learning classifiers for speech emotions corpus using combinations of prosodic features. *International Journal of Computers and Applications*, *76*(2).

Ang, J., Dhillon, R., Krupski, A., Shriberg, E., & Stolcke, A. (2002). Prosody-based automatic detection of annoyance and frustration in human-computer dialog. *Proceedings of international conference on spoken language processing*, 2037-2039.

Bitouk, D., Verma, R., & Nenkova, A. (2010). Class-level spectral features for emotion recognition. *Speech Communication*, 52(7-8), 613–625. doi:10.1016/j.specom.2010.02.010 PMID:23794771

Bosch, L. (2003). Emotions, speech and the ASR framework. *Speech Communication*, 40(1-2), 213–225. doi:10.1016/S0167-6393(02)00083-3

Chandrasekar, P., Chapaneri, S., & Jayaswal, D. (2014, April). Automatic speech emotion recognition: A survey. In *2014 International Conference on Circuits, Systems, Communication and Information Technology Applications (CSCITA)* (pp. 341-346). IEEE. 10.1109/CSCITA.2014.6839284

Cheng, X. M., Cheng, P. Y., & Zhao, L. (2009). A study on emotional feature analysis and recognition in speech signal. In *Proc. International Conference on Measuring Technology and Mechatronics Automation* (pp. 418-420). IEEE. 10.1109/ICMTMA.2009.89

Chul Min Leeand Shrikanth, S. N. (2005). Toward Detecting Emotions in Spoken Dialogs. *IEEE Transactions on Speech and Audio Processing*, 13(2), 293–303. doi:10.1109/TSA.2004.838534

Davis, S. B., & Mermelstein, P. (1980, August). Comparison of Parametric Representations for Monosyllabic Word Recognition in Continuously Spoken Sentences. *IEEE Transactions on Acoustics, Speech, and Signal Processing*, 28(4), 357–366. doi:10.1109/TASSP.1980.1163420

Dellaert, F., Polzin, T., & Waibel, A. (1996), Recognizing emotion in speech, *Proceedings of international conference on spoken language processing*, 3, 1970-1973.

Devillers, L., & Vidrascu, L. (2006). Real-life emotions detection with lexical and paralinguistic cues on human–human call center dialogs. Proceedings of Interspeech, 801-804.

El Ayadi, M., Kamel, M. S., & Karray, F. (2011, March). Survey on speech emotion recognition: Features, classification schemes, and databases. *Pattern Recognition*, 44(3), 572–587. doi:10.1016/j.patcog.2010.09.020

Farrell, Mammone, & Assaleh. (1994). Speaker Networks Recognition Using Neural and Conventional Classifiers. *IEEE Transactions on Acoustics, Speech, and Signal Processing*, 2(1), 194–205.

Fragopanagos, N., & Taylor, J. G. (2005). Emotion recognition in human–computer interaction. *Neural Networks*, 18(4), 389–405. doi:10.1016/j.neunet.2005.03.006 PMID:15921887

Fulmare, N. S., Chakrabarti, P., & Yadav, D. (2013). Understanding and estimation of emotional expression using acoustic analysis of natural speech. *International Journal on Natural Language Computing*, 2(4), 37–46. doi:10.5121/ijnlc.2013.2503

Hayes, M. H. (1996). *Statistical Digital Signal Processing and Modeling*. John Wiley and Sons.

Haykin, S. (2005). Neural Networks: A comprehensive foundation (2nd ed.). Essex, UK: Pearson Education.

He, L., Lech, M., Maddage, N. C., & Allen, N. B. (2011). Study of empirical mode decomposition and spectral analysis for stress and emotion classification in natural speech. *Biomedical Signal Processing and Control*, 6(2), 139–146. doi:10.1016/j.bspc.2010.11.001

Hermansk, H. (1990). Perceptual linear predictive (PLP) analysis of speech. *The Journal of the Acoustical Society of America*, 87(4), 1739–1752. PMID:2341679

Huber, R., Batliner, A., Buckow, J., Nöth, E., Warnke, V., & Niemann, H. (2000). Recognition of emotion in a realistic dialogue scenario. *Proceedings of international conference on spoken language processing*, 665-668.

Javidi, M. M., & Roshan, E. F. (2013). Speech emotion recognition by using combinations of C5. 0, neural network (NN), and support vector machines (SVM) classification methods. Journal of mathematics and computer. *Science, 6*(3), 191–200.

Javidi, M. M., & Roshan, E. F. (2013, April). Speech Emotion Recognition by Using Combinations of C5.0, Neural Network (NN), and Support Vector Machines (SVM) Classification Methods. *Journal of Mathematics and Computer Science, 6*, 191–200.

Joshi, D. D., & Zalte, M. B. (2013), Speech Emotion Recognition: A Review. *IOSR Journal of Electronics and Communication Engineering, 4*(4), 34-37.

Kolodyazhniy, V., Kreibig, S. D., Gross, J. J., Roth, W. T., & Wilhelm, F. H. (2011). An affective computing approach to physiological emotion specificity: Toward subject-independent and stimulus-independent classification of film induced emotions. *Psychophysiology, 48*, 908–922. PMID:21261632

Laukka, P., Neiberg, D., Forsell, M., Karlsson, I., & Elenius, K. (2011). Expression of affect in spontaneous speech: Acoustic correlates and automatic detection of irritation and resignation. *Computer Speech & Language, 25*(1), 84–104. doi:10.1016/j.csl.2010.03.004

Lee, C. M., & Narayanan, S. (2003). Emotion recognition using a data driven fuzzy inference system. Proceedings of Eurospeech, 157-160.

Lee, C. M., & Narayanan, S. (2003). Emotion recognition using a data-driven fuzzy inference system. *Eighth European conference on speech communication and technology*.

Lee, C. M., Narayanan, S., & Pieraccini, R. (2001). Recognition of negative emotions from the speech signal. In *IEEE Workshop on Automatic Speech Recognition and Understanding, 2001. ASRU'01* (pp. 240-243). IEEE. 10.1109/ASRU.2001.1034632

Li, Y., & Zhao, Y. (1998). Recognizing emotions in speech using short-term and long-term features. *Fifth International Conference on Spoken Language Processing*.

Liscombe, J., Hirschberg, J., & Venditti, J. J. (2005). Detecting certainness in spoken tutorial dialogues. *Proceeding of European conference on speech communication and technology*, 1837-1840.

Litman, D. J., & Forbes-Riley, K. (2006). Recognizing student emotions and attitudes on the basis of utterances in spoken tutoring dialogues with both human and computer tutors. *Speech Communication, 48*(5), 559–590. doi:10.1016/j.specom.2005.09.008

Loizou, P. C. (2007). *Speech enhancement: theory and practice*. CRC Press. doi:10.1201/9781420015836

Makhoul, J. (1975). Linear prediction: A tutorial review. *Proceedings of the IEEE, 63*(4), 561–580. doi:10.1109/PROC.1975.9792

Mihir Narayan Mohanty, H. K. P., & Chandra, M. (2014). Design of Neural Network Model for Emotional Speech Recognition. *Artificial Intelligence and Evolutionary Algorithms in Engineering Systems*, *325*, 291–300.

Mohanty, Routray, & Kabisatpathy. (2010, December). Voice Detection using Statistical Method. *Int. J. Engg. Techsci.*, *2*(1), 120–124.

Mohanty, Mishra, & Routray. (2009). A Non-rigid Motion Estimation Algorithm for Yawn Detection in Human Drivers. *International Journal of Computational Vision and Robotics*, *1*(1), 89–109.

Mohanty, M. N., & Jena, B. (2011). Analysis of stressed human speech. *International Journal of Computational Vision and Robotics*, *2*(2), 180–187. doi:10.1504/IJCVR.2011.042273

Mohanty, M. N., & Routray, A. (2014, December). Machine Learning Approach for Emotional Speech Classification. In *International Conference on Swarm, Evolutionary, and Memetic Computing* (pp. 490-501). Springer.

Ntalampiras, S., & Fakotakis, N. (2012). Modelling the Temporal Evolution of Acoustic Parameters for Speech Emotion Recognition. *IEEE Transactions on Affective Computing*, *3*(1), 116–125. doi:10.1109/T-AFFC.2011.31

Nwe, T. L., Foo, S. W., & De Silva, L. C. (2003). Speech emotion recognition using hidden Markov models. *Speech Communication*, *41*(4), 603–623. doi:10.1016/S0167-6393(03)00099-2

Palo, Mohanty, & Chandra. (2015). Novel Feature Extraction Technique for Child Emotion Recognition. In *International Conference on Electrical, Electronics, Signals, Communication and Optimization (EESCO)* (pp. 1848-1852). IEEE. 10.1109/EESCO.2015.7253839

Palo, H. K., & Mohanty, M. N. (2016). Modified-VQ Features for Speech Emotion Recognition. *Journal of Applied Sciences (Faisalabad)*, *16*(9), 406–418. doi:10.3923/jas.2016.406.418

Palo, H. K., & Mohanty, M. N. (2017). *Wavelet based feature combination for recognition of emotions. Ain Shams Engineering Journal.*

Palo, H. K., Mohanty, M. N., & Chandra, M. (2015). *Statistical feature based child emotion analysis.* Academic Press.

Palo, H. K., Mohanty, M. N., & Chandra, M. (2015). Use of different features for emotion recognition using MLP network. In *Computational Vision and Robotics* (pp. 7–15). New Delhi: Springer. doi:10.1007/978-81-322-2196-8_2

Palo, H. K., Mohanty, M. N., & Chandra, M. (2018). Speech Emotion Analysis of Different Age Groups Using Clustering Techniques. *International Journal of Information Retrieval Research*, *8*(1), 69–85. doi:10.4018/IJIRR.2018010105

Polzehl, T., Schmitt, A., Metze, F., & Wagner, M. (2011). Anger recognition in speech using acoustic and linguistic cues. *Speech Communication*, *53*(9-10), 1198–1209. doi:10.1016/j.specom.2011.05.002

Quatieri, T. F. (1996). *Discrete-Time Speech Signal Processing* (3rd ed.). Prentice-Hall.

Ram, Palo, & Mohanty. (2013). Emotion Recognition with Speech for Call Centres using LPC and Spectral Analysis. *International Journal of Advanced Computer Research, 3*(11), 189–194.

Ramakrishnan, S. (2012). Recognition of emotion from speech: A review. In *Speech Enhancement, Modeling and recognition-algorithms and Applications.* IntechOpen. doi:10.5772/39246

Reynolds, D. A., & Rose, R. C. (1995, January). Robust Text-Independent Speaker Identification Using Gaussian Mixture Speaker Models. *IEEE Transactions on Speech and Audio Processing, 3*(1), 72–83. doi:10.1109/89.365379

Samal, Parida, Satpathy, & Mohanty. (2014). On the use of MFCC Feature Vectors Clustering for Efficient Text Dependent Speaker Recognition. Advances in Intelligence System and Computing Series, 247, 305-312.

Sant'Ana, R., & Rosângela, C. A. A. (2006, May). Text-Independent Speaker Recognition Based on the Hurst Parameter and the Multidimensional Fractional Brownian Motion Model, IEEE Transactions on Audio. *Speech And Language Processing, 14*(3), 931–940. doi:10.1109/TSA.2005.858054

Schuller, B., Batliner, A., Seppi, D., Steidl, S., Vogt, T., Wagner, J., ... Aharonson, V. (2007). The relevance of feature type for the automatic classification of emotional user states: low level descriptors and functionals. *Eighth Annual Conference of the International Speech Communication Association.*

Seehapoch, T., & Wongthanavasu, S. (2013, January). Speech emotion recognition using support vector machines. In *2013 5th international conference on Knowledge and smart technology (KST)* (pp. 86-91). IEEE. 10.1109/KST.2013.6512793

Sheikhan, M., Bejani, M., & Gharavian, D. (2012). *Modular neural-SVM scheme for speech emotion recognition using ANOVA feature selection method. In Neural Comput & Applic.* Springer-Verlag London. doi:10.100700521-012-0814-8

Sivanandam, S. N., & Deepa, S. N. (2011). *Principles of Soft Computing* (2nd ed.). Wiley India.

Smruti, S., Sahoo, J., Dash, M., & Mohanty, M. N. (2015). An approach to design an intelligent parametric synthesizer for emotional speech. In *Proceedings of the 3rd International Conference on Frontiers of Intelligent Computing: Theory and Applications (FICTA) 2014* (pp. 367-374). Springer. 10.1007/978-3-319-12012-6_40

Tolkmitt, F. J., & Scherer, K. R. (1986). Effect of experimentally induced stress on vocal parameters. *Journal of Experimental Psychology. Human Perception and Performance, 12*(3), 302–313. doi:10.1037/0096-1523.12.3.302 PMID:2943858

Ververidis, D., & Kotropolos, C. (2004, May). Automatic emotional speech classification. *Proceedings of the IEEE International Conference on Acoustics, Speech, and Signal Processing, 1,* 593–596.

Ververidis, D., & Kotropoulos, C. (2006). Emotional speech recognition: Resources, features, and methods. *Speech Communication, 48*(9), 1162–1181. doi:10.1016/j.specom.2006.04.003

Vogt, T., & André, E. (2005, July). Comparing feature sets for acted and spontaneous speech in view of automatic emotion recognition. In *2005 IEEE International Conference on Multimedia and Expo* (pp. 474-477). IEEE. 10.1109/ICME.2005.1521463

Wu, S., Falk, T. H., & Chan, W. Y. (2011). Automatic speech emotion recognition using modulation spectral features. *Speech Communication*, *53*(5), 768–785. doi:10.1016/j.specom.2010.08.013

Xiang, B., & Berger, T. (2003, September). Efficient Text-Independent Speaker Verification with Structural Gaussian Mixture Models and Neural Network. *IEEE Transactions on Acoustics, Speech, and Signal Processing*, *11*(5), 447–456.

Yacoub, S., Simske, S., Lin, X., & Burns, J. (2003). Recognition of emotions in interactive voice response systems. *Proceeding of European conference on speech communication and technology*, 729–732.

Yang, B., & Lugger, M. (2010). Emotion recognition from speech signals using New Harmony features. *Signal Processing*, *90*(5), 1415–1423. doi:10.1016/j.sigpro.2009.09.009

Zão, L., Cavalcante, D., & Coelho, R. (2014). Time-Frequency Feature and AMS-GMM Mask for Acoustic Emotion Classification. *IEEE Signal Processing Letters*, *21*(5), 620–624. doi:10.1109/LSP.2014.2311435

Zeng, Z., Pantic, M., Roisman, G. I., & Huang, T. S. (2009). A survey of affect recognition methods: Audio, visual, and spontaneous expressions. *IEEE Transactions on Pattern Analysis and Machine Intelligence*, *31*(1), 39–58.

Chapter 9
Analysis of Speaker's Age Using Clustering Approaches With Emotionally Dependent Speech Features

Hemanta Kumar Palo
Siksha 'O' Anusandhan (Deemed), India

Debasis Behera
ⓘ https://orcid.org/0000-0002-3983-0891
C. V. Raman College of Engineering, India

ABSTRACT

Emotions are age, gender, culture, speaker, and situationally dependent. Due to an underdeveloped vocal tract or the vocal folds of children and a weak or aged speech production mechanism of older adults, the acoustic properties differ with the age of a person. In this sense, the features describing the age and emotionally relevant information of human voice also differ. This motivates the authors to investigate a number of issues related to database collection, feature extraction, and clustering algorithms for effective characterization and identification of human age of his or her paralanguage information. The prosodic features such as the speech rate, pitch, log energy, and spectral parameters have been explored to characterize the chosen emotional utterances whereas the efficient K-means and Fuzzy C-means clustering algorithms have been used to partition age-related emotional features for a better understanding of the related issues.

INTRODUCTION

The understanding and identification of human affective states have been a study of research during the last few decades. These emotional attributes are manifested in the form of facial expressions, gestures, postures or during a spoken dialogue. Among these modalities, speech remains an important and lone

DOI: 10.4018/978-1-7998-1021-6.ch009

medium of communication via phone. Nevertheless, the acoustic features describing human speech emotions vary with age, gender, culture, physical and mental conditions of a speaker. Thus, the design and development of an efficient Emotional Speech Recognition (ESR) system for human-computer interaction remains a complex domain of research until today. In this regard, the age of a speaker plays an important role with varying acoustic properties that can influence the performance of an ESR system drastically (Lyakso, & Frolova, 2015A; Lyakso, et al., 2015B). Absence of adequate research in this direction motivates the authors to consider the age and emotional relevant acoustic cues that influence the performance of an ESR system. It is a well-known fact that the speech production mechanism goes many structural changes during different stages of a human life-cycle. The vocal tract and vocal folds of a child take time to develop until he becomes a fully grown-up adult. Thus, the prosodic characteristics that describe the voice of a child and his affective states arguably differ from that of adults. As a result, an ESR system destined for a particular age group may influence the accuracy of a machine learner if applied to other age groups (Palo, Mohanty, & Chandra, 2018D; Chaudhari, & Kagalkar, 2015A; Hämäläinen, et al., 2011). The system requires suitable features which are discriminating, reliable, and can provide emotional relevant information across different age. Alternatively, the features can be used to partition people of different age groups and their affective states with some efficient clustering algorithms. The outcomes of these ESR systems can provide psychological assistance to children affected with psychological trauma or negative emotions. Service industries in the area of telecommunications, meeting browser, speech translation, human-robotic interfaces, assessment systems, smart call center, smart workspaces, intelligent tutoring, dialogue and language learning systems, forensic labs, etc. can be managed more efficiently using these systems. The criminal investigators, lawmakers, psychologists, etc. can use the system to counsel or interrogate both victims and culprits irrespective of their age. An accurate evaluation of the intended emotional states will assist the law enforcement agencies in decision making during court hearings. The paralanguage information identification system based on the age of anti-social elements, radicals, fanatic individuals, and influential people can help the law administrators monitor the defaulters. It can serve as a deterrent to persons involved with intimidating calls, false alarms, kidnappings, etc. These factors motivate this piece of work and lay the foundation for the current investigation. It focuses on the issues, algorithms and the current trends that influence this field in the present scenario. Most of the issues related to database generation and collection, feature extraction and clustering algorithms, emphasizing a speaker's age have been analyzed elaborately. A few simulation results to characterize and cluster the chosen state of emotions across different age groups have been graphically portrayed for a better understanding of the related issues.

The rest of the paper has been organized as follows. The related literature is provided in section 2. The issues that motivate this piece of research is briefed in section 3. An overview of the different database corresponding to different age groups has been made in section 4. The application domain of different feature extraction techniques related to ESR has been investigated in section 5 whereas section 6 provides information on the clustering algorithms discussed in this work. A brief overview of the fuzzy and k-means clustering algorithms has also been depicted in this section. Section 7 concludes the work with possible future directions.

Related Literature

The effect of age on speech information can be studied using discriminative parameters such as the pitch, jitter, formants, shimmer, Mel Frequency Cepstral Coefficients (MFCC), harmonic to noise ratio (HNR), etc. The study conducted on 60 older and younger adults in age groups of 60-80 years and 20-40 years shows that the ESR accuracy indeed varies with a speaker's age. Due to a wide variation in acoustic cues with age, separate models have been suggested by the authors corresponding to each age group [Das et al., 2013]. The variation in the fundamental frequency varies with age has been investigated using the speech utterances of 187 males and 187 females spanned across different age groups. The observation shows the least significant change in the speaking fundamental frequency or SFF with a slight increase in age. Nevertheless, in older adults above 70 years, the SFF founds to be lower as compared to their younger counterpart. A lower SFF has also been manifested with female speakers in the age group of 30-40 years as compared to females in their 20s. It shows that the SFF reduces with an increase in the age of a person and is more prominent in the case of female and children (Nishio, & Niimi, 2008). A study on the emotional perception from voices of 165 individuals in the age group of 4years to 22 years has been conducted to determine the effect of age (Morton, & Trehub, 2001). The adult participants are psychology students and children from the local community. They spoke fluent English and are made to judge the emotionally relevant happy and sad utterances to identify the affective state. The observation shows, a few participants tend to emphasize more on either the paralanguage or on the content of the utterance irrespective of their age. On the contrary, the adults have emphasized more on the paralanguage information of an utterance in comparison to the children. The adults have judged the emotions based on the way the sentences are uttered. There has been a gradual increase in the understanding of the paralanguage information with an increase in the age of the participant. For the children in the age group of 9 or below, the speaker emotion has been authenticated based on what the speaker has uttered. The lack of experience to capture the emotional cues from the spoken utterances by children has been the major reason for this discrepancy. On the other hand, although the emotionally oriented intelligibility is similar across different age groups, the younger listeners are more capable to recognize the words than the older ones (Dupuis, & Pichora-Fuller, 2014). The recognition rate has been better for high arousal emotions such as the feared speech than the emotions of lower energy such as sadness. The claimed accuracy has been better for younger adults and the talker influence on ESR accuracy has been insignificant. Among other higher arousal emotional state, the happy state has shown better accuracy as compared to the low arousal sad or neutral states (Gordon, & Hibberts 2011). The claimed accuracy is due to the portrayal of happy articulation and the positive stimuli contained in this state as advocated in the literature.

Authors in their work attempt to identify the speech emotions across younger (26 years) and older (64 years) age groups using the Toronto emotional speech dataset. The older adult listeners have been reported with a lower recognition of emotions from voice signals as claimed by the authors (Dupuis & Pichora-Fuller 2011; Ryan, Murray, & Ruffman, 2010; Mitchell 2007). Further, it is difficult for the older individual to perceive the change in amplitude modulation in the speech envelope (Grose, Mamo, & Hall, 2009; Sheldon, Pichora-Fuller, & Schneider, 2008; Souza & Boike 2006; Purcell et al. 2004). On account of removal of the vocal fine structure, by the vocoder, the cues of the amplitude envelope remain in every speech frequency bands of older adults makes it essential for the older adults to use more frequency bands for a given word recognition accuracy. Such age-related reduction in the supra-threshold auditory temporal processing is likely to prevent the older individuals to extract the essential gap, periodicity, and continuously occurring Envelope fluctuation. Hence, it is difficult for them to perceive the variation in speech and paralanguage information of human being.

An age driven ESR system using Support Vector Machine (SVM) classifier has been proposed (Verma, & Mukhopadhyay, 2016). The authors have extracted the spectral and prosodic features with their statistics to characterize the age of the speakers. The Toronto emotional speech dataset has been used to build

Table 1. The ESR accuracy (word recognition rate) across high arousal emotions (M: mean, SD: standard deviation

Parameters	Angry		Happy		Fear		Surprise		Disgust	
	M	SD	M	SD	M	SD	M	SD	M	SD
Younger adults	69.1%	17.9	69.5%	17.8	78.79%	14.91	76.5%	15.1	73.5%	16.2

separate identification system models to identify the age of the speaker. Further, ESR models are framed separately for different age groups in the SVM platform. Improved accuracy of 7% has been manifested with age-related information in modeling speech emotions as compared to the conventional ESR models without age parameters. Similarly, many few hypotheses have been tested by earlier researchers to study the effect of age on ESR or word recognition performance (Dupuis, & Pichora-Fuller, 2014). Due to perceived threat, the fear has shown the highest intelligibility followed by the surprise state and sad has shown the lowest accuracy irrespective of the chosen age groups as shown in Table 1 and Table 2.

Among the conventional clustering algorithms, the hierarchical, fuzzy c-means (FCM), K-means clustering, Grid-Based, Density-Based, Partitioning, Model-Based, etc. remain quite popular in the field of pattern recognition (Trabelsi, Ayed, & Ellouze, 2016; Morales, & Levitan, 2016; Kaur, & Vashish, 2013). The ESR accuracy using FCM and statistical parameters of speech features founds to be 63.97% approximately with SROL as reported by these authors (Zbancioc, & Ferarua, 2012). The K-means clustering algorithm with low-level descriptors such as the energy or spectral components and functionals in Weka has been used for depression detection. The authors have attempted to model the human depression states accurately with different values of 'k' in their proposed work (Morales, & Levitan, 2016). To study the proximity of the affective states, K-means clustering has been applied to the integrated corpus of the Kismet/BabyEars in Weka (Shami, & Verhelst, 2007). However, results show the ESR performance does not improve significantly due to the clustering in many cases. For a small number of clusters, the improvement has been uniform with a lower mean absolute error. Due to the presence of a small number of training features, the performance becomes worse as the value of k increases. Thus, the size of the data plays a significant role in limiting an affective state's recognition performance.

THE ISSUES

As people become older, they go in a myriad change psychologically as well as biologically. The neuro-physiological and neuroanatomical changes occur with age vary the speaking style and human affective states to a large extent. Arguably, emotional understanding and judgment differ due to a change in the

Table 2. The ESR accuracy (word recognition rate) across low arousal emotions (M: mean, SD: standard deviation)

Parameters	Sad		Neutral	
	M	SD	M	SD
Younger adults	59.57%	22.51	75.6%	17.1

linguistic and acoustic correlates. These factors make the study of human emotions across different age groups complex and challenging. For example, the unpredictable cognitive and neural functions of older adults make the study largely speculative, though testable sometimes (Glisky, 2007). Hence, the acoustic attributes describing the voice or affective states of older adults, such as the speech rate, energy, pitch, etc. are likely to differ either from that of a child or a young adult. The complexity further aggravates due to difficulties in the generation, collection, and procurement of a suitable emotional data set for SER analysis. The available emotional speech datasets are mostly recorded either from adults or children under different conditions. Most of the adult emotional speech dataset comprises of utterances of either professional actors (Jackson, & Haq, 2014; Burkhardt et al., 2005), or psychiatry patients in a clinical environment (Lyakso, et al., 2015A; Kaya, et al., 2014). The SER performance tends to vary with these datasets due to involvements of different language, genders, emotional states, speakers, etc. On the contrary, most of the child emotional datasets are spontaneous in nature. In these, the emotional clips are collected by simulating a child's affective states using the props, electronic gadgets, robots, card games, movie scenes, etc. (Pérez-Espinosa, Reyes-García, & Villaseñor-Pineda, 2011; Batliner, Steidl, & Nöth, 2008). Nevertheless, the procurement of children emotional speech corpus has to tackle many few issues such as accessibility, availability, legality, ethnicity, etc. It further demands the development of a suitable communicative scenario to simulate the veridical emotional expressions from a child. The complexity in reading the emotional aspects of a child actor from his speech makes the acted children emotional speech datasets a far reach to researchers. Finally, an emotional speech dataset involving different age groups is neither available nor accessible.

Another problem associated with developing a suitable Emotional Speech Recognition (ESR) system modeling is the adaptability and applicability of the recognizer to different age groups. Normally, a child has an underdeveloped vocal cord system with the vocal folds and vocal tract still growing. Arguably, the acoustic properties representing their emotional cues tend to be different from that of adults (Palo, Mohanty, & Chandra, 2017B; Tanner, & Tanner, 2004). Thus, a recognition system trained to characterize and identify a child emotion may not give the desired ESR accuracy in case of adults. Further, the features containing emotional information such as the fundamental frequency (F0), energy, formants, speech rate, etc. vary widely across different age groups (Lyakso, et al., 2015B). Among efficient features, the MFCC has been a widely acknowledged spectral representation of speech emotion found in most literature. It has been successfully employed in the field of ESR using different feature selection algorithms such as the PCA (Principal Component Analysis) or Supervised PCA (SPCA) (Chaudhari, & Kagalkar, 2015). The authors have focused on ESR systems that cater to different age groups. However, the ability of other acoustic parameters to identify age-related speech emotions as compared to the traditional MFCC has been rarely explored in this field. It has made the design and development of an ESR system model with discriminating and reliable feature sets across different age groups a challenging domain of research till today (Porat, Lange, & Zigel, 2010; Feld, Burkhardt, & Müller, 2010).

From these pieces of work, it can be inferred that the characterization and classification of speech emotion of people belonging to different age groups have to overcome many challenges. These issues are mainly associated with the difficulties in procurement of a suitable database of the desired size which must be balanced with gender and age. Further, the choice of reliable feature sets that performs the adequate classification task conducive to age is another issue yet to be tackled in the given scenario. Finally, the size of the feature sets and the choice of an efficient classification algorithm are few influencing factors need further attention for better ESR analysis. These factors have laid the necessary foundation for the present work. It aims to provide a comprehensive review of those factors capable to benefit the ESR accuracy with age-related human attributes.

THE DATABASE

The generation or procurement of a reliable and authenticated emotional speech dataset of human being belonging to different age group remains an ever-growing challenge. A few important issues that always creep in the collection of an authenticated database are explained briefly in this section.

- Collection of spontaneous speech emotions always associated with legal, ethical and cultural issues. It requires extensive planning, provision of suitable recording machines at the site of recording, setting the desired recording environment, removal of environmental and background disturbances or noises, selection of suitable speakers/ actors, deciding the duration of recordings, etc.
- A separate emotional speech database involving different age groups remains difficult due to the unavailability of the desired number of speakers/ volunteers/ actors. For example, in the case of children, it necessitates the desired permission from the parents/guardians or teachers to record or collect the spontaneous emotional clips using some forms of simulators or props or electronic gadgets.
- It is easy to record, procure or collect the acted emotional speech database. However, the selection of suitable professionals at different age categories makes the scheme costly. Further, the provisioning of the recording environment to all classes of people often poses difficulties
- Although there are a few adult and children databases available for research, these are not easily accessible. Additionally, the database lacks the desired number of speakers, emotions, and the number of utterances per emotions. Further, most of the datasets are not gender or age balanced and contains neutral or everyday sentences to make it linguistic independent.
- Emotional speech database of very older adults is either not available or not accessible.
- The acoustic properties characterizing the emotional content of children speech is quite different than that of an adult due to the variation in the shape and size of the vocal tract and vocal folds. This makes the comparing platform cumbersome for characterization and classification of emotions across different age groups.
- The emotions are mostly overlapped and confusing in nature such as anger/disgust/annoyance, happy/jubilant/ elation, sorrowful/ sadness/ depression, etc. Thus, the dataset requires proper labeling since the emotional descriptions are highly subjective. The choice of evaluators or multiple experts of the desired number is essential for proper annotation of the emotional states.
- To maintain generalizability, scalability, and reliability, it is essential to record a dataset of adequate size and number of emotional states. However, all the existing and accessible emotional datasets are either small or moderate size that creates difficulties in developing a suitable ESR system. Table 3 provides some frequently used emotional database by researchers.

Table 3. Details of emotional database used frequently for ESR

Database	Availability	Size	Language	Source	Age group	Number of Emotions
Berlin (EMO-DB) [Burkhardt, et al., 2005]	Free for public	493 Utterances	German	Acted	Adults (25 to 35 years)	7
SAVEE [Jackson, & Haq, 2014]	Free for public	480 utterances	English	Acted	Adults (27 to 31 years)	7
FAU Aibo[Batliner, Steidl, & Nöth, 2008]	Not free	9.2 hours of speech	German	Spontaneous	Children (10-13 years)	11
EmoChildRu [Lyakso, et al., 2015A]	Not free	20K recordings	Russian	Spontaneous	Children (3-7 years)	3
EISVDB [Wang, et al., 2016]	Not free	810 utterances	Chinese	Acted	Older adults	7
BabyEars [Slaney, & McRoberts, 2003]	Not free	509 utterances	English	Acted	Young Parents	3
Danish emotional database [Engberg, et al., 1997	Free with license	4actors _5 emotions(2words + 9sentences+2passages	Danish	Acted	Adults	5

Application of Feature Extraction Algorithms

Extraction of a reliable set of features and their judicious selection remains key to an effective recognition system (Palo, & Mohanty, 2018A; Palo, & Mohanty, 2018). The parameters describing the acoustic properties of a speech signal have often discussed by many researchers since last few decades in the field of ESR (Palo, & Mohanty, 2016C; Ayadi, Kamel, & Karray, 2011). Most of the features have been used to recognize either the children or adult emotions. The ESR system oriented to detect or cluster emotions belonging to different age groups has been rarely attempted. This motivates the author to work in this direction and as such attempts to overview the characterization and classification of emotions across different age groups. Thus, the features that describe the age information of an affected speaker have been mostly discussed. These features are confined mostly to the amplitude/ arousal level/ energy, F0, speech rate, etc. Figure 1 below provides the stages of an ESR system.

Figure 1. The stages of an ESR system

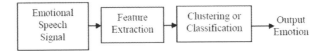

Figure 2. The variation of F0 with age for different speech emotional states

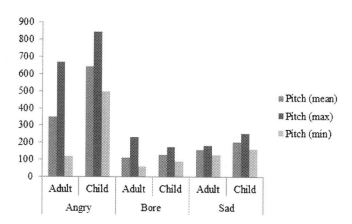

Pitch or Fundamental Frequency (f0)

The pitch (f0) depends on the vocal tract vibration that manifests the affecting states of a human being. It tends to be more in the case the speaker is either a child or a female than that of a male speaker. The variation is due to a variation in the shape, size or length of the vocal tract or the vocal fold as a person attains different age. Usually, older adults are identified with a lower pitch than younger adults (Benjamin, 1981). This has been observed by the author on experimenting forty adult speakers (20 younger and 20 older). The value of f0 continues to decrease with an increase in age, irrespective of genders (Winkler, 2007; Das, et al., 2013). The value of f0 also differs with the type of emotional attributes in a speech signal. It is higher for emotions such as angry, happy, surprise, fear, etc. as compared to the boredom or sadness. The level of arousal plays an important part in a higher pitch in these states since a person speaks with higher energy when either elated or excited or agitated [Palo, & Mohanty, 2016C; Ayadi, Kamel, & Karray, 2011].

For a speech signal '$x(n)$', the autocorrelation coefficients (ACF) can be computed using the relation

$$x(\tau) = \frac{1}{N} \sum_{n=0}^{N-1} x(n) x(n + \tau)$$

(1)

where 'τ' is the shift parameter and the term 'N' denotes the number of samples in a sequence. A higher value of ACF represented as $x(0)$ can be witnessed when $x(n)=x(n+\tau)$. The value of ACF reduces as 'τ' increases. The peaks of the ACFs can be observed at $\tau=IT$, where T denoted the time period of a signal and I is an integer. The locations of these ACFs peaks will provide us the desired f0 of a signal. The variation of f0 with the age of different speakers is shown in Figure 2 corresponding to different emotional states.

As observed from this Figure, the pitch of an adult remains low in comparison to that of a child. This is due to the large vocal tract of an adult that vibrates slower than that of the child. Further, the fully developed facial skeleton and lower larynx in adults make the f0 value low. The value of f0 in the plot forms a zigzag pattern as the database comprises samples of both genders. Among the affective states, a

Figure 3. Comparison of log energy features of chosen emotional states based on age

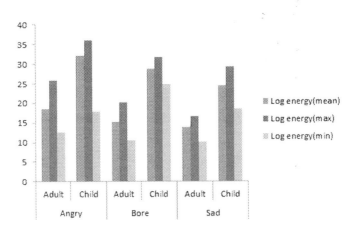

lower f0 value has been resulted from the sad or bore states as compared to the angry state irrespective of the age of the speaker. The angry state is defined by a high arousal or excitation level that results in a higher value of f0 magnitude.

Log Energy

The stress or the state of arousal varies among the different states of emotions. The energy or intensity contained in the emotional speech varies as per the type of emotions. In general, emotions described by a higher level of arousal have more high-frequency components. The speech utterance contains a large magnitude of energy/ amplitude/ intensity due to a rise in the voice of the subject during excitation of agitation. On the contrary, relaxed or dull voices have a low level of arousal, hence represented by a lower level of amplitude/ energy/ intensity. The logarithmic value of energy has been an important parameter that found useful in the field of ESR. It is preferred in contrast to the energy, to approximate the logarithmic human hearing system. The log energy of a signal can be computed as

$$E_{log}(n) = 10 log \sum_{n=1}^{N} |x(n)|^2 \qquad (2)$$

In Figure 3, the log energy values of different emotions have been compared across different age groups. As shown, the angry state is described by a higher value of log energy as compared to the sad or bore emotional states. The results are found to be true irrespective of the age of the speaker.

Figure 3 compares the variation in the log-energy magnitudes in the emotional utterances of both the children and the adults. The energy remains higher in the case of a child than that of an adult due availability of more higher-frequency components as seen in this Figure.

Speech Rate

The number of syllables or words spoken at a certain time is denoted by the speech. It signifies the time for communication during a conversation. It can serve to indicate the arousal or energy level. In general, human being speaks both faster and louder during the state of excitation or agitation. However, as a person becomes older, he suffers from a change in speech production mechanism, which again reduces the speech rate as compared to younger adults (Skoog Waller, Eriksson, & Sörqvist, 2015; Jacewicz, Fox, & Wei, 2010). The reason for this may be attributed to the psychological, hormonal, cognitive changes, the aging of the speech organs, and the deterioration of hearing mechanism (Rodr_ıguez-Aranda & Jakobsen, 2011; Xue & Hao, 2003). Thus, speech rate can serve as an important framework to determine the age as well as emotional states of a person in the field of speech science, emotional analysis, speech pathology, Neuropsychology, behavioral psychology, etc. It can be extracted as

$$SR\left(s\right) = \frac{N_V\left(s\right)}{D\left(u\right)} \tag{3}$$

where $N_v(s)$ is the number of vowel segment and $D(u)$ is the duration of an utterance.

The variation in speech rate values between two age groups (children and adult) extracted from their emotional utterances is examined in Figure 4. As shown, a child has a small speech rate due to the presence of social anxiety, as well as the reading disorder. Among other factors, the neuromuscular parameters and the biologists are the other major ingredients that reduce the speech rate of the child. As the child grows up, he/ she develop many linguistic skills (phonological, semantic, and lexical) as well as the oral-motor skills. These parameters enhance his/ her motor planning specificity which increases the articulation rate. As the child attains adulthood, the cognitive developments increase the speaking fluency hence the speech rate. In general, most of the children often take some time to find a suitable vocabulary/ words even when emotionally affected. This is due to a limited exposure either to the environment or to the language spoken. Further, a child imagines his or her own vocabulary and words as per the situations or environment rather than depending on the learning vocabularies, unlike the adults. As such, the reaction time and the speech rate reduce and the child is experienced with a lower speech rate.

Figure 4. Comparison of speech rate of the chosen emotions based on the speaker's age

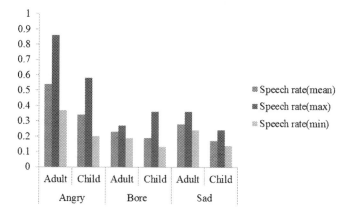

Linear Prediction Cepstral Coefficients (LPCC)

Frequency domain representation of signal remains more informative than its time domain representation. This is particularly true in case of the speech signal, as the identity of a speaker and its affective states can be easily determined by the vibration and resonance structure of the vocal cords or vocal tracts. Further, most of the prominent prosodic features such as the pitch, formants or short-time energy, describing a speaker's age, gender or qualities are spectral dependents. Among the spectral features, the Linear Prediction (LP) based features such as the LP coefficients (LPC), LP Cepstral Coefficients (LPCC), and the Perceptual LP (PLP) coefficients have been quite popularly used in the field of ESR. As compared to spectral vectors, the Cepstral vector components are usually uncorrelated, hence only means and variances are sufficient to develop an appropriate statistical model representing speech emotions and the covariance terms are not necessary. These factors have made researcher opt for an advanced LPC based technique known as LPCC [Palo, & Mohanty, 2018A, Palo, Mohanty, & Chandra, 2015]. In this method, the LPC parameters are converted into Cepstral coefficients using a recursive algorithm as given by [Palo, & Sagar, 2018E]

$$a_0' = \ln \rho^2, \qquad k = 0$$
$$a_m' = a_m + \sum_{k=1}^{m-1} \left(\frac{k}{m} \right) a_k' a_{m-k}, \quad \text{for } 1 \leq m \leq p \qquad (4)$$
$$a_m' \qquad \sum_{k=m-p}^{m-1} \left(\frac{k}{m} \right) a_k' a_{m-k}, \qquad m > p$$

where a and a' denotes the *LPC* and *LPCC* coefficients respectively, m is the number of samples per frame, ρ^2 represents the LPC model gain term and p is the number of previous samples linearly combined. The block diagram representation of the LPCC feature extraction technique is given in Figure 5.

The clustering of the LPCC features extracted from angry states of emotions has been plotted in Figure 6. The first coefficients of LPCC have been chosen to characterize the desired state of the emotions. The features in the age group of 19-34 years and 30-40 years are closely clustered to each other. These states represent the adult groups and are quite distant clustered from the angry state of children in the age group of 8-14 years. The magnitudes of LPCC coefficients are also higher in the case of adults than children. It indicates that the adults express emotion at more energy than the children.

Figure 5. The steps of LPCC feature extraction technique

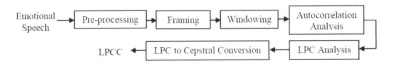

Mel-Frequency Cepstral Coefficients (MFCC)

Among other Cepstral based features, the MFCC has been widely acknowledged in the field of ESR during last few decades [Palo, Chandra, & Mohanty, 2018C; Palo, Chandra, & Mohanty, 2016B]. . The The baseline accuracy has been 65.5%, 68.1%, 68.5%, and 69.1% using the stand-alone MFCC, MFCC+ jitter, MFCC+ shimmer, MFCC + jitter+ shimmer respectively (Ayadi, Kamel, & Karray, 2011). The technique takes into account both the non-linear loudness and pitch perception. It has outperformed the prosodic as well as the LP based features that include the LPCC and PLP (Farhoudi, Setayeshi, & Rabiee, 2017; Pan, Shen, & Shen, 2012). The reported ESR accuracy has been 56.1% with LPCC technique whereas, it has been 59.0% with MFCC features (Nwe, Foo, & De Silva, 2003). The authors have experienced the performance when the Hidden Markov Model (HMM) classifier has been simulated to features extracted from a locally generated Burmese emotional database having six emotional states. Figure 7 provides a method of MFCC feature extraction. It uses a Mel scale and the feature extraction procedure is similar to the PLP technique in which a Bark scale is employed.

MFCC technique uses a Mel-scale in the filter bank so as to space the frequency to approximate the critical band. The Mel-scale frequency is given by [Davis, & Mermelstein, 1980]

$$F^m = 2595 \ \log_{10} \left(\frac{F}{700} + 1 \right) \tag{5}$$

Figure 8 plots the distribution of MFCC magnitude by forming different cluster centers using the K-means algorithm. The first MFCC coefficients extracted from emotional speech database in the age

Figure 6. Clustering using LPCC coefficient for angry state of across different age groups

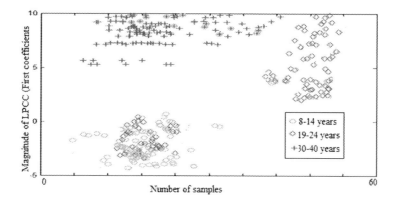

Figure 7. The steps of MFCC feature extraction technique

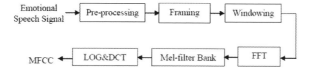

Figure 8. Clustering using MFCC coefficient for happy state across different age groups

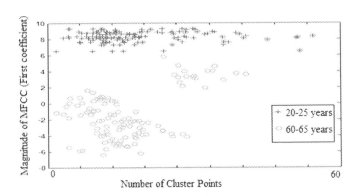

group of 20-25 years and 60-65 years have been used to characterize the happy emotional state. As observed, the features belonging to younger adults (20-25 years) are found to have higher energy components or first MFCC magnitudes than that of older people (60-65 years). It shows, the degradation of voice quality, production mechanism, and age related issues has the effect that segments the older people from adult groups.

THE CLUSTERING TECHNIQUES

Among these different clustering approaches, the work emphasizes on Fuzzy C-means (FCM) and K-means clustering algorithms. Use of these algorithms has been explored to characterize and classify the emotional states earlier [Palo, Mohanty, & Chandra, 2017A]. The authors emphasize on clustering of prosodic features extracted from the emotional utterance belonging to different age groups. The investigated emotions are sadness, boredom, and anger. It has been observed that while the K-means follows hard clustering, the FCM relies on soft clustering. The K-means approach has the ability to solve known clustering problems and is simple to simulate. It produces more dense clusters in comparison to the conventional hierarchical clustering and is faster. An improved in speech emotional accuracy has been manifested with K-means as compared to the Fuzzy C-means using Gaussian Mixture and Support Vector Models using an exclusive clustering approach [Trabelsi, Ayed, & Ellouze, 2016]. On the other hand, the FCM is a compatible and overlapped clustering algorithm used in the identification of patterns associated with a variation in clusters.

K-Means Clustering

It is a simple unsupervised learning clustering algorithms which classify a chosen feature sets using k-clusters fixed a priori corresponding to k-centroids. While clustering, each feature seeks to search the nearest centroid and get associated with it. Let, 'L' signifies the numbers of feature coefficient's corresponding to a specific category that have been extracted from the voice samples of all emotional states. In order to segment these feature values into P number of clusters, we need to define cluster center D_p, $p=1,2,\ldots,P$ corresponding to each cluster. The approach minimizes an objective function 'b' using a squared error function to form clusters. In the process, it ensures an adequate emotional cluster by seeking an optimal convergence of 'b' (Palo, Mohanty, & Chandra, 2016A). The objective function can be represented as

$$b = \sum_{p=1}^{P}\sum_{l=1}^{L} s_l^{(p)} - D_p^{\;2} \tag{6}$$

where $\|\;\|$ denotes a distance norm between D_p and the data point $s_l^{(p)}$. The application of K-means clustering can be solemnized in the following steps.

From every P feature point, choose the corresponding centroid.

1. Compute P cluster iteratively, by assigning all the extracted feature values to its corresponding closest centroid.
2. Update the centroids by iteratively computing the cluster centers until the further variation in the cluster center is not manifested.

Although the algorithm is said to converge in some cases, it is not a necessary condition. Further, the algorithm is sensitive to the selection of initial random cluster centers. Thus, the algorithm needs to run multiple times to obtain the desired degree of convergence and a level of clustering.

In Figure 9 the K-means algorithm has been used to cluster the speech rate across different age groups.

It can be observed that the feature coefficients extracted from the utterances of in the age group of 19-24 years and 30-40 years are clustered very close to each other. These groups are considered to fall in a similar category with features having a similar range of values. As compared to this, the feature values of the children (age group of 8-14 tears) found to be widely separated from these above categories.

A comparison among sad emotional states across different age groups has been made using the K-means algorithm in Figure 10 using the pitch. The cluster points of the pitch features are widely separated as expected when the age groups of 8-14 years and 30-40 years are compared.

Figure 9. K-means clustering of speech rate extracted from the angry speech utterances across different age groups

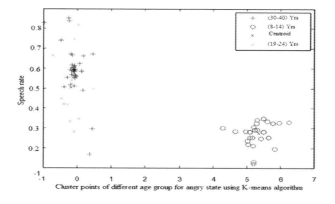

Figure 10. K-means clustering of pitch features extracted from the angry speech utterances across different age groups

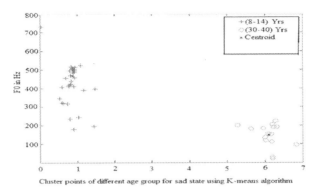

Figure 11. K-means clustering of log energy features extracted from the bore speech utterances across different age groups

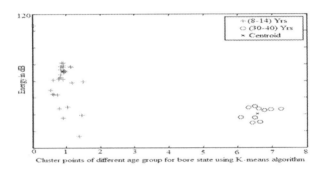

The K-means clustering has been used to partition the boredom state across different age group using the log energy features in Figure 11 for boredom state. It has been possible to cluster these age groups separately using the extracted features as observed from this Figure.

Fuzzy C-Means (FCM) Clustering

It is possible to associate a single parameter to more than one cluster using the FCM clustering algorithm. The application of fuzzy logic in the field of ESR has been explored earlier using the spectral and prosodic parameters (Ram, et al., 2016). The focus has been to classify adult speech emotions rather than clustering. Nevertheless, it has been used to cluster sad state of emotions with effective results [Palo, Mohanty, & Chandra, 2016A]. The authors used the FCM clustering algorithm to segment emotions across different age groups. In this approach, every feature value has been involved with more than one cluster. An iterative optimization algorithm has been used to approximate the objective function 'b' to the minimum. Let's define a feature space Q^l with the desired feature vectors with each feature vector comprised of L real numbers $x = \{x_1, x_2, \ldots, x_l\}$, $s \in Q^l$. For each subset x' corresponding to Q^l, an objective function $b' : x' \rightarrow [0,1]$ is assigned in the fuzzy set x' for every $x \in x'$ with a membership grade. The process allocates a weighting exponent of '*m*' to the corresponding membership grade so as to partition the desired feature groups or class.

Assuming a feature subset $x' \subseteq Q^l$, $x' = \{x_1, x_2, \ldots, x_n\}$, The fuzzy partition set c of x' can be described by a matrix $U \in R_{fc}$, $U = \{x_1', x_2', \ldots, x_n'\}$, $2 \leq c \leq n$. Here, '*n*' denotes the number of feature values in a subset whereas, the FCM functional $P_m : R_{fc} \times Q^{cL} \rightarrow Q^+$ is given as

$$P_m(U, x') = \sum_{i=1}^{n} \sum_{j=1}^{c} (v_{ji})^m (d_{ji})^2 \tag{7}$$

where $x_j' \in Q^L$, $1 \leq j \leq c$, represents *j*-the class cluster center, $d_{ji} = \|x_i - x_j'\|$, $\|\ \|$ is the distant norm and $x' = (x_1', x_2', \ldots, x_c') \in Q^{cL}$ respectively. The mth power of the squared distance weighting corresponding to the jth cluster membership of datum '*x*' has been used here. In this case, 'P_m' is considered to possess the squared error criterion. It is minimized iteratively to optimize the clustering using a fuzzy set. The algorithm provides the fuzzy c partition of the feature set described by $x' = \{x_1, x_2, \ldots, x_n\}$. The FCM algorithm is implemented using the following steps.

- Fix the weighting exponent '*m*'and the number of clusters '*c*' where $2 \leq c \leq n$ and, $1 \leq m \leq \infty$.
- Choose $\|\ \|$ and initialize the fuzzy c partition $U^{(0)}$ using $x - x_B'^2 = (x - x')^T B(x - x')$, where $B \in R_{LL}$ is positive definite.
- Follow step 'k', $k=0,1,2,\ldots,$.
- Compute '*c*' number of cluster centers using $\left\{ x_j'^{(k)} \right\}$ with $U^{(0)}$. The jth cluster center is computed as

$$x_{jp}' = \frac{\sum_{i=1}^{n} (x_{ji}')^m . x_{ip}}{\sum_{i=1}^{n} (x_{ji}')^m}, p = 1,2,\ldots, L \tag{8}$$

- Update $U^{(k)}$ to find the memberships in $U^{(k+1)}$ as per the given procedure.
  For i=1 to n,compute J_i and $\bar{J}_i$ using

$$J_i = \left\{ j \mid 1 \leq j \leq c, d_{ji} = x_i - x_j' = 0 \right\}, \bar{J}_i = \left\{ 1,2,\ldots, c \right\} - J_i ;$$

  b) Estimate the new membership functions with respect to the feature values i
      If J_i=δ,

$$x'_{ji} = \cfrac{1}{\sum_{p=1}^{c} \left(\cfrac{d_{ji}}{d_{pi}} \right)^{2/(m-1)}} \tag{9}$$

ii)   else make $x'_{ji} = 0$ for all $j \in \overline{J}_i$ and $\sum_{j \in J_i} x'_{ji} = 1$;

- Stop iteration if $U^{(k)}\text{-}U < \tau$, where τ denotes the error threshold in a convenient matrix norm
- Else, set $k=k+1$ and continue with the above procedure.

The FCM algorithm has been used to cluster the emotions across different age groups by plotting the objective function 'b' against the number of iterations. In the FCM clustering process, every feature values of an utterance are assigned with membership grade or MG. The desired cluster is achieved by updating the MG iteratively. For optimum clustering, the objective function is minimized by shifting the specific cluster center and updating the MG weights correspondingly. In this work, a default value of 2.0 has been used as the exponent partition or the membership function matrix. A different number of iterations have been used to implement the algorithm with an improvement factor of 0.00001. The stopping criterion is fixed either when the designated maximum iteration has been reached or when the objective functions between two consecutive iterations unable to improve further below the set improvement factor. Figure 12 represents the variation in the 'b' versus the number of iterations during the process of clustering with log energy features for the sad state across different age groups. It has been observed that the objective function converges at a value of 3004.49 with 22 iterations.

The convergence of the objective function vs. the number of iterations during the process of clustering across different age groups for the angry state of emotion is shown in Figure 13. The convergence founds to fall at a value of 377.6 with 12 iterations using the pitch values. The convergence is found to occur at 0.269 with 23 iterations for the speech rate parameters of bore state as shown in Figure 14. Observation of Figures 12 through Figure 14 indicates that the rate of decay of the objective function and its exponential smoothness remains more effective for speech rate as compared to either the pitch or the Log energy.

The FCM clustering using the speech rate of bore emotional state across different age groups is shown in Figure 15. The features form close proximity among the age groups of 19-24 years and 30-40 years

Figure 12. The graphical representation of the objective function 'b' vs. the number of iteration for sad state using the log energy features indicating the progress of clustering

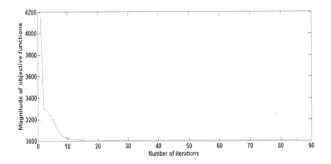

Figure 13. The graphical representation of the objective function 'b' vs. the number of iteration for angry state using the pitch features indicating the progress of clustering

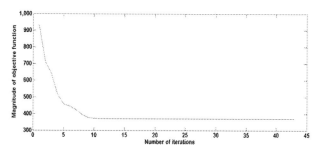

Figure 14. The graphical representation of the objective function 'b' vs. the number of iteration for bore state using the speech rate features indicating the progress of clustering

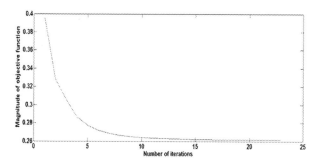

respectively. The magnitudes of the speech rate values mostly fall above 0.5 with adult database containing bore utterances. However, the values for children bore utterances are clustered below 0.5. When the FCM clustering using the pitch value is investigated, we observe similar closeness among two adult age groups (19-24 years and 30-40 years). The result is found to be true even when angry utterances have been used as shown in Figure 16. However, the magnitude of the fundamental frequency remains higher in the case of children as compared to adults.

An investigation of the FCM clustering across different age groups has been made using the log energy magnitudes in Figure 17. An analysis of a sad state with this set-up allows a boundary to demarcate the different age groups as observed in this Figure. The adult groups tend to be closely clustered similar to the observation made in Figure 15 and figure 16 earlier.

Table 4 provides a comparison of different gender independent prosodic features that have been analyzed for adult emotional states by the different researcher in this domain.

A Comparison of prosodic features, among children and adults emotional states has been tabulated in Table 5. The statistical log energy values such as the mean, minimum, and maximum remain higher for a child's voice as observed from this table. A child remains more enthusiastic and excited during an emotional encounter or when subjected to a certain abnormal situation. This has been manifested with a higher level of energy in children as compared to that of an adult. On the other hand, the adults remain judgmental and well-matured thus, emotionally more controlled and balanced that suppressed their energy level. On the other hand, the adults remain judgmental and well-matured, thus, emotionally more

Figure 15. FCM clustering of speech rate features extracted from the bore speech utterances across different age groups

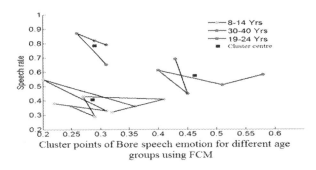

Figure 16. FCM clustering of pitch features extracted from the angry speech utterances across different age groups

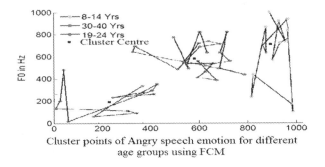

Figure 17. FCM clustering of log energy features extracted from the sad speech utterances across different age groups

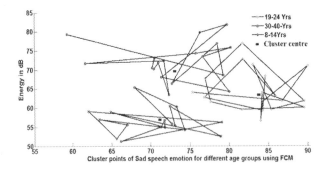

controlled and balanced that suppressed their energy level. Similarly, higher statistical pitch values have been observed with child's utterances than that of adults. These results are observed to be true irrespective of the type of emotion tested. Similar experiments have been conducted by earlier researchers using the variation in pitch values and the statistical parameters (Rathina, Mehata, & Ponnavaikko, 2012; Banse, & Scherer, 1996; Sauter, et al., 2010). The authors have investigated different gender independent adult emotional states such as anger, boredom, and happiness. A highest mean f0 has been observed by anger,

Table 4. Comparative study of the state of art age and gender dependent feature extraction techniques

Features	Emotions					
	Angry	Sad	Fear	Happy	Bore	Disgust
Speech rate [Laukka, et al., 2005]	↑↑	↓↓	↑↑↑	↑	↓	↑↑↑
F1 [Banse & Scherer, 1996; Laukka, et al., 2005; Sauter, et al., 2010; Rathina, et al., 2012]	↑↑↑	↓↓	↑	↑↑	↓	↑↑
F0 Variance [Banse & Scherer, 1996; Rathina, et al., 2012]	↑↑↑	↓	↑	↑↑	↓↓	↓
F0 mean [Banse & Scherer, 1996; Rathina, et al., 2012]	↑↑↑	↓	↑	↑↑	↓↓	↓↓↓
Energy [Maca, et al., 2016; Palo, & Mohanty, 2016C]	↑↑↑	↓↓	↑	↑↑	↓↓	↑↑
Spectral centroid [Sauter, et al., 2010]	↑↑↑	↓↓	↑	↑↑	↓↓↓	↓
Duration [Sauter, et al., 2010]	↓↓	↑↑↑	↑	↑	↑↑	↓
↑= increase, ↓= decrease						

Table 5. Comparison of prosodic features among children and adults

Features	Angry		Bore		Sad	
	Adult	Child	Adult	Child	Adult	Child
Speech rate(mean)	0.54	0.34	0.23	0.19	0.28	0.17
Speech rate(max)	0.86	0.58	0.27	0.36	0.36	0.24
Speech rate(min)	0.37	0.20	0.19	0.13	0.24	0.14
Pitch (mean)	350.7	643.5	109.3	127.9	155.3	204.2
Pitch (max)	667	844	231	175	183	255
Pitch (min)	120	495	61	89	126	162
Log energy(mean)	18.5	32.1	15.2	28.8	13.9	24.6
Log energy(max)	25.9	36.1	20.2	31.7	16.8	29.3
Log energy(min)	12.7	17.8	10.5	24.9	10.2	18.5

emotional state followed by the happy state, whereas, the lowest mean f0 has been experienced with the boring state. The statistical parameters of the speech rate show a lower value for children's utterances across all the emotional states. The fear and the angry state have shown a higher magnitude of speech rate as compared to either the sadness or poor state as reported in this field (Laukka, Patrik, & Roberto, 2005; Sauter, et al., 2010). From these surveys and our results, it can be concluded that the speech rate or time is taken by a person during emotional expression has been lower when Meticulous observation of the duration feature indicates that a person is quick to express his affective states during the state of aggression or agitation or elation.

Table 6 compares the real-time computation factor between the K-means and the FCM algorithm. The time of clustering varies with the type of features extracted as observed in the Table. It is lowest in the case of the speech rate as compared to either the f0 or the log-energy features. The K-means clustering algorithm founds to outperform the FCM with better clustering and the computation time. Involvement of fuzziness and the soft clustering approach in the FCM has been the major reason of its drawbacks.

Table 6. A comparison of computation time to cluster different features using the FCM and K-means clustering techniques

Computation Time (in seconds)			
Clustering Algorithm	**Time to Cluster**		
	Log energy	**Pitch**	**Speech rate**
FCM	0.30	0.29	0.24
K-means	0.20	0.23	0.18

Further, the K-means remains a better algorithm for exclusive clustering which suits our case since the extracted features comprising of exclusive age group.

CONCLUSION

This paper provides an overview of the feature extraction techniques that provide age-related information on affective states of a human voice signal. A detailed survey of the databases pertaining to emotional speech information across different age groups has been tabulated. It describes the importance of clustering algorithms in characterizing and segmentation of speech emotions belonging to different age groups. In particular, the FCM and K-means algorithms have been explored with few simulation results of different emotions. The relative advantages and the limitations of these feature extraction techniques and the clustering algorithms are analyzed to explore their application domain. It is possible to demarcate human age using age-related prosodic features with the discussed clustering algorithms. The investigation of other clustering algorithms and discriminating features will provide new avenues in this field for future researchers. The outcomes of these ESR systems can provide psychological assistant to children affected with psychological trauma or negative emotions. Service industries in the area of telecommunications, meeting browser, speech translation, human-robotic interfaces, assessment systems, smart call center, smart workspaces, intelligent tutoring, dialogue and language learning systems, forensic labs, etc. can be managed more efficiently using these systems. However, the availability of databases spanning different age groups has been quite difficult to access or collect in the current scenario. In future, such efforts towards database generation and reliable feature extraction may help in modeling a suitable ESR model more efficiently.

REFERENCES

Ayadi, M. E., Kamel, M. S., & Karray, F. (2011). Survey on speech recognition: Resources, features and methods. *Pattern Recognition*, *44*, 572–587. doi:10.1016/j.patcog.2010.09.020

Banse, R., & Scherer, K. R. (1996). Acoustic profiles in vocal emotion expression. *Journal of Personality and Social Psychology*, *70*(3), 614–636. doi:10.1037/0022-3514.70.3.614 PMID:8851745

Batliner, A., Steidl, S., & Nöth, E. (2008, May). Releasing a thoroughly annotated and processed spontaneous emotional database: the FAU Aibo Emotion Corpus. *Proc. of a Satellite Workshop of LREC*, 28.

Benjamin, B. J. (1981). Frequency variability in the aged voice. *Journal of Gerontology, 36*(6), 722–726. doi:10.1093/geronj/36.6.722 PMID:7299089

Burkhardt, F., Paeschke, A., Rolfes, M., Sendlmeier, W. F., & Weiss, B. (2005). A database of German emotional speech. *Ninth European Conference on Speech Communication and Technology.*

Chaudhari, J. S., & Kagalkar, R. M. (2015A). Methodology for Gender Identification, Classification and Recognition of Human Age. *International Journal of Computer Applications.*

Chaudhari, S. J., & Kagalkar, R. M. (2015B). Automatic speaker age estimation and gender dependent emotion recognition. *International Journal of Computers and Applications, 117*(17), 5–10. doi:10.5120/20644-3383

Das, B., Mandal, S., Mitra, P., & Basu, A. (2013). Effect of aging on speech features and phoneme recognition: A study on Bengali voicing vowels. *International Journal of Speech Technology, 16*(1), 19–31. doi:10.100710772-012-9147-3

Davis, S., & Mermelstein, P. (1980). Comparison of parametric representations for monosyllabic word recognition in continuously spoken sentences. *IEEE Transactions on Acoustics, Speech, and Signal Processing, 28*(4), 357–366. doi:10.1109/TASSP.1980.1163420

Dupuis, K., & Pichora-Fuller, M. K. (2011). Recognition of emotional speech for younger and older talkers: Behavioural findings from the Toronto Emotional Speech Set. *Canadian Acoustics, 39*(3), 182–183.

Dupuis, K., & Pichora-Fuller, M. K. (2014). Intelligibility of emotional speech in younger and older adults. *Ear and Hearing, 35*(6), 695–707. doi:10.1097/AUD.0000000000000082 PMID:25127327

Engberg, I. S., Hansen, A. V., Andersen, O., & Dalsgaard, P. (1997). Design, recording and verification of a Danish emotional speech database. *Fifth European Conference on Speech Communication and Technology.*

Farhoudi, Z., Setayeshi, S., & Rabiee, A. (2017). Using learning automata in brain emotional learning for speech emotion recognition. *International Journal of Speech Technology, 20*(3), 553–562. doi:10.100710772-017-9426-0

Feld, M., Burkhardt, F., & Müller, C. (2010). *Automatic speaker age and gender recognition in the car for tailoring dialog and mobile services.* Interspeech.

Glisky, E. L. (2007). Changes in cognitive function in human aging. Brain aging: Models, Methods, and Mechanisms, 3-20.

Gordon, M. S., & Hibberts, M. (2011). Audiovisual speech from emotionally expressive and lateralized faces. *Q J Exp Psychol (Hove), 64*(4), 730–750. doi:10.1080/17470218.2010.516835 PMID:20945268

Grose, J. H., Mamo, S. K., & Hall, J. W. III. (2009). Age effects in temporal envelope processing: Speech unmasking and auditory steady state responses. *Ear and Hearing, 30*(5), 568–575. doi:10.1097/AUD.0b013e3181ac128f PMID:19633565

Hämäläinen, A., Meinedo, H., Tjalve, M., Pellegrini, P., Trancoso, I., & Dias, M. S. (2011). Improving speech recognition through automatic selection of age group–Specific Acoustic Models. ADFA, 1.

Jacewicz, E., Fox, R. A., & Wei, L. (2010). Between-speaker and within-speaker variation in speech tempo of American English. *The Journal of the Acoustical Society of America, 128*(2), 839–850. doi:10.1121/1.3459842 PMID:20707453

Jackson, P., & Haq, S. (2014). *Surrey audio-visual expressed emotion (savee) database*. Guildford, UK: University of Surrey.

Kaur, J., & Vashish, S. (2013). Analysis of different clustering techniques for detecting human emotions variation through data mining. *International Journal of Computer Science Engineering and Information Technology Research, 3*(2), 27–36. doi:10.5815/ijitcs.2013.07.03

Kaya, H., Salah, A. A., Gürgen, S. F., & Ekenel, H. (2014, April). Protocol and baseline for experiments on Bogazici University Turkish emotional speech corpus. In *2014 22nd Signal Processing and Communications Applications Conference (SIU)* (pp. 1698-1701). IEEE. 10.1109/SIU.2014.6830575

Laukka, P., Patrik, J., & Roberto, B. (2005). A dimensional approach to vocal expression of emotion. *Cognition and Emotion, 19*(5), 633–653. doi:10.1080/02699930441000445

Lyakso, E., & Frolova, O. (2015B, September). Emotion state manifestation in voice features: chimpanzees, human infants, children, adults. In *International Conference on Speech and Computer* (pp. 201-208). Springer. 10.1007/978-3-319-23132-7_25

Lyakso, E., Frolova, O., Dmitrieva, E., Grigorev, A., Kaya, H., Salah, A. A., & Karpov, A. (2015A). EmoChildRu: emotional child Russian speech corpus. *Speech and Computer, 17*th *International Conference*, 144-152.

Maca, V. M. M., Espada, J. P., Diaz, V. G., & Semwal, V. B. (2016). Measurement of viewer sentiment to improve the quality of television and interactive content using adaptive content. *International conference on electrical, electronics, and optimization techniques*, 4445-4450.

Mitchell, R. L. C. (2007). Age-related decline in the ability to decode emotional prosody: Primary or secondary phenomenon? *Cognition and Emotion, 21*(7), 1435–1454. doi:10.1080/02699930601133994

Morales, M. R., & Levitan, R. (2016). Mitigating confounding factors in depression detection using an unsupervised clustering approach. *Proceedings of the 2016 Computing and Mental Health Workshop*.

Morton, J. B., & Trehub, S. E. (2001). Children's understanding of emotion in speech. *Child Development, 72*(3), 834–843. doi:10.1111/1467-8624.00318 PMID:11405585

Nishio, M., & Niimi, S. (2008). Changes in speaking fundamental frequency characteristics with aging. *Folia Phoniatrica et Logopaedica, 60*(3), 120–127. doi:10.1159/000118510 PMID:18305390

Nwe, T. L., Foo, S. W., & De Silva, L. C. (2003). Speech emotion recognition using hidden Markov models. *Speech Communication, 41*(4), 603–623. doi:10.1016/S0167-6393(03)00099-2

Palo, H. K., Chandra, M., & Mohanty, M. N. (2017B). Emotion recognition using MLP and GMM for Oriya language. *International Journal of Computational Vision and Robotics, 7*(4), 426–442. doi:10.1504/IJCVR.2017.084987

Palo, H. K., Chandra, M., & Mohanty, M. N. (2018C). Recognition of Human Speech Emotion Using Variants of Mel-Frequency Cepstral Coefficients. In *Advances in Systems, Control and Automation* (pp. 491–498). Singapore: Springer. doi:10.1007/978-981-10-4762-6_47

Palo, H. K., & Mohanty, M. N. (2016B). Modified-VQ Features for Speech Emotion Recognition. *Journal of Applied Sciences (Faisalabad)*, *16*(9), 406–418. doi:10.3923/jas.2016.406.418

Palo, H. K., & Mohanty, M. N. (2016C). Performance analysis of emotion recognition from speech using combined prosodic features. *Advanced Science Letters*, *22*(2), 288–293.

Palo, H. K., & Mohanty, M. N. (2018A). Comparative analysis of neural networks for speech motion recognition. *IACSIT International Journal of Engineering and Technology*, *7*(4), 112–116.

Palo, H. K., & Mohanty, M. N. (2018B). Wavelet based feature combination for recognition of emotions. *Ain Shams Engineering Journal*, *9*(4), 1799–1806. doi:10.1016/j.asej.2016.11.001

Palo, H. K., Mohanty, M. N., & Chandra, M. (2015). Design of neural network model for emotional speech recognition. In *Artificial intelligence and evolutionary algorithms in engineering systems* (pp. 291–300). New Delhi: Springer. doi:10.1007/978-81-322-2135-7_32

Palo, H. K., Mohanty, M. N., & Chandra, M. (2016A). Sad state analysis of speech signals using different clustering algorithm. In *2016 2nd International Conference on Next Generation Computing Technologies (NGCT)* (pp. 714-718). IEEE. 10.1109/NGCT.2016.7877504

Palo, H. K., Mohanty, M. N., & Chandra, M. (2017A). Emotion Analysis from Speech of Different Age Groups. *Proceedings of the Second International Conference on Research in Intelligent and Computing in Engineering*, 283–287. 10.15439/2017R21

Palo, H. K., Mohanty, M. N., & Chandra, M. (2018D). Speech Emotion Analysis of Different Age Groups Using Clustering Techniques. *International Journal of Information Retrieval Research*, *8*(1), 69–85. doi:10.4018/IJIRR.2018010105

Palo, H. K., & Sagar, S. (2018E, September). Comparison of Neural Network Models for Speech Emotion Recognition. In *2018 2nd International Conference on Data Science and Business Analytics (ICDSBA)* (pp. 127-131). IEEE. 10.1109/ICDSBA.2018.00030

Pan, Y., Shen, P., & Shen, L. (2012). Speech emotion recognition using support vector machine. *International Journal of Smart Home*, *6*(2), 101–108.

Pérez-Espinosa, H., Reyes-García, C. A., & Villaseñor-Pineda, L. (2011). EmoWisconsin: an emotional children speech database in Mexican Spanish. In *Affective Computing and Intelligent Interaction* (pp. 62–71). Berlin: Springer. doi:10.1007/978-3-642-24571-8_7

Porat, R., Lange, D., & Zigel, Y. (2010). *Age recognition based on speech signals using weights super vector.* Interspeech.

Purcell, D. W., John, S. M., Schneider, B. A., & Picton, T. W. (2004). Human temporal auditory acuity as assessed by auditory steady state responses. *The Journal of the Acoustical Society of America*, *116*, 3581–3593. doi:10.1121/1.1798354 PMID:15658709

Ram, R., Palo, H. K., Mohanty, M. N., & Suresh, L. P. (2016). Design of FIS-Based Model for Emotional Speech Recognition. *Proc. of the International Conference on Soft Computing Systems, Advances in Intelligent Systems and Computing*, 77-88. 10.1007/978-81-322-2671-0_8

Rathina, X. A., Mehata, K. M., & Ponnavaikko, M. (2012). Basic analysis on prosodic features in emotional speech. *International Journal of Computer Science Engineering and Applications*, 2(4), 99.

Rodrıguez-Aranda, C., & Jakobsen, M. (2011). Differential contribution of cognitive and psychomotor functions to the age-related slowing of speech production. *Journal of the International Neuropsychological Society*, 17, 1–15.

Ryan, M., Murray, J., & Ruffman, T. (2010). Aging and the perception of emotion: Processing vocal expressions alone and with faces. *Experimental Aging Research*, 36(1), 1–22. doi:10.1080/03610730903418372 PMID:20054724

Sauter, D. A., Eisner, F., Calder, A. J., & Scott, S. K. (2010). Perceptual cues in nonverbal vocal expressions of emotion. *Quarterly Journal of Experimental Psychology*, 63(11), 2251–2272. doi:10.1080/17470211003721642 PMID:20437296

Shami, M., & Verhelst, W. (2007). Automatic classification of expressiveness in speech: a multi-corpus study. In *Speaker classification II* (pp. 43–56). Berlin: Springer. doi:10.1007/978-3-540-74122-0_5

Sheldon, S., Pichora-Fuller, M. K., & Schneider, B. A. (2008). Effect of age, presentation method, and learning on identification of noise-vocoded words. *The Journal of the Acoustical Society of America*, 123(1), 476–488. doi:10.1121/1.2805676 PMID:18177175

Skoog Waller, S., Eriksson, M., & Sörqvist, P. (2015). Can you hear my age? Influences of speech rate and speech spontaneity on estimation of speaker age. *Frontiers in Psychology*, 6, 978. doi:10.3389/fpsyg.2015.00978 PMID:26236259

Slaney, M., & McRoberts, G. (2003). BabyEars: A recognition system for affective vocalizations. *Speech Communication*, 39(3-4), 367–384. doi:10.1016/S0167-6393(02)00049-3

Souza, P. E., & Boike, K. T. (2006). Combining temporal-envelope cues across channels: Effects of age and hearing loss. *Journal of Speech, Language, and Hearing Research: JSLHR*, 49(1), 138–149. doi:10.1044/1092-4388(2006/011) PMID:16533079

Tanner, D. C., & Tanner, M. E. (2004). *Forensic aspects of speech patterns: voice prints, speaker profiling, lie and intoxication detection*. Lawyers & Judges Publishing.

Trabelsi, I., Ayed, D. B., & Ellouze, N. (2016). Comparison between GMM-SVM sequence kernel and GMM: Application to speech emotion recognition. *Journal of Engineering Science and Technology*, 11(9), 1221–1233.

Udhan, T. (2016). Emotion Recognition using Fuzzy Clustering Analysis. Georgia Southern University.

Verma, D., & Mukhopadhyay, D. (2016, April). Age driven automatic speech emotion recognition system. In *2016 International Conference on Computing, Communication and Automation (ICCCA)* (pp. 1005-1010). IEEE. 10.1109/CCAA.2016.7813862

Wang, K., Zhu, Z., Wang, S., Sun, X., & Li, L. (2016, June). A database for emotional interactions of the elderly. In *2016 IEEE/ACIS 15th International Conference on Computer and Information Science (ICIS)* (pp. 1-6). IEEE. 10.1109/ICIS.2016.7550902

Winkler, R. (2007). Influences of pitch and speech rate on the perception of age from voice. *Proc. of ICPhS*, 1849-1852.

Xue, S. A., & Hao, G. J. (2003). Changes in the human vocal tract due to aging and the acoustic correlates of speech production: A pilot study. *Journal of Speech, Language, and Hearing Research: JSLHR*, *46*(3), 689–701. doi:10.1044/1092-4388(2003/054) PMID:14696995

Zbancioc, M., & Ferarua, M. (2012). *A Study about the Statistical Parameters Used in the Emotion Recognition*. In 11th International Conference on development and application systems, Suceava, Romania.

198

Chapter 10
Some Aspects of Reliability Estimation of Loosely Coupled Web Services in Clustered Load Balancing Web Server

Abhijit Bora
Gauhati University, India

Tulshi Bezboruah
Gauhati University, India

ABSTRACT

Reliability of loosely coupled services through the paradigm of service-oriented computing and observing their fault tolerance against massive load in clustered load balancing web server plays an important role while evaluating the quality aspects of software-as-a-service (SaaS), grid, and distributed systems. This chapter shows some aspects of service execution while observing their failure records against massive execution of server-side instruction. A novel reliability estimation framework is proposed that can be deployed for evaluating the reliability of service execution over clustered load balancing web server. A load generating tool is used to generate massive load over the service execution. In this study we will discuss an experimental system and its architecture by using clustered load balancing web server, the reliability estimation framework along with the goodness of fit study through statistical analysis. The overall assessment of the work will validate the applicability of the proposed framework for the loosely coupled service in clustered load balancing web server.

INTRODUCTION

Web Service (WS) provides a framework for deploying computational task in a flexible manner. It provides a platform where one can deploy different architecture of grid and distributed system, Internet of Things (IoT) and Software as a system (SaaS) applications. It supports interoperability among heterogeneous modules of loosely coupled software models. It follows the methodology of discovering, consuming and

DOI: 10.4018/978-1-7998-1021-6.ch010

publishing over public domains, which are key principles of Service Oriented Architecture (SOA). It enhances the principles of reusability and integration of remote service. The SOA is not bound to technology. Different programming languages over network based protocol can be followed for deployment. The powerful features of Extensible Markup Language (XML) can be included for sharing different services among business modules. Recently, WSs are deployed for inter machine communication. It supports different adaptability of connections over different platform independent terminals.

The WS supports modularity, interoperability and reusability. However, numbers of studies are carried out for observing the quality aspects of such deployment. From the perspective of software industry, the stakeholders such as consumers and service providers are keen interested for evaluating the quality report of such service. Basically, the service consumers are interested for evaluating the quality aspects of service, while the service providers are interested for evaluating the execution aspects of service. The validity and applicability of the service is also verified by the consumer before deploying such WS for their own business needs. The service providers publish their services over public registries where the service consumer can identify and consume it as required. Different WS may have different business parameters and decision model. Based on the requirement of the organization, the consumer usually termed as WS client establishes necessary communication with the service providers.

Many prominent consumers are utilizing the features of WS in their respective business models. They deploy to provide better and quality service to end users. The primary goal of service providers is to satisfy their consumer through flexible and in a better manner. However, over years, the end users of WS are increasing prominently. As such, delivering the service during high usage of service period is becoming an important concern. However, clustering the web server and deploying a load balancer machine can provide a better service towards the heavy usage of service. From the perspective of the exponential growth of requirement demands and organizational infrastructure, the deployment of loosely coupled WS and assessing their reliability against high usages has become a key concern among researchers. As such, this study will highlight a novel reliability evaluation framework and some important aspects of loosely coupled WS execution against high usage of service. The contribution in this chapter is an extension of the work that was discussed elsewhere (Bora et al., 2018b).

BACKGROUND

WS is the platform where one can deploy software modules as service agents. It supports configuration of loosely or tightly coupled software modules for business process. It provides a programmable interface where the integration of different functional logic can be executed (Matthew et al., 2005). The internal configuration files and data structure of WS is omitted from outside world. As such, the consumer simply utilizes the basic operation of WS. The overall service computing that comprises of service delivery, execution and publishing is defined as Service Oriented Computing (SOC). However, based on computational logic, the deployment of SOC primarily follows loosely or tightly coupled WSs. The publicity of WSs is primarily executed through Web Service Description Language (WSDL), that generates necessary executable files in server side for successful establishment of communication among platforms (WSDL, 2016). The XML is used to communicate external remote service. This is carried out along with the Simple Object Access Protocol (SOAP) features (SOAP, 2016). The Universal Description Discovery and Integration (UDDI) is a showcase of service parameters for end users (Peiris et al., 2007). The WSs can communicate in different ways and is discussed elsewhere (Bora et al., 2016).

The WS helps in executing software agent along with the supporting business logic and process model. The roles of WS coupling can be achieved as required in business model. The loosely coupled WSs have less dependency among them. However, tightly coupled WSs have strong dependency. The utilization of tightly or loosely coupling WSs may vary based on requirement. In many scenarios, the deployment of lightly coupled WS is observed in software industries and is observed due to its flexibility in delivering multi service multi functional operations. The WSs can play the role of consumer, broker and parent. In tightly coupled WS, the participating agents are aware of such role. However, in lightly coupled WSs the participating agents are not aware of such roles of participating WSs. In both cases, the features of SOAP, UDDI and WSDL is being used for service execution.

The web server is solely responsible for execution of WS request in server side. In different studies of authors, it is observed that the web servers fails during massive execution of server side request (Saddik, 2006; Kalita et al., 2011a; Bora et al., 2013; Bora et al., 2014). The author had discussed that while processing multi request, the web server may throw server error after a specific capacity limit. However, a study of author had reveal that the utilization of clustered load balancing server can increase the efficiency of service execution (Bryhni et al., 2000). It was discussed that, the deployment of such server can be carried out through multi or single machines. The web servers can be clustered into multiple service nodes. Each node can be utilized for service execution of similar properties. The load balancer periodically validates the service node. During service execution, if a specific node fails, the incoming request as received from end user is redirected to other active service node. Such deployment can enhance the availability, scalability and reliability of the system. The author of (Goel, 1985) discussed that reliability of service can be defined as the availability of system over specific period of time. However, the observation of WS execution in such server and finding their limits of reliability is getting comparatively more concern in the research community.

Related Work

Many authors have carried out their investigation over deployment of single service oriented WS for different business logic. In that perspective, Pacifici et al. (2005) had presented a novel methodology for management of server side stress during peak usages hours. They had discussed that management of performance metrics can enhance the quality aspects of the service. In the same year, Anzbock et al. had developed a model that can be followed for deployment of service. The study was carried out through recorded data sample of WS execution. Their study had demanded the importance of WS model for different business logic. As such, Castro et al. (2006) had proposed a novel principle that WS model should be followed for data processing. However, their study lack of experimental validation. In that case, Zhang et al. (2008) had presented a novel model for developing the quality aspects of service execution. Their study concluded that response time and rejection rate of server request is correlated. Further, Medhi et al. (2014) discussed about the performance aspects of WS oriented application that can execute for specific financial operation. The experimental results had shown the viability of .NET framework for WS development. In the same year, Kilintzis et al. had presented a different experimental setup and system metrics that were found to be necessary for end users. In the year 2015,, Ismail et al. had discussed a novel assessment framework for service deployment and execution. The applicability of their study was observed throughout the execution and recorded results. However, the discussion over importance of reliability was not highlighted. As such, Medhi et al. (2017) had carried out the matter and introduced a novel reliability evaluation strategy for WS oriented system based on Microsoft Windows Communication Foundation (WCF) service. Similarly, in the same year, Jiang et al. had contributed over the study of reliability for WSs. Abdelfattah et al. had introduced additional key aspects of service execution that can have impact over the reliability metric estimation. In the same year, the Zhou et al. had stated that security policies of WS can also impact the performance aspects of service execution. However, the impact of different application server over reliability metrics was not carried out by other studies. As such, Bora et al. (2018b) had presented a novel strategy for observing the failure and reliability of WS execution using Microsoft IIS and Tomcat web server. The study had presented a comparative assessment of deploying such service. In the same year, Yamada et al. had discussed performance aspects of aggregation of WS for grid based system. However, the testing methodology of such scenario was omitted. As such, Neto et al. (2018) proposed a test bed scheme for characterization of system execution.

The novelty of the proposed study focuses on deployment of loosely coupled WS for clustered load balancing web server and observing their reliability against different stress of usages. The system will be evaluated through statistical analysis for finding the applicability of the work.

FOCUS OF THE CHAPTER

The study will focus some aspects of reliability estimation of lightly coupled WS using clustered load balancing web server. The estimation will be evaluated against massive usage of such system. The work will primarily focus on a framework that can be followed for reliability estimation of service execution. It will emphasize how the lightly coupled WS will execute beyond its capacity in clustered load balancing web server.

Figure 1. The architecture of loosely coupled WS in clustered load balancing web server

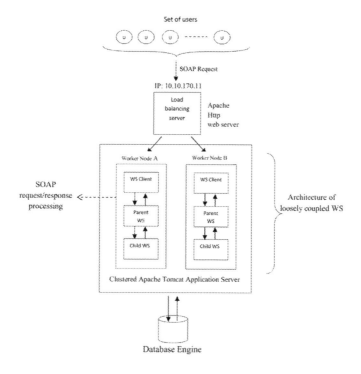

The framework of reliability estimation is carried out using an experimental arrangement that comprises lightly coupled multi WS deployed in two clustered working nodes. The architecture of service deployment is shown in Figure 1. The Apache Tomcat Application server is used due to its open source nature. It is clustered into two working nodes. The features of mod_jk tomcat connector and Apache Http Web Server is utilized for the deployment. The JAVA programming language is used to develop necessary instructions for the lightly coupled WS. The 2.5 version of Model View Controller (MVC) and MySQL database engine is used for server side query execution and information retrieval. A database having 15000 tuples of record for clinical instruction is prepared for the system. The 8.1 version of Mercury LoadRunner, a load testing tool is deployed for generating massive load over the system. It has the features of generating massive stress over the system and records the system metrics for the assigned load time (Mercurry LoadRunner, 2018). The flowchart of the proposed reliability evaluation framework is shown in Figure 2.

Figure 2. Flowchart for reliability evaluation of loosely coupled WS in clustered load balancing web server

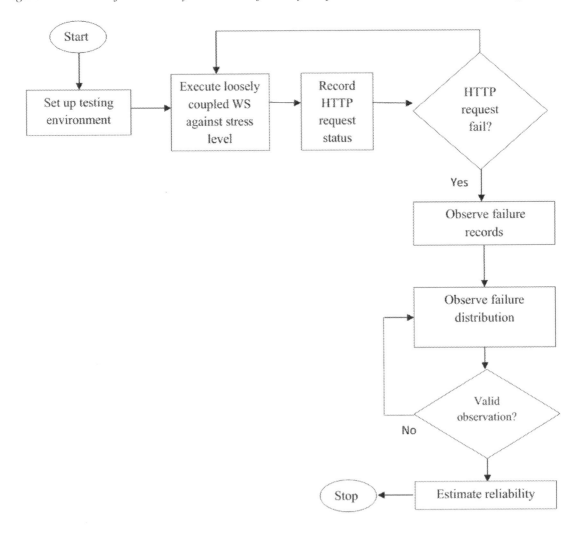

A system test case is created using the tool. The test case contains all necessary instruction that is followed by all stress level. The test case and different environmental parameters are discussed elsewhere (Bora et al., 2014). Different extensive stress is generated over the system and the data sample of Hyper Text Transfer Protocol (HTTP) transaction passed and failed is recorded. The server machine is configured for deployment of the loosely coupled WS. The server has a hardware configuration of Intel® Xeon® CPU E5620 @ 2.40 GHz processor, operating system of Windows Server 2008 with 64 bit, RAM of 8 GB, application server of Apache Tomcat version 7, web server of Apache HTTP version 2.2.4, MySQL version 5.0, Mod JK Tomcat connector, 600 GB hard disk, JDK verion 7, JRE version 7, Metro WS stack, Spring MVC 2.5 frameowrk, NetBeans IDE version 7 and Google Chorme as web browser. The load is generated from an external machine with hardware configuration as Intel® Pentium® Dual CPUE2200 @ 2.20 GHz processor, Windows XP operating system, 150 GB hard disk, 1 GB RAM and load testing tool Mercury LoadRunner version 8.1.

TESTING AND EVALUATION

The deployment of system testing and statistical analysis can play an important role for evaluating the effectiveness of a service (Kalita et al., 2011b). The loosely coupled WS along with the clustered load balancing web server is evaluated against the stress level of 50, 100, 800, 1500, 1700, 1800 and 2000 users. All stress level of users follows the same test case. The load testing tool records the failure record against the different stress level of users. It is shown in Table 1.

The number of recorded frequency against different fault count range and the clustered cylinders is shown in Table 2 and Figure 3. The clustered cylinders of recorded fault count show that the highest fault count is 13 and is in the range of 40529.5 to 43753.2. To observe the distribution of data sample, we evaluate Cumulative Distribution Function (CDF) plot against the recorded data sample. The CDF plot is shown in Figure 4. Here, the data points are following the continuous distribution. As such, continuity of failure distribution is observed.

Table 1. Recorded fault count of loosely coupled WS in clustered load balancing web server (TP: Transaction passed; TF: Transaction failed, FR: Failure rate)

Stress level of usage	TP	TF	FR (%) = TF/(TF+TP)
50	287	0	0
100	695	0	0
800	19,566	0	0
1500	62,968	0	0
1700	80,040	0	0
1800	82387	43525	0.34
2000	91345	69251	0.43

Table 2. Fault count and frequency range

Fault count	Frequency
37306	1
40529.6	5
43753.2	13
46976.8	7
50200.4	2
>50200.4	2

Figure 3. The clustered cylinders of fault count recorded against the stress level of 1800 users.

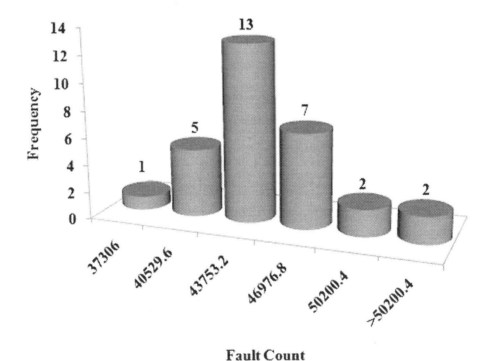

Goodness of Distribution through Chi Square (χ²) Testing

The goodness of continuous distribution is carried out through χ^2 testing. It shows "how good the frequency distribution of failure data fits the expected distribution" (Levin et al, 2009; Raj Jain, 2012). Two hypothesis (H_p) is taken considering observed and expected distribution. The null H_p states about fitness of distribution. The alternate H_p states about not fitness of distribution. The different estimated parameters of χ^2 test are shown in Table 3.

At 95% confidence level, the $\chi^2_{(0.95;\ 5)}$ is observed to be 11.0705. From Table 3, the total calculated χ^2 is less than 11.0705, i.e. $\chi^2 < 11.0705$. As such, null H_p is accepted for the observed data sample.

Figure 4. CDF of recorded fault count against the stress level of 1800 users

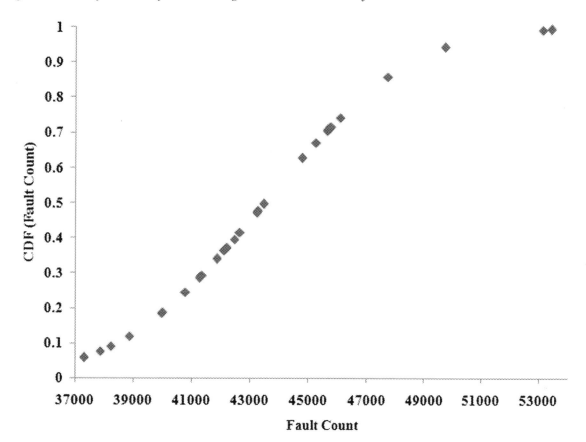

Table 3. Estimated parameter of χ^2 test (Observed value:OV, Expected value: EV)

Failure range	OV	EV	OV-EV	(OV-EV)²	(OV-EV)²/EV
0-37306	1	3% of 30 =0.9	0.1	0.01	0.0111
>37306-40529.6	5	16.66% of 30 =4.99	0.01	0.0001	0.00002
>40529.6-43753.2	13	43.33% of 30 =12.99	0.01	0.0001	0.000007
>43753.2-46976.8	7	23.33% of 30 =6.99	0.01	0.0001	0.00001
>46976.8-50200.4	2	6.6% of 30 =1.98	0.02	0.0004	0.0002
>50200.4	2	6.6% of 30 =1.98	0.02	0.0004	0.0002
Total calculated χ^2					0.011537

RELIABILITY, ESTIMATION OF SERVICE EXECUTION

The reliability is evaluated over the recorded data sample of service execution. From Table 1, the first HTTP fault count is recorded for the stress level of 1800 users. The equation (1) is used for evaluating the reliability of loosely coupled WS. It is defined by (Shooman, 2002, Rahmani et al., 2014, Medhi et al.,2017, Bora et al., 2018a).

Table 4. A comparative study of the proposed work with other methodology

Stress level	FR % of proposed study	FR % of earlier study done by other researchers			
		Saddik, 2006	Kalita et al., 2011b	Medhi et al., 2014	Bora et al., 2018b
50	0	No test carried out	0	0	0
100	0	60.28%	50%	0	0
500	No test carried out	87.9%	No test carried out	0	No test carried out
800	0	No test carried out	No test carried out	No test carried out	0
1000	No test carried out	92.06%	No test carried out	37%	32%
1500	0	No test carried out	No test carried out	75%	66%
1700	0	No test carried out	No test carried out	No test carried out	No test carried out
1800	34%	No test carried out	No test carried out	No test carried out	No test carried out
2000	43%	No test carried out	No test carried out	No test carried out	81%

$$R_L = e^{-ft} \qquad (1)$$

Here, R_L is the parameter for reliability of service, 'f' is the parameter for failure rate during 't' time of stress level execution. The R_L assumes a value from 0 to 1. A closer to 1 will predict strong reliability of service. The poor reliability may degrade the quality aspects of the service. That means, the reliability of the service is poor if R_L is closer to 0. For the stress level of 1800 users, the 'f' is evaluated to be 0.34%. As such, the R_L is evaluated to be 0.71%. This concludes that, for peak usage of 1800 users, strong reliability of the loosely coupled WS may be estimated up to 71% of service execution through clustered load balancing web server.

A comparative study is carried out with other existing works that are contributed by other authors. It is shown in Table 4.

The Table 4 shows that during the stress level of 1700 users the failure rate is recorded to be 0%, whereas for Saddik (2006), the failure rate is 92.06% for stress level of 1000 usres, for Kalita et al (2011b), the failure rate is 50% for stress level of 100 users, for Medhi et al (2014), the failure rate is 75% for 1500 users and for Bora et al. (2018b), the failure rate is 66% for 1500 users. As such, from the overall assessment of the proposed methodology, it can be concluded that the proposed system delivers a better reliability than other techniques.

FUTURE RESEARCH DIRECTIONS

The future study of the work will be to conclude about the feasibility of deployment using the proposed framework for reliability estimation of tightly coupled WSs in grid based system. A proper server resource management scheme will be developed to enhance the reliability of the clustered load balancing web server.

CONCLUSION

The study introduces a novel reliability estimation framework for loosely coupled WS by using clustered load balancing web server. It concludes that for a specific limit of stress level, the system throws HTTP failure records and increases gradually. The strong reliability of the WS can be achieved up to 1700 users. Beyond that, it is showing failure rate. As such moderate service reliability can be assumed for stress level of 1800 users. The statistical evaluation of the data sample reveals that the data points follow continuous distribution. The fitness of data distribution through χ^2 test is observed at 95% confidence level. The reliability of loosely coupled WS decreases with increase in fault count. During the usage level of 1800 users, a system reliability of up to 71% of valid data processing can be assumed. From the overall assessment, it can be concluded that the proposed framework is valid and viable for estimating the reliability of loosely coupled WS by using clustered load balancing web server. From the comparative study of the proposed work, it can be concluded that the propose system is better than the other techniques that are primarily followed for information retrieval and data processing in server side. The experimental arrangement, architecture and the statistical evaluation can help different researcher and software practitioner to get some aspects of reliability of service execution in such platform.

ACKNOWLEDGMENT

The authors express their sincere thanks to All India Council of Technical Education (AICTE), Govt of India for financial support towards the work (Grant No. 8023/BOR/RID/RPS (NER)-84/2010-2011 31ˢᵗ March 2011).

REFERENCES

Abdelfattah, A., & Abdelkader, T., & EI-Horbaty, E. (2017). RSAM: An enhanced architecture for achieving web services reliability in mobile cloud computing. *Computer and Information Sciences*, *30*, 164–174. doi:10.1016/j.jksuci.2017.03.002

Anzbock, R., & Dustdar, S. (2005). Modeling and implementing medical Web services. *Data & Knowledge Engineering*, *55*(2), 203–236. doi:10.1016/j.datak.2005.03.009

Bora, A., & Bezboruah, T. (2014). Testing and Evaluation of a Hierarchical SOAP based Medical Web Service. *International Journal of Database Theory and Application*, *7*(4), 169–188. doi:10.14257/ijdta.2014.7.4.13

Bora, A., & Bezboruah, T. (2016). *Some Aspects of QoS for High Performance of Service Oriented Computing in Load Balancing Cluster Based Web server. In Handbook of Research on Recent Developments in Intelligent Communication Application* (pp. 566–603). IGI- Global. doi:10.4018/978-1-5225-1785-6

Bora, A., & Bezboruah, T. (2018b). Some aspects of reliability evaluation of multi service multi functional SOAP based web services. *International Journal of Information Retrieval Research*, *8*(4), 24–39. doi:10.4018/IJIRR.2018100102

Bora, A., Bhuyan, M. K., & Bezboruah, T. (2013). Investigations on Hierarchical Web service based on Java Technique. *Proceedings of the World Congress on Engineering (WCE).*

Bora, A., Medhi, S., & Bezboruah, T. (2018a). *Investigations on Failure and Reliability Aspects of Service Oriented Computing Based On Different Deployment Technique. In Advanced Computational and Communication Paradigms. Lecture Notes in Electrical Engineering* (Vol. 475). Springer. doi:10.1007/978-981-10-8240-5_60

Bryhni, H., Klovning, E., & Kure, O. (2000). A Comparison of Load Balancing Techniques for Scalable Web Servers. *IEEE Network, 14*(4), 58–64. doi:10.1109/65.855480

Castro, V., Sanz, M., & Marcos, E. (2006). Business Process Development based on Web Services: a Web Information System for Medical Image Management and Processing. *IEEE International Conference on Web Services*, 807 – 814. 10.1109/ICWS.2006.41

Goel, A. L. (1985). Software Reliability Models: Assumptions, Limitations, and Applicability. *IEEE Transaction of Software Computing, SE-11*(12), 1411–1423. doi:10.1109/TSE.1985.232177

Ismail, H., Issa, K., & Abdallah, K. (2015). Designing High Performance Web-Based Computing Services to Promote Telemedicine Database Management System. *IEEE Transactions on Services Computing, 8*(1), 47–64. doi:10.1109/TSC.2014.2300499

Jain, R. (2012). *The art of computer systems performance analysis: Technique for experimental Design, Measurement, Simulation and Modeling.* Wiley Professional Computing.

Jiang, P., Elag, M., Kumar, P., Peckham, S. D., Marini, L., & Rui, L. (2017). A service-oriented architecture for coupling web service models using the Basic Model Interface (BMI). *Environmental Modelling & Software, 92*, 107–118. doi:10.1016/j.envsoft.2017.01.021

Kalita, M., & Bezboruah, T. (2011a). Investigations on performance testing and evaluation of PReWebD: A. NET technique for implementing web application. *IET Software, 5*(4), 357–365. doi:10.1049/iet-sen.2010.0139

Kalita, M., Khanikar, S., & Bezboruah, T. (2011b). Investigation on performance testing and evaluation of PReWebN: A JAVA technique for implementing web application. *IET Software, 5*(5), 434–444. doi:10.1049/iet-sen.2011.0030

Kilintzis, V., Beredimas, N., & Chouvarda, I. (2014). *Evaluation of the performance of open-source RDBMS and triplestores for storing medical data over a web service.* doi:10.1109/EMBC.2014.6944623

Levin, I., Richard, S., & Rubin, D. (2009). Statistics for management, Pearson education, Inc. *South Asia.*

Matthew, M. C., Laskey, K., McCabe, F., Brown, P., & Metz, R. (2005). *Reference Model for Service Oriented Architectures. Published on the internet.* OASIS Working Draft.

Medhi, S., & Bezboruah, T. (2014). Investigations on implementation of e-ATM Web Services based on. NET technique. *International Journal of Information Retrieval Research, 4*(2), 42–51. doi:10.4018/ijirr.2014040103

Medhi, S., Bora, A., & Bezboruah, T. (2017). Investigations On Some Aspects of Reliability of Content Based Routing SOAP based Windows Communication Foundation Services'. *International Journal of Information Retrieval Research, 7*(1), 17–31. doi:10.4018/IJIRR.2017010102

Mercury LoadRunner. (n.d.). Available at: https://qageek.files.wordpress.com/2007/05/loadrunner_tutorial.pdf

Neto, J., Moreira, A., & Musicante, M. (2018). Semantic Web Services testing: A Systematic Mapping study. *Computer Science Review, 28*, 140–156. doi:10.1016/j.cosrev.2018.03.002

Pacifici, G., Spreitzer, M., Tantawi, A. N., & Youssef, A. (2005). Performance Management for Cluster-Based Web Services. *IEEE Journal on Selected Areas in Communications, 23*(12), 2333–2343. doi:10.1109/JSAC.2005.857208

Peiris, C., Mulder, D., Cicoria, S., Bahree, A., & Pathak, N. (2007). *Pro WCF: Practical Microsoft SOA Implementation.* Apress Press.

Rahmani, M., Azadmanesh, A., & Siy, H. (2014). Architectural reliability analysis of framework-intensive applications: A web service case study. *Journal of Systems and Software, 94*, 186–201. doi:10.1016/j.jss.2014.03.070

Saddik, A. E. (2006). Performance measurement of Web Service based application. *IEEE Transactions on Instrumentation and Measurement, 55*(5), 1599–1605. doi:10.1109/TIM.2006.880288

Shooman, M. L. (2002). *Reliability of Computer Systems and Networks: Fault Tolerance, Analysis, and Design.* New York: John Wiley & Sons. doi:10.1002/047122460X

SOAP. (n.d.). Available at http://www.w3.org/TR/soap12-part1/]

WSDL. (n.d.). Available at http://www.w3.org/TR/wsdl20-primer/

Yamada, T., Suzuki, K., & Ninagawa, C. (2018). Scalability Analysis of Aggregation Web Services for Smart Grid Fast Automated Demand Response. *2018 IEEE International Conference on Industrial Technology (ICIT).* 10.1109/ICIT.2018.8352363

Zhang, Z., & Fan, W. (2008). Stochastics and Statistics Web server load balancing: A queueing analysis. *European Journal of Operational Research, 186*, 681–693. doi:10.1016/j.ejor.2007.02.011

Zhou, B., Zhang, Q., Shi, Q., Yang, Q., Yang, P., & Yu, Y. (2017). Measuring web service security in the era of Internet of Things. *Computers & Electrical Engineering*, 1–11. doi:10.1016/j.compeleceng.2017.06.020

Chapter 11
Multi–Agent System Based on Data Mining Algorithms to Detect Breast Cancer

Imane Chakour
Sultan Moulay Slimane University, Morocco

Yousef El Mourabit
Sultan Moulay Slimane University, Morocco

Mohamed Baslam
Sultan Moulay Slimane University, Morocco

ABSTRACT

Recently, data mining and intelligent agents have emerged as two domains with tremendous potential for research. The capacity of agents to learn from their experience complements the data mining process. This chapter aims to study a multi-agent system that evaluates the performance of three well-known data mining algorithms—artificial neural network (ANN), support vector machines (SVM), and logistic regression or logit model (LR)—based on breast cancer data (WBCD). Then the system aggregates the classifications of these algorithms with a controller agent to increase the accuracy of the classification using a majority vote. Extensive studies are performed to evaluate the performance of these algorithms using various differential performance metrics such as classification rate, sensitivity, and specificity using different software modules. In the end, the authors see that this system gives more autonomy and initiative in the medical diagnosis and the agent can dialogue to share their knowledge.

INTRODUCTION

We live in the data evolution. Since the data come from a wide range of sources, including social networking sites, supply chains and databases; it is usually unstructured in the absence of a particular format or layout. Therefore, the researchers must process the incoming data for useful information. Data mining is the process in which intelligent methods can extract interesting data models and knowledge from large

DOI: 10.4018/978-1-7998-1021-6.ch011

amounts of data (Rao, 2017). However, the speed at which data is produced is very high, and they need efficient methods of operating to keep up to date. Distributed Data Mining (DMD) aims at extracting a useful model from distributed heterogeneous databases in order, for example, to compose them within a distributed knowledge base and use it for decision-making purposes. DMD can also be useful in environments with multiple computing nodes connected over high speed networks. Although data can be quickly centralized using the relatively fast network, proper compute load balancing between a group of nodes may require a distributed approach. The distributed nature of agent extraction brings several benefits to data mining, such as scalability, scalability, reliability, security, interactivity, and high speed (Bellifemine, Caire, Poggiet, & Rimassa, 2008). Agents can be used to automate various tasks such as data selection, data cleansing, and data preprocessing for classification and representation of knowledge. As an emerging field, a lot of research can be done in this area. for this chapter authors have found that, moreover, it is difficult for a specialist to diagnose in a patient whether the patient has breast cancer or not, to confirm his presence or to determine his characteristics (his extension, his aggressiveness, ...). The current situation has motivated research in this field and the need to automate medical diagnosis has become indispensable. The aim of this system is to give more autonomy and initiative to the various software modules specialized in medical diagnosis and which can interact for share their knowledge as human experts. Breast cancer remains the first female cancer in the world, it is a real social problem. The frequency of breast cancer varies greatly from country to country and the factors involved are multiple: genetic factors, role of diet. The issue of breast cancer detection leads researchers, specialists in the field to look at other trends, new technologies other than human to address this real social problem. The goal of this chapter is to create a new approach that will help determine whether a patient has benign or malignant cancer following multiple descriptors. To achieve this goal, researchers propose a solution based on the concept of multi-agent systems. they perform a coupling between two major areas of Medicine and Computer Science for the diagnosis of breast cancer and the agent paradigm respectively. The purpose of this coupling is to improve the performance and efficiency of medical diagnostic systems. The peculiarity of their the approach is the development and definition of a model based on an architecture composed of distinct parts, each part will diagnose whether the cancer is malignant or benign from a database in a specific way, but able to communicate to share their knowledge. The multi agent paradigm in their approach would be applied in several contexts: Each agent in this system will make its own diagnosis for the same learning base (autonomy). The final decision will be made after a majority vote: the patient will be assigned to the class that has been appointed by the large number of agents.

Background

Authors shortly describe the multi-agent system based on data mining as well as the precedent algorithms to evaluate the performance of the classification and refer the reader to (Soares, & Souza, 2016) for more details.

MULTI-AGENT SYSTEM

It is rather rare for agent designers to need only one agent in the environment they build. When several agents find themselves in the same environment and these agents need to interact with each other, this is called a multi agent system. A multi-agent system (MAS) can be defined as a macro-system composed of autonomous agents that interact in a common environment in order to achieve a coherent collective activity (Ellouzi, Ltifi, Ben Ayed, 2017). The result of the organization of these agents, the links linking them, defines the identity of the multi-agent system.

Interests of MAS

The most important contributions of multi-agent systems are summarized as follows (Nizalizadeh, Moghadam, Ravanmohr, 2018):

- Automation and improvement of decision-making processes.
- Decentralization of a system into cooperative subsystems.
- Reuse by creating new systems by interoperating with existing ones.
- The representation of knowledge in a distributed way.
- The simulation of the workings of organizations, as they are used to simulating many mechanisms in order to verify the hypotheses of numerous researches.

Principe of MAS

In addition to the notion of environment, which as explained, is fundamental in the definition of MAS, two other concepts characterize these. The concept of interaction that allows agents to exchange and the concept of organization which structures. A MAS can be opened (the agents enter and leave freely) or closed, homogeneous (the agents come from the same model) or heterogeneous. In terms of its design, it imposes a local and decentralized vision.

DATA MINING TECHNIQUES

The term Data Mining refers to the analysis of data from different perspectives and transforming that data into useful information, establishing relationships between data or identifying patterns. Very simply, the tools (classification, Clustring, visualization with methods such as Principal Component Analysis (PCA), Factorial correspondence analysis (FCA), Association for Computing Machinery (ACM), Neural Networks, etc.) of data mining process the immense amount of data to highlight trends, models, correlations and summarize them with simple quantitative models, is one of the great challenges of information: turning data into information and turning information into knowledge.

To perform the tasks of Data Mining, there are several techniques from various scientific disciplines (statistics, artificial intelligence, database) to reveal hidden correlations in data sources to build models from these data (Han, Kamber, & Pei, 2011). depending on the nature of the data and the type of study that is to be undertaken, this report deals with the classification problem, in particular the classification algorithms, the algorithms chosen for this chapter are detailed in the following.

First of all, what is a classification problem? Consider the following example. Researchers place themselves in the plane, and they have two categories: rounds and squares, each occupying a different region of the plane. However, the border between these two regions is not known. What want is that when authors present a new point whose position in the plane they only know, the classification algorithm will be able to predict whether this new point is a square or a circle.

Figure 1. Linear separation of data

Here is their classification problem: for each new entry, be able to determine to which category this entry belongs. In other words, one must be able to find the boundary between the different categories. If they know the frontier, which side of the frontier does the point belong to, and therefore which category does it belong to?

Linear Classifier

Linear classifiers are classifiers that use a linear separation (a straight line) of data, and will eventually see that each classification algorithm used in this report has its own method for finding the boundary between categories as the left of Figure 1 shows.

After defining what is the problem of classification, in right of Figure 1 it is found later that there are data that are linearly separated and others not linearly separate.

Non-Linear Classification

Since rounds are surrounded by squares on all sides, it is impossible to find a straight line that is a boundary: it is said that the training data are not linearly separable. However, imagine that researchers can find a transformation that makes our problem look like left of Figure 2:

From right of Figure 2, it is easy to find a linear separation. So just find a transformation that goes well to classify objects. In this chapter, authors present how the selected classification algorithms will learn from these data either linearly or non-linearly separate.

Support Vector Machines

SVMs (Support Vector Machines) are a useful technique for data classification technique. The goal of SVM is to produce a model (based on the training data) which predicts the target values of the test data

Figure 2. Non- linear separation of data

given only the test data attributes. Also, Support Vector machines can be defined as systems which use hypothesis space of a linear function in a high dimensional feature space, trained with a learning algorithm from optimization theory that implements a learning bias derived from statistical learning theory (Cao, Zeng, Symeonidinis, & Gorodetsky, 2014).

Logistic Regression

Logistic regression is a predictive technique. It aims at constructing a model allowing to predict / explain the values taken by a qualitative target variable (most often binary, one speaks about binary logistic regression, if it has more than 2 modalities, one speaks about polytomic logistic regression) from a set of quantitative or qualitative explanatory variables (coding is necessary in this case). It is widely used in the medical field (healing or not of a patient), in sociology, in epidemiology, in quantitative marketing (purchase or not of products or services following an action) and in finance for risk modeling (scoring). The principle of the logistic regression model is to relate the occurrence or non-occurrence of an event to the level of explanatory variables. For example, in the phytosanitary field, it is sought to evaluate from which dose of a chemical agent, an insect will be neutralized.

Artificial Neural Network

Artificial neural networks are simply systems inspired by the functioning of biological neurons. The most famous of these is the multilayer perceptron (also written multi-layered), an artificial system capable of learning by ... experience! Introduced in 1957 by Franck Rosenblatt, it is only really used since 1982 after its improvement. Thanks to the computing power of the 2000s, the perceptron has become widely democratized and is increasingly used. Neural networks, made of artificial cellular structures, provide an approach to approach the problems of perception, memory, learning and reasoning in the same way as genetic algorithms. They are also very promising alternatives to circumvent some of the limitations of conventional numerical methods. Through their parallel processing of information and their mechanisms inspired by nerve cells (neurons), they infer emerging properties to solve complex problems.

DISTRIBUTED DATA MINING AND MULTI-AGENT SYSTEM

Several researchers have been involved in agent technology research and data mining. An effort has been made to eliminate the boundary between the two technologies, it is the interaction and integration between agent technology and Data Mining that can contribute the most. The combination between agents and Data Mining is driven by difficulties faced by both communities, and the need to develop more advanced data processing approaches, and smarter systems (Nizalizadeh, Moghadam, Ravanmohr, 2018). Datamining technology has emerged as a way to identify hidden patterns and trends in large amounts of data. Data Mining technology normally adopts a data integration method to generate data warehouses, where all data is gathered in a central site, and then run an algorithm on that data to extract new knowledge. However, only one Data Mining technique was not revealed appropriate for each domain. Data Mining techniques also involve the complex environment that dynamic changes due to changes in the system face, which can affect the overall performance of the system. Agent technology aimed at dealing with complex systems has revealed the potential for improving distributed systems in a number of ways. Multi-Agent Systems

Figure 3. General Distributed Data Exploration Framework

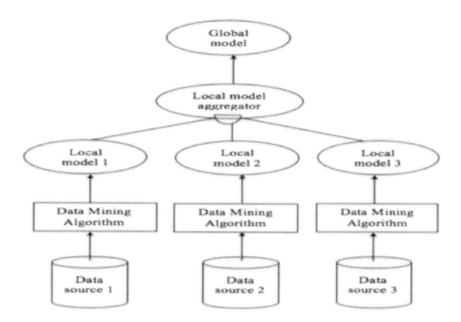

(MAS) are often complex applications that require distributed problem solving. In many applications, the individual and collective behavior of agents depends on data observed from distributed sources. In Figure 3, a general framework for distributed data mining is presented. In essence, the success of various DDM algorithms lies in aggregation. Each local model represents locally consistent models, but lacks the detail that may be needed to generate globally significant knowledge. For this reason, various DDM algorithms require centralizing a subset of local data to compensate for it. The overall approach has been applied in various fields to increase the accuracy of the predictive model to learn. It produces several models and combines them to improve accuracy. Generally, the voting scheme (weighted or unweighted) is used to aggregate the base model in order to obtain a global model. DDM algorithms have minimal data transfer which is another key attribute of DDM's success. Distributed data mining is a new area of research put forward in recent years. Because he has a tempting first plan, at the moment, there is a lot of personal research devoted to research on this subject and having achieved some results. The two basic steps of the typical distributed data mining algorithm are: Partial data analysis and production of a partial data model (partial knowledge). Combine a partial data model into different data points and then obtain the global data model (general knowledge).

In Agent-based Data Mining, an agent is a software entity characterized by the following capabilities:

1. Interact with the data source and / or other agents
2. Receive / collect raw data,
3. Process data from one or more data sources allowing it to produce knowledge,
4. Coordinates these actions with the other agents to produce the relevant and useful knowledge.

An agent-based Data Mining system positively contributes to the Data Mining process in several cases:

First, an MADM system guarantees parallelism that improves speed, efficiency and accuracy. The distributed nature of the agent system allows the parallel execution of Data Mining processes without worrying about the number of remote data sources involved. This means that conventional Data Mining algorithms can still be applied to local (agent-related) data because information about other data is not needed for local operations. Then agents must collaborate to integrate information from many local sources.

Secondly. Agent concepts provide users of a Data Mining system with the ability to progressively follow the process of discovering knowledge in different steps, for example a user may want to visualize the knowledge model obtained by a particular agent before the integration takes place. The details reported at each step depend on the implementation of the MADM system. Another benefit of adopting a MADM system is the agent's ability to gather, retrieve, and process information beyond a data source. This is possible thanks to the mobility attribute of a software agent (Bellifemine, Caire, Poggiet, & Rimassa, 2008).Although it offers the means to do Distributed Data Mining, Data Mining-based agents are not spared the inherent problems of Data Mining techniques, such as missing data, and the scalability problem. In addition, agent-based data mining systems in many cases are more difficult to design and implement than conventional data mining systems. The technology of multi-agent systems has sparked a lot of excitement in recent years thanks to the promises it makes committing a new paradigm of design and implementation of software systems. These promises are particularly attractive for creating software that works in distributed and open environments. Artificial intelligence is the "search for ways to equip computer systems with intellectual capabilities comparable to those of human beings". AI is based on the sciences of man: Linguistic Psychology, Sociology, Neuro Biology, Biosphere. Distributed Artificial Intelligence: DAI=IA: Modeling the knowledge of agents (competence)+ Distribution: Modeling their interactions (social organization). An Agent is an entity who acts autonomously, to achieve the goals for which it was designed, can communicate with other agents, equipped with abilities similar to living beings and agent can be a process, a robot, a human being, etc. A multi-agent system (MAS) is a distributed system: composed of a set of distributed agents, located in a certain environment and interacting according to some organizations. A MAS solves complex problems by exploiting the collective intelligence of agents that compose it. Jade platform for the multi-agent system is to simplify the development of multi-agent systems: Ensuring compliance of standards with a complete set of services and agents. Complying with FIPA standards: Name Service, Yellow Pages Service, Transported Messages and Analysis Service, and a FIPA Interaction Protocol Library to use. Jade has three main modules required by FIPA standards. DF "Directory Facilitator" provides a "yellow pages" service to the platform. ACC "Agent Communication Channel" manages communication between agents. AMS "Agent Management System" oversees agent registration, authentication, access, and system usage (Nizalizadeh, Moghadam, Ravanmohr, 2018).

The concepts object and distributed agent are very close but it is not the same of the agent like intentional entity. Indeed, the objects have no goal of satisfaction and the mechanism of sending messages is a simple procedure call. There is no communication language per se. The interaction mechanisms are therefore the responsibility of the programmer. The essential difference between an object and an agent is that an object is defined by the set of services it offers (its methods) and that it can't refuse to execute if another object requests it. On the other hand, agents have objectives that give them autonomy of decision with respect to the messages they receive. In addition, they establish complex interactions involving high-level communications. In fact, an agent can be considered as an object endowed with additional capacities: searches for satisfactions (intentions, impulses) on the one hand, and on the other hand communication based on more advanced languages. Conversely, an object can be considered as a "degenerate" agent that has become a mere executor, any message being considered as a request (Han, Kamber, & Pei, 2011).

MADM: MULTI-AGENT BASED ON DATA MINING SYSTEM CONCEPTION

The MADM approach proposed in this section is that of a collection of persistent, autonomous but also cooperative agents operating in a distributed environment. To study the nature of the proposed MADM system, its operation, and its architecture, authors propose the design of a system that reflects their proposed approach. To realize the MADM system a development methodology has been adopted that goes from the definition and analysis of the problem to the detailed design. In this section provides a detailed description in terms of the needs of the design and architecture of such a system. Developing a datamining system that uses specialized agents with the ability to communicate with multiple data sources, as well as with other agents, requires great flexibility. For example, adding a new data source should simply involve adding a new agent and publishing its capabilities to other agents that form the MADM system, a process that should be easy so that it is as simple as possible (Rao, 2017). As noted above the main motivation for researching and implementing an MADM system was to look closely at the different research challenges to build a MADM system. In this section, the different types of agents used in the proposed approach are detailed. The discussion focuses on agent functionality, and implementation is discussed later in this section. On the basis of the problems identified in the beginning of this section, several types of agents have been proposed. However, regardless of the type of these agents, they conform to the general definitions of agents described in (Bellifemine, Caire, Poggiet, & Rimassa, 2008). The types of agents present in our approach are: User Agent, Spot Manager Agent, Registrar, Facilitator, Datamining agent, Data Agent, and Coordinating Agent.

Data agents and users are all identified as interface agents because they all provide "interfaces" to users or data sources. User agents provide the interface between system end users and the system, while

Figure 4. The general architecture of the system

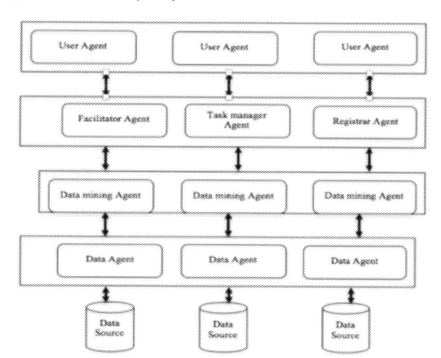

data agents provide the interface between the data sources and the rest of the system. The data mining agents and task manager are identified as processing agents, their roles are to process and respond to user requests.

Figure 4. shows that the agents must be housed in each component of the domain identified in the structural design analysis. The task manager receives a request, and requests the facilitating agent to check all available data sources (data agent s) and datamining agents to find: the data to be used, and the data mining algorithm most appropriate for the data source (datamining agent). The task manager then passes the task to the datamining agent and monitors its progress. Each data source (database) must have a data agent to determine the characteristics of the data source and to accurately select the most appropriate datamining agent.

MADM SYSTEM IMPLEMENTATION

In this section, authors give the detailed implementation of (MADM) Multi-agent based on Data mining, which uses three classifications algorithms together with Multi-agent system. utilizing MAS, it will be possible to mine the data in a distributed environment using agents. In MADM, each classification algorithm used in this approach are associated with an agent in such a way that can act as an agent in, processing units, Agent 1 to Agent 3 in Figure 5.

Figure 6 used to determine the interaction of the agents. Agent UML is a support notation for agent-oriented development systems. It consists of using the modeling language UML and its extension to represent the agents, their behaviors and their interactions between them. Agent UML is not limited to the use of UML, it is adapted even by other approaches. In system Figure 6, the platform consists of a

Figure 5. Proposed Multi-agent system

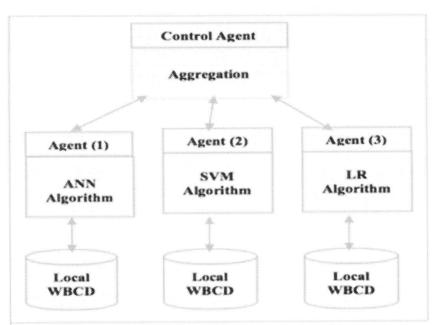

Figure 6. AUML sequence diagram for MADM

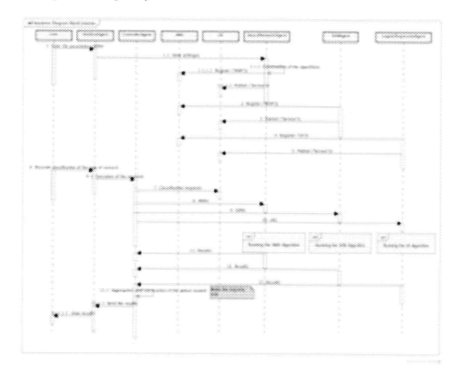

Main Container, let recall that is consists mainly of two main agents. The agents 'AMS' which manages the identification of the agents including the assignment of the ID to each agent and the agent 'DF' which consists of a director in which researchers will publish the services and through which they discovered the services that they use in approach. Then, authors created three containers to create Neural Network, SVM, Logistic regression agents to classify the patient to their associated class. before these agents start, they will register at the agent '' AMS '', practically it has all the identities of the agents and suddenly it will allow to find the agents in the platform. The starting point of the system is the classification agents. The latter, will make the final decision that will be taken after a majority vote: the patient will be assigned to the class that has been appointed by the large number of agents.

RESULTS AND DISCUSSIONS

The medical diagnosis is a process of classification, this classification of pathologies is to gather the cases which have biological similarities and which are likely to share certain etiopathological factors. Although the expert's decision is the most important factor in the diagnosis, classification systems provide substantial support.

What are Classification Algorithms?

The classification algorithms chosen in this chapter seek to find the boundaries between classes in the hyperspace of data. for this reason, the resolution methods, which learn by example, are able to reproduce the expert's classification. The sample of their study is partitioned into a learning set and a test set. The idea is to have a set to test the quality of the induced classification procedure.

Test Phase (Evaluation)

This phase must allow the assignment of a new object to one of the classes, by means of a decision rule integrating the results of the learning phase.

Classification Measures- Classification Rate, Sensitivity and Specificity

There is no perfect classifier algorithm; all of them are subjected to errors and biases. The following table depicts a simple 2 x 2 matrix shows how many of a given class's records were correctly classified and therefore how many were wrongly classified:

In disease diagnosis, which is the subject of this chapter, the concept of a binary confusion matrix is applied in the sense that a false diagnosis may be either a false positive or a false negative. The idea is to obtain the most accurate estimate possible of the behavior of the classifier under real conditions of use. That's why, conventional criteria such as classification rates, error rates are almost always used and for the rate of false results can be measured by using sensitivity and specificity indexes.

$$Classification\ Rate = \frac{Numbers\ of\ true\ Posotives\ And\ Negatives}{Total\ of\ Actual\ Negative\ and\ posotive\ Records}$$

Sensitivity denotes the true positive rate; for authors, the sensitivity of the test its ability to give a positive result when the disease is present.

$$Sensitivity = \frac{Number\ of\ True\ Positives}{Total\ of\ Actual\ Positive\ Records}$$

Specificity, in turn, represents the true negative rate; for authors, the specificity of the test its ability to give a positive result when the disease is absent.

$$Specificity = \frac{Number\ of\ True\ Negtives}{Total\ of\ Actual\ Negative\ Records}$$

Table 1. Confusion matrix 2x2

Real class	Inferred class	
	malignant (1)	benign (0)
malignant (1)	True Positive	False Negative
benign (0)	False positive	True Negative

Results

In this section, researchers create a new multi-agent approach that will help determine whether a patient has benign or malignant cancer from the universal database WBCD "Wisconsin Breast Cancer Database" to evaluate their model following multiple descriptors. The breast cancer database contains the medical information of 699 breast cancer clinical cases classified as benign or malignant: 458 patients (i.e. 65.5%) are mild cases and 241 patients (34.5%) are malignant cases. The database contains 16 missing data (Soares, & Souza, 2016), for this reason they restricted ourselves to working on 683/699 patients; Table 2 point that the patients are characterized by 11 attributes: the first one refers to the patient's identifier and the last one represents the class: the diagnosis is 0 if the case is benign, 1 if the case is malignant as for the 9 others, they represent following clinical cases:

- **Clump Thickness:** The thickness of the plasma membrane of a cancer cell is greater than that of a normal cell.
- **Uniformity of Cell Size:** Cancer cells are characterized by anisocytosis, which is an inequality in size compared to healthy cells.
- **Uniformity of Cell Shape:** Cancer cells are marked with irregular contours and incisions.
- **Marginal Adhesion Shape:** over expression of the integrin beta3 protein at the surface of the cancer cell.
- **Single Epithelial Cell Size:** Since epithelial cells are naturally absent in the bone marrow and are not detected in healthy individuals, bone marrow can, therefore, be considered as an indicator of metastatic disease in patients with primary breast cancer.
- **Bare Nuclei:** In the normal state, the nucleoli are inside the nucleus. In the case where its last are confused with the cytoplasm it indicates that the cell presents an anomaly and that it is likely to become cancerous.
- **Bland Chromatin:** H2az is a protein that induces the expression of the estrogen receptor gene.
- The overproduction of this protein is a marker of the presence of cancer cells in the breast since they are hormone dependent.
- **Normal Nucleoli:** DNA is naturally protected by a nuclear membrane. A failure observed at this membrane may reflect tumor growth.
- **Mitosis:** Mitosis is a process of regulated cell division that reproduces daughter cells that are genetically identical to the parental cell.

Malignant cells are characterized by anarchic and intense cell division compared to a normal cell population. The following table shows the configuration of this dataset.

To distribute the 683 patients: researchers kept (600) for the learning phase and (83) for the test phase. the following table shows the results obtained by the three classification algorithms chosen for this analysis by generating the confusion matrix, the sensitivity and the specificity of the test data set.

ANN classifier gave a better performance especially in the recognition of malignant cases. This performance is mainly to the optimization of the structure and the modification of the weights, in addition to the neuronal learning (2 inputs Input3 and Input8) were eliminated, the latter two represent respectively: Uniformity of cell shape and Noarmal Nucleioli. From a medical point of view, they are the least significant (confirmed by experts in the field).

Table 2. Configuration of the database

Variable name	Type	Maximum value and minimum value
Diagnosis Result	Output	[0;1]
Clump Thickness	Input#1	[1 ;10]
Uniformity of Cell Size	Input#2	[1 ;10]
Uniformity of Cell Shape	Input#3	[1 ;10]
Shape Marginal Adhesion	Input#4	[1 ;10]
Single Epithelial Cell Size	Input#5	[1 ;10]
Bare Nuclei	Input#6	[1 ;10]
Bland Chromatin	Input#7	[1 ;10]
Normal Nucleoli	Input#8	[1 ;10]
Mitoses	Input#9	[1 ;10]

Table 3. Results of the three classification agents

Classifier	Confusion matrix	Classification Rate	sensitivity	Specificity
ANN	13.0 1.0 1.0 68.0	0.9759	0.9285	0.9855
SVM	11.0 1.0 1.0 60.0	0.9726	0.9166	0.9836
LR	14.0 1.0 1.0 63.0	0.9747	0.9333	0.9843

Figure 7. Performance histogram of ANN, SVM and LR

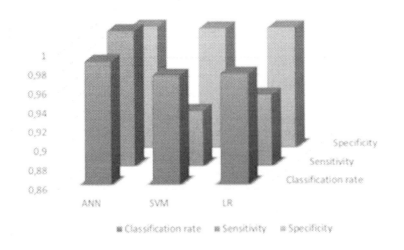

Table 4. Configuration of the database

ControlAgent		
Classification rate	**Sensitivity**	**Sensitivity**
0,975	0,982	0,973

Figure 8. Performance histogram of ControlAgent

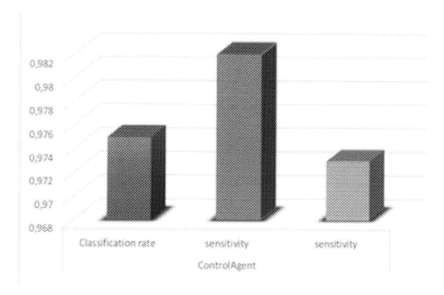

Authors adopted the distributed approach (MAS) to take advantage of the contributions of the three models (CANN, CSVM, CLR) each representing an agent to which they have integrated a fourth agent that they have named "ControlAgent". Beforehand, these different agents have been named as follows:

1- Agent Classifier for neural networks artificial CANN.
2- AgentClassiffeur1 for SVM CSVM.
3- Agent Classifier 2 for logistic regression CLR.

The ControlAgent retrieves the results of the three agents then it calculates its own performance in order to establish the final diagnosis the results obtained are presented in the following table:

Researchers note that the ControlAgent has benefited from the best results obtained by the three agents (majority vote) to calculate its own performance, which has visibly increased its results.

FUTURE RESEARCH DIRECTIONS

This system of course is far from complete, and still requires effort and perseverance. And if authors have the chance to continue in this area of research the next steps would be focused on the following points:

Apply their system to a large database, with potentially inconsistent data; harmoniously complete the development of the different agents; Increased communication between different agents and they need to develop systems that explicitly take this into account, by combining data mining with game theory.

CONCLUSION

In this chapter, Researchers focused on the study of three different domains that are Distributed Data Mining, the agent paradigm, and the use of agents in Data Mining with the ultimate goal of providing a Data Mining based agent approach and to design the multi-agent system to implement it. Agent-based data mining is a new discipline that combines two major technologies that are Data Mining, and multi-agent systems. From this discipline derive two new lines of research. One is interested in improving the Data Mining process by using the paradigm agent advantages, and the other leverages Data Mining techniques for the development and realization of intelligence in agent technology. this case study was conducted while trying to choose the best technical tools. She highlighted the mechanism of the proposed approach. Authors hope to have given a good idea about Data Mining systems based agents, their characteristics, their objectives and explicitly underlined the nature of the problems posed by these systems. From the points we have quoted, they can judge that the two areas of data mining and intelligent agents are evolution-capable and research-rich areas that is waiting, one that comes to meet its challenges.

REFERENCES

Bellifemine, F., Caire, G., Poggi, A., & Rimassa, G. (2008, January). JADE: A software framework for developing multi-agent applications. Lessons learned. *Information and Software Technology*, *50*(1-2), 10–21. doi:10.1016/j.infsof.2007.10.008

Cao, Z., An, S., & Gorodetsky, C., & Yu. (Eds.). (2014). *Agents and Data Mining Interaction. 10th International workshop, ADMI 2014*, Paris, France.

Ellouzi, H., Ltifi, H., & Ben Ayed, M. (2017, April). Multi-agent modelling of decision support systems based on visual data mining. *Multiagent Grid Syst.*, *13*(1), 31–45. doi:10.3233/MGS-170260

Han, Kamber, & Pei. (2011). Data Mining: Concepts and Techniques. *Lecture Notes in Computer Science*, 9145.

Niazalizadeh Moghadam, A., & Ravanmehr, R.. (2018, January). Multi-agent distributed data mining approach for classifying meteorology data: Case study on Iran's synoptic weather stations. *International Journal of Environmental Science and Technology*, *15*(1), 149–158. doi:10.100713762-017-1351-x

Perner, P. (2017). *Advances in Data Mining. Applications and Theoretical Aspects. 17th Industrial Conference, ICDM 2017*, New York, NY.

Rao, V. S. (n.d.). Multi Agent-Based Distributed Data Mining: An Over View. *Lecture Notes in Computer Science, 10357.*

Soares, F. M., & Souza, A. M. F. (2016). *Neural network programming with Java: unleash the power of neural networks by implementing professional Java code*. Birmingham, UK: Packt Publishing.

Chapter 12
Split and Merge–Based Breast Cancer Segmentation and Classification

Ichrak Khoulqi
University of Sultan Moulay Slimane Beni-Mellal, Morocco

Najlae Idrissi
University of Sultan Moulay Slimane Beni-Mellal, Morocco

ABSTRACT

Breast cancer is the most frequent cancer in morocco with 36.1%. It is the second leading cause of death for women all over the world. The effective way to diagnose and treat breast cancer is the early detection because it increases the success of treatment and the chances of survival. Digitized mammographic images are one of the frequently used diagnosis tools to detect and classify the breast cancer at the early stage. To improve the diagnosis accuracy, computer-aided diagnosis (CAD) systems are beneficial for detection. Generally, a CAD system consists of four stages: pretreatment, segmentation, features extraction, and classification. In this chapter, the authors present some work in the development of a CAD system in order to segment a breast tumor (microcalcifications) on mammographic images and classify it by choosing the algorithm that gives a good rate using a technique of a vote.

INTRODUCTION

Breast cancer is a malignant tumour that originates in breast cells. The word "malignant" means the tumor can spread (metastasize) to other parts of the body (Institut National du Cancer, 2016) . Breast cells sometimes undergo changes that make their growth or behaviour abnormal. These changes can lead to benign breast conditions, such as atypical hyperplasia and cysts. In some cases, changes in breast cells can cause breast cancer. In the context of prevention it is necessary to use a radiography tool that allows to better visualize the different parts of the breast and one of the best tools is Mammography which is a technique of radiography, particularly adapted to the breasts of the woman. It is intended to detect abnormalities as soon as possible before they cause clinical symptoms (IMENE CHEIKHROUHOU,2012).

DOI: 10.4018/978-1-7998-1021-6.ch012

The mammography image is the result of attenuation of a beam of Xrays passing through the different mammary tissues. The attenuation of this beam depends essentially on the composition of the tissues through which it passes. Indeed, the grease is considered a transparent radio zone since it has a very light physical density. As a result, it appears very dark on a mammogram. The opaque radio zones appear clear and correspond to the fibroglandular tissue and calcium which is the essential component of the mammary lesions (IMENE CHEIKHROUHOU,2012).Mammography is usually taken in different directions called incidences. A good incidence is to visualize the maximum breast tissue by spreading it as much as possible on the X-ray plate. Depending on the part of the breast examined, different implications are used. The most frequently used incidences are the incidence of the face also called Cranio Caudale (CC), the oblique external incidence called Medio Lateral Oblique (MLO) and the incidence of profile.

The mammography is an essential examination for the diagnosis of breast diseases in the presence of a symptom: palpable nodule, skin changes, discharge, inflammation.

Background

In the detection of breast cancer, several studies have been performed using mammographic images to determine microcalcifications.

This first work (M.Nafi Gurcan, Yasemin Yardimci, A.Enis, Cetin and Rashid Ansari,1997) consists in improving the digital mammographic images in order to use them in the diagnostic process, so in this work the detection of microcalcifications is performed in the sub-band domain (application of a filter bank to have an image decompose into sub-band),the resulting sub image is analyzed to detect microcalcifications groupings using third and fourth order correlation parameters (asymmetry and kurtosis) to find microcalcifications clusters, then the obtained sub-images will be divided into square regions whose asymmetry and Kurtosis will be estimated, if a region has a positive and high value of asymmetry and kurtosis then it is considered to be a region of interest.

The second work (T.Balakumaran, Dr.Ila.Vennila,C.Gowri shankar,2010) consists in improving the microcalcifications using the wavelet transform, and for the detection phase they used the fuzzy shell method.

- **Microcalcifications Improvement:** wavelet analysis allows image decomposition at different resolution levels according to a two-dimensional structure .
- **Microcalcifications Detection:** this involves identifying the region of interest(ROI), after improving the mammographic image by the wavelet transform, the resulting detailed horizontal or vertical image is used to identify the region by surrounding the microcalcification clusters,the third and fourth order statistical parameters, asymmetry and Kurtosis are used to find the microcalcification regions.Then Fuzzy shell clustering is used to perceive the nodular structure of the ROI.

In (Saranya R, M. Bharathi Ph.D, Showbana.R, 2014), their work is based on four main steps:

- **Preprocessing:** They use the median filter which is a nonlinear digital filtering technique, often used to eliminate noise and also it keeps the edges while eliminating noise.
- **Segmentation:** The segmentation method used is the region growth method, this method takes an initial set of points as input and these initial points mark each of the objects to be segmented. Regions magnified iteratively by comparing all the neighboring pixels not allocated to the regions

Figure 1. Two-dimensional structure of dyadic wavelets

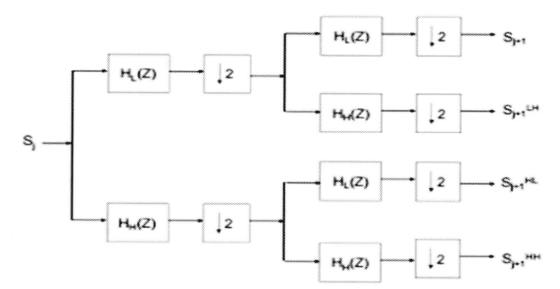

and the difference between the intensity value of the pixel and the average of the region is used as a measure of similarity. The pixel with the smallest difference value is assigned to the corresponding region. This process continues until all pixels are allocated to a region.

- **Extraction of Characteristics**: The feature extraction step is the most critical in the context of microcalcifications segmentation and classification. In this work, they proposed the use of 10 different parameters in the first step of feature extraction. The parameters they considered are sub-divided into: geometric characteristics and characteristics of the texture. The first is related to the shape of the microcalcifications, the distance between them and to many statistics, the second set of characteristics deals with the interior of microcalcifications, taking into account the variation of intensity in each microcalcifications. Finally, they used texture features called Haralick parameters. A combination of three characteristics, such as entropy, energy, and number of pixels, is a combination that distinguishes the pathological stage from microcalcifications.

- **Classification:** After extracting the necessary characteristics, they proceeded to the classification phase using artificial neural networks (ANN) is a set of algorithms whose design is originally very schematically inspired by the functioning of biological neurons, and which later came closer to statistical methods.

Another work (Anuj Kumar Singh, Bhupendra Gupta, 2015) consists in creating a diagnostic aid system for breast cancer, and to do this they passed through several stages:

- **Preprocessing:** They take a mammography image of a size M*N and they make an average filter of size s*s to smooth the pixels which have a value of intensity close to or similar to that of the cancerous region.

- **Segmentation:** In this step they performed a thresholding to separate the pixels of the cancerous region from the normal region. but they find that there are still white patches that cover the area of interest, to solve this problem they used the Max-Mean and Least-Variance technique, which first creates a small rectangular window along the white spot and applies this window to the image, then they divide this window into sub windows of size w*w to find the local mean and variance in each sub window .Then highlighting all the pixels of the sub windows found in the previous step identifies the region of interest and to extract this region from the input image they used the morphological close and gradient of the image.

Also in (Danilo Cesar Pereira, Rodrigo Pereira Ramos, Marcelo Zanchetta do Nascimento, 2014), they used mammographic images using both CC and MLO views, their work proceeds in three stages:

- **Artefacts Removal**: to ensure the performance of the segmentation algorithm it is first necessary to remove the artefacts from each image using the top-hat method of mathematical morphology with a 60 pixel(radius) structuring element, after a subtraction is performed between the original image and the resulting image .
- **Enhancement based on Wavelet Multiresolution Processing**: the analysis of images with multiple scales makes it possible to modify the resolution of the images in order to treat the least possible data, it is a question of representing an images on several sub images of great resolution to the smallest and then to analyze them in the domain of the frequencies.
- **Segmentation using Wavelet Analysis and Genetic Algorithm**: Wavelet theory and genetic algorithm (GA) determine the threshold number for each mammographic image by calculating the histogram of grey levels to see the graphical representation of grey levels, and to accelerate convergence of GA the size of the histogram is reduced by the dyadic wavelet transformation.

THE PROPOSED APPROACH

With the aim to increase the chances of detecting the evolution of breast cancer, we proposed an automatic early breast cancer detection based on digital mammograms analysis and interpretation using the tools of medical imaging, the use of digital mammograms allows us to better visualize the lesion in order to detect the ROI and classify it. for the purpose of increasing the chances of an effective treatment to regress the evolution of microcalcifications.

The essential steps through which our system passes are: Pretreatment, Segmentation, Description and Classification of mammography images.

In this section, we will detail the different preprocessing, segmentation and classification algorithms designed during this work as illustrated in Figure below:

Preprocessing Step

Digital mammography images often contain significant quantities of noise, so filtering must be done to attenuate noise and increase the homogeneity of the image to make it as clean as possible, and to do this we proposed to use median filter (P. BONNET) because it allows to remove impulsive noise and it respects the edges.

Figure 2. General structure of our system of detection and classification of Breast Cancer

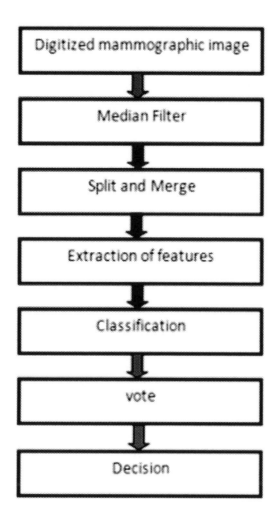

Figure 3. a: The original image, b: The filtered image

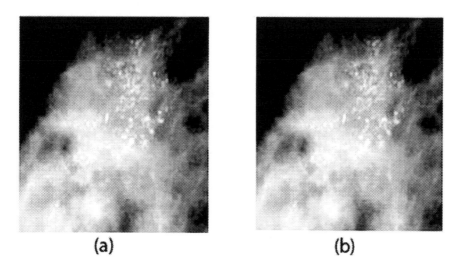

(a) (b)

Segmentation Step

Image segmentation is the most critical task of image analysis, it consists in partitioning an image into multiple regions, it is used to detect and locate objects and boundaries. The aim of segmentation is to make the representation of an image significant and easy to be analysed.

Split and Merge Approach

The split and merge(SM)algorithm (S.L. Horowitz et T. Pavlidis, 1976) was first introduced in 1974 by Pavlidis and Horowitz. This algorithm is similar in principle to the region growing algorithm. The main difference stems from the nature of the aggregate elementary regions.

This technique is used for image segmentation, it allows the image to be divided into four regions based on the homogeneity criterion and similar regions are merged to construct the result (the segmented image).

The SM is based on the quadtree structure, the steps through which this algorithm passes are as follows:

- Specifying the homogeneity criterion that will be used in the test;
- Divide the image into four regions of the same size;
- Calculate the criteria for each region;
- This process will be repeated until all regions pass the homogeneity test.

There are several ways to define the criterion of homogeneity, among these methods we cite:

- Variance:the gray level variance will be defined as follows.

$$\sigma^2 = \frac{1}{N-1}\sum(I(i,j) - \overline{I})^2 \tag{1}$$

- Local and global mean: If the mean of a region is high in comparison to the mean of the original image, then this region is homogeneous.
- Uniformity: the region is homogeneous if its grey levels are constant or inside a given threshold.

Figure 4. Segmentation of Digitized mammography using SM

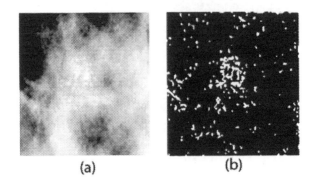

(a)   (b)

We applied this method to detect MCCs contained in mammography images because this technique is a global and local method: globally during division, and local during merging. The result of this application provides information on the Microcalcifications and their distribution in digitized mammography.

Features' Extraction Step

The extraction of discriminating characteristics is a fundamental step in the recognition process, prior to classification. The characteristics are usually numerical, but they can be strings, graphs or other quantities. it consists in producing a vector regrouping the information extracted from the image called descriptor. This descriptor translates information from an image into a more compact form. In the following section we will present all the methods used in this work to extract the characteristics.

Local Binary Pattern

Local binary patterns were initially proposed by Ojala in 1996 (Lotfi HOUAM, 2012) in order to characterize the textures present in images in gray levels. They consist in attributing to each pixel P of the image I (i,j) to be analyzed, a value characterizing the local pattern around this pixel. These values are calculated by comparing the gray level of the central pixel P with the values of the gray levels of the neighboring pixels.

The concept of LBP is simple, it proposes to assign a binary code to a pixel according to its neighbors. This code describing the local texture of a region is calculated by thresholding a neighbor with the gray level of the central pixel, in order to generate a binary pattern, all neighbors will then take a "1" value if their value is greater than or equal to the current pixel and "0" otherwise . The pixels of this binary pattern are then multiplied by weights and summed in order to obtain an LBP code of the current pixel.

Figure 5. Construction of a binary pattern and calculation of the LBP code

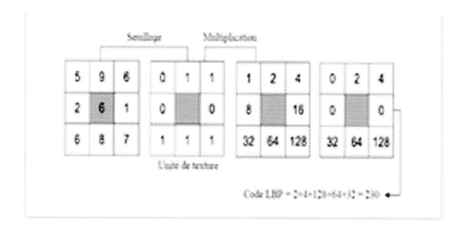

Tamura

The Tamura approach (N. Idrissi, 2008) is interesting for the search of images by content, it describes the possible textures, because it adopts an approach based on psychological studies and on visual perception. The authors propose six visual texture parameters:

- Coarseness
- Contrast;
- Direction;
- Presence of lines;
- Regularity;
- Roughness.

These parameters are calculated to construct a texture vector. The first three parameters (coarseness, direction, contrast) have a strong connection with human perception. It would seem that the human eye is most sensitive to the coarseness of the texture, then to its contrast and finally to the direction. This type of characteristics may seem interesting to compare the visual content of the images because it corresponds directly to the way in which the human perceives them.

Gabor Filters

GABOR (A. Pujol, 2009) or Gaussian filters are a special class of linear filters, they are oriented filters. These filters have an impulse response i. e. applied by convolution, which are composed of a sinusoidal component and a Gaussian component these filters correspond to a weighting by a Gaussian function in the frequency domain.

$$h\left(x,y\right) = g\left(X,Y\right)e^{2\pi j\left(Ux+Vy\right)} \tag{2}$$

where

$(X,Y) = (x\cos\phi + y\sin\phi, -x\sin\phi + y\cos\phi)$

the rotation angle ϕ of (X,Y) in regard to (x,y) gives the orientation of the Gaussian envelope in the space domain. And

$$g\left(X,Y\right) = \frac{1}{2\pi\sigma^2}e^{\frac{-\left(\frac{X}{\lambda}\right)^2 + Y^2}{2\sigma^2}}$$

is a two-dimensional Gaussian function of axis ratio λ and the expansion factor σ.

CLASSIFICATION STEP

Classification allows to group all the pixels of the image into a limited number of classes corresponding to the major structural components of the image, it is a method to establish a cartography for the image.

Two types of classifications can be distinguished: unsupervised classifications where information about the objects to be classified is not previously relied upon, and supervised calssifications based on the identification of the objects known as "reference sites".

In our case, we adopted the supervised classification in order to have information on the pathological aspects of the lesion and for this purpose we chose three classifiers that allow us to give better rates for the classification of mammographic images.

K-Nearest Neighbor

The k nearest neighbors(KNN) approach is a powerful non-parametric method for estimating and determining the class of an image, this method (W. Lahbib., 2013) consists in determining for each new individual who is to be classified the list of k-nearest neighbors among the individuals already classified. The KNN method is a technique that is generally based on the calculation of the Euclidean distance between an unclassified image and the other images contained in the learning base according to the chosen value of k.

Let's take for example an input sample y_i with m features $(y_{i1}, y_{i2}, \ldots, y_{im})$, so the Euclidean distance between y_i and y_l with m features $(y_{l1}, y_{l2}, \ldots, y_{lm})$ is as follows:

$$d\left(y_i, y_l\right) = \sqrt{\left(y_{i1} - y_{l1}\right)^2 + \left(y_{i2} - y_{l2}\right)^2 + \ldots + \left(y_{im} - y_{lm}\right)^2} \tag{3}$$

Finally, classification is done by assigning the class of the element that occurs most frequently among the k training samples and is closest to the element in question.

Support Vector Machine

The Support Vector Machine (SVM) (O. Bousquet,2001), also called the "Large Margin Separator",it is an algorithm of the automatic learning family that solves the classification problem, its purpose is to separate the data points by using a separating surface in a way that the distance between the data points and the separating surface is maximum, this distance called the "Margin".

The separating surface assumes that the data are linearly separable, which is not possible in most cases,thus the need to separate the data in a greater vector space\cite{svmthese}, this is called the kernel trick.

We consider the separation of the vectors of the training base into two separate classes:

$$D=\{(x^1,y^1),\ldots,(x^l,y^l)\} \tag{4}$$

where $x \in R^n$ and $y \in \{-1,1\}$. With the equation of the hyperplan:

$(w,x)+b=0$ (5)

If there is a maximum separation between the vector closest to the hyperplane, then we have the redundancy at the equation mentioned above. therefore it is necessary to consider a vapnik (1995) canonical hyperplane, where the parameters w and b will be constrained by:

$\min_i |(w,x^i)+b|=1$ (6)

This parameter setting is necessary to simplify the formulation of the problem. The hyperplane of separation in canonical form will be as follows:

$Y^i[(w,x^i)+b]>1, i,=1,\dots,l$ (7)

And the distance between the hyperplane and the data point x is as shown below:

$$d\left(w,b;x\right) = \frac{\left|\left(w,x^i\right)+b\right|}{\left\|w\right\|}$$ (8)

Hence the hyperplane that optimally separates the data is the one that minimise:

$$\phi\left(w\right) = \frac{1}{2}\left\|w\right\|^2$$ (9)

Decision Tree (Algorithm C4.5)

The algorithm C4.5 was developed by Quinlan in 1993 (R. Marée, 2005). The decision trees are a very effective method of supervised training. The aim is to partition a data set into groups that are as homogeneous as possible in terms of the variable to be predicted. We take as input a set of classified data, and we provide as output a tree that looks like an orientation diagram where each end node (sheet) represents a decision (a class) and each non-end node (internal) represents a test. This method uses a more elaborated "gain ratio" criterion, the purpose of which is to limit the proliferation of the Tree by penalizing variables that have many modalities, C4.5 practices pruning to classify the attributes and build the decision tree.

First we will calculate the entropy which represents the information contained in a distribution:

$Entropy(D) = -p_+\log(p_+)-p_-\log(p_-)$ (10)

And now we will define a function that allows to choose the test that should label the current node by calculating the gain information, its formula is as follows:

$$Gain\left(D,T\right) = Entropy\left(D\right) - \sum_{i=1}^{n}(p_i * Entropy\left(p_i\right)) \tag{11}$$

with T is a test.

EXPERIMENTAL RESULTS

The description and classification allow us to classify our mammography images. In the figure below we present the result obtained for the rate of classification by using a proposed descriptors and classifiers.

In this work, we have made a hybridization of descriptors (Gabor and Tamura) in order to obtain a better rate of good classification, the graph below illustrates the results obtained.

In our computer aided diagnostic system, we were based on majority voting to give a reliable and correct classification according to the different results obtained from the selected classifiers.

To measure the quality of segmented images, we used the structural similarity measure (SSIM) (David M. Rouse, Sheila S. Hemami) which employs a local spatial correlation measure between the reference image pixels and the test images that is modulated by distortions, his expression is given by the following formula:

$$SSIM\left(I_o, I_s\right) = \frac{\left(2\mu_o\mu_s + c_1\right)\left(2\sigma_{os} + c_2\right)}{\left(\mu_o^2 + \mu_s^2 + c_1\right)\left(\sigma_o^2 + \sigma_s^2 + c_2\right)} \tag{12}$$

where:

Figure 6. Rate of Classification

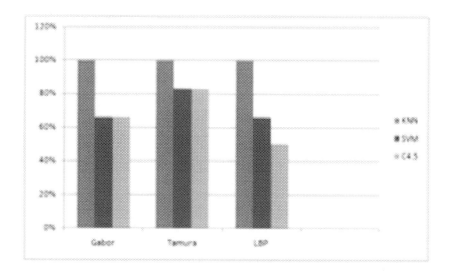

Figure 7. Rate of Classification

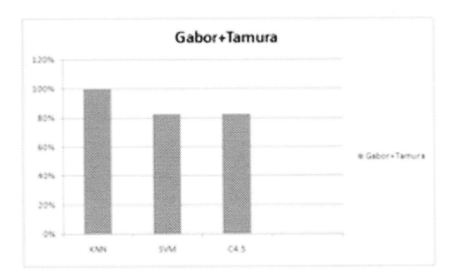

μ_o The average of O;

μ_s The average of S;

μ_o^2 the variance of O;

μ_s^2 the variance of S;

σ_{os} the covariance of O and S;

$c_1=(k_1L)^2$, $c_2=(k_2L)^2$ two variables to stabilize the division with weak denominator;

L The dynamic range of the pixel-values ((typically this is $2^{bitsperpixels-1}$));

$k_1=0.01$ and $k_2=0.03$ by default.

Also we used the PSNR Peak Signal-to-Noise Ratio (Yusra A, Y. Al-Najjar, Dr. Der Chen Soong, 2012) is an estimate of the reconstructed image quality relative to the original image, it represents a mathematical measure based on the difference in pixels between these two images, his expression is given by the following formula:

$$PSNR = 10log\frac{s^2}{MSE} \tag{14}$$

where s = 255 for an 8-bit image. And MSE is the Mean Square Error computed by averaging the squared intensity of the original(input) image and the resultant (output) image pixels.

$$MSE = \frac{1}{MN}\sum_{m=0}^{M-1}\sum_{n=0}^{N-1}e\left(m,n\right)^2 \tag{15}$$

where e(m,n) is the error difference between the original and the distorted images, and M*N represent the size of the images.

Table 1. The values of the SSIM and PSNR indices using the Split & Merge Approach

Experiments	SSIM	PSNR
	0,9662	41,10
	0,8986	35,54
	0,9491	39,79
	0,9591	41,98
	0,9569	41,60
	0,9183	38,27
	0,9629	35,97

Table 1 summarize the overall results obtained for the approach based on Split and Merge using the two evaluation metrics cited above.

CONCLUSION

The objective we fixed at the beginning of this work was to propose a decision support system for the detection of breast cancer at an early stage in order to increase the chances of survival and cure. To achieve this objective, we have studied several segmentation algorithms that will detect lesions in breast tissue and determine their degree of malignancy in order to improve the prevention of these diseases that attack women and that are fatal causes in women.

REFERENCES

Association Lalla Salma de lutte contre le cancer. (2011). Guide de détection précoce des cancers du sein et du col de l'utérus. Author.

Balakumaran, Vennila, & Shankar. (2010). Detection of Microcalcification in Mammograms Using Wavelet Transform and Fuzzy Shell Clustering. *International Journal of Computer Science and Information Security*, 7(1).

Bonnet. (n.d.). Image processing courses. USTL.

Bousquet. (2001). Introduction to Vector Machine Support (SVM). Academic Press.

Cheikhrouhou. (2012). Description et classification des masses mammaires pour le diagnostic du cancer du sein. Universite D'evry Val D'essonne Laboratoire d'Informatique, Biologie Intégrative et Systèmes Complexes.

Gurcan, Yardımcı, & Cetin, Enis,, & Ansari. (1997). Detection of Microcalcifications in Mammograms Using Higher Order Statistics. *IEEE Signal Processing Letters*, 4(8).

Horowitz, S. L., & Pavlidis, T. (1976). Picture segmentation by a directed split and merge procedure. Computer Methods in Images Analysis.

Idrissi, N. (2008). *La navigation dans des bases d'images: prise en compte des attributs de texture* (PhD thesis). Université de Nantes.

Institut National du Cancer. (2016). *Cancers du sein.* Author.

Lahbib. (2013). Algorithm KNN: K-nearest neighbor. Academic Press.

Lotfi, H. (2012). *Contribution à l'analyse de textures de radiographies Osseuses pour le diagnostic précoce de l'ostéoporose.* Thèse de Doctorat.

Marée. (2005). *Automatic classification of images by decision tree.* Academic Press.

Pereira & Ramos. (2014). Segmentation and detection of breast cancer in mammograms combining wavelet analysis and genetic algorithm. *Marcelo Zanchetta do Nascimento., 114,* 88–101.

Pujol. (2009). Contribution à la classification sémantique d'imageAcademic Press..

Rouse & Hemami. (n.d.). The Role of edge information to estimate the perceived utility of natural images. Visual Communications Lab, School of Electrical and Computer Engineering. *Cornell University.*

Saranya, R., & Bharathi Ph, M. D. (2014). Automatic Detection and Classification of Microcalcification on Mammographic Images. *IOSR Journal of Electronics and Communication Engineering, 9*(3), 65-71.

Singh & Gupta. (2015). A Novel Approach for Breast Cancer Detection and Segmentation in a Mammogram. Eleventh International Multi-Conference on Information Processing-2015.

Yusra, Al-Najjar, & Soong. (2012). Comparison of Image Quality Assessment:PSNR, HVS, SSIM, UIQI. *International Journal of Scientific & Engineering Research, 3*(8).

Chapter 13

Mammogram Classification Using Nonsubsampled Contourlet Transform and Gray–Level Co–Occurrence Matrix

Khaddouj Taifi
University Sultan Moulay Slimane Beni, Morocco

Naima Taifi
University Sultan Moulay Slimane Beni, Morocco

Mohamed Fakir
University Sultan Moulay Slimane Beni, Morocco

Said Safi
University Sultan Moulay Slimane Beni, Morocco

Muhammad Sarfraz
ⓘD https://orcid.org/0000-0003-3196-9132
Kuwait University, Kuwait

ABSTRACT

This chapter explores diagnosis of the breast tissues as normal, benign, or malignant in digital mammography, using computer-aided diagnosis (CAD). System for the early diagnosis of breast cancer can be used to assist radiologists in mammographic mass detection and classification. This chapter presents an evaluation about performance of extracted features, using gray-level co-occurrence matrix applied to all detailed coefficients. The nonsubsampled contourlet transform (NSCT) of the region of interest (ROI) of a mammogram were used to be decomposed in several levels. Detecting masses is more difficult than detecting microcalcifications due to the similarity between masses and background tissue such as F) fatty, G) fatty-glandular, and D) dense-glandular. To evaluate the system of classification in which

DOI: 10.4018/978-1-7998-1021-6.ch013

k-nearest neighbors (KNN) and support vector machine (SVM) used the accuracy for classifying the mammograms of MIAS database between normal and abnormal. The accuracy measures through the classifier were 94.12% and 88.89% sequentially by SVM and KNN with NSCT.

INTRODUCTION

In spite of evolution of new technologies for progressing quality of the mammographic images, the interpretation process and the images analysis are still difficult tasks. The same difficulty is true for the radiologist. This is due to the abundant texture and/or noise. It is expected to develop the analysis system and automatic interpretation of the mammographic images as a tool of the aid to make decision for detecting and classifying cancer. Currently, breast cancer is the most frequently found cancer for women worldwide and such incidences are increasing at a large scale. Therefore, search for analyzing images of the breast to aid diagnostic system (HD. Cheng et al., 2006) attracts the attention of many researchers. There are, at present, a number of techniques used for the medical images for breast cancer diagnosis which are: Ultrasound (imaging ultrasound), MRI (Magnetic resonance imaging) and mammography. Many of the studies have agreed the idea that the early stage of detection of the breast cancer may improve prognosis and improve survival rate for breast cancer patients (Smart CR et al., 1995; B.Cady et al., 2001).

Mammography technique remains the essential part of detecting breast. It is the most efficient in monitoring and early detection of breast cancer (L. Tabár et al.,1985; RE. Bird et al., 1992). All radiologists suffer from the difficulty in interpreting mammograms which further increased with type of examined breast tissue. Mammographic images show a contrast between the two main components of the breast fatty tissue and Connective-Fibrous Matrix. In general, it is very difficult to define normality of mammographic images: Indeed, the appearance of the mammary gland is extremely variable depending on the patient age and the period in which the mammogram is done. That's why many researchers have proposed the algorithms for mass.

An approach for Mammogram classification (S. Beura et al., 2015) was presented using two dimensional Discrete Wavelet Transform and Gray-Level Co-occurrence Matrix for detecting breast cancer. The work in (Yu. Zhang et el., 2010) came up with new segmentation method for identifying mass regions in mammograms. For each ROI, an enhancement function was applied and proceeded with filters. Then, energy features based on the co-occurrence matrix of pixels were computed. The paper (P. Rahmati et el., 2009) presented a region-based active contour approach to segmentation of masses in digital mammograms. The work in (M.M. Eltoukhy et al., 2010) presented an approach for breast cancer diagnosis in digital mammogram using Curvelet Transform. After suggested mammogram images in Curvelet basis, a special set of the biggest coefficients is extracted as feature vector. A Computer-aided diagnosis (CAD) for characterization of Mammographic Masses was presented in (Jiazheng Shi et al., 2009). It is based on Level Set Segmentation with New Image Features. The Patient Information is based on the level set method, and includes two new types of image features related to the presence of microcalcifications with the mass and patient age. A linear discriminant analysis (LDA) classifier with stepwise feature selection was used to merge the extracted features into a classification score.

The literature survey reveals the existing classification schemes for digital mammogram images. However, most of them are not able to provide a good accuracy. In this chapter, we have proposed an effective algorithm for detecting and extracting texture features, using Nonsubsampled Contourlet Trans-

Figure 1. Block diagram of the proposed scheme for classification of mammograms using SVM and KNN

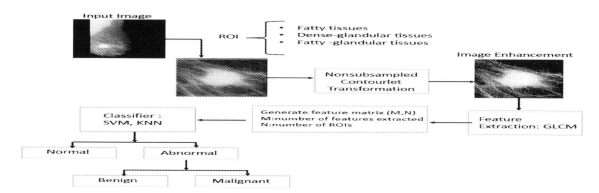

formation and the Wavelet transform Discrete with gray-level co-occurrence matrix (GLCM). To classify features, we used SVM and KNN, whether it is a normal or abnormal. Algorithm proposed extraction and classification is shown in (see Figure 1).

The rest of this chapter is organized as follows. Section 2 deals with the proposed scheme, where extraction of features and classification is discussed in detail. Section 3 describes the experimental results and analysis. Section 4 gives the concluding remarks.

METHODOLOGY

This section is dedicated to the proposed methodology, it proposes extraction and classification. The whole methodology is summarized in the designed Algorithm as shown in Figure 1.

Extraction of Region of Interest (ROI)

It may be noticed that Mammography images are, often, affected by different types of noise that are due to acquisition of parameters. These parameters include the exposure time and the strength of compression of the breast, artifacts in their background. The object area also contains the pectoral muscles. A human visual system can easily ignore these artifacts in the interpretation process. It's not the same case for the automated system, and these artifacts may interfere with this process. For this reason, many studies have, recently, worked on extracting breast area and removing artifacts in mammography (M. Wirth et al.,2005; L. Belkhodja et al., 2009; J. Nagi et al.,2011) have proved the effectiveness in the development of the automatic diagnosis in mammography.

All these areas are unwantedly creating obstacles in extracting descriptor features by which mammographic images can classify between normality and abnormality. Therefore, the regions of interests containing the abnormalities must be extracted, excluding the unwanted areas of the image.

We used in our work images "MIAS": "http://peipa.essex.ac.uk/ipa/pix/mias/" and the following link provides information about the nature and the location of present abnormality: "http://peipa.essex. ac.uk/info/mias.html". The MIAS link gives us the center of clusters of the abnormal area as the center of ROI as shown in Figure 2. From the center one can extract regions of interest. The size of original images is 1024 ×1024, and the size of regions of interest can be either 256 × 256, 128 ×128 or 64 ×64 depending on user choice.

Figure 2. Mammographic ROIs of MIAS database (J. Suckling, et al., 1994). The sub-figures indicate different type tissues present in mammograms. The levels a, b and c of ROIs represent normal, malignant and benign classes respectively: (1) Fatty tissue; (2) Fatty-glandular tissues; and (3) Dense-glandular tissues.

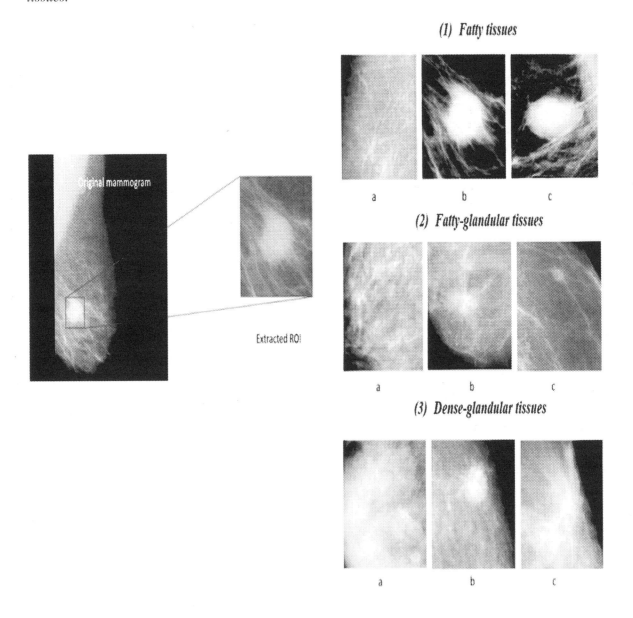

Nonsubsampled Contourlet Transformation

Contourlet Transform was proposed in (MN. Do et all., 2005) as a directional multiresolution image representation that can efficiently capture and represent smooth object boundaries in natural images. The contourlet transform is constructed as a combination of the Laplacian Pyramid (Lu. Yue et al., 2006) and the directional filter banks (DFB) (PJ. Burt et al., 19983). The Contourlet Transform can efficiently

Figure 3. Nonsubsampled contourlet transform. (a) NSFB structure that implements the NSCT; (b) Idealized frequency partitioning

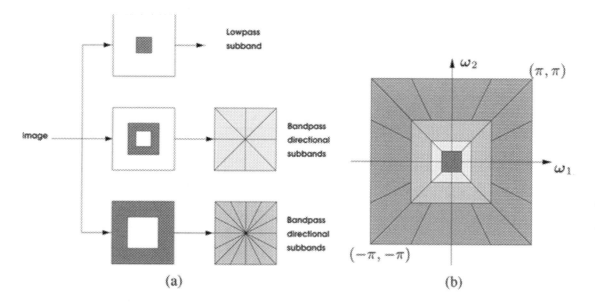

capture the basic geometric structures such as contours in an image and can achieve better expression of image than the Wavelet Transform. Moreover, it is easily adjustable for detecting fine details in any orientation along curvatures, which results in more potential for effective analysis of images.

However, the Contourlet Transform has lack of shift-invariance due to the down sampling and up sampling. In 2006, Cunha et al. suggests the Non-Subsampled Contourlet Transformation (NSCT) (RH. Bamberger et al.,1992) which is a fully shift-invariant, multiscale, and multidirectional expansion has better directional frequency localization and a fast implementation. NSCT consists of two filter banks, i.e. the nonsubsampled pyramid filter bank (NSPFB) and the nonsubsampled directional filter bank (NSDFB) as shown in Figure 3.a. They split the 2-D frequency plane in the sub-bands illustrated in Figure 3.b. The NSPFB provides nonsubsampled multi-scale decomposition and captures the point discontinuities. The NSDFB provides nonsubsampled directional decomposition and links point discontinuities into linear structures.

Gray-Level Co-Occurrence Matrix

Haralick (1973) proposed the gray-level co-occurrence matrix. This approach is about exploring the spatial dependency of texture by constructing a co-occurrence matrix in an orientation and a distance between the pixels of the image. Then, extracting information, which are based on the parameter of the Haralick, are defined as: contrast, entropy, homogeneity of the variance, the average sum, energy, uniformity, the correlation information1, and the correlation. The success of this method depends on the choice of parameters: the orientation and the distance between two neighboring pixels.

A co-occurrence matrix measures the probability of occurrence of pixel pairs located at a certain distance in the image; it is based on calculating probability P (i, j, d, θ). The angular directions used in the calculation of GLCM are respectively: θ = 0, 45,90,135 degrees with the distance D = 1,2, 3..., see Figure 4.

Figure 4. Directionality used in the gray level co-occurrence matrix

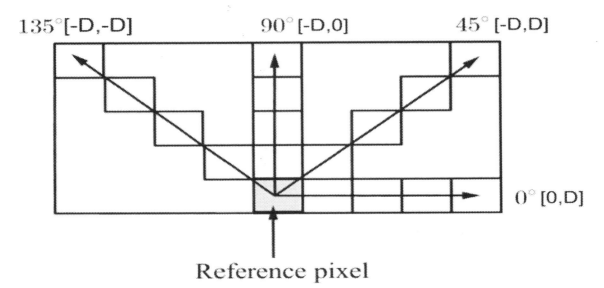

The texture descriptors derived from GLCM used in this work are: contrast, energy, Homogeneity and Correlation. The GLCM gives a joint distribution of gray level pairs of neighboring pixels within an image (*Haralick, R.M..*, 1973). In Table 1, we have the computation of feature descriptors.

with

$$\mu_i = \sum_i \sum_j i.P_{d,\theta}(i,j) \tag{1}$$

Table 1. Computation of feature descriptors for mammographic ROIs

Feature descriptor	Name	Computation
FD_1	Contrast	$C = \sum_{i=0}^{n}\sum_{j=0}^{n}(i-j)^2 P_{d,\theta}(i,j)$
FD_2	Correlation	$Cor = \dfrac{\sum_{i=0}^{n}\sum_{j=0}^{n} ij P_{d,\theta}(i,j) - \mu_i \mu_j}{\sigma_i \sigma_j}$
FD_3	Energy	$E = \sum_{i=0}^{n}\sum_{j=0}^{n} P_{d,\theta}(i,j)^2$
FD_4	**Homogeneity**	$H = \sum_{i=0}^{n}\sum_{j=0}^{n} \dfrac{1}{1+(i-j)^2} P_{d,\theta}(i,j)$

$$\mu_j = \sum_i \sum_j j.P_{d,\theta}(i,j) \tag{2}$$

$$\sigma_i = \sum_i \sum_j \left(i - \mu_i\right)^2 P_{d,\theta}(i,j) \tag{3}$$

$$\sigma_j = \sum_i \sum_j \left(i - \mu_j\right)^2 P_{d,\theta}(i,j) \tag{4}$$

Classification

During the classification of feature stage that characterizes the images, we use the Nearest Neighbor classifier (KNN) (O. Boiman et al., 2008) and Support Vector Machine (SVM) (J. C. Burges et al.,1998; B. Scholkopfand et all., 2002; U. Krebel., 1992).

EXPERIMENTAL RESULTS AND ANALYSIS

This section is dedicated to various experiments for the proposed method. A detailed analysis also makes a part of this section.

Experiment on the MIAS Dataset

To validate the proposed feature extraction and mammogram classification scheme (see Figure 5), simulations have been used in the MATLAB environment and mammographic images are taken from database such as Mammographic Image Analysis Society (MIAS) database: http://peipa.essex.ac.uk/ipa/pix/mias/ providing us with appropriate information based on types of background tissues for classifying mammograms into normal and abnormality; the abnormality is divided in to two classes: benign and malignant. The MIAS database contains 322 images. 207 images are normal, 115 images are abnormal and again among abnormal images, there is number of benign and malignant types, which are 64 and 51 respectively, which are categorized into three tissue types: fatty, fatty-glandular and dense-glandular.

Although MIAS database consists of 322 images, in this work we used only 94 ROI$_S$, which contain abnormality and normality. These are characterized by three background tissue types: fatty, fatty-glandular and dense-glandular. The number of training and testing is shown in Table 2.

Enhancement Mammographic ROIs by Nonsubsampled Contourlet Transform

Before extracting features, we have firstly to use the method of enhancement Mammographic ROIs by Nonsubsampled Contourlet Transform. It is easily adjustable for detecting fine details in any orientation as shown in Figure 6.

Figure 5. The proposed Breast Tissues Diagnosis system

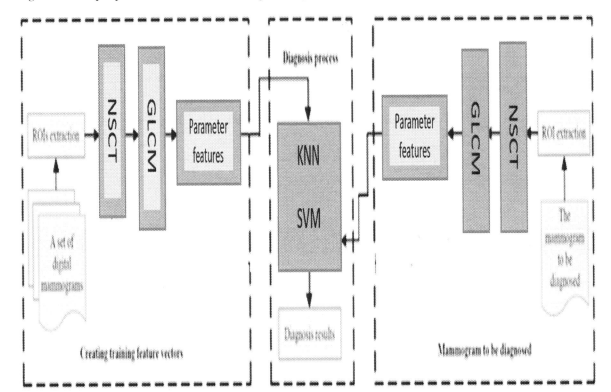

Table 2. Number of Training and Testing samples

Type of tissues	Abnormal	Normal	Training	Testing
Fatty	24	24	31	17
Fatty-glandular and dense tissues	26	20	28	18

Different Features

Extracting contrast, correlation, energy and homogeneity features of the images result of nonsubsampled contourlet transform method requires using GLCM characterized by four directions $\theta = 0, 45, 90, 135$ and distance parameter (D). In this work, we have taken the value of D = 1 and 2.

In order to evaluate the performance of the proposed method, we have to know the value D, the orientation and chosen features influencing on the final result. It can be done through a series of experiments which are made on the MIAS database.

Tables 3, 4, 5, 6 mention all the feature descriptors mentioned D =1 and $\theta = 0, 45, 90, 135$ respectively. To classify this features, we used some classifiers such as SVM and K Nearest Neighbor (KNN).

Figure 6. Enhancement Mammographic ROIs by Nonsubsampled Contourlet Transform. The sub-figures indicate different type tissues present in mammograms. The levels a, b and c of ROIs represent normal, malignant and benign classes respectively: (1) Fatty tissues; (2) Fatty-glandular tissues; (3) Dense-glandular tissues.

(1) Fatty tissues

(2) Fatty-glandular tissues

(3) Dense-glandular tissues

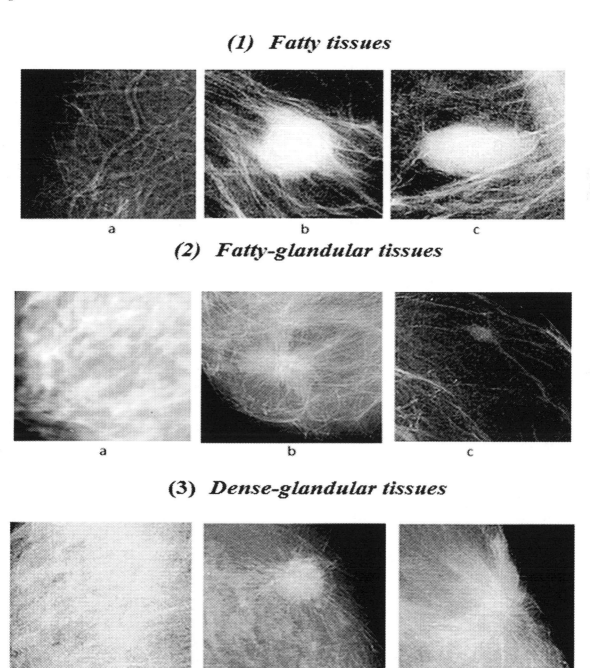

Different Classifiers

We use some typical classifiers such as SVM and KNN for the comparison: (1) SVM has recently received a widely considerable attention in pattern recognition. In the experiment, we selected Rbf, linear and quadratic types of kernel function. (2) KNN is a non-parametric method to label each testing sample's class based on its feature vector. The process of the classification is performed by calculating the similarity between a testing feature vector, each training feature vector and finding out the K nearest training cases. Therefore, the testing case is labeled by the class of the majority in these K cases. In our experiment, K is chosen between 1 and 10.

Table 3. Different values of various feature descriptors at $\theta=0$ with set distance $D=1$ for Fatty tissues

Type of ROI	FD_1	FD_2	FD_3	FD_4
mdb028 maligne	0,24	0,86	0,20	0,87
mdb134 maligne	0,25	0,71	0,34	0,87
mdb132 begnin	0,24	0,80	0,30	0,87
mdb025 begnin	0,27	0,78	0,20	0,86
mdb006 normal	0,23	0,39	0,48	0,88
mdb299 normal	0,25	0,45	0,41	0,87
mdb294 normal	0,23	0,79	0,37	0,88

Table 4. Different values of various feature descriptors at $\theta=45$ with set distance $D=1$ for Fatty tissues

Type of ROI	FD_1	FD_2	FD_3	FD_4
mdb028 maligne	0,29	0,83	0,19	0,85
mdb134 maligne	0,29	0,66	0,32	0,85
mdb132 begnin	0,28	0,77	0,29	0,85
mdb025 begnin	0,32	0,75	0,19	0,84
mdb006 normal	0,28	0,29	0,47	0,86
mdb299 normal	0,30	0,35	0,39	0,85
mdb294 normal	0,28	0,75	0,35	0,86

Table 5. Different values of various feature descriptors at $\theta=90$ with set distance $D=1$ for Fatty tissues

Type of ROI	FD_1	FD_2	FD_3	FD_4
mdb028 maligne	0,24	0,86	0,20	0,87
mdb134 maligne	0,25	0,70	0,34	0,87
mdb132 begnin	0,25	0,80	0,30	0,87
mdb025 begnin	0,27	0,78	0,20	0,86
mdb006 normal	0,24	0,39	0,48	0,88
mdb299 normal	0,26	0,44	0,41	0,86
mdb294 normal	0,24	0,78	0,36	0,87

Table 6. Different values of various feature descriptors at θ=135 with set distance D=1 for Fatty tissues

Type of ROI	FD_1	FD_2	FD_3	FD_4
mdb028 maligne	0,27	0,84	0,19	0,86
mdb134 maligne	0,29	0,66	0,32	0,85
mdb132 begnin	0,30	0,76	0,29	0,85
mdb025 begnin	0,33	0,74	0,18	0,83
mdb006 normal	0,28	0,28	0,46	0,86
mdb299 normal	0,31	0,34	0,39	0,84
mdb294 normal	0,28	0,75	0,35	0,86

Nearest Neighbor Classifier

The nearest neighbor classifier is used to compare between the feature vector of the input image and feature vectors stored in the database. It is obtained by finding the distance between the prototype image and the database. The class is found by measuring the distance between a feature vector of input image and feature vectors of images. The Euclidean distance measurement d, shown in Equation 5, is used in this chapter, but other distance measurements can be used as well (Boiman. O., 2008).

$$d = \sqrt{\sum_{i=1}^{n}(x_i - y_i)^2} \tag{5}$$

Support Vector Machine

Recently, the SVM has been gaining popularity in the field of pattern classification due to its encouraging experimental performance. More details about SVM can be found in (Burges, J. C., 1998). SVM are binary classifiers and different approaches like one-against-all; one-against-one are built to expand SVM to the multi-class classification case (Burges, J. C., 1998). For a K-class classification, the common method is to use one-against-all (Scholkopfand. B., 2002). Each SVM distinguishes one class from all other classes. The final output is the class that corresponds to the SVM with the highest output value. Another main method is the one-against-one. The first use of this strategy on SVM was done by (Kreel, U., 1999). This method works on building up all possible K(K 1)=2 binary SVMs representing all possible pairs out of K classes. Each one of them is used to distinguish between two of the K classes only.

Measuring Performance Evaluation

The performance metric used to evaluate the accuracy of the proposed classification system is the confusion matrix. It represents information about actual and classified cases produced by a classification system. Performance of such system evaluated by showing the normal and abnormal cases is shown in Figure 7.

To measure Accuracy for medical test, we tested some people. Some of these people have the disease, and our test says that they are positive. They are called true positives (TP). Some have disease, but the

Figure 7. Confusion matrix for two-class problem with different performance measures

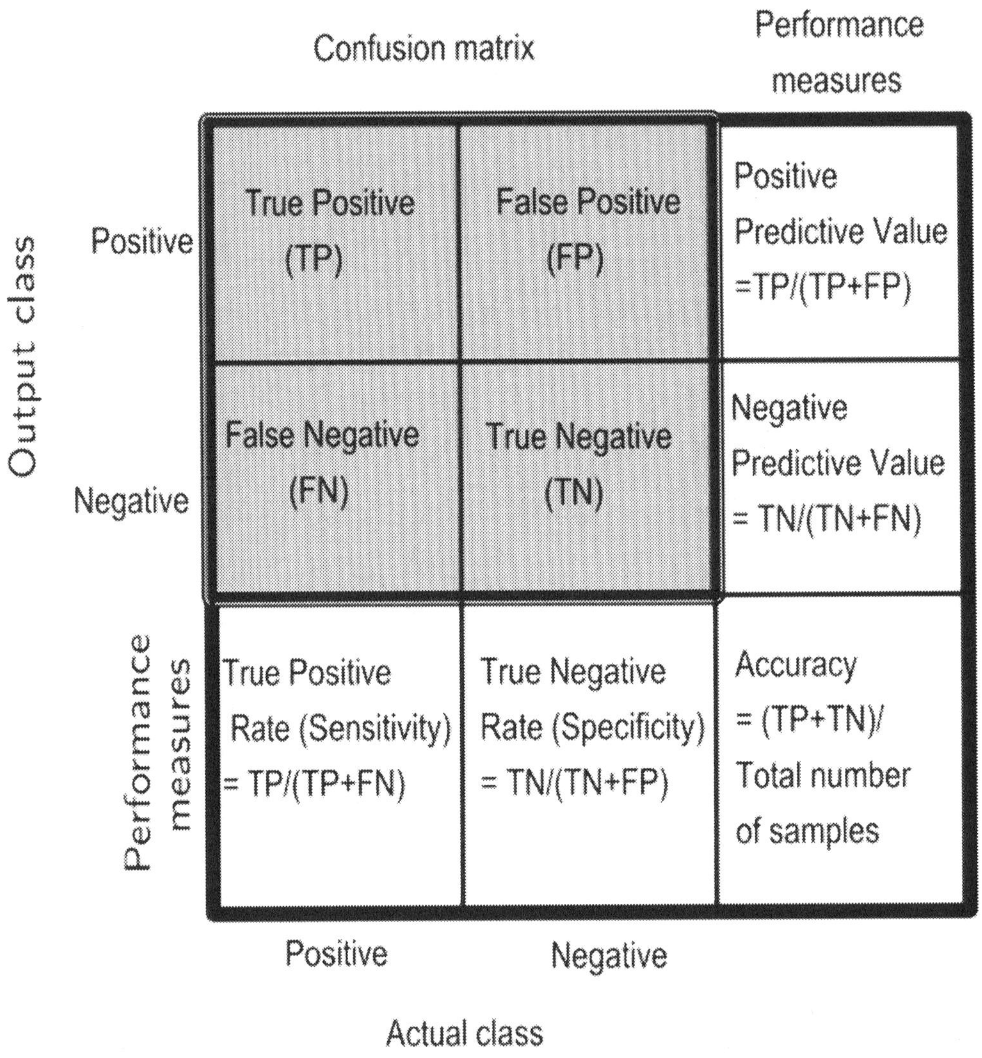

	Confusion matrix		Performance measures
Positive	True Positive (TP)	False Positive (FP)	Positive Predictive Value =TP/(TP+FP)
Negative	False Negative (FN)	True Negative (TN)	Negative Predictive Value = TN/(TN+FN)
Performance measures	True Positive Rate (Sensitivity) = TP/(TP+FN)	True Negative Rate (Specificity) = TN/(TN+FP)	Accuracy = (TP+TN)/ Total number of samples
	Positive	Negative	

Output class

Actual class

test says they don't. They are called false negatives (FN). Some don't have disease, and the test says they don't - true negative (TN). Finally, there were people in good health who have a positive result - false positive (FP). Thus, the number of true positives, false negatives, true negatives and false positives add up to 100% of the whole as shown in (Figure 7). A number of different measures are commonly used to evaluate performance of the proposed method. These measures including accuracy (Ac) is calculated from confusion matrix (R. Nithya et al., 2011).

The notations TP, FP, TN, and FN are explained as follows:

TP: Correct classification of abnormal.
FP: Incorrect classification of abnormal.
TN: Correct classification of normal.

Table 7. Accuracy the NSCT by SVM for classification with set distance D=1 for Fatty and Dense-glandular tissues

Methods	orientation	Fatty tissues			Dense-glandular tissues		
		rbf	linear	quadratic	rbf	linear	quadratic
NSCT	θ =0	0,94	0,88	0,70	0.72	0.6	0.38
	θ =45	0,94	0,88	0,70	0.66	0.50	0.50
	θ =90	0,94	0,88	0,70	0.66	0.44	0.38
	θ =135	0,88	0,88	0,76	0.66	0.61	0.44

FN: Incorrect classification of normal.

RESULTS AND DISCUSSIONS

This section provides various results for the proposed method. A detailed and useful related discussions also make a part of this section.

The Influence of Classifiers and Texture of Background on the Final Results

Table 7 shows the accuracy of classification of SVM for the descriptors GLCM. It can be noticed that the best accuracy of classification is obtained by Kernel function 'rbf' and 'linear' which is 94.12%. We can remark that extraction of descriptors from the images containing fatty tissues gives better performance than descriptors calculated from the images containing Dense-glandular tissues.

Figure 8. Accuracy KNN classifier of various descriptors feature at θ=0,45,90 and 135 with set distance d=1 for Fatty tissues

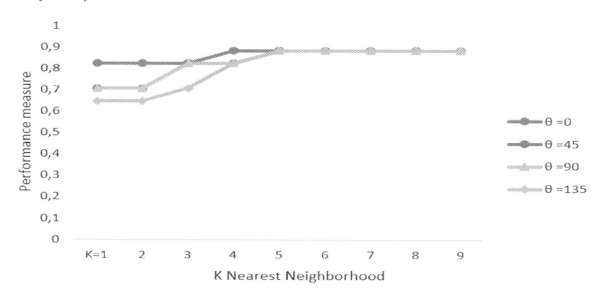

The Influence of Direction of GLCM on the Final Results

Figure 8 presents the calculation of the accuracy which shows the efficiency of the algorithm to classify tissues of the mammographic images between normal and abnormal. In this chapter, KNN has been used as a classifier. As seen from Figure 8, we can also observe the best results from all the transforms NSCT the Fatty tissues are always obtained for θ=0 the GLCM features.

The Figure 8 traces the classification texture of KNN for the descriptors of GLCM for different directions.

We can easily notice that the descriptor GLCM gives better performance of direction θ=0 at D=1 than the other directions for different values of KNN.

The Influence of D of GLCM on the Final Results

From Figure 9 and Figure 10, the best results of classification for the Fatty tissues and Dense glandular tissues, θ=0, 45, 90 and 135 are always obtained for D = 1.

Figure 9. The accuracy KNN classifier of various descriptors feature at θ=0,45,90 and 135 with set distance D=1, D=2 for Fatty tissues

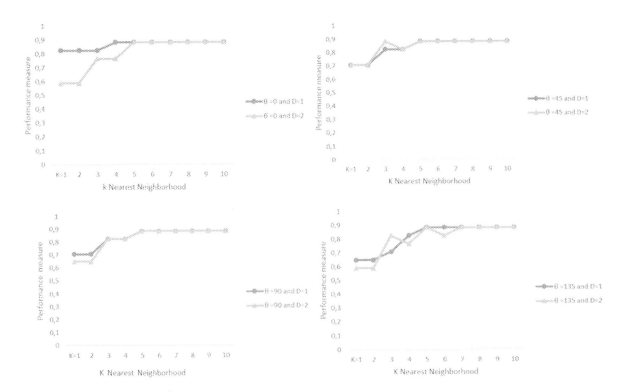

Figure 10. The Accuracy KNN classier of various descriptors feature at θ=0,45,90 and 135 with set distance D=1, D=2 for Fatty glandular tissues and Dense-glandular tissues

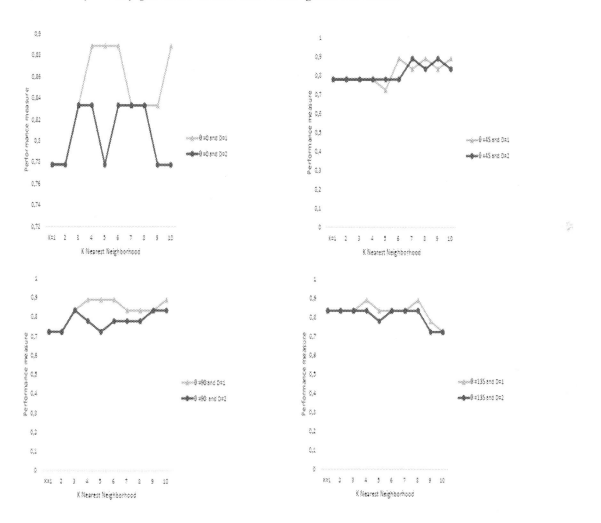

CONCLUSION

In this chapter, we propose an efficient mammogram classification scheme to support the decision of radiologists. The scheme uses NSCT and GLCM in succession to derive feature matrix form mammograms. To validate the efficiency of the suggested scheme, we used MIAS database in simulation. In conclusion, the obtained results show that NSCT and GLCM with θ=0 and D = 1 gives the best results for Fatty tissues. An accuracy of 88.89% has been obtained by KNN. For SVM with kernel function 'rbf' and 'linear' shows the best accuracy rate of 94.12%.

REFERENCES

Bamberger, R. H., & Smith, M. J. T. (1992). A filter bank for the directional decomposition of images: Theory and design. *IEEE Trans. Signal Processing, 40*(4), 882–893.

Belkhodja, L., & Benamrane, N. (2009) Approche d'extraction de la région globale d'intérêt et suppression des artefacts radiopaques dans une image mammographique. IMAGE'09 Biskra.

Beura, S., Majhi, B., & Dash, R. (2015). Mammogram classification using two dimensional discrete wavelet transform and gray-level co-occurrence matrix for detection of breast cancer. *Neurocomputing, 154*, 1–14. doi:10.1016/j.neucom.2014.12.032

Bird, R. E., & Wallace, T. W. (1992). *Yankaskas BC Radiology*. PMID:1509041

Boiman, O., Shechtman, E., & Irani, M. (2008). In defense of nearest neighbor based image classification. *Proceedings of the IEEE Conference on Computer Vision and Pattern Recognition (VPR)*.

Burges, J. C. (1998). A tutorial on support vector machines for pattern recognition. *Data Mining and Knowledge Discovery, 2*(2), 121–167. doi:10.1023/A:1009715923555

Burt, P. J., & Adelson, E. H. (1983). The Laplacian pyramid as a compact image code. *IEEE Trans. Comm., 31*, 532–540.

Cady, B., & Michaelson, J. S. (2001). The life-sparing potential of mammographic screening. *Cancer, 91*(9), 1699–1703. doi:10.1002/1097-0142(20010501)91:9<1699::AID-CNCR1186>3.0.CO;2-W PMID:11335893

Cheng, H. D., Shi, X. J., Min, R., Hu, L. M., Cai, X. P., & Du, H. N. (2006). Approaches for automated detection and classification of masses in mammograms. *IEEE Transactions on Systems, Man, and Cybernetics*, (6): 610–621.

Do, MN., & Vetterli, M. (2005). The contourlet transform: an efficient directional multiresolution image representation. IEEE Trans. Image Proc., 14(12).

Eltoukhy, M.M., Faye, I., & Samir, B.B. (2010). Breast cancer diagnosis in digital mammogram using multiscale curvelet transform. Comput. Med. Imag.Graphics, 34.

Jiazheng, Sahiner, Chan, Ge, Hadjiiski, Helvie, … Cui. (2010). Characterization of Mammographic Masses Based on Level Set Segmentation with New Image Features and Patient Information. *Medical Physics*.

Kreßel, U. (1999). Pairwise classification and support vector Machines. In *Advances in Kernel Methods: Support Vector Learnings* (pp. 255–268). Cambridge, MA: MIT Press.

Mallat, S. G. (1989). A theory for multiresolution signal decomposition: The wavelet representation. *IEEE Transactions on Pattern Analysis and Machine Intelligence, 11*(7), 674–693. doi:10.1109/34.192463

Nagi, J., Sameem, A., Nagi, F., & Syed, K. (2011). *Automated breast profile segmentation for ROI detection using digital mammograms*. In *IEEE Biomedical Engineering and Sciences*. IECBES.

Nithya, R., & Santhi, B. (2011). *Comparative study on feature extraction method for breast cancer classification*. Academic Press.

Rahmati & Ayatollahi. (2009). Maximum Likelihood Active Contours Specialized for Mammography Segmentation. *Biomedical Engineering and Informatics. BMEI '09. 2nd International Conference.*

Scholkopfand, B. A., & Smola, J. (2002). *Learning with Kernels.* MIT Press.

Smart, C. R., Hendrick, R. E., Rutledge, J. H., & Smith, R. A. (1995). Benefit of mammography screening in women ages 40 to 49 years: Current evidence from randomized controlled trials. *Cancer, 75*(7), 1619–1626. doi:10.1002/1097-0142(19950401)75:7<1619::AID-CNCR2820750711>3.0.CO;2-T PMID:8826919

Suckling, J. (1994). The mammographic image analysis society digital mammogram database, Exerpta Medica. *International Congress Series, 1069*, 375–378.

Tabár, L., Fagerberg, C. J., Gad, A., Baldetorp, L., Holmberg, L. H., Gröntoft, O., ... Eklund, G. (1985, April 13). Reduction in mortality from breast cancer after mass screening with mammography. *Lancet, 1*(8433), 829–832. doi:10.1016/S0140-6736(85)92204-4 PMID:2858707

Vetterli, M., & Herley, C. (1992). Wavelets and filter banks: Theory and design. *IEEE Trans. Signal Processing, 40*, 2207–2232.

Wirth, M., & Nikitenko, D. (2005). *Suppression of stripe artifacts in mammograms using weighted median filtering.* Springer Link. doi:10.1007/11559573_117

Yue, Lu., & Minh, N. (2006). A new contourlet transform with sharp frequency localization. *Proc. of IEEE International Conference on Image Processing.*

Zhang, Y., Tomuro, N., Furst, J., & Stan Raicu, D. (2010). *A Contour-based Mass Segmentation in Mammograms.* Scientific Commons.

Chapter 14

Enhancing HE Stain Images Through an Advanced Soft Computing–Based Adaptive Ameliorated CLAHE

Dibya Jyoti Bora
The Assam Kaziranga University, India

ABSTRACT

HE stain images play a crucial role in the medical imaging process. Often these images are regarded as of golden standards by physicians for the quality and accuracy. These images are fuzzy by nature, and hence, traditional hard-based techniques are not able to deal with this. Thereby, a decrease in the accuracy of the analysis process may be experienced. Preprocessing of these images is utmost needed so that the fuzziness may be removed to a satisfactory level. A new approach for tackling this problem is introduced in this chapter. The proposed technique is soft computing-based advanced adaptive ameliorated CLAHE. The experimental results demonstrate the superiority of the proposed approach than the other traditional techniques.

INTRODUCTION

In histology and pathology laboratories, HE Stain images are regarded as of gold standard (Paxton, Peckham, and Adele, 2003) (HE stain, n.d.). Most cells are colorless and transparent and hence, it is very difficult to analyze them (Bora, 2019). The histological sections are thus stained to make the cells distinct and visible (Paxton, Peckham, and Adele, 2003) (HE stain, n.d.) (Bora, 2019). HE stain is one such popular technique where hematoxylin and eosin are used to color nuclei and cytoplasm differently. Hematoxylin is a dark blue or violet stain which is basic/positive and Eosin is a red or pink stain that is Acidic / Negative. From there combination, the following color produces blues, violets, and reds. Although HE Stain images are very helpful for the diagnosis process but it is found that mostly these images suffer from vagueness. So, there is a greater tendency of misleading results if the problem of vagueness is dealt with beforehand.

DOI: 10.4018/978-1-7998-1021-6.ch014

So, in this chapter, advanced soft computing based Adaptive Ameliorated CLAHE is introduced to deal with this problem. The proposed technique can be considered as a hybrid version coming out of the techniques that we have introduced in (Bora, 2018 A) (Bora, 2018 B).

The remaining part of the chapter is organized as follows: In section 2, a review on the recent works in the field and motivation towards the proposed approach is mentioned. The flowchart of the proposed approach i.e. the steps involved in the proposed technique are mentioned in section 3. Section 4 is the discussion of the methods and materials involved in the proposed approach. Experiments and results discussion is carried in section 5. Finally, the conclusion is drawn in section 6. After the conclusion section, we have a reference section.

RELATED WORKS AND MOTIVATION

Following are some important contribution in this field. These works are carefully studied and the methodology behind them are mentioned below:

In (Ensafi and Tizhoosh, 2005), the authors proved that the type-2 fuzzy logic system is able to perform better contrast enhancement than the type-1 fuzzy counterpart. They have introduced a new membership function for the type-2 fuzzy enhancement; this technique is actually an extended type-2 version of the type-1 adaptive fuzzy histogram hyperbolization.

A novel method FACE (Fuzzy Automatic Contrast Enhancement) is introduced in (Lin and Lin, 2016) which first performs fuzzy clustering to segment the input image where the pixels with similar colors in the CIELAB color space are classified into similar clusters with smaller characteristics. In each cluster, pixels are spread out from the center to enhance the contrast. The authors introduced a universal contrast enhancement variable and optimize its value to maximize entropy value.

Chaira introduced a medical image contrast enhancement technique based on type-2 fuzzy set (Chaira, 2013) (Chaira, 2014). Hamacher T co-norm is used as an aggregation operator to form a new membership function with proper upper and lower membership function. The enhanced image is the one with the new membership function.

Tizhoosh et al. (1995) used fuzzy histogram hyperbolization for contrast improvement. The local adaptive feature is used in two previous fuzzy enhancement techniques: minimization of fuzziness and fuzzy histogram hyperbolization and obtained results far better than their global version (Tizhoosh, Krell, and Michaelis, 1997). Tizhoosh (2005) in used the type-2 fuzzy set-based technique for thresholding images through a new measure of ultrafuzziness. The efficiency of the proposed technique is verified by thresholding laser cladding images.

A fingerprint image enhancement technique is proposed by Bansal et al (2009) where Hong's algorithm is used for preprocessing the image. After that, a type-2 fuzzy logic is used to produce the final enhancement. This technique is found to be efficient when applied to several images.

A new enhancement technique for medical color image enhancement is proposed by Gu et al. (2015), where they perform Y-H (Young-Helmholtz) transformation with the adaptive equalization of intensity numbers matrix histogram. The contrast is enhanced by adaptive histogram equalization and as a result, it suppresses the noises present in the input original image. Then reverse transformation from Y-H to RGB is carried out thereby presenting the enhanced the color image without affecting hue and saturation values. The low computational complexity is one of the pros of this technique.

A modified color histogram equalization based technique is proposed by Hsu et al. (2015) for medical image enhancement. Here they focus on hue preservation while doing the enhancement for which two methods are employed. With the first one, an equalized color image is obtained preserving hue by using the ratio of the original grayscale image and the equalized image. And the second method achieves hue preservation by applying the difference between the original gray version of the image and the equalized one obtaining the final equalized color image.

Unsharp masking based technique is also found to be used for medical image enhancement. One such technique is proposed by Zhao et al. (2016). In this technique, the authors suppress the background noise by embedding the PLIP multiplication into the unsharp masking framework.

Kuru (2014) in introduced a bilinear interpolation based approach for improving the quality of H&E stain images. LAB color model is used efficiently without losing any essential detail. The color information of nuclei (hematoxylin stained sections) is preserved.

Li et al. (2018) proposed a medical image enhancement technique based on CLAHE and unsharp masking in the NSCT domain. They first process the image with CLAHE and then the resultant image is decomposed into one low-frequency component and several high-frequency components with non-subsampled contourlet transform (NSCT). After that, the linear stretching is used to process the low-frequency component for improving the contrast. To suppress the noise of the high-frequency components, adaptive thresholding is employed. The inverse NSCT is then used to reconstruct the processed coefficients of low-frequency sub-band and high-frequency sub-bands. And lastly, the unsharp masking is applied to enhance the edge details. The superiority of the proposed technique can be observed from the experimental results.

Dhal et al. (2018) proposed an enhancement and segmentation technique for the overexposed color skin cancer images through exact hue-saturation-intensity (eHSI) color model and contrast limited adaptive histogram equalization (CLAHE). The reason behind using eHSI color model is because of its capability for hue preserving and gamut problem free nature. An unsupervised clustering approach with the assistance of seven different gray level thresholding methods is used for the segmentation task.

In Yadav et al. (2014) have introduced an enhancement technique for enhancing the visibility level of the foggy image with CLAHE. The video frames are read one at a time. Intensity is adjusted for the foggy frame. First RGB image is converted to gray level and then CLAHE is applied. The resultant enhanced frame is a new structure. Finally, the enhanced De-foggy video is obtained after processing every frame with the above-mentioned step.

Hitam et al. (2013) proposed a new method called mixture Contrast Limited Adaptive Histogram Equalization (CLAHE) color models for underwater image enhancement. This technique operates CLAHE on RGB and HSV and both, and then Euclidean norm. is used to combine the results together. From the experimental results, it is clear the contrast of underwater images is improved as well as reduces noise and artifacts.

Wen et al (2016) proposed an image enhancement algorithm based on wavelet-domain homomorphic filtering and CLAHE for the contrast improvement of medical X-ray image with low brightness, low contrast, and noise.In the proposed technique, the image is first decomposed into low-frequency and high-frequency coefficients of 1st layer of wavelet domain using wavelet transformation. The low-frequency coefficients are then processed and linearly amplified with an improved homomorphic filter and the high-frequency coefficients are processed by wavelet threshold shrinkage followed by wavelet reconstruction. CLAHE is used as at the final step for modifying the image histogram and thereby generating the final enhanced version of the image. Through the subjective and objective evaluation, it is proved that the proposed technique is able to effectively enhance the texture details of medical X-ray images, increasing the brightness and contrast, suppress noise far better than the other traditional techniques.

Al-Ameen et al (2015) introduced an improved version of CLAHE to provide a good brightness with decent contrast for CT images. An initial phase of a normalized gamma correction function is added in this technique to adjust the gamma of the processed image and with that, the common errors of the basic CLAHE like the excess brightness and imperfect contrast can be avoided. No visible artifacts are found in the experimental results and also the proposed technique outperforms other techniques considered for comparison.

Magudeeswaran et al. (2017) proposed a technique namely Contrast limited fuzzy adaptive histogram equalization (CLFAHE) to improve the contrast of MRI Brain images. Three stages are involved in the proposed technique: in the first stage, the gray level intensities are transformed into membership plane and membership plane is modified with Contrast intensification operator. In the second stage, CLAHE is employed on the modified membership plane to prevent excessive enhancement in contrast by preserving the original brightness. And in the final stage, membership plane is mapped back to the gray level intensities. Different qualitative measures such as entropy, PSNR, AMBE, and FSIM are used to compare the efficiency of the proposed technique. The main credit of this technique goes to its ability in preserving the local information of the original image during the contrast improvement process.

So, from the above literature review, we have noted that image enhancement is the critical and most important part in any image analysis part. Especially, if the analysis is concerned for medical images, then this preprocessing part is utmost necessary as most of the medical images suffer from a high level of fuzziness and thereby creating problems for the diagnosis process to be conducted accurately. HE stain images are the most popular ones in the current scenario of medical imaging. We have already introduced two novel methods (Bora 2018 A) (Bora, 2018 B) for image enhancements. Now, from the mentioned methods in the above literature review and already proposed method (Bora 2018 A) (Bora, 2018 B), we have been motivated to introduce an enhancement technique for HE stain images. The proposed technique is a hybrid of (Bora 2018 A) (Bora, 2018 B) and of new of its kind.

PROPOSED APPROACH AND METHODOLOGIES

In this section, first, the steps involved in the proposed approach are stated in brief. Then a flow chart is also presented to illustrate them sequentially in a better understandable way.

Steps Involved in The Proposed Approach

Step 1: Input HE Stain color image.
Step 2: RGB to HSV Conversion
Step 3: Separate V channel.
Step 4: The extracted V-channel has to be processed with Type-2 fuzzy set-based technique for initial vagueness reduction. Say, the resultant V-channel is V' .
Step 5: V' is then sent for final stage of contrast improvement using AA_CLAHE() technique.Say, it implies V''.
Step 6: The old V-channel is then replaced by V''.

Figure 1. Flowchart for the proposed approach

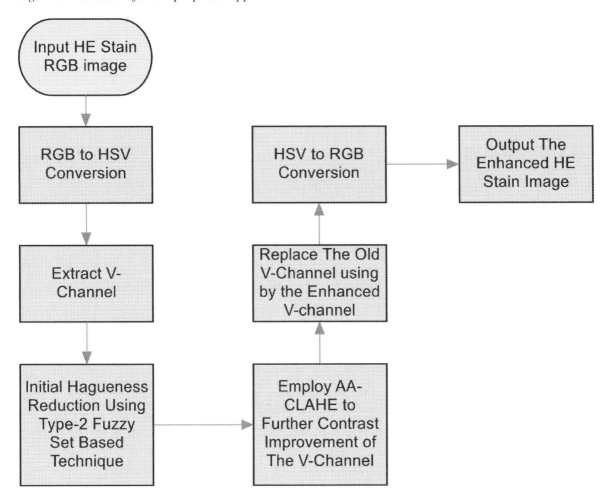

Step 7: Conversion from HSV color space to RGB is done to obtain the final enhanced color image of the original HE stain image.

Flowchart for the proposed approach is shown in Figure 1.

HE Stain Images

In histology and pathology laboratories, HE stain image is often regarded as of gold standard as they lead to accurate diagnosis process (HE stain, n.d.) (Anon., 2018). As most cells are found colorless and transparent, so, it is a very difficult process to analyze them, and also, a high level of accuracy cannot be expected from such colorless images. In the staining technique, like HE Staining, the histological sections are stained in such a way these cells should be visible. Here, for coloring the nuclei and cytoplasm differently, hematoxylin and eosin are used. Hematoxylin, which is basic/positive by nature, is a dark blue or violet stain. And, Eosin, which is Acidic / Negative by nature, is a red or pink stain. From their combination, colors blues, violets, and reds are produced. H&E is a well-established method, and

Figure 2. A Sample HE Stain Image (Medisp.bme.teiath.gr., 2018).

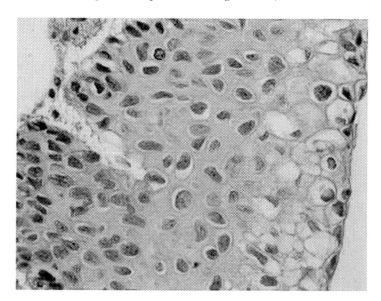

with a good amount of data and publications, it will continue to be the universal practice over the next 50 years [25]. Although HE Stain images are often admired for its good quality, still, due it has been found suffering from fuzziness near or on the boundaries (Bora, 2019). And because of this, it becomes very hard to distinguish the boundaries separating different cells or ROIs. Traditional hard computing based techniques are not able to deal with this vagueness. Only soft computing based techniques have the ability to remove the fuzziness level to an acceptable level. So, in this chapter, we are focusing on proposing an advanced fuzzy set-based technique for HE stain image enhancement. Below is a sample HE stain image collected from (Medisp.bme.teiath.gr., 2018).

HSV Color Space

Color space can be defined as an abstract mathematical model with the help of which colors can be represented in terms of intensity values following a specific three-dimensional coordinate system. With respect to different applications, we have a number of different types of color spaces. Each such color space may carry a different feature or characteristic with it that may be suitable to a particular application but may not be for some other application. In general, every device or application uses RGB as a default color space. In RGB color space, all the three channels Red, Green, and Blue are associated with intensity values, and there arises a very big problem when we need a colo space with a devoted intensity channel. It may lead to color misclassification if changes occur to any of these channels. To deal with this problem, we have an alternative color space: HSV color space. This color space has three channels: Hue (H), Saturation(S) and Value (V) (Bora, 2017). Here, hue is defined as an angle in the range $[0,2\pi]$. This channel is directly related to color as with respect to different hue angles, different colors can be obtained. Then, the saturation channel is used to describe how pure the hue is with respect to a white reference. This is generally measured as a radial distance from the central axis with values between 0 at the center to 1 at the outer surface. The V channel or value channel represents a percentage value goes

Figure 3. Coordinate System for HSV Color Space

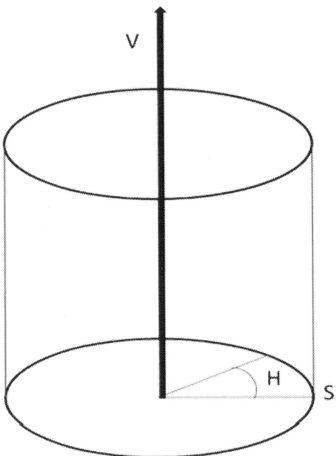

from 0 to 100 and it expresses the amount of light illuminating a color. The V channel in HSV color space acts as a devoted channel for intensity level measurements. This is the reason, why we have selected HSV color space for our proposed approach. The enhancement task is employed on the V-channel and hence there is not a chance for color miss-classification. Details and in-depth study on color space and HSV color space is presented in (Bora, 2017).

Type-2 Fuzzy Set

The concept of the fuzzy set was introduced by Zadeh introduced in 1965 (Zadeh, 1965). Although the fuzzy set-based technique like fcm has more capability in dealing with vagueness than its hard computing based counterpart for various problems like enhancement, segmentation, etc (Bora, 2017 A) (Bora, 2017 B), but still it has a drawback that it does not count the uncertainty involved in the membership function. So, a type-1 fuzzy set is not able to completely remove the fuzziness. But, removing the fuzziness to a greater extent is the only way to ensure accuracy in any medical image analysis process. Zadeh tried to encounter this problem by introducing the concept of type-2 fuzzy set in 1975 (Zadeh). The type-2 fuzzy

Figure 4. (a) Type-1 Membership Function, and (b) Bluriness invokes the type-2 membership function

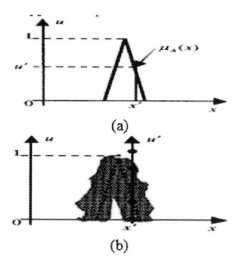

(a)

(b)

set can be defined as an extension of the type-1 fuzzy set and is found very useful in such cases when it is very difficult to agree on the accuracy of the type-1 membership function because of uncertainty in its shape, location or other such parameters. In the case of type-2 fuzzy set, proper upper and lower bounds are used to bound the membership function. So, the type-1 membership function is blurred to obtain the type-2 membership function. The following figure introduced by Mendel in (Mendel and John, 2002) more clearly depicts the relation between the type-1 fuzzy set and type-2 fuzzy set.

Mathematically, type-2 fuzzy set can be described with the following equation (Hitam, Yussof, Awalludin and Bachok, 2013):

$$A_{TYPEII} = \left\{ x, \widehat{\mu}_A\left(x, \mu\right) \mid \forall x \in X, \forall u \in J_x \subseteq \left[0,1\right] \right\} \tag{1}$$

where $\widehat{\mu}_A\left(x, \mu\right)$ represents the Type II membership function, J_x represents the primary membership function.

The upper and lower limits can be calculated through the following equations:

$$\mu^{upper} = \left[J_x\right]^{\alpha} \mu^{lower} = \left[J_x\right]^{1/\alpha} \tag{2}$$

where $0 < \alpha \leq 1$.

Again, the relation of upper and lower bound in a type-2 fuzzy set with respect to type-1 fuzzy set can be depicted through the Figure 5 (Bora, 2019).

FOOTPRINT OF UNCERTAINTY (FOU) is an important terminology related to type-2 fuzzy set. It is used to express the uncertainty in the primary membership of a type-2 fuzzy set. The following equation clearly shows FOU in terms of the primary membership function J_x:

Figure 5. Upper and Lower Limit defining Membership area With Respect to Type-1 and Type-2 Fuzzy Set

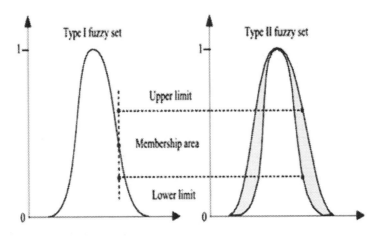

$$FOU(A_{TYPEII}) = \bigcup_{x \in X} J_x \tag{3}$$

We have adopted a type-2 fuzzy set in our proposed technique as it has the capability of dealing with the fuzziness involved in medical images like HE stain images more accurately than its type 1 fuzzy set based counterparts. For this, we have introduced a type-2 fuzzy set-based technique in (Bora, 2018 B). The methodology involved is an advanced of the same is introduced in section 3.5.

Type_2 (V-channel)

Type_2(V-channel) is an advanced interval based type-2 fuzzy set based technique (Bora, 2018 B).

The methodology of this technique is described below. After the HSV conversion of the input HE Stain RGB color image, the V-channel is being extracted from it.

Now, this extracted V channel of size M×N is fuzzified using the following primary membership function J_x as:

$$J_x = \frac{V - V_{min}}{V min_{max}} \tag{4}$$

where V is the value channel of the input HE stain image (say I_h) of the range 0 to L-1, V_{min} is the minimum V value and V_{max} is the maximum V value.

After that upper and lower bounds are framed so that an interval based type-2 fuzzy set can be constructed. These upper and lower bounds can be easily calculated with the equations (2) (section 3.4). An optimal value of α can be easily found through trial and error strategy.

An important fact to be considered while designing a new membership function is that a darker region should look brighter in the enhanced version, and to implement this fact, we need to somehow make a higher value of μ^{upper} for dark portion. Since in that case, it will lead to having higher gray values for them. So, considering this issue, the following membership is designed:

$$\hat{\mu}_A = k \cdot \left(\frac{\mu_{low} \cdot \lambda + \mu_{high} \cdot (1-\lambda)}{1-(1-\lambda) \cdot \mu_{low} \cdot \mu_{high}} \right) \tag{5}$$

where λ is calculated using the equation below:

$$\lambda = \frac{V_{mean}}{L} \tag{6}$$

where V_{mean} is the mean gray value calculated from the image and L is the number of gray levels in the image. And, k >0 is the contrast enhancement factor as by manipulating its value we can change the contrast from low to high. For this chapter k value taken is 1.

So, when the V-channel is sent as an input to this method, we will get an image with low fuzziness values surrounding the ROIs.

Adaptive Ameliorated Clahe, AA_Clahe()

Contrast management is an important part of the image enhancement process. Histogram equalization is one of the frequently adopted global contrast enhancement technique. It has the advantage of low complexity and easy to be implemented. The working methodology of global histogram equalization is properly explained in (Bora, 2018 A). But in maximum cases, global histogram equalization results in amplified noise when there exists a high peak in the histogram of the image. So, local adaptive histogram equalization is a better option than a global histogram equalization.

AA_CLAHE() is a local adaptive histogram equalization technique (Bora, 2018 A). The use of BSB_T() for histogram clipping and redistribution; and bicubic interpolation merge up the neighboring tiles: these tow techniques makes AA_CLAHE()more powerful and efficient.The steps involved in AA_CLAHE() are:

Algorithm: AA_CLAHE()

Input: V'-Channel(obtained as an output from Type_2(V-channel)).
Output: Enhanced V''-Channel.
Step 1: *Consider the window of size N×N. Initialize N value as 3*
Step 2: *Analyze the histogram of every tile of the image.*
Step 3: *Employ BSB_T() for the clipping and redistribution and after that histogram equalization takes place from the CDF of the clipped histogram.*
Step 4: *Bicubic Interpolation is carried out to obtain the final contrast-enhanced image.*
Step 5: *Calculate Entropy, E_i. The entropy will be calculated using the following equation:*

$$E=-sum(p.*\log_2(p)) \tag{7}$$

where p contains the histogram counts evaluated from the histogram of the enhanced image. A higher value of entropy signifies a better enhancement.

Step 6: $N \leftarrow N+2$
Step 7: *Repeat step 2 to 5, with the new window size, finally calculate the entropy E_{i+1} of the enhanced image in the current step.*
Step 8: *Stop if $E_{i+1} < E_i$ else repeat until N<=128.*
Step 9: *Output the enhanced image with the largest E value.*

The techniques BSB_T() and Bicubic Interpolation are described below:

BSB_T()

For clipping the histogram and redistribute the clipped pixels, this technique is proved to be an efficient one (Bora, 2017 B). The algorithm for this technique is:

Algorithm: BSB_T()

Step 1: Say *T* is the top and *B* is the bottom of the concerned ClipLevel.
Step 2: Repeat until $T-B<\in$, where $\in>0$ is negligibly small
    [a]   Find *M* where *M* is the middle between *T* and *B*
    [b]   Find *S* where *S* is the sum of excess above *M* in each bin of the histogram
    [c]   if *S+M>ClipLevel* then assign *T=M*
    [d]   if *S+M<ClipLevel* then assign *B=M*
    [e]   if *S+M==ClipLevel* then *M* is the required value at which clipping should be done. So, break binary search loop.
Step 3: Clip the histogram at *M* and redistribute the excess into each bin equally.

So, BSB_T(), is used to determine where the clipping should be done. According to that clipping is done and redistribute the clipped pixels by calculating the CDF.

Figure 6. Clip Limit & Redistribution of clipped pixels

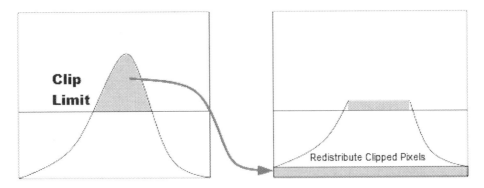

Bicubic Interpolation

Bi-cubic interpolation can be used to merge up the neighboring tiles to eliminate any artificial boundaries. In fact, it works much better than bilinear interpolation (Han, 2013). Mathematically, interpolation is defined as a process of estimating approximate continuous values of a function. And, in image processing, interpolation is used to transfer an image from one resolution to another so that the quality of the image will be improved by removing artificially induced boundaries. There are two types of Interpolation methods: adaptive and non-adaptive. The first one considers different features like texture, edge information, intensity transformation, etc, while the later one directly manipulates pixels without considering any feature like adaptive ones. DDT, ICBI, NEDI, etc. are some of the selective adaptive interpolation methods. While, nearest neighbor, bilinear and bicubic are few important non-adaptive interpolation techniques. The reason behind choosing adopted non-adaptive based interpolation technique is because the cost involved here is less in comparison to those of adaptive ones. Bicubic interpolation is the one of the best techniques among the non-adaptive interpolation techniques, since here sixteen closest pixels' weighted average is used to fill the interpolated point, while in case of nearest neighbor interpolation, only the nearest pixel is used to fill the interpolated point, and in case of bilinear interpolation technique, the interpolated pixel is filled with four closest pixels' weighted average.

Figure 7 shows the consideration of sixteen nearest neighbor pixels in bicubic interpolation algorithm.

Figure 7. Bicubic Interpolation

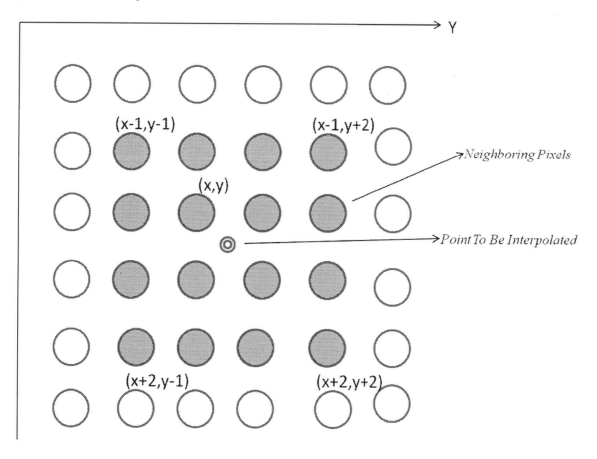

The equation to calculate the interpolation kernel, u (which must be symmetric) for bicubic interpolation (Keys, 1981) is calculated using the following equation:

$$u(d) = \begin{cases} \frac{3}{2}|d|^3 - \frac{5}{2}|d|^2 + 1 & 0 \leq d < 1 \\ -\frac{1}{2}|d|^3 + \frac{5}{2}|d|^2 - 4|d| + 2 & 1 \leq d < 2 \\ 0 & 2 < d \end{cases} \tag{8}$$

where d is the distance between the interpolated point and the grid point to be considered.

In our proposed technique AA_CLAHE(), we have used bicubic interpolation as the last stage for merging the contrast limited histogram equalized tiles of the original image to obtain the final enhanced version of the same.

EXPERIMENT AND RESULT DISCUSSION SECTION

Experiment and result analysis is demonstrated in this section. The proposed approach has been implemented in Matlab (2014 A). The system used for conducting the experiments possesses an Intel Core i5 processor with 64-bit Windows 10 operating system. The test images are collected from (HE stain, n.d.) (Shamir, Orlov, Eckley, Macura, and Goldberg, 2008). The results are compared with the traditional algorithm Histogram Equalization and one recent technique Bora et al. (2018 C) to compare the efficiency and superiority of the proposed approach. Both subjective and objective evaluations are adopted for performance evaluation. Subjective evaluation is very important as the human visual perception is the best technique for measuring the quality of enhancement carried out (Jenifer, Parasuraman, and Kadirvelu, 2016). For objective evaluation, PSNR and entropy are adopted.

So, from the above series of images (figure 8), the steps involved in the proposed technique is very much clear through the output generated at each of them. An RGB color image (i.e. the input the HE Stain image) has three channels, and with each of them intensity values are associated. These three channels are separated and shown them in the figures 8(b),8(d) and 8(f); and their respective histograms are shown in the figures 8(c),8(e) and 8(g) respectively. RGB to HSV conversion is done and the resultant HSV converted image is shown in figure 8(h). V-channel is extracted and shown in figure 8(i) and its histogram is shown in 8(j). Now, the output obtained from Type_2(V-channel) is shown in 8(k). Then this result is sent as input to AA_CLAHE() and it produces 8(l). Our final output is shown in 8(m). One recent technique (based on advanced fuzzy set) (Bora, 2018 C), and two traditional techniques Histogram Equalization and CLAHE are considered for the result comparison. The results produced by them are shown in 8(n), 8(o) and 8(p). It is very clear that the result produced by our proposed approach is far better in terms of quality than the other methods into consideration. The ROIs are distinctly visible, the nuclei, cell are very much distinct through sharp edges as the fuzziness removed to a satisfactory level by Type_2(V-channel) and contrast is improved through AA_CLAHE(). The technique in (Bora, 2018 C) is no doubt producing better than Histogram Equalization and CLAHE, but not better than our

Figure 8. (a) Original Image; (b)R-channel;(c) Histogram of the R-channel; (d) G-channel; (e) Histogram of the G-Channel; (f) B-channel; (g) Histogram of the B-channel; (h) HSV Converted image; (i) V-channel; (j) Histogram of the V-channel; (k)Output from Type_2(V-channel); (l) Output from AA_CLAHE( ); (m) Final output of our proposed technique; (n)Result obtained from Bora Method[37]; (o) Result obtained from Histogram Equalization; and (p) Result obtained from CLAHE.

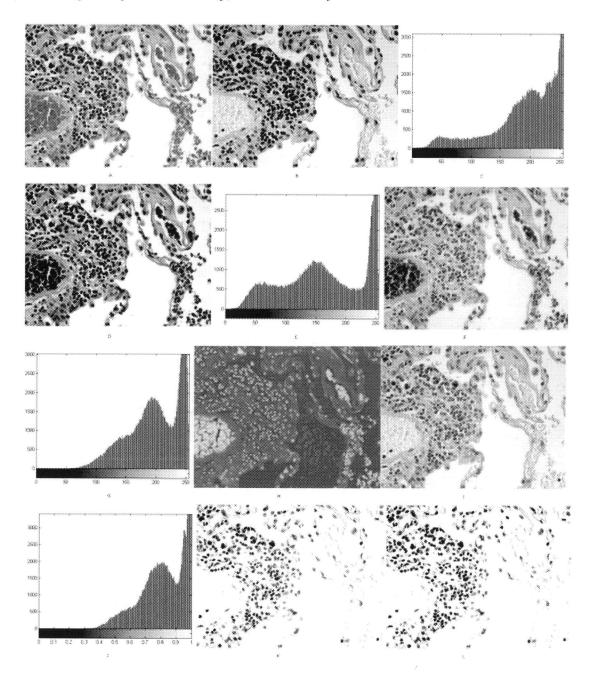

Figure 9. (a) Original Image; (b)Result obtained from Histogram Equalization; (c) Result obtained from CLAHE; (d) Result obtained from Bora Method[37]; (e) Result obtained from our proposed technique

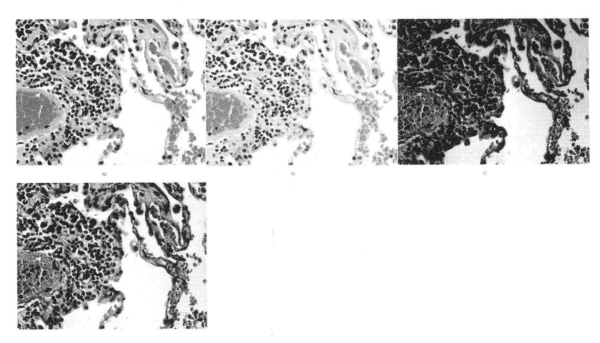

Figure 10. (a) Original Image; (b)Result obtained from Histogram Equalization; (c) Result obtained from CLAHE; (d) Result obtained from Bora Method[37]; (e) Result obtained from our proposed technique

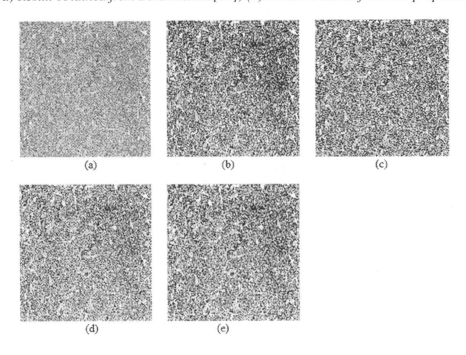

Figure 11. (a) Original Image; (b)Result obtained from Histogram Equalization; (c) Result obtained from CLAHE; (d) Result obtained from Bora Method[37]; (e) Result obtained from our proposed technique

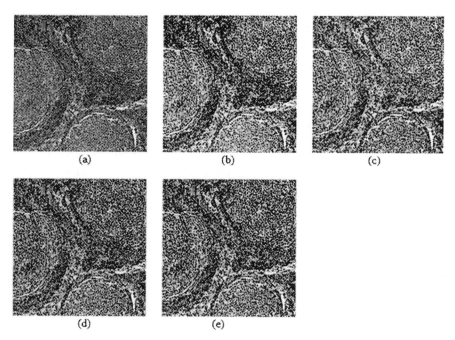

proposed approach. CLAHE's result is better than Histogram Equalization, but, in both the cases, color information is not properly maintained.

So, the proposed approach succeeds to produce better results than the other techniques in two aspects mainly: (a) reduction of fuzziness ; (b) an improved contrast management ;and (c) color information preservation.

Figures 9-11 show the results for some other HE stain images.

SUBJECTIVE EVALUATIONS

6 Experts are selected for the subjective evaluation of the experimental results. They have evaluated the result on the basis of up to what amount the fuzziness is reduced, up to how much color information restored with fewer color artifacts and brightness preserving which as a whole determine the quality of enhancement done on the input HE Stain images. Following table 1 present their report:

So, from the above table 1 of the subjective evaluation, it is found that our proposed approach on average succeeds to obtain a score of 8.33 which implies that it succeeds to produce an efficient enhancement on the input HE stain image

Table 1. Subjective Evaluation

Expert	Is Fuzziness Level Reduced to An Accepted Level	Is Overall Visual Improvement Done After Enhancement: Yes/No	Visual Improvement Rating(Value Ranges from 1 to 10,1 is the lowest and 10 is the highest rating)
1	Yes	Yes	9
2	Yes	Yes	9
3	Yes	Yes	8
4	Yes	Yes	7
5	Yes	Yes	8
6	Yes	Yes	9
Average	*Yes*	*Yes*	*8.33*

OBJECTIVE EVALUATION

To conduct the objective evaluation, we have adopted two metrics: Entropy and PSNR(Peak Signal to Noise Ratio). The entropy of an image can be calculated using the equation no. (5) in section 3.3. The PSNR of an image can be calculated using the following equation.

$$PSNR = 10\log_{10}(MAXi^2/MSE) \tag{7}$$

Where MAX_i is the maximum possible pixel value of the image and MSE is the Mean Squared Error which can be calculated using the following equation no.(8):

$$MSE = \sum_{y=1}^{M}\sum_{x=1}^{N}\left[I\left(x,y\right) - I'\left(x,y\right)\right]^2 \tag{8}$$

where, M, N are the dimensions of the image and I(x,y) is the original image, I'(x,y) is the enhanced image.

We have selected entropy and PSNR for the objective evaluation of these two metrics include both the enhancement impact and also the noise sensitivity issue. For better enhancement, the entropy value should be high. And, for better suppression of noises, the PSNR value is high. So, the higher the values of entropy and PSNR, the better are the enhancement achieved by an enhancement technique.

From the above table and figures, it is very clear that the entropy and PSNR values for the proposed approach for each image and also for overall average is higher than the same of Histogram Equalization, CLAHE and Bora (2018 C) method. So, the objective evaluation also proves the superiority of the proposed technique in HE stain image enhancement.

So, it is seen that (from Table 3 and Figure 13) time taken by the proposed approach is comparatively longer than the time taken by the other algorithms in comparison. So, a high time complexity may be considered as one limitation of the proposed approach.

Table 2. Objective Evaluation

Image No.	Objective Evaluation	Histogram Equaization	CLAHE	Bora[37]	Proposed Approach
Image 1	Entropy	0.01901	0.0180	0.0206	0.0240
	PSNR	21.8160	21.8171	23.5021	23.5641
Image 2	Entropy	0.0101	0.0107	0.0156	0.0170
	PSNR	10.1223	10.1610	13.7056	14.4619
Image 3	Entropy	0.0103	0.0113	0.0127	0.0133
	PSNR	17.5701	17.5613	19.0781	19.9038
Image 4	Entropy	0.0107	0.0108	0.01471	0.01783
	PSNR	18.1358	19.0121	20.3136	21.3290
Average	Entropy	0.0125275	0.0127	0.0159025	*0.0180325*
	PSNR	16.91105	17.137875	19.14985	*19.8147*

Figure 12. (a) Entropy Comparison; (b) PSNR Comparison

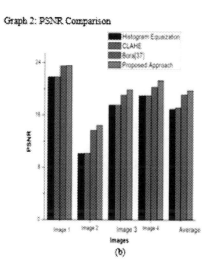

Table 3. Time Comparison

Techniques	Average Time Taken (in Seconds)
Histogram Equalization	0.952919
CLAHE	1.627595
Bora[37]	5.182051
Proposed Technique	5.489127

Figure 13. Time Comparison

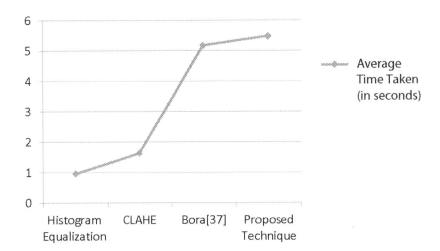

CONCLUSION

HE stain images play an important part in accurate medical diagnosis. The accuracy can be further enhanced if the quality of such images can be improved. And this is very important as these images suffer from vagueness since the level of fuzziness surrounding the nuclei and cell is very high in this case. So, a proper preprocessing technique is required to deal with this problem. Also, as these images are color images, so, proper care should be taken while employing the enhancement technique so that color miss-classification will not occur after the enhancement process. In this proposed technique, both of these two problems are taken into consideration, and thereby a hybrid approach is developed as an assemble of one type 2 interval fuzzy set-based technique, Type_2(V-channel) and an adaptive contrast limited histogram equalization technique, AA_CLAHE(). The experimental results prove the superiority of the proposed approach.

As future work, this work will be integrated with one segmentation framework to find out how much efficiency it will bring to the same.

REFERENCES

Al-Ameen, Z., Sulong, G., Rehman, A., Al-Dhelaan, A., Saba, T., & Al-Rodhaan, M. (2015). An innovative technique for contrast enhancement of computed tomography images using normalized gamma-corrected contrast-limited adaptive histogram equalization. *EURASIP Journal on Advances in Signal Processing*, *2015*(1), 32. doi:10.118613634-015-0214-1

Bansal, R., Arora, P., Gaur, M., Sehgal, P., & Bedi, P. (2009). Fingerprint Image Enhancement Using Type-2 Fuzzy Sets. *2009 Sixth International Conference on Fuzzy Systems and Knowledge Discovery*. 10.1109/FSKD.2009.396

Bora, D. (2017). AERSCIEA: An efficient and robust satellite color image enhancement approach. *Proceedings of the Second International Conference on Research in Intelligent and Computing in Engineering*. 10.15439/2017R53

Bora, D. J. (2017). *Importance of image enhancement techniques in color image segmentation: a comprehensive and comparative study*. arXiv preprint arXiv:1708.05081

Bora, D. J. (2017). Performance Comparison of K-Means Algorithm and FCM Algorithm with Respect to Color Image Segmentation. *International Journal of Emerging Technology and Advanced Engineering*, *7*(8), 460–470.

Bora, D. J. (2018). An Efficient Innovative Approach Towards Color Image Enhancement. *International Journal of Information Retrieval Research*, *8*(1), 20–37. doi:10.4018/IJIRR.2018010102

Bora, D. J. (2018). An Ideal Approach for Medical Color Image Enhancement. In *Advanced Computational and Communication Paradigms* (pp. 351–361). Singapore: Springer. doi:10.1007/978-981-10-8237-5_34

Bora, D. J. 2019. HE Stain Image Segmentation Using an Innovative Type-2 Fuzzy Set-Based Approach. In Histopathological Image Analysis in Medical Decision Making (pp. 276-299). IGI Global. doi:10.4018/978-1-5225-6316-7.ch012

Chaira, T. (2013) Contrast enhancement of medical images using type II fuzzy set. *2013 National Conference on Communications (NCC)*. 10.1109/NCC.2013.6488016

Chaira, T. (2014). An improved medical image enhancement scheme using Type II fuzzy set. *Applied Soft Computing*, *25*, 293–308. doi:10.1016/j.asoc.2014.09.004

Dhal, K. G., Ray, S., Sen, M., & Das, S. 2018. Proper Enhancement and Segmentation of the Overexposed Color Skin Cancer Image. In Intelligent Multidimensional Data and Image Processing (pp. 240-258). IGI Global. doi:10.4018/978-1-5225-5246-8.ch009

Ensafi, P., & Tizhoosh, H. (2005). Type-2 Fuzzy Image Enhancement. *Lecture Notes in Computer Science*, *3656*, 159–166. doi:10.1007/11559573_20

Gu, J., Hua, L., Wu, X., Yang, H., & Zhou, Z. (2015). Color medical image enhancement based on adaptive equalization of intensity numbers matrix histogram. *International Journal of Automation and Computing*, *12*(5), 551–558. doi:10.100711633-014-0871-9

Han, D. (2013).Comparison of Commonly Used Image Interpolation Methods. *Proceedings of the 2nd International Conference on Computer Science and Electronics Engineering (ICCSEE 2013)*. 10.2991/iccsee.2013.391

HE Stain. (n.d.). Retrieved from https://en.wikipedia.org/wiki/H\%26E_stain

Hitam, M., Yussof, W., Awalludin, E., & Bachok, Z. (2013). Mixture contrast limited adaptive histogram equalization for underwater image enhancement. *2013 International Conference On Computer Applications Technology (ICCAT)*. 10.1109/ICCAT.2013.6522017

Hsu, W., & Chou, C. (2015). Medical Image Enhancement Using Modified Color Histogram Equalization. *Journal of Medical and Biological Engineering*, *35*(5), 580–584. doi:10.100740846-015-0078-8

Jenifer, S., Parasuraman, S., & Kadirvelu, A. (2016). Contrast enhancement and brightness preserving of digital mammograms using fuzzy clipped contrast-limited adaptive histogram equalization algorithm. *Applied Soft Computing*, *42*, 167–177. doi:10.1016/j.asoc.2016.01.039

Keys, R. (1981). Cubic convolution interpolation for digital image processing. *IEEE Transactions on Acoustics, Speech, and Signal Processing*, *29*(6), 1153–1160. doi:10.1109/TASSP.1981.1163711

Kuru, K. (2014). Optimization and enhancement of H&E stained microscopical images by applying bilinear interpolation method on lab color mode. *Theoretical Biology & Medical Modelling*, *11*(1), 9. doi:10.1186/1742-4682-11-9 PMID:24502223

Li, L., Si, Y., & Jia, Z. (2018). Medical image enhancement based on CLAHE and unsharp masking in NSCT domain. *Journal of Medical Imaging and Health Informatics*, *8*(3), 431–438. doi:10.1166/jmihi.2018.2328

Lin, P., & Lin, B. (2016). Fuzzy automatic contrast enhancement based on fuzzy C-means clustering in CIELAB color space. *2016 12th IEEE/ASME International Conference on Mechatronic and Embedded Systems and Applications (MESA)*. doi: 10.1109/mesa.2016.7587156

Magudeeswaran, V., & Singh, J. F. (2017). Contrast limited fuzzy adaptive histogram equalization for enhancement of brain images. *International Journal of Imaging Systems and Technology*, *27*(1), 98–103. doi:10.1002/ima.22214

Medisp.bme.teiath.gr. (2018). Available at: http://medisp.bme.teiath.gr/hicl/Images/staining/HE.png

Mendel, J., & John, R. (2002). Type-2 fuzzy sets made simple. *IEEE Transactions on Fuzzy Systems*, *10*(2), 117–127. doi:10.1109/91.995115

Paxton, S., Peckham, M., & Adele, K. (2003). *The Leeds Histology Guide*. Academic Press.

Shamir, L., Orlov, N., Eckley, D. M., Macura, T. J., & Goldberg, I. G. (2008). IICBU 2008: A proposed benchmark suite for biological image analysis. *Medical & Biological Engineering & Computing*, *46*(9), 943–947. doi:10.100711517-008-0380-5 PMID:18668273

Tizhoosh, H. (2005). Image thresholding using type II fuzzy sets. *Pattern Recognition*, *38*(12), 2363–2372. doi:10.1016/j.patcog.2005.02.014

Tizhoosh, H. R., & Fochem, M. (1995). Image Enhancement with Fuzzy Histogram Hyperbolization. *Proceedings of EUFIT'95*, *3*, 1695 - 1698.

Tizhoosh, H. R., Krell, G., & Michaelis, B. (1997). Locally adaptive fuzzy image enhancement. In B. Reusch (Ed.), Lecture Notes in Computer Science: Vol. 1226. *Computational Intelligence Theory and Applications. Fuzzy Days 1997*. Berlin: Springer.

Wen, H., Qi, W., & Shuang, L. (2016). Medical X-Ray Image Enhancement Based on Wavelet Domain Homomorphic Filtering and CLAHE. *2016 International Conference On Robots & Intelligent System (ICRIS)*, 249-254. 10.1109/ICRIS.2016.50

Yadav, G., Maheshwari, S., & Agarwal, A. (2014). Contrast limited adaptive histogram equalization based enhancement for real time video system. *2014 International Conference on Advances in Computing, Communications and Informatics (ICACCI)*, 2392-2397. 10.1109/ICACCI.2014.6968381

Zadeh, L. (1965). Fuzzy sets. *Information and Control, 8*(3), 338–353. doi:10.1016/S0019-9958(65)90241-X

Zadeh, L. A. (1975). The concept of a linguistic variable and its application to approximate reasoning—I. *Information Sciences, 8*(3), 199–249. doi:10.1016/0020-0255(75)90036-5

Zhao, Z., & Zhou, Y. (2016) PLIP based unsharp masking for medical image enhancement. *2016 IEEE International Conference on Acoustics, Speech and Signal Processing (ICASSP)*. 10.1109/ICASSP.2016.7471874

Chapter 15
Enhanced Ant Colony Algorithm for Best Features Selection for a Decision Tree Classification of Medical Data

Abdiya Alaoui
  https://orcid.org/0000-0002-4879-3850
Djillali Liabes University Sidi Belabbes, Algeria

Zakaria Elberrichi
  https://orcid.org/0000-0002-3391-6280
Djillali Liabes University Sidi Belabbes, Algeria

ABSTRACT

Classification algorithms are widely applied in medical domain to classify the data for diagnosis. The datasets have considerable irrelevant attributes. Diagnosis of the diseases is costly because many tests are required to predict a disease. Feature selection is one of the significant tasks of the preprocessing phase for the data. It can extract a subset of attributes from a large set and exclude redundant, irrelevant, or noisy attributes. The authors can decrease the cost of diagnosis by avoiding numerous tests by selection of features, which are important for prediction of disease. Applied to the task of supervised classification, the authors construct a robust learning model for disease prediction. The search for a subset of features is an NP-hard problem, which can be solved by the metaheuristics. In this chapter, a wrapper approach by hybridization between ant colony algorithm and adaboost with decision trees to ameliorate the classification is proposed. The authors use an enhanced global pheromone updating rule. With the experimental results, this approach gives good results.

DOI: 10.4018/978-1-7998-1021-6.ch015

INTRODUCTION

One important task of data mining is the supervised classification, which allows predicting if an instance will be assigned to a predefined class. It has many human applications: it is especially appropriate for automated decision making problems such as medical diagnosis. For some application areas, it is essential to produce the explicit classification procedures for the user. For example a decision trees for a medical diagnosis. The medical data is with many Features, diagnosis of the diseases is expensive as many tests are required to predict the disease.

The computational complexity of a classification algorithm may suffer from the curse of dimensionality caused by numerous features. Often a dataset has too many irrelevant features. Selecting only the most important ones can only be beneficial. Dimensionality reduction plays an important role in the domain of medicine as it contains many attributes.

Feature selection is often one of the imperative tasks in data preprocessing for data mining that has been used in different domains, it used to solve many problems in Bioinformatics (Dif & Elberrichi, 2019; Fan, Tang, Tian, & Wu, 2019), opinion classification (Sangam & Shinde, 2019), text categorization (Tang, Dai, & Xiang, 2019), cancer Classification (Lindqvist & Price, 2018) and sentiment analysis (Zheng, Wang, & Gao, 2018).

It consists in removing irrelevant, redundant, and noisy data. It reduces automatically the number of features, and has an immediate effect for the applications: speeding up the data mining algorithm, improving the model performance such as predictive accuracy.

Many problems connected to feature selection have been shown to be NP-Hard (Cotta & Moscato, 2003) and can be solved by using metaheuristics. Many optimization techniques such as genetic algorithms (Feng, Xuezheng, Yanqing, & Bourgeois, 2007), Tabu Search (Hongbin & Guangyu, 2002), Simulated Annealing (Ronen & Jacob, 2004) and Particle swarm optimization (Bing, Mengjie, & Will, 2014; Liam, Bing, Mengjie& Lin, 2012) have been used for solving the feature selection problem. Among these approaches, the Ant Colony Optimization (ACO) has been explored significantly to solving these problems. It is thought to be a promising method for a good selection of features (Al-Ani, 2005; Kumar, 2011; Shahzad, 2010).

Table 1. Filter and Wrapper Feature selection methods.

References	Algorithms	Type	Datasets
(Subanya & Rajalaxmi, 2014)	Binary Artificial Bee Colony/ K–Nearest Neighbor (BABC k–NN)	Wrapper	Heart disease
(Harb & Desuky, 2014)	Particle Swarm Optimization (PSO)	Filter and Wrapper	Breast Cancer, Heart Statlog, Dermatology
(Ravi et al., 2014)	Genetic algorithm /SVM	Wrapper	Wisconsin Breast, cancer Pima Diabetes, Dermatology, Thoracic Surgery, Mammographic,
(Brezocnik et al., 2018)	Swarm Intelligence Algorithms, Review	Filter, Wrapper and embedded	Medical Data and Other
(Darwish et al., 2018)	bio-inspired algorithms	Wrapper	breast cancer (WBCD and WPBC)
(Nematzadeh et al., 2019)	whale algorithm with Mutual Congestion	Filter	Colon

Many approaches have been proposed in the literature for feature selection problem in medical domain, some approaches are shown in Table 1. Where the metaheuristics are used to determine the optimal feature subset with improved classification accuracy in disease diagnosis.

Feature selection methods are Filter and wrapper based on evolutionary and swarm algorithms.

In this chapter, an optimization of the classification task by features selection with hybrid method improved Ant Colony Optimization (ACO) and Adaboost with Decision Trees (C4.5) is proposed. In the next section, a general description of feature selection for classification of medical data is presented. The Ant Colony Optimization is presented in Section 3. The Decision Trees is presented in Section 4. Section 5 presents Adaboost Algorithm. Section 6 describes the proposed approach. Section 7 presents experimental results obtained with a comparative study.

RELATED WORK

Some features in the dataset may not be useful for diagnosis and thus can be eliminated before learning. This section explores the research works which are related to the proposed work.

A Novel Feature Selection Algorithm for Heart Disease Classification is proposed in (Subanya & Rajalaxmi, 2014). The Researchers uses a metaheuristic algorithm to determine the optimal feature subset with improved classification accuracy in heart disease diagnosis. A Binary Artificial Bee Colony (BABC) algorithm is used to find the best features in the disease identification. The fitness of BABC is evaluated using K–Nearest Neighbor (KNN) method.

Wang and Ma (2009) proposed a rough set-based feature selection for medical dataset. It says that rough set feature selection known as feature forest algorithm can improve classification accuracy.

Feature Selection Using Genetic Algorithm and Classification using Weka for Ovarian Cancer is proposed in (Khare & Burse, 2016).The aim of this paper to investigate the performance of different classification methods on clinical data. Before applying classification algorithm relevant feature are selected by applying genetic algorithm (Khare & Burse, 2016).

Feature Selection for Classification Incorporating Less Meaningful Attributes in Medical Diagnostics is proposed in (Wosiak & Zakrzewska, 2014) in the first step feature set classification is applied, then taking into account the selected set of attributes clustering is performed. Two different algorithms of classification with two methods of clustering were combined (J48 + k-means, J48 + EM, AdaBoost + k-means, and AdaBoost + EM) during experiments, conducted on real data.

Feature Selection on Classification of Medical Datasets based on Particle Swarm Optimization is proposed in (Harb & Desuky, 2014), this paper proposes the filter and wrapper approaches with Particle Swarm Optimization (PSO) as a feature selection methods for medical data. The performance of the proposed methods is compared with another feature selection algorithm based on Genetic approach.

The authors (Rizwan et al., 2017) proposed approach based on Ant Colony Optimization and maximum Relevance and Minimum Redundancy for efficient subset evaluation.

This paper guarantees the choice of attributes which are highly pertinent with the target concept, weakly redundantly with each other and helpful predictor for classification algorithms. They use Mutual Information to measure redundancy between the attributes and pertinence with the class. The performance of the proposed method is compared with three popular machine learning classifiers over eleven dataset. It was concluded that this approach with an existing methods achieves better classification accuracy and uses reduced number of attributes.

As perspective, the authors proposed to look forward for hybrid searching mechanisms to enhance the approach. Moreover, parameter tuning can produce better optimized search. And, feature selection can be extended to contain the data stream mining.

The authors (El Houby, et al., 2017) proposed an Ant Colony Optimization approach for feature selection. The sequential forward feature selection is employed, so it chooses from the highest recommended attributes sequentially until the accuracy is enhanced. The accuracy was measured by K-Nearest Neighbor classifier.

The authors used the Class-Separability (CS) value of the feature as heuristic information, the pheromone value is based on the classification accuracy produced by adding an attribute.

The proposed method is applied on diverse medical datasets giving good results.

The authors (Khan & Baig, 2016) proposed an approach to find the pertinent feature subset by employing ant colony optimization minimum-redundancy-maximum-relevance. The proposed method considers the importance of each attribute while increasing the dimensionality.

The performance of proposed approach has been compared with available feature subset selection algorithms on eight selected datasets from UCI machine learning repository for experimentation.

It was concluded that the presented algorithm with an existing approaches achieves better classification accuracy and uses decreased number of features.

The authors (Jameel & Saif, 2018) proposed an optimal wrapper ant colony optimization based feature selection mechanism, the authors used a symmetrical uncertainty to compute the heuristic function. Symmetry is a required characteristic for measuring correlations among features. It reduces the number of comparisons. It is not influenced by multi valued attributes as the information gain, and its values are normalized in the range [0, 1].

The fitness function is the classification accuracy obtained by naïve Bayes classifier. The proposed method enhanced the accuracy by 5% on average through experimentation on all datasets employed when the subset feature selection is performed.

ANT COLONY OPTIMIZATION

Ant colony optimization (ACO) is a population-based metaheuristic that can be used to find approximate solutions to difficult optimization problems, it is inspired by the behavior of real ants in their search for the shortest paths to food sources. In ACO, a set of software agents called artificial ants search for good solutions to a given optimization problem. To apply ACO, the optimization problem is transformed into the problem of finding the best path on a weighted graph. The artificial ants (hereafter ants) incrementally build solutions by moving on the graph. The solution construction process is stochastic and is biased by a pheromone model, that is, a set of parameters associated with graph components (either nodes or edges) whose values are modified at runtime by the ants (Dorigo, 2007).

The Ant Colony Optimization has been successfully applied to optimization problems including telecommunications networks, vehicle routing and data mining.

The basic Ant Colony Optimization (ACO) Procedure:

Procedure ACO_MetaHeuristic

```
While (not_terminated)
    Generate_Solutions()
    Daemon_Actions() //Calculate fitness of the generated solution
    Pheromone_Update()
End while
End procedure
```

DECISION TREE

The author Waseem Shahzad (Shahzad, 2010) used approach Ant Colony Optimization with ID3 decision trees, ID3 does not apply any pruning procedures nor does it handle numeric attributes or missing values (Quinlan,1986).

C4.5 is an algorithm used to generate a decision tree developed by Ross Quinlan (Quinlan, 1993). C4.5 is an extension of Quinlan's earlier ID3 algorithm. The decision trees generated by C4.5 can be used for classification. C4.5 is an evolution of ID3, presented by the same author Quinlan (Quinlan, 1993).

It uses gain ratio as splitting criteria. The splitting ceases when the number of instances to be split is below a certain threshold. Error–based pruning is performed after the growing phase. C4.5 can handle numeric attributes. It can induce from a training set that incorporates missing values by using corrected gain ratio criteria.

Given a set S of cases, C4.5 first grows an initial tree using the divide-and-conquer algorithm as follows:

- If all the cases in S belong to the same class or S is small, the tree is a leaf labeled with the most frequent class in S.
- Otherwise, choose a test based on a single attribute with two or more outcomes. Make this test the root of the tree with one branch for each outcome of the test, partition S into corresponding subsets S1, S2, . . . according to the outcome for each case, and apply the same procedure recursively to each subset. There are usually many tests that could be chosen in this last step.

C4.5 uses two heuristic criteria to rank possible tests: information gain, which minimizes the total entropy of the subsets {Si} (but is heavily biased towards tests with numerous outcomes), and the default gain ratio that divides information gain by the information provided by the test outcomes. The initial tree is then pruned to avoid overfitting.

ADABOOST

Boosting is an approach to machine learning based on the idea of creating a highly accurate prediction rule by combining many relatively weak and inaccurate rules to improve their performance (Freund, 1995).

The AdaBoost algorithm, short for "Adaptive Boosting", is a machine learning meta-algorithm formulated by (Freund & Schapire, 1996). It was the first practical boosting algorithm.

AdaBoost generates a set of hypotheses (classifiers), and combines them through weighted majority voting of the classes predicted by the individual hypotheses.

Hypotheses are generated by training a weak classifier; samples are drawn from an iteratively updated distribution of the training set.

This distribution update ensures that instances misclassified by the previous classifier are more likely to be included in the training data of the next classifier.

Consecutive classifiers are trained on increasingly hard-to-classify samples.

In this paper, boosting was used in combination with the decision-tree learning algorithm C4.5 as the weak learner.

THE PROPOSED APPROACH

Approach Ant Colony Optimization with ID3 decision trees is proposed by (Shahzad, 2010), in this Article, the approach is oriented to c4.5 decision trees.

The important element of this approach is to find a subset of feature from a connected graph N^2 where N is the number of features present in Datasets excluding target attribute.

The graph is the search space for the ants to move, where the links represent the connection between features of a dataset and nodes are the features. Each ant probabilistically selects features on the basis of pheromone and heuristic values associated with each link. When an ant completes its tour (it constructs a candidate solution in this search space by traversing a path of nodes and links) then for evaluating the fitness of the subset of features selected by it, the authors use Adaboost with Decision Trees (C4.5 classifier) based only on the features in the subset and then evaluate the accuracy of the classifier which is considered the fitness of the solution found by the ant. For evaluating the accuracy of the classifier the authors use 10-fold cross validation. The proposed approach is wrapper approach (the wrapper approach searches through the features subset space using the estimated accuracy from an induction algorithm as a measure of subset suitability).

This process continues until a stopping criterion is met. The authors find features subset that has the best accuracy. All the steps of approach proposed are shown below.

Search Space

The search space contains N^2 nodes (N features of dataset excluding target attribute) and "END" node (Shahzad, 2010), where the link between nodes denote the choice of the next node (next feature).The "END" node is used to terminate the search of subset of features (nodes), it is connected to each node of the graph, when an ant selects 'END' node, its path is complete and it stops adding nodes (Figure 1).

Figure 1 presents the search space of features, where A1, A2,… are the features present in dataset. There are as many layer as the number of features and each layer has all the features, each feature is connected to all other features in the next layer (each vertical line represents a single layer of all features). If an ant selects a feature then it cannot select that feature again in its current path (avoid adding duplicate features in the same set) for example from N=5 Features (A1, A2, A3, A4, A5) present in dataset, the found best subset is (A2, A4, A5) with 3 features.

Figure 1. N² search space for ant path

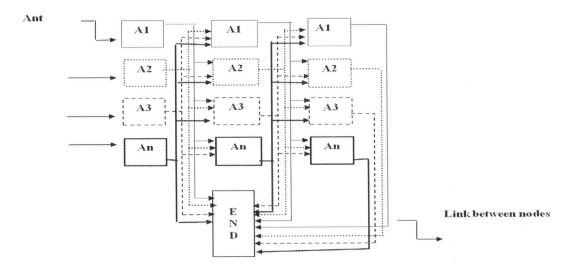

Pheromone Values

The pheromone value is associated with each link between the nodes. At the start of algorithm, the pheromone values are initialized with the same random value (Dorigo, 2007; Shahzad, 2010) (no feature is preferred over other features), the initial pheromone is calculated with (1).

$$\tau_{ij}(t=1)=1/N \tag{1}$$

where t=1 is the first iteration of algorithm.

N: number of features present in dataset excluding target attribute.
i: current node (feature), j: next node (feature).

Selection of a Feature

An ant moves from the present node to the next node with a probability, this probability is calculated with two components (2): pheromone value (it is present on the edge between current node and next node) and heuristics values (it represents the worth of the next node).

$$\rho_{ij} = \frac{\left[\tau_{ij}\right]^{\alpha} \left[\eta_{ij}\right]^{\beta}}{\sum_{k \in S}\left[\tau_{ik}\right]^{\alpha} \left[\eta_{ik}\right]^{\beta}} \tag{2}$$

τ_{ij}: The pheromone values between the current node i and the next node j.
η_{ij}: The heuristic value of node j.

S: The set of nodes that not have been visited by current node i, the parameters α and β are influencing factors of pheromone value and heuristic value respectively.

Heuristic Values

The heuristic value indicates the worth of the feature, an ant uses this value for the decision of the move from node to other. The gain ratio of each feature is used as a heuristic value, the authors calculate the gain ratio of each feature in the dataset (3), the gain ratio "normalizes" the information gain as follows (Quinlan, 1993):

$$GainRation(a_i, S) = \frac{InformationGain(a_i, S)}{Entropy(a_i, S)} \quad (3)$$

Where a_i is an attribute and S is a sample from dataset.

Note that this ratio is not defined when the denominator is zero. Also the ratio may tend to favor attributes for which the denominator is very small. Consequently, it is suggested in two stages. First the information gain is calculated for all attributes. As a consequence, taking into consideration only attributes that have performed at least as good as the average information gain, the attribute that has obtained the best ratio gain is selected.

It has been shown that the gain ratio tends to outperform simple information gain criteria, both from the accuracy aspect, as well as from classifier complexity aspects (Quinlan, 1988).

When an ant wants to select the next node, the corresponding feature gain ratio is used as heuristic value and is used in (2).

Fitness Function

The worth of the subset of features (S) selected by an ant is measured by fitness function (Evaluate(S)), the authors use Adaboost (C4.5) with 10-fold cross validation for building model from the selected feature subset and then evaluate learned model (classifier).

In 10-fold cross validation, the authors execute these steps:

- Randomly, Break dataset into 10 subsets (Ten equally sized);
- Train on 9 subsets and test on 1;
- Repeat 10 times and take a mean accuracy (the average).

This average is used as fitness of the features subset. The fitness of a particular feature subset is measured by (4).

$$fitness = {}^{\sigma}/_{N} \quad (4)$$

where σ is the number of instances incorrectly classified by the classifier and N is the total number of test instances. This fitness is calculated for each fold and then averaged.

Evaluate (S)

Evaluate features subset S (with (Adaboost (C4.5)) and return fitness (4)).

Improved Global Pheromone Updating Rule

The pheromone values are updated after all ants complete its tours (each iteration), at the next iteration, the ants can use this value in their search. At iteration t+1, the amount of pheromone on each link existing in the current features subset (Li et al., 2017) is updating according to (5, 6):

$$\tau_{ij} = (1-\rho) . \tau_{ij}(t) + \Delta\tau_{ii}(t) \tag{5}$$

$$\Delta\tau_{ii}(t) = \begin{cases} Q \,/\, fitness, t < A \\ Q \,/\, fitness_{opt}, t >= A \end{cases} \tag{6}$$

where:

$\tau_{ij}(t)$: The pheromone value between $node_i$ and $node_j$ in present iteration (t)
P: The pheromone evaporation rate.
Q: The pheromone Intensity Factor.
Fitness: The quality of the best path (features subset) constructed by an ant in iteration t.
$Fitness_{opt}$: The quality of the best path (features subset) constructed by all ant in iteration t.

Constant A is linked to the predetermined iteration number.
When t <A, pheromone value is updated for all traversed paths to locate the best one.
When t ≥ A, the ant colony algorithm only updates the pheromone value on the optimal path in each iteration.
The aim of the pheromone update is to increase the pheromone values associated with good or promising solutions (features), and to decrease those that are associated with bad ones.

The Proposed Method Improved ACO/Adaboost (C4.5)

```
Begin
    Load the dataset.
    Calculate gain ratio (heuristic value) of each feature (3).
    Generate a population of Ants (K ants).
    Initialize the parameters of ACO (Pheromone (1), α, β, ρ, criterion stop-
ping).
    T=1 (initial iteration)
    Repeat
        For each Ant (i=1 to k)
```

```
        Generate a subset S (each feature of subset is selected with prob-
ability (2)).
        Evaluate(S)
    End For
    Return the best subset of iteration t (with best fitness)
    If the fitness (current iteration) > previous global best (previous it-
eration).
        Set the current subset S accuracy as global best accuracy.
    End IF
    Update the pheromone values (5,6).
  Until (stopping criteria is met).
    Return best features subset as final more appropriate set.
End.
```

In this algorithm, the authors load the dataset and they initialize the different parameters, the search space which is an N^2 graph where N is the number of features in the dataset excluding target feature. The pheromone values are initialized on all links between nodes (1), a population of ants is defined and the parameters (α, β, ρ) are initialized.

The authors calculate heuristic values (gain ratio) for each feature in Datasets (3). In an iteration of the algorithm, each ant selects an initial feature randomly, it completes its path (selects other features). When an ant starts its search it selects the next node (feature) according to (2). Each ant completes its path (terminate with "END" node) it has a subset of different features, each features subset are used to construct decision tree Adaboost(C4.5) classifier, the authors return fitness (4) of each subset generated by the ants, they search the best subset with best accuracy (best fitness) from all the subset generated of this iteration.

If the accuracy (fitness) of the current features subset is best than previously best features subset then this current features subset will become the global best subset and its fitness will be the global best accuracy. In the next iteration the same procedure is applied for all ants. This process continues until a stopping criterion is met, in our approach the authors use a defined number of iterations, and they use error rate of classifier as fitness. Finally the global best subset is returned as final features subset.

EXPERIMENTAL RESULTS WITH A COMPARATIVE STUDY

The authors have implemented the proposed approach in java as the programming language, with Weka (open source code developed in java, University of Waikato, Hamilton, New Zealand) There are no standard values of parameters used in algorithm ACO in the literature; it depends to the experimentations and its results.

The proposed method is experimented on seven benchmarked datasets of the UCI Machine Learning Repository for handling medical dataset classification, it is a collection of databases, domain theories, and data generators that are used all over the world as a primary source of machine learning datasets for the empirical analysis of machine learning algorithms (Blake & Merz, 1998).

The details of the Medical datasets are shown in Table 2.

Table 2. Datasets of UCI

Datasets	Number of Features	Number of Instances	Number of Class
Anneal	38	898	6
Ecoli	7	336	8
Breast-w	9	699	2
Heart-disease	13	303	5
Primary-tumor	17	339	22
Mammographic_masses	5	961	2
Postoperative_patient_data	8	90	3

For example, the dataset primary-tumors contains 17 attributes, one class attribute and 339 instances. It contains total 22 classes of primary tumor. The rest of the attributes indicate the areas from where primary tumors start.

In Table 2, first column is the name of dataset, second column presents the number of features, third column presents the number of instances and fourth column presents the number of class. The datasets are selected with different characteristics: some of them have a higher number of features and other have lesser, some of them have two class and other have more class, some of them have a higher number of instances and other have lesser, some features are nominal and other are numeric.

The best results on these datasets in related work are shown below:

- A metaheuristic BABC k–NN (Subanya & Rajalaxmi, 2014) is proposed to determine the best features in heart disease diagnosis. It gives an accuracy of 92.4% for this datatset;
- PSO with Correlation based feature selection as subset evaluating mechanism has been used (Harb & Desuky, 2014) with a medical datasets Breast Cancer the proposed method applied on the five Weka classifiers like Decision tree C4.5 with accuracy 74.13%;
- Ravi, Ramachandra & Nagamani(2014) proposed a Genetic algorithm based optimization algorithm, which can optimize the parameter values for SVM, the GA-SVM method was applied to remove insignificant features and effectively find best parameter values in medical datasets Mammographic Mass (With accuracy 0.781% and F -Measure 0.78%) and Wisconsin Breast Cancer (With accuracy 0.97% and F –Measure 0.97%);
- A novel feature selection algorithm FEAST is proposed in (Wang & Song, 2012) based on association rule mining. The results on the real world data sets show that FEAST give a competent result in terms of average classification accuracy for example decision tree c4.5 with algorithm FEAST for the primary tumor are with accuracy 43.65%;
- A feature selection method called: filtered and supported sequential forward search (FS_SFS) with support vector machines (SVM) are proposed in (Liu & Zheng, 2005), for example the accuracy result of the Postoperative Patients data set (PO Patients) is equal to 73.1%.

Another approach hybrid (Genetic Algorithm/ Adaboost (Decision trees C4.5)) is implemented to be compared with our approach (ant colony optimization / Adaboost (decision Trees C4.5), this approach

Table 3. The initial values of the parameters.

Ant Colony Optimization	Genetic Search	Adaboost Algorithm
Number of ants used: 50 α (Importance of pheromone values): 01 β (Importance of heuristic values): 01 criterion stopping: 50 Evaporation rate (p): 0.1 Constant A: 25 Pheromone Intensity Factor (Q): 01	Probability of crossover that two population members will exchange genetic material: 0.6 Number of generations to evaluate: 20 Probability of mutation occurring: 0.033 Population size (even number), this is the number of individuals (attribute sets) in the population: 20	Number of iterations to be performed: 10 Random number seed to be used: 01 Weight threshold for weight pruning: 50

is available under Weka software, Genetic Search Performs a search using the simple genetic algorithm described in Goldberg (Goldberg, 1989).

The Genetic Search (GS) and Ant colony Optimization (ACO) are population based metaheuristics.

For each dataset, the original number of features is used, when the authors implement features selection (our approach and genetic search with Adaboost (C4.5) approach), they obtain features subset that can be decrease or increase the error rate of supervised classification (Adaboost(C4.5)).

The values of the parameters were therefore used for the Ant colony optimization, Genetic Search and Adaboost Algorithm are shown in table 3.

The comparison is based on the number of reduced features (compared to the original dataset) and the best accuracy of learning model i.e. lesser error rate and the F-Measure (compared to C4.5 algorithm).

The classical evaluation metrics of F-measure is used to evaluate the efficiency of the proposed approach, F-measure is calculated by the precision and the recall (the precision is the proportion of positive predictions that are correct and the recall is the proportion of positive samples that are correctly predicted positive.

The results of the experiments are given below (table shows the comparison of proposed approach with Genetic search/Adaboost (C4.5) and C4.5 Algorithm) Table 4.

The medical data Primary-tumor is with 17 Features and 339 instances, the diagnosis of the diseases is expensive as many tests are required to predict the disease. Selecting the most important ones can be beneficial (relevant features: 08) by our approach with lesser error rate (0.540) and F-Measure (0.387).

Table 4. Comparison of error rate of classification, number of features and F-Measure

Datasets	Improved ACO/ AdaBoost (C4.5)			Genetic Search/ Adaboost(C4.5)			C4.5	
	Error Rate	F-Measure	Number of Features	Error Rate	F-Measure	Number of Features	Error Rate	F-Measure
Anneal	**0.001**	**0.999**	16	0.001	0.99	16	0.016	0.984
Ecoli	**0.155**	**0.842**	6	0.167	0.836	6	0.158	0.836
Breast-w	**0.049**	**0.951**	5	0.038	0.946	9	0.054	0.946
Heart-disease	**0.178**	**0.819**	3	0.171	0.814	3	0.224	0.774
Primary-tumor	**0.540**	**0.387**	8	0.546	0.383	10	0.602	0.358
Mammographic_ masses	**0.166**	**0.834**	3	0.166	0.765	3	0.178	0.822
Postoperative_ patient_data	**0.289**	**0.591**	1	0.289	0.591	1	0.3	0.586

The number of features selected by the proposed algorithm (the fourth column) is significantly smaller than the total number of the features in the original datasets (the second column, Table 2) in the majority of the datasets.

Based on the error rate of classification obtained by the C4.5 algorithm (it is implemented on the original set of features), the proposed approach gave a lesser error rate of classification

For example, with our approach, the datasets Primary-tumor have a lesser error rate (0.540) compared with Genetic search/AdaBoost (C4.5) (0.546) and the same compared with C4.5 algorithm (0.602).

Based on the F-Measure, the proposed approach gives a significant result of classification for all datasets compared to C4.5 Algorithm.

These first experimental results indicate that the proposed feature subset selection approach (Ant Colony Optimization with Adaboost (C4.5)) selects relevant features from the Medical datasets causing a decrease in the error rate, a significant decrease in the number of features and a significant increase in the F-Measure.

In the original ant colony algorithm, the pheromone values are updated after all ants complete its paths. In the beginning, the search for the optimal path is yet at the phase of exploration, the ants can track some detours, if the pheromone update is do it on each phase for the paths that are not linked with the optimal path, it is likely that the next ants will be misled, to ovoid the slow convergence (Li et al., 2017), the authors use an improved global pheromone updating rule. With the first experimental results, the improving algorithm gave a good result in term of accuracy and F-Measure compared to previous version of algorithm (Alaoui & Elberrichi, 2018).

CONCLUSION

In this chapter, the authors presented a feature subset selection based on the improved Ant Colony Optimization metaheuristic and Adaboost (C4.5 Decision Trees) for a Medical Data. ACO is an important approach for feature selection problem. Ant Colony Optimization is used to search for more appropriate features (relevant) from the original set of features and Adaboost (C4.5) is used to build robust learning models. The performance of the proposed approach is compared with those of the hybrid Genetic Search/Adaboost (C4.5) and C4.5 Algorithm. The authors conclude that the metaheuristic Ant colony optimization and Adaboost (C4.5) algorithm are really helpful for dimensionality reduction of features and also for building cost effective model for disease prediction.

Experimental results show that this approach is competitive. The results are promising in terms of the solution quality and the number of selected features in the medical datasets.

To improve the solutions and avoid converging to local optimum, the parameters (evaporation rate, alpha and beta) can be optimized.

REFERENCES

Al-Ani, A. (2005). Ant Colony Optimization for feature subset selection. In *Proceedings Of World Academy Of Science*. Engineering and Technology.

Alaoui, A., & Elberrichi, Z. (2018). Feature Subset Selection Using Ant Colony Optimization for a Decision Trees Classification of Medical Data. *International Journal of Information Retrieval Research*, *8*(4), 39–50. doi:10.4018/IJIRR.2018100103

Bing, X., Mengjie, Z., & Will, B. (2014). Particle swarm optimization for feature selection in classification: Novel initialization and updating mechanisms. *Applied Soft Computing*, (18): 261–276.

Blake, C., & Merz, C. (1998). *UCI Repository of machine learning DataBases*. Irvine, CA: University of California.

Brezocnik, L., Fister, I., & Podgorelec, V. (2018). *Swarm Intelligence Algorithms for Feature Selection: A Review*. Applied Sciences Journal. doi:10.3390/app8091521

Cotta, C., & Moscato, P. (2003). The k-feature set problem is w[2]-complete. *Journal of Computer and System Sciences*, *686-690*. doi:10.1016/S0022-0000(03)00081-3

Darwish, A., Sayed, G. I., & Aboul Hassanien, E. (2018). Meta-Heuristic Optimization Algorithms Based Feature Selection For Clinical Breast Cancer Diagnosis. *Journal of the Egyptian Mathematical Society*, *26*(3).

Dif, N., & Elberrichi, Z. (2019). An Enhanced Recursive Firefly Algorithm for Informative Gene Selection. *International Journal of Swarm Intelligence Research*, *10*(2), 21–33. doi:10.4018/IJSIR.2019040102

Dorigo, M. (2007). *Ant colony optimization*. Retrieved from http://www.scholarpedia.org/article/Ant_colony_optimization

El Houby, E.M.F., Yassin, N., & Omran, S. (2017). A Hybrid Approach From Ant Colony Optimization And K-Nearest Neighbor For Classifying Datasets Using Selected Features. *Informatica*, *41*(4).

Fan, S., Tang, J., Tian, Q., & Wu, C. (2019). A robust fuzzy rule based integrative feature selection strategy for gene expression data in TCGA. *BMC Medical Genomics*, *12*(1), 14. doi:10.118612920-018-0451-x PMID:30704464

Feng, T., Xuezheng, F., Yanqing, Z., & Bourgeois, G. (2007). *A genetic algorithm-based method for feature subset selection*. Springer-Verlag.

Freund, Y. (1995). Boosting a weak learning algorithm by majority. *Information and Computation*, *121*(2), 256–285. doi:10.1006/inco.1995.1136

Freund, Y., & Schapire, R. (1996). Experiments with a New Boosting Algorithm. *Machine Learning: Proceedings of the Thirteenth International Conference*.

Goldberg, E. (1989). *Genetic algorithms in search: optimization and machine learning*. Addison-Wesley.

Harb, M., & Desuky, A. (2014). Feature Selection on Classification of Medical Datasets based on Particle Swarm Optimization. *International Journal of Computers and Applications*, *104*(5).

Hongbin, Z., & Guangyu, S. (2002). Feature selection using Tabu Search method. *Pattern Recognition*, *701–711*.

Jameel, S., & Rehman, S. U. (2018). An Optimal Feature Selection Method Using A Modified Wrapper Based Ant Colony Optimization. *Journal of the National Science Foundation of Srilanka, 46*(2), 143–151.

Khan, A., & Baig, A. (2016). Multi-objective feature subset selection using MRMR based enhanced ant colony optimization algorithm. *Journal of Experimental & Theoretical Artificial Intelligence, 28*(6), 1061–1073. doi:10.1080/0952813X.2015.1056240

Khare, P., & Burse, K. (2016). Feature Selection Using Genetic Algorithm and Classification using Weka for Ovarian Cancer. *International Journal of Computer Science and Information Technologies, 7*(1), 194–196.

Kumar, S., & Mewada, P. (2011). ACO based Feature subset Selection for multiple K-Nearest Neighbor Classifiers. *International Journal on Computer Science and Engineering.*

Li, P., Wang, H., & Li, X. (2017). Improved ant colony algorithm for global path planning. *Advances in Materials, Machinery, Electronics,* I.

Liam, C., Bing, X., Mengjie, Z., & Lin, S. (2012). Binary Particle Swarm Optimization for Feature Selection: A Filter Based Approach. *Proceedings of the IEEE World Congress on Computational Intelligence.*

Lindqvist, N., & Price, T. (2018). *Evaluation of Feature Selection Methods for Machine Learning Classification of Breast Cancer.* Academic Press.

Liu, Y., & Zheng, F. (2005). FS_SFS: A novel feature selection method for support vector machines. *The Journal of Pattern Recognition Society.*

Nematzadeh, H., Enayatifar, R., Mahmud, M., & Akbari, E. (2019). Frequency based feature selection method using whale algorithm. *Genomics.* doi:10.1016/j.ygeno.2019.01.006 PMID:30660788

Quinlan, R. (1986). Induction of decision trees. *Machine Learning, 1*(1), 81–106. doi:10.1007/BF00116251

Quinlan, R. (1988). Decision Trees and Multivalued Attributes. *Machine Intelligence,* (11), 305 – 318.

Quinlan, R. (1993). *C4.5: Programs for machine learning.* Morgan Kaufmann Publishers.

Ravi Kumar, G., Ramachandra, G. A., & Nagamani, K. (2014). An Efficient Feature Selection System to Integrating SVM with Genetic Algorithm for Large Medical Datasets. *International Journal of Advanced Research in Computer Science and Software Engineering, 4*(2).

Rizwan, M., Waseem, S., & Ejaz, A. (2017). Maximum Relevancy Minimum Redundancy Based Feature Subset Selection using Ant Colony Optimization. *Journal of Applied Environmental and Biological Sciences, 7*(4), 118–130.

Ronen, M., & Jacob, Z. (2004). Using simulated annealing to optimize feature selection problem in marketing applications. *European Journal of Operational Research, 171*(3), 842–858.

Sangam, S., & Shinde, S. (2019). Most Persistent Feature Selection Method for Opinion Mining of Social Media Reviews. Information and Communication Technology for Competitive Strategies, 213 – 221.

Shahzad, W. (2010). Classification and Associative Classification Rule Discovery Using Ant Colony Optimization, these. Islamabad, Pakistan: Academic Press.

Subanya, B., & Rajalaxmi, R. (2014). A Novel Feature Selection Algorithm for Heart Disease Classification. *International Journal of Computational Intelligence and Informatic, 4*(2).

Tang, X., Dai, Y., & Xiang, Y. (2019). Feature selection based on feature interactions with application to text categorization. *Expert Systems with Applications, 120*, 207–216. doi:10.1016/j.eswa.2018.11.018

Wang, G., & Song, Q. (2012). Selecting Feature Subset via Constraint Association Rules. Advances in Knowledge Discovery and Data Mining. doi:10.1007/978-3-642-30220-6_26

Wang, Y., & Ma, L. (2009). Feature selection for medical dataset using rough set theory. In *Proceedings of 3rd WSEAS international conference on Computer engineering and applications*, (pp. 68 – 72). Academic Press.

Wosiak, A., & Zakrzewska, D. (2014). Feature Selection for Classification Incorporating Less Meaningful Attributes in Medical Diagnostics. In *Proceedings of the 2014 Federated Conference on Computer Science and Information Systems*, (pp.235–240). Academic Press. 10.15439/2014F296

Zheng, L., Wang, H., & Gao, S. (2018). Sentimental feature selection for sentiment analysis of Chinese online reviews. *International Journal of Machine Learning and Cybernetics, 9*(1), 75–84. doi:10.100713042-015-0347-4

KEY TERMS AND DEFINITIONS

Best Fitness: Best accuracy of best subset found.

Feature Selection: By this task removing irrelevant, redundant, and noisy data.

Global Best Subset: Selecting only the most important ones can only be beneficial.

Improved Ant Colony Optimization: Ant colony optimization with improved global pheromone updating rule.

Medical Datasets: Set of instances for diagnosis and prognosis.

Relevant Features: Helpful attributes for diagnosis and thus can't be removed before learning.

Supervised Classifier: Allows predicting if an instance will be assigned to a predefined class to classify the data for diagnosis and prognosis.

294

Chapter 16
Load Balancing in Cloud Computing:
Challenges and Management Techniques

Pradeep Kumar Tiwari
https://orcid.org/0000-0003-0387-9236
Manipal University Jaipur, India

Geeta Rani
Manipal University Jaipur, India

Tarun Jain
Manipal University Jaipur, India

Ankit Mundra
Manipal University Jaipur, India

Rohit Kumar Gupta
Manipal University Jaipur, India

ABSTRACT

Cloud computing is an effective alternative information technology paradigm with its on-demand resource provisioning and high reliability. This technology has the potential to offer virtualized, distributed, and elastic resources as utilities to users. Cloud computing offers numerous types of computing and storage means by connecting to a vast pool of systems. However, because of its large data handling property, the major issue the technology facing is the load balancing problem. Load balancing is the maximum resource utilization with effective management of load imbalance. This chapter shares information about logical and physical resources, load balancing metrics, challenges and techniques, and also gives some suggestions that could be helpful for future studies.

DOI: 10.4018/978-1-7998-1021-6.ch016

INTRODUCTION

An effective Load balancing mechanism enhances the fair workload distribution among the VMs. Load balancing use the mechanism of hyper threading to use a single processor as multiple processors. Load balancing intends to minimize the resource and maximize the resource utilization. The core concept of effective load balancing technique maximizes the throughput and minimizes the response time with fault tolerance (Rathore and Chana, 2014).

The load balancing mechanism is a key mechanism to manage the User Bases resources request from Data Centers (Zhang, Cheng, and Boutaba, 2010).

Load balancing provide effective management of resources by resource allocation policy using the task scheduling in distributed environment. The load management mechanism should ensure the:

- Resource availability on time to reduce Service Level Agreement (SLA) violation
- Effective resource utilization during the high or low load.
- Cost effective by using effective management of resources.
- Increasing the Quality of Service (QoS) with robust fault tolerance mechanism.

That is, load balancing help to continue the service by implementing fail over in the cases where the failure of one or more component occurs. Maximization of the throughput, minimization of the response time and avoidance of the overload are the other major advantages of the load balancing. Above all, by keeping resource consumption at minimum, the load balancing techniques help to reduce costs and create the enterprises greener.

All these features make load balancing atop a prioritized subject among computer science researchers and numerous different load balancing approaches were proposed by multifarious researchers. The present chapter is conducting an in depth review of the studies regarding the existing load balancing techniques in Cloud networking and attempt to find shortcomings exist in those proposals as a mean to come up with a novel proposal which can overcome these shortcomings. The review also targets the studies which deal with the factors such as, parameters for identifying hotspots, an algorithm that can evaluate how balanced a system is, a prediction algorithm for estimating the workload after a migration has occurred and an algorithm to determine how costly a migration will be.

The operating system and the applications of a VM function autonomously without any mutual interference. VM is migrated without downtime and VM failure does not affect the distribution of resources among VMs. The service level agreement (SLA) and the Quality of Service (QoS) must be managed by the Load Balance (LB) policy. The main causes of SLA violation are scattered data among heterogeneous servers, hot spot, load imbalance, and weak resource management (Rathore et al., 2014). The occurrence of the load imbalance is when the demands in the heterogeneous environments are frequently changing. Load imbalance can be managed through LB between high load and low load machines. The management of LB is difficult on high resource demands that change frequently. The factors that help in the management of LB are information policies, location to migrate VM, selection of VM, and transfer of load (Zhang et al., 2010).

In order to attain High Performance Computing (HPC) and utilization of computing resources, the elementary concept of the distributed system is utilized to perform cluster, grid and cloud computing. The distributed application determines the distributed paradigms. Virtual Machines (VMs) can comprise of separately functioning operating systems and applications. Virtualization is the core concept of resource

Figure 1. Type 1 hypervisor

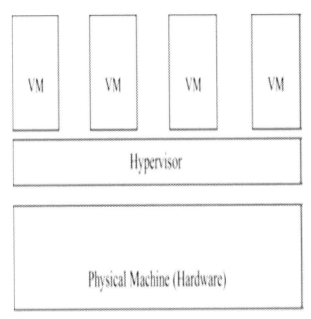

Figure 2. Type 2 hypervisor

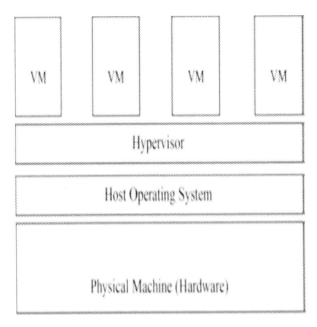

pool and management. Hypervisor assists in attaining hardware virtualization and is segregated into Type 1 and Type 2. The Type 1 hypervisor is the bare-metal hypervisor that is installed directly on the x86-based hardware and renders direct access to the hardware resources (Figure 1). The Type 2 hypervisor is the hosted hypervisor that is installed and run as an application on an operating system (Figure 2).

Many recommendations are on the anvil despite a huge number of LB managing mechanisms being posited by researchers. In environments that have scattered servers and multi-tenants, the management of memory, computer and network is cumbersome. The CPU and memory management policies and the consequent impact on load management form the basis of these approaches. Static approach, dynamic approach and dynamic consolidation approach are the approaches that are available. The load can automate the modern load balancing mechanism. Cost minimization, dynamic load requirement, energy saving, and high performance are rendered by the modern mechanisms. The crucial role of resource management is executed by the efficient dynamic load management during frequently varying environment and high resource demands. Only the resources that are available on physical machine (PM) can be possessed by VMs. A situation in which the VM's demand for resources is larger than those available on PMs is termed as a hotspot. On the contrary, a situation in which the PM's resources are not utilized to their full potential is termed as a cold spot. VMs can be moved for managing hotspot and coldspot. The selected VM and hot spot mitigation are moved to those PMs, which have a less load (Vinothina, Sridaran, and Ganapathi, 2012).

The primary objective of the current research is to formulate and create an effective load balancing algorithm within a heterogeneously distributed environment termed as cloud. VMs possess their own identity, processing power, bandwidth, memory and number of CPUs. In order to facilitate a single failure point and to elude bottleneck, the suggested algorithm is decentralized.

Figure 3. Types of resources

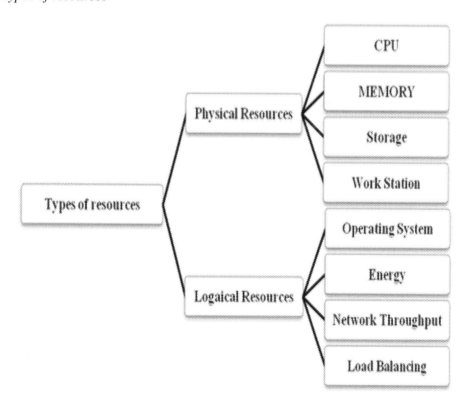

PHYSICAL AND LOGICAL RESOURCES OF CLOUD COMPUTING

The physical and logical components available in a physical computing machine are known as resources. Cloud computing uses physical resources (CPU, memory, secondary storage, work station) and logical resources (operating system, energy, network throughput, load balancing mechanism). Figure 3 shows the type of physical and logical resources of Cloud computing (Singh, Juneia, and Malhorta, 2015).

Physical Resources

Physical resources are Central Processing Unit (CPU), memory, storage and work station. Feasible utilization of physical resources maximizes the throughput. Physical resources are the hardware components of Cloud computing service.

Central Processing Unit (CPU)

CPU is known as the processing resource and its execution capacity is mapped by MIPS. The CPU has either a single core or a multi-core. An individual core capacity is utilized by VM and the multiple cores are assigned to multiple VMs. The maximal utilization of the CPU increases the throughput.

Memory

The dynamic allocation of jobs requires more memory space. The virtualization component makes the pool of memory for its effective management. This helps to fulfill the huge demand of memory for the process execution.

Storage

Storage is the component that stores the user data in a huge memory. The storage system may be managed by a third party.

Work Station

Physical machines are used as grid, cluster, or cloud-based computing systems. The virtualization component divides the single machine in to multiple VMs. A work station may have more than 30 GB memory as well as a big CPU and the available capacity is utilized by VMs (L.D. and Krishna, 2013).

Logical Resource

Logical resources control and manage the available physical resources. Logical applications not only use the available physical resources effectively, but also distribute resources among VMs, i.e., they manage the physical resources.

Operating System (OS)

An OS controls and manages the virtualized resources to utilize the available resources according to the process requirements. The OS management policy takes care of the device management, fault tolerance, and firewall security.

Energy

The energy application minimizes the use of PMs and shutdown to the ideal (non-utilized) node. This helps to reduce energy consumption and also helps to promote green computing.

Network Throughput

Network throughput is a measurement and distribution of bandwidth. It helps to transfer the file from one work station to another work station.

Load Balancing

The management of demanded resources is known as load balancing mechanism in which the workload is distributed among the VMs. The mechanism of load balancing is a vital component of the hypervisor, which dynamically or statically manage the load imbalance in a distributed manner on the available VMs. The CPU, memory and network components are virtualized to maximize the utilization of resources. In computing, the distribution of workloads across multiple computing resources, such as disk drives, CPUs, network links, computer clusters, or computers, is enhanced by load balancing (Xiao et al., 2015).

Researchers objectives are maximizing the CPU utilization of VMs with efficient results in load balancing metrics (Liao et al., 2012) (Sammy, Shengbing and Wilson, 2012) (Lau, Lu, and Leung, 2006) (Lu and Lau, 1995) (Rotithor, 1994) (Buyya, Rangan and Calheiros, 2010) (Gupta, Gardner and Vahdat, 2006) (Nathan, Kulkarni, and Bellur, 2013) (pubs.vmware.com). The load balance manager distributed the users requested load among the VMs. It maps the requested resource capacity to the available capacity and also checks the physical machine capacity from hosted VMs. During the high demand load balancer migrate the jobs either VM to VM or DC to DC (Cao et al., 2003) (Ferreto, netto, Calheiros, and De Rose, 2011) (Forsman, Glad, Lundberg, and Ilie, 2015) (Kalra and Singh, 2015) (Bitam, 2012) (Lin, Wang, Liang, and Qi, 2011) (Calheiros, Ranjan, Belglazov, De Rose and Buyya, 2011) (Wickrmasinghe, Calheiros, and Buyya, 2010) (Kabalan, Smari and Hakimian, 2002) (Kopaneli, Kousiouris, Velez, Evangelinou, and Varvaigou, 2015) (Andreolini, Casolari, Colajannni, and Messori, 2009).

ACCOUNTING AND PROCESS PARAMETERS

The load balancing mechanism manges the resource distribution according to the UB request. The UB's high resource demand causes load imbalance and the highly loaded VMs transfer the load to low loaded VM during load imbalance. The load balance manager migrate the jobs from high load VMs to low load VMs. The migration time of the job should be the minimum. Otherwise, the waiting time of job migration will increase, thereby causing service level agreement (SLA) violation.

The migration ID, which is a discrete sequence number, together with the migration issuer forms a unique ID that will identify a migration process. Each ID also has the following seven parameters:

- Maximum CPU capacity
- Current CPU load
- Maximum memory capacity
- Used memory
- Maximum bandwidth
- Used bandwidth
- CPU load history

The CPU load history is a list of the previous consecutively recorded load values. Load history helps to easily distinguish between high load and low load VMs. Each DC [ID] has a list of information for 'n' VMs.

Each item in that list is defined as follows:

- VM [ID]
- Number of virtual cores
- Current CPU load of VM
- Memory size of VM
- Used bandwidth
- CPU load history

Stored Data - There are several parameters stored in every DC in the system:

- Data about itself.
- Information about all VMs it hosts.
- Data about all neighboring DCs, including PM and VM information.
- VM candidates [ID].
- Information history and current state for all VMs.

These basic parameters are used during the mapping of the load of VM, DC, and specific migration management.

Literature Review

This section reviews the multiple studies regarding the various live (dynamic) migration algorithms proposed by multifarious researchers.

Andreolini et al. (2009) proposed the re-allocation of management algorithms of VMs in a Cloud networking, which consist of large numbers of hosts. The proposed novel algorithms take decisions without recurring to typical thresholds and identify only the real critical instances. Furthermore, they consider the load trend behavior of the resources. Experimental findings indicated that proposed algorithms provided good results invariable contexts by reducing system instability and limiting the migrations to only when it is really necessary. However, the major drawback of the study is that the study was not contained in the heterogeneous infrastructures and platforms. Furthermore, the study did not consider the guests that can migrate only within certain subsets of hardware and operating systems.

Akoush et al. (2010) proposed a hybrid migration approach for balancing the load. The study designed two simulation algorithms to execute fast and accurate live migration. . The algorithms used a lot of useful information state, including multiple devices and frequently accessed pages of functioning VM. The findings revealed that the proposed algorithms are capable of predicting the migration times with 90% accuracy for both real world and simulative benchmarks. However, the study was conducted in the limited environment using LAN. Hence, the compatibility of this algorithm with big distributed networks, which uses WAN networking, is yet to be proved.

Hu et al. (2011) proposed an algorithm to support the live wide-area migration of virtual machines which used local storage for their persistent state. The main advantage of this approach is the transparency to the migrated VM. Furthermore, this new approach does not interrupt open network connections from and to the VM during wide area migrations, which in turn ensure consistency of the VM's local constant state at the source and the destination after migration. Another advantage of the proposed algorithm was its ability to handle highly intensive workloads. However, the study failed to highlight the performance effectiveness of the proposed algorithm.

Ferreto et al. (2011) designed Heuristics based on Linear Programming (LP), namely, First Fit Decreasing (FFD), Best Fit Decreasing (BFD), worst fit decreasing (WFD), and Almost Worst Fit Decreasing (AWFD). The heuristic approach is a two-way resource management method. The PMs are shortlisted according to their capabilities by one method; whereas, the VMs are identified and the capacity from the existing PMs is mapped by another method. The minimization of the required PM and the mapping of the VMs' resource availability from the hosted PM constitute the LP's objectives. The study was conducted using Google data center and TU-Berlin workloads in order to compare the proposed migration algorithm control strategy against existing eager-migration-based solutions. The findings exhibited that the proposed algorithm provided less migration time in comparison with the existing migration techniques with the minimal penalty in the number of PMs. However, the success level in the implementation of this algorithm in the commercial platforms, such as VMware and Citrix is yet to be proved.

Chen et al. (2012) offered a whole-system live migration technique in order to transfer the whole system run time state, such as CPU state, local disk storage and memory data of the virtual machine. The proposed algorithm was a three phase migration algorithm along with an additional incremental migration algorithm, which is used to migrate the virtual machine back to the source machine in a short span of migration time. According to the findings, significant load balancing is achieved using the algorithm. However, the limited use of nodes and the comparatively small environment throws doubts on the algorithm's effectiveness in big data centers.

Xianqin and Xiaopeng (2012) proposed an optimized iterative pre-copy algorithm to improve the performance of live migration. The findings revealed that the newly proposed algorithm is effective in reducing the dirty rate of VM.

Zaw and Thein (2012) proposed a Network aware VM Migration algorithm. This algorithm chiefly uses network traffic and network latency for migration of VM. The model itself includes the pre-processing phase, which contains a prediction working set algorithm, for reducing the amount of transferred data. The valuation of the effectiveness of the working set prediction algorithm with various workloads proved that the proposed framework can reduce 23.67% of the total data transferred during migration compared with XEN's default pre-copy based migration algorithm, and it can also save a 11.45% of total migration time on average. However, even though the study exhibited considerable amount of time saved during migration, it still is not enough in big distributive networks.

Li et al. (2011) presented a novel approach to the optimal placement of virtual machine within data centers for predicable and time-constrained load peaks. The study developed a method based on binary integer programming for optimal load balancing. Furthermore, the study also introduced the methods to pre-process the optimization problem before solving it as a mean for tradeoffs between quality of solution and computation time. In order to reduce the time required to compute a final solution, upper bound based optimizations are used. This helped to solve the larger problems. The study also presented three approximation algorithms, based on heuristics and/or greedy formulations for further scalability. Synthetic data sets are used to evaluate the proposed algorithms. The findings of the evaluation exhibited that the proposed algorithms are feasible and these can be combined to achieve desired trade-offs between execution time and quality of solution.

Sammy, Shengbing and Wilson (2012) proposed an energy-aware provisioning of Cloud computing resources in virtualized platforms. The simulation results exhibited the feasibility of the proposed VMs migration using Dynamic Round-Robin algorithm for server consolidation so as to reduce energy consumption in a data center without having any compromise on security. The proposed algorithm has also resulted lower SLA violations compared with existing strategies like ST. However, the present study did not consider the measurement of VM migration cost in a cluster. Also the study did not focus on the multiple threats which need to be studied in future.

Yang et al. (2013) proposed Automatic Dynamic Migration to balance resources in the OpenStack environment. The proposed algorithm was aimed to solve traditional migration problem of manually determining the machine overloading. The proposed algorithm automatically detected the virtual machine load level. Furthermore, the study also integrates the proposed algorithm with resource monitoring open source software for real-time monitoring of resources. Thus the system automatically performs live migration, while the load imbalance of resources occurs, as a mean to manage the load on the system.

Farahnakian, Liljeberg and Plosila (2013) offered a CPU usage prediction method based on the linear regression technique for energy-efficient consolidation of virtual machines in Cloud data centers. The prediction function was estimated by linear regression method. In accordance with the past utilization values the linear regression created the function in a host which is used to forecast the future short-term utilization. This forecast is based on the current requested utilization in each host. The migration of virtual machine will start as soon as prediction utilization is greater than the current utilization capacity and the host will be overloaded.

Beloglazov and Buyya (2015) proposed OpenStack Neat as a mean to provide a framework for dynamic consolidation of VMs, based on the OpenStack platform. The study used their public APIsto interact with the core OpenStack services. A benchmark suite was also designed to evaluate and compare the dynamic VM consolidation algorithms. Even though the findings indicated promising results of the proposed algorithm in energy consumption, it failed to highlight the capability of the algorithm in load balancing.

Maini and Mazzocca (2014) proposed a model to support the design of a network architecture based on Software Defined Networking (SDN) and network Function Virtualization (NFV) principles. The proposed framework has been used to evaluate the performance of the virtual machine live migration in terms of migration time and downtime. The main proposed algorithm was used to analyze the influence of the parameters such as page dirty rate and link speed of the network on the migration time and downtime. This finding indicates that the page dirty rate and link speed causes non-linear effects on migration and downtime due to the use of some stop conditions in the migration algorithm which force the migration to the final round. Future research efforts will be oriented on the development of other aspects related to architecture components. However, the major drawback of the study is that it only considers the influence of migration time and downtime, meanwhile the other performance indicators, such as throughput, latency, and jitter etc. have been left out.

Deng et al. (2014) applied Shannon's information entropy to identify the imbalance in a cluster storage system. A prediction prototype that utilizes the Exponentially Weighted Moving Average (EWMA) is produced to "anticipate future bursts in the resource requirements" when dealing with network monitoring, or more generally, continuous traffic queries. However, the fact that the proposed system observes only CPU cycles remains as its core drawback.

Upadyay and Lakkadwala (2015) conducted a study with the aim of allocating requests resources by proposing two different algorithms one to deal with virtual migration and other to deal with resource scheduling. The study used limited number of nodes of Cloud computing environment. However, even though the findings highlight the efficiency of the scheduling algorithm, it failed to provide a crystal picture regarding the efficiency of the proposed migration algorithm. Furthermore, since the study was conducted in the small environment using the limited nodes, its efficiency in big data centers is needed to prove.

Joseph, Chandrasekaran and Cyriac (2015) proposed a genetic algorithm based approach in order to minimize the migration time and energy consumption. A contract is made by a user with the service provider and the requirement of services and resources is specified by the user, which is referred to as the SLA. A superior level of SLA must be maintained by a Cloud service provider. The findings revealed that the minimization of VM migrations and energy consumption is achieved by the suggested algorithm. The number of active hosts is maintained at a minimal level, while the SLA level is simultaneously increased by the proposed algorithm. However, the experiment was conducted in limited distributed environment. The effect of the algorithm in the wide Cloud networks should yet to be proved.

Malik and Barde (2015) presented a live migration technique that possesses the dynamic virtual machine consolidation using adaptive utilization threshold based on CPU usage prediction. The CPU usage prediction is assumed to manage the high level of SLA and reduces the number of VM migration in between the host. This approach explains the phenomenon of the under load and overload detection, in which all the virtual machines from the host migrated to another host, and the particular host is switched off for a small interval of time whenever the host has under load. Also, whenever the requested amount CPU demand exceeds the available capacity on that host then some VMs migrate to another host for maintaining the SLA level.

Forsman et al. (2015) proposed an algorithm which was based on Pull and Push strategy to balance the load on the system with multiple VM. In the proposed algorithm, the Push strategy will migrate workload to less loaded hosts whenever it goes overloaded. On the other hand, the Pull strategy can quickly re-distribute the load of the system when the load is in the range of low-to medium. Two load-sharing schemes, namely, receiver scheme and sender scheme, are depicted in Push-Pull. The initiative is taken by the underutilized host for finding work in the receiver scheme; whereas, the initiative is taken by the overloaded host for sharing its load in the sender scheme. The receiver scheme is resembled by the developed pull strategy and the sender scheme is resembled by the developed push strategy. A Push-Pull distributed resource scheduling model, termed as GridIS, is applied for grid environments. The push algorithm and the pull algorithm simultaneously run at the producer and at the consumer, respectively. In accordance with the monitored resources' changed status and the user's requirements, the two algorithms enable the resource monitoring system to switch intelligently between Push and Pull operations. The findings indicated that the push and Pull strategies complement each other. The push operation identifier is pushed and the Pull operation identifier is pulled. These identifiers are set to be reciprocally exclusive in order to avert the simultaneous occurrence of the Pull and push operations in the same period. This may ensue in the reduction of updating times. Furthermore, the value of the pull interval is minimized by the push and Pull algorithm. Both Push and Pull algorithms act frequently and the aforementioned position is in the center of these two cases. However, larger amounts of time taken for the response acts are the major drawback of this approach.

Chen et al. (2015) presented a dynamic Cloud environment Virtual Machine Migration algorithm, Virtual Machine Dynamic Forecast Migration (VM-DFM) to reduce the amount of virtual machine migration. As per the author's argument the algorithm can be applied to excessive memory consumption load in Cloud environment of physical nodes as a mean to provide the appropriate VM live migration.

Xiao et al. (2015) proposed a novel migration algorithm by using the evolutionary game theory to solve the problem of energy optimization. First, the study built a model of energy consumption to provide a supporting atmosphere for computing the amount of energy consumed during the dynamic adjustment of VMs placement. Further, the study modeled three parts of energy consumption, which can be taken into account for the first time while building an energy model for VMs dynamic placement. Then the study proposed an algorithm based on the evolutionary game theory which takes the initial solution into account, using the initial state of VMs distribution. The findings of the experiment exhibited that the proposed algorithm outperformed the other algorithms compared, both in the short run-time snapshots and a relatively long period of time. One of the drawbacks of this study is that some energy consuming accessories like the cooling equipment are not considered.

Rastogi and Sushil (2016) conducted the study to analyze the performance of VM migration using KVM virtualization. The study conducted both the offline and live VM migration to analyze total downtime and total migration time. The findings of the comparative analysis showed that the downtime during live migration was very less when compared with the offline migration. At the same time the total migration time taken by live migration was higher in comparison with the offline migration. From the experiment, the study concluded that live migration is an apt choice if VM is running an important application/s which should not be down for a longer time. If the requirement is less time, then offline migration is preferable.

Duggan et al. (2016) proposed Autonomous Network Aware VM migration algorithm that performed suitable action depends on the observed and experienced current demand level of the network. Furthermore, the study also proposed a dynamic Reinforcement Learning (RL) network aware approach to learn the most favorable time to migrate a group of VM's. This is performed by enabling a single RL agent. The functioning of this approach depends on the current utilization of Cloud's network resource. This autonomous approach is sensitive to high demand request to a network resource and makes efficient use of resource available.

Load Balancing Strategies

Genetic Approach

Joseph et al. (2015) proposed Genetic Approach for VM Allocation this approach is focused on minimization of energy consumption and number of VM migrations. The proposed algorithms are divided in three sub-algorithms first algorithm is based on the Family Genetic algorithm, second algorithm work on the fitness value of each chromosome and the third algorithm takes as input an individual and returns a chromosome representing a feasible assignment. Kaur and Verma [45] proposed a meta-heuristic based modified genetic algorithm, proposed algorithm focus on minimizes execution time and cost. This work is merger of two existing scheduling algorithms. The outcome of mechanism performing exhibits a good performance under the heavy loads. Greene et al. [46] developed a Genetic algorithm. This algorithm periodically schedules the incoming task to the available processors. The research objectives are well scheduled in available processor. And the second objective is dynamic scheduling in affordable cost. Dam et al. [47] suggests load balancing mechanism to search low loaded node to manage the imbalance node. Researchers use the CloudAnalyst simulator to implement the proposed mechanism. Result of proposed algorithm is compared with Genetic Algorithm (GA), Stochastic Hill Climbing (SHC), First Come First Serve (FCFS), and Ant Colony Optimization (ACO). This algorithm is based on minimization of Makespan and VMs migration. Ye et al. [48] Researchers contribute the genetic algorithm to manage QoS model and present the analysis research approach among other algorithm. The proposed algorithm is based on random selection mechanism.

Adaptive Approach

Kanagaraj et al. (2012) suggested a mechanism to dynamically manage load imbalance using service queue, where in every server computes its load value by summing the load parameters (i.e. Memory utilization, CPU utilization, and network utilization) and exchange load value with a central node in a certain cyclic period. Central node selects the least loaded server among farm of servers to process the request. Each server at the central node waits in a queue. This queue is called service queue and they wait for turn to request process. Researcher's categories threshold in high, low and normal states. And also check the memory, CPU and network traffic load in every five second. Kopaneli et. al. [25] work use the Adaptive Cloud Target Selection approach which is near to the real work simulation environment. Kabalan et al. [24] proposed Adaptive Load Sharing with Never Queue Policy. Researchers use heterogeneous computing system and simulate the work on the modified SED, NQ and GT policies. Lau et al. [9], Authors proposed Load Distribution(LD) algorithm ensure the negation of sender and receiver pair to negotiate to perform the batch size which is suitable to execute first. The proposed protocol considers the processing speed of jobs and ensures the maximal utilization of resources in negotiation session.

Agent Base Approach

Cao et al. (2003) proposed Agent-based grid management mechanism this work is based on performance-driven task scheduler with maximum use of resource utilization. Researchers use PACE resource tool to simulate proposed work they also recommend the other simulation tool (e.g. Globus MDS and NWS) to check the efficiency of the proposed mechanism.

Adaptive Approach

Singh et al. (2015) proposed Autonomous Agent Based Dynamic Load Balancing mechanism. The authors' objective is maximizing resource utilization, throughput, and minimize the response time. Meera et al. [50] Proposed an Agent Based approach to CPU and memory utilization. The monitor agent collects VMs usage resources and display performance metrics of CPU and memory utilization. This report provides the flexible administration with resource utilization policy. Sim et al. [51] research work focus on to develop software tools and test beds for cloud resource management. This work contribution to proposed Cloudlet develop agent based search tool for cloud service discovery. Its best suited for automatic service selection for user from service provider. Cosenza et al. [52] Proposed scheme used agent based simulation to manage distributed load balancing. This mechanism achieves high scalability to manage distributed load and calculate the load in computational step to manage the imbalance of load.

Honey Bee

Bitam et al. (2012) proposed Bees Life Algorithm (BLA) schedules the jobs among the VMs on DCs. Job scheduling problem is considered as NP-Complete problem and its main goal is proper distribution of load among the VMs. Mechanism is able to minimization of execution time and improves utilization of cloud resources. Experimental result shows makespan with the least complexity. Krishna et al. [5] Researchers proposed honey bee based load balancing (HBB-LB). Proposed mechanism objective of is attaining effective load balanced among VMs for maximizing the throughput by priorities the task on the machine in the way of waiting time in the queue. Result shows the its effective management of load strategy. Kruekaew et al. [53] Introduce Artificial Bee colony (ABC) to provides best scheduling of VMs. This work key function reduces the makespan of data processing time. The scheduling of job is based on job size and longest job schedule first give the best result to manage imbalance.

Dynamic

Xiao et al. [6] Proposed mechanism dynamically manages the VMs placement to minimize the energy consumptions by using game theory. This mechanism reduces the 30-40% energy consumption. Lin et al. [21] proposed the resource allocation at the application level rather than physical resources to virtual resource. Algorithm manages the threshold based dynamically allocation of resources in VMs from the computing application. Threshold helps to manage the resource allocation and reallocation. Saraswathi et al. [54] This research focus on allocation of VMs in non-priorities manner, jobs are dynamically allocating the VM resources within the dead line. Ahn et al. [55] Introduce the NUMA aware scheduling to manage the hot page migration with cluster level VMs scheduling technique. The main advantage of this technique is no need of prior knowledge of VMs behavior.

TYPES OF VIRTUAL MACHINE MIGRATION

There exist two different techniques for the migration of virtual machines from one physical machine to another physical machine without interrupting the users. They are 1) static (off-line) virtual machine migration and 2) dynamic (live) virtual machine migration. Dynamic virtual machine migration is further categorized into pre-copy and post copy migrations.

Static (Off-line) Virtual Machine Migration

This technique involves the pausing of source host while the transferring of all files in the source host to the destination host and then finally resume the working of virtual machine at the destination host.

The major drawback of it is that it results in larger down time, which in turn invites the notice from the user (2012).

Dynamic (Live) Virtual Machine Migration

This involves the transfer of virtual machines from one host to another with minimum possible interruptions in the services. This process involves following metrics.

1. **Preparation Time:** It is the time between the beginning of the migration process and the trsferring of the processor of the migration machine to the destination node. During this time the virtual machine run continuously and creates page faults.
2. **Resume Time:** It is the time between the restarting of the virtual machine's processing and the completion of the migration. During this time total dependencies on the source host are removed.
3. **Pages Transferred:** The total number of pages, including the copies of pages, transferred.
4. **Down Time:** The amount of time during which the processing of virtual machine is clogged. It is during this time that the state of the processor sends to the destination.
5. **Total Migration Time:** It is the total amount of time taken by the migration process. That is, it is the time period between the starting of the migration process and the end of the migration process. This is an important parameter since it influences the resource releasing on both the source and destination nodes.
6. **Application Degradation:** It is the degradation which occurs in the performance of the application as a result of migration of virtual machine from one host to another.

There exist three different techniques/algorithms using which we can perform the live machine migration, they are, pre-copy, post copy and hybrid copy techniques (Xiao et al., 2015).

Pre-Copy Techniques

The pre-copy algorithm enjoys the position of the most popular technique in live VM migration process. The reduction of the downtime in the migration process through the maximization of the memory emulating synchronization between the source and the destination host is the core idea behind the pre-copy algorithm. The pre-copy algorithm involves two phases, namely iteration phase and stop and copy phase.

Iteration Phase

This phase includes the repetitive copying of the memory data from source to destination so as to maximize the memory mirroring synchronization between the source and the destination host. In this phase, a partial modification of memory pages occurs during the previous transmission turn since the source VM continues to work. The synchronization of the memory pages should be happened until the number of the remaining memory pages is less than a threshold.

Stop-And-Copy Phase

This phase involves the halting of the source VM and copying of remaining pages to the destination VM. After the copying, the new VM in the destination host will start to work.

The major advantage of the pre-copy algorithm is that it significantly shortens the downtime in a read-intensive VM. However, for write–intensive VM, the iteratively copy behavior would just waste bandwidth resources and increase the total migration time, as the speed of memory write is faster than the network transmission speed (Hu et al., 2011).

Post-Copy Algorithms

In the post-copy algorithm, the transfer of the memory data to the destination occurs only after the new VM in the destination host begins to function. The entire process of the post-copy algorithm began with suspending the functioning of VM at the source. Then, some kernel data the VCPUs and device states are transferred to the destination. After that, the new VM at the destination resumed to work. Finally, the transfer of memory data from the source to the destination occurs. This transfer is performed in two ways; on-demand paging and active pushing. In on–demand paging, as soon as the VM starts to work at the destination and did not find the memory page which the machine searched, will immediately signal as page faults. Then the corresponding pages will be sent from the source. However, this causes network delay which in turn causes a serious degradation in the performance of VM. This is the major shortcoming of this memory transfer method. Besides, the migration process may continue for a long time unless there is no other mechanism. This can happen because some part memory pages of the VM may not have been visited in a long term. Active pushing is another method which is used for transferring the memory data. This technique is used to reduce the duration of enduring dependencies on the source node. In this process, the source will stay as long as the migration process continues and the source will proactively push the remaining memory pages to the destination (Joseph et al., 2015).

Hybrid Copy Algorithms

The hybrid-copy algorithm uses the pre-copy at its first phase as the initiator of the process. In this phase, the data service to the user provided by the source VM will continue while performing the copying of all the memory data to the destination. Then, source VM is suspended and its processor state is copied to the destination. This step will ensure that no memory pages will remain without copying. After this process, immediately VM restarts at the destination and the post-copy algorithm began to execute. At this stage, the rest of the memory pages will be synchronized in the post-copy phase. Even though page faults in post-copy phase causes significant performance loss, it can be avoided to a certain extent by the use of pre-copy algorithm, used in the hybrid-copy technique. Moreover, the page faults occurring in the post-copy phase can be further reduced by executing more iteration. Apart from these, the hybrid-copy algorithm can also overcome the write intensive workload problem caused in the pre-copy technique, by the use of post copy technique. Table 1 discuss the authors used technique and description.

Table 1. Authors technique and description

Author(s)	Technique	Description
Singh et al. [4]	Autonomous Agent Based	Agent based approach maximize the throughput; minimize the response time and migration time
Cao et al. [16]	Agent-based grid management	Researchers uses the PACE resource management tool to maximize the resource utilization
Ferreto et al. [17]	LP formulation and heuristic	Uses the heuristic approach to maximize the utilization of resources by automatic live migration of VMs
Forsman et al. [18]	Push and Pull Strategy	Maximizes the utilization of physical machines by using bidding policy
Bitam [20]	Honey Bee	Job Scheduling mechanism considered the NP-Complete formulation for proper distribution of load among the all available nodes
Lin [21]	Threshold based Dynamic Approach	Resource allocation at the application level rather than physical management of resources
Kabalan et al. [24]	Adaptive Load Sharing	Manages the heterogeneous computing system by never queue policy
Kopaneli et al. [25]	Adaptive Cloud Target Selection CTS) tool methodology	Adaptive target selection mechanism approach and utilization of resources in near to real environment
Kruekaew [53]	Honey Bee	Reduces the time of data processing
Joseph et al. [39]	Genetic	Minimizes the energy consumption by reduction of VM migrations

Research Gaps

This chapter conducted a comprehensive review of studies pertained to the various load balancing techniques. On the basis of that in depth review the following research gaps are identified.

- The studies regarding the static task allocation techniques reveal some of the prime drawbacks which include the inability to measure the output metrics like response time and processing time and its non-compatibility with complex infrastructures and changing user requirements (Deng et al., 2014). Furthermore, the study by Radojevic and Zagar (Radoievic and Zagar, 2011) revealed the compromise in the stability of the system due to the introduction of new elements and the possible single point failure due to the implantation of algorithm as a central management module which influences both the load balancing decisions, and virtual server resources. Another issue indicated by the authors is that the static algorithms always tend to enter into the unforeseen loops and start to flap its decision between nodes, resulting in poor performance and end-user experience. The lack of parameters to check the availability of VM and the implementation difficulty highlighted by Nayak and Patel (2015), lack of flexibility and the inability to measure the other parameters, such as scalability, throughput, resource availability etc. exhibited by Patel and Shah, (2016) and the incompatibility to the heterogeneous systems by Aswathi, Sharma and Mahesh (2016) and Kokilavani and Amalarathinem, (2011) are some of the other drawbacks the review came across. The inability to properly measure the output metrics such as, throughput, scalability, etc., the shortfall in the consideration of deadline of each task and the geography location of tasks and resources, revealed in the review of the study Chen et al. (2015) presents some more drawbacks existing in the different static approaches. Apart from these gaps, the left out of the multi pass blocking that assigns multiple blocks per entity (Gopinath and Vasudevan, 2015) and the problem of deadlocks and server overflow (Xu, Han and Bhyan, 2007) also found out by the present review.

- The review of the studies related to the dynamic task allocation load balancing techniques reveals the lack of studies which consider the possibility of precedence constraint between tasks and the dependency between tasks. The review of the studies, such as Casalicchion and Colajanni (2001) and Xu, Han and Bhuyan (2007) exhibits lack of compatibility with the wide distributed systems and high overhead for the load communication between the servers respectively. The review of the study Chen et al. (2012) revealed the problem of bottleneck created by the event driven algorithm. Another drawback of event driven was exposed in the review of Lu, Parkin and Morgan (2006). This study revealed the complexity of the algorithm which made it unsuited for fast-paced FPS game. The review of the studies regarding the honey bee foraging algorithm uncovered the drawbacks, such as lack of clarity in the performance of the algorithm using other output parameters, such as reliability and scalability, the skepticism regarding the efficiency of the algorithm in the wide Cloud network, and its compatibility with other alternative QoS factors. The lack of studies regarding the performance in fluencies factors, such as connectivity. The silence of the studies regarding the consideration of conservation law in assessing the performance of the algorithms and the relationship between load balancing and Job Selection for the available appropriate Cloud resource between the scheduler in the real Cloud environment and distributed in nature, are the some of the other shortfall revealed in the review.

- The major gap that can be highlighted from the review of the studies which proposes the algorithms for virtual machine migration, is their lack of adaptability to the big distributed Cloud networks (e.g. Akoush and Sohan (2010), Chen et al. (2012), Upadyay and Lakkadwala (2015) etc.). The study result by Joseph, Chandrasekaran and Cyriac (2015) also substantiates this argument. The skepticism regarding the successful implementation of the proposed algorithms in the commercial platforms, (VM ware, Citrix etc.), as indicated by Ferreto et al. (2011), is another drawback. The deficiency of studies which targets the use of migration algorithm in balancing the load in Cloud networking is also evident. The study of Beloglazov and Buyya (2015) highlighted the ability of the proposed algorithm in reducing the energy consumption, however, kept silent on the capability of the algorithm in load balancing mechanism. In addition, even after proposing the algorithms to balance the load, the studies like Hu et al. (2011), Xianqin and Xiaopeng (2012), etc. failed in highlighting the performance and the effectiveness of the proposed algorithm in balancing the load in a Cloud networking environment. The lack of comprehensive studies which highlights the performance of entire outcome parameters is the next major drawback highlighted by the review. The study of Maini and Mazzocca (2014) considers only the limited number of performance parameters, such as migration time and downtime and conveniently left out the others, such as throughput, scalability, reliability and availability etc. Meanwhile the study by Deng et al. (2014) which used an EWMA to "anticipate future bursts in the resource requirements" when dealing with network monitoring, or continuous traffic queries, exhibits the drawback of observing only the CPU cycles. Furthermore, the study like Forsman et al. (2015) exhibits larger response time, which in turn stands as a vital shortcoming that affect the performance of the migration. Again, the study by Andreolini et al. (2009) pointed out the gaps, such as the lack test results in the heterogeneous infrastructures and platforms and neglect of the guests that can migrate

Table 2. Simulator tools analysis

Simulator Tool	Platform/Support Language	Availability	Support Model
CloudSim	Eclipse, NetBeans, Java	Open Source	Cloud computing infrastructures services
OMNet++	C++ simulation library and framework	Open Source	Protocol modeling Modeling of multiprocessors and other distributed hardware systems Validating of hardware architectures
GENI (Global Environment for Network Innovations)	Apache HTTP Server	Free of Charge for Research and Classroom Use	Experimental Heterogeneous Network Structure, Distributed System and Security
Google App Engine	Execution of web application, Java and Python	Freeware Platform	Experimental Heterogeneous Network Structure, Distributed System and Security
Grids Lab Aneka	.NET-based Framework	On-demand	Multiple application models, persistence, and security solutions
Open Stack	Web-Based Dashboard	Open Source	Large network of VM, Storage System, Resource Management
Sun Network.com (Sun Grid)	C, C++ and FORTRAN based Application	Open Source	Job Management

only within certain subsets of hardware and operating systems. The gap revealed in the study by Sammy et al. (2012) which indicated the exemption of the measurement of VM migration cost in a cluster and lack of focus on the multiple threats, also needed to be studied. Table 2 depicts the simulator tool analysis.

CONCLUSION

The chapter conducted a set of research-literature reviews to decide what kind of infrastructure the system will use and to identify the appropriate algorithms and parameters. The reviews targeted various load balancing algorithms and approaches that can either be modified with minimal effort or can fit the study objectives directly. The study also conducted an in depth review of the research papers which are closely related to the interest of the present study. Considering these factors, the present study conducted a comprehensive review of the studies pertained to a various task allocation based load balancing algorithms (static and dynamic) and the load balancing algorithms which uses virtual machine migration (non-live and live). The review analyzed the efficiency of the proposed algorithms in term of their performance metrics such as scalability, throughput, reliability, response time, migration time, etc. The analysis revealed a number of research gaps in the existing algorithms proposed by multifarious researchers.

REFERENCES

Ahn, J., Kim, C., Han, J., Choi, Y. R., & Huh, J. (2012, June). Dynamic Virtual Machine Scheduling in Clouds for Architectural Shared Resources. HotCloud.

Akoush, S., Sohan, R., Rice, A., Moore, A. W., & Hopper, A. (2010, August). Predicting the performance of virtual machine migration. In *Proceedings of the Modeling, Analysis & Simulation of Computer and Telecommunication Systems (MASCOTS), 2010 IEEE International Symposium on* (pp. 37-46). IEEE. 10.1109/MASCOTS.2010.13

Andreolini, M., Casolari, S., Colajanni, M., & Messori, M. (2009, October). Dynamic load management of virtual machines in cloud architectures. In *Proceedings of the International Conference on Cloud Computing* (pp. 201-214). Springer.

Aswathi, M., & Nisha, N., & Mahesh A. S. (2016). An Enhancement of Throttled Load Balancing Algorithm in Cloud using Throughput. *IJCTA, 9*(15), 7603–7611.

Beloglazov, A., & Buyya, R. (2015). OpenStack Neat: A framework for dynamic and energy efficient consolidation of virtual machines in OpenStack clouds. *Concurrency and Computation, 27*(5), 1310–1333. doi:10.1002/cpe.3314

Bitam, S. (2012 Feb) Bees life algorithm for job scheduling in cloud computing. In *Proceedings of the Third International Conference on Communications and Information Technology*, (pp. 186-191). Academic Press.

Buyya, R., Ranjan, R., & Calheiros, R. N. (2010, May). Intercloud: Utility-oriented federation of cloud computing environments for scaling of application services. In *Proceeding of International Conference on Algorithms and Architectures for Parallel Processing* (pp. 13-31). Springer. 10.1007/978-3-642-13119-6_2

Calheiros, R. N., Ranjan, R., Beloglazov, A., De Rose, C. A., & Buyya, R. (2011). CloudSim: A toolkit for modeling and simulation of cloud computing environments and evaluation of resource provisioning algorithms. *Software, Practice & Experience, 41*(1), 23–50. doi:10.1002pe.995

Cao, J., Spooner, D. P., Jarvis, S. A., Saini, S., & Nudd, G. R. (2003, April). Agent-based grid load balancing using performance-driven task scheduling. In *Proceedings of Parallel and Distributed Processing Symposium*. IEEE.

Casalicchio, E., & Colajanni, M. (2001). A client-aware dispatching algorithm for web clusters providing multiple services. *Proceedings of the 10th International World Wide Web Conference*, 535-544. 10.1145/371920.372155

Chen, H., Kang, H., Jiang, G., & Stage, Y. Z. (2012). *Network-aware migration control and scheduling of differentiated virtual machine workloads*. IEEE Computer Society.

Chen, J., Qin, Y., Ye, Y., & Tang, Z. (2015, August). A Live Migration Algorithm for Virtual Machine in a Cloud Computing Environment. In *Proceedings of the Ubiquitous Intelligence and Computing and 2015 IEEE 12th Intl Conf on Autonomic and Trusted Computing and 2015 IEEE 15th Intl Conf on Scalable Computing and Communications and Its Associated Workshops (UIC-ATC-ScalCom), 2015 IEEE 12th Intl Conf on* (pp. 1319-1326). IEEE. 10.1109/UIC-ATC-ScalCom-CBDCom-IoP.2015.239

Cosenza, B., Cordasco, G., De Chiara, R., & Scarano, V. (2011, February). Distributed load balancing for parallel agent-based simulations. In *Parallel, Distributed and Network-Based Processing (PDP), 2011 19th Euromicro International Conference on* (pp. 62-69). IEEE. 10.1109/PDP.2011.22

Dam, S., Mandal, G., Dasgupta, K., & Dutta, P. (2015, February). Genetic algorithm and gravitational emulation based hybrid load balancing strategy in cloud computing. In *Computer, Communication, Control and Information Technology (C3IT), 2015 Third International Conference on* (pp. 1-7). IEEE. 10.1109/C3IT.2015.7060176

Deng, W., Liu, F., Jin, H., Li, B., & Li, D. (2014). Harnessing renewable energy in cloud datacenters: Opportunities and challenges. *IEEE Network*, *28*(1), 48–55. doi:10.1109/MNET.2014.6724106

Duggan, M., Duggan, J., Howley, E., & Barrett, E. (2016, September). An autonomous network aware vm migration strategy in cloud data centres. In *Proceedings of the Cloud and Autonomic Computing (ICCAC), 2016 International Conference on* (pp. 24-32). IEEE. 10.1109/ICCAC.2016.9

Farahnakian, F., Liljeberg, P., & Plosila, J. (2013, September). LiRCUP: Linear regression based CPU usage prediction algorithm for live migration of virtual machines in data centers. In *Proceedings of the Software Engineering and Advanced Applications (SEAA), 2013 39th EUROMICRO Conference on* (pp. 357-364). IEEE.

Ferreto, T. C., Netto, M. A., Calheiros, R. N., & De Rose, C. A. (2011). Server consolidation with migration control for virtualized data centers. *Future Generation Computer Systems*, *27*(8), 1027–1034. doi:10.1016/j.future.2011.04.016

Forsman, M., Glad, A., Lundberg, L., & Ilie, D. (2015). Algorithms for automated live migration of virtual machines. *Journal of Systems and Software*, *101*, 110–126. doi:10.1016/j.jss.2014.11.044

Gopinath, P. G., & Vasudevan, S. K. (2015). An in-depth analysis and study of Load balancing techniques in the cloud computing environment. *Procedia Computer Science*, *50*, 427–432. doi:10.1016/j.procs.2015.04.009

Greene, W. A. (2001, November). Dynamic load-balancing via a genetic algorithm. In *Tools with Artificial Intelligence, Proceedings of the 13th International Conference on* (pp. 121-128). IEEE.

Gupta, D., Cherkasova, L., Gardner, R., & Vahdat, A. (2006, November). Enforcing performance isolation across virtual machines in Xen. In *Proceedings of the ACM/IFIP/USENIX 2006 International Conference on Middleware* (pp. 342-362). Springer-Verlag. 10.1007/11925071_18

Hu, B., Lei, Z., Lei, Y., Xu, D., & Li, J. (2011). A Time-series Based Precopy Approach for Live Migration of Virtual Machines. *Proceedings of the 17th International Conference on Parallel and Distributed Systems (ICPADS)*. 10.1109/ICPADS.2011.19

Joseph, C. T., Chandrasekaran, K., & Cyriac, R. (2015). A novel family genetic approach for virtual machine allocation. *Procedia Computer Science*, *46*, 558–565. doi:10.1016/j.procs.2015.02.090

Kabalan, K. Y., Smari, W. W., & Hakimian, J. Y. (2002). Adaptive load sharing in heterogeneous systems: Policies, modifications, and simulation. *International Journal of Simulation, Systems, Science and Technology*, *3*(1-2), 89–100.

Kalra, M., & Singh, S. (2015). A review of metaheuristic scheduling techniques in cloud computing. *Egyptian Informatics Journal, 16*(3), 275-295.

Kanagaraj, G., Shanmugasundaram, N., & Prakash, S. (2012). Adaptive Load Balancing Algorithm Using Service Queue. In *2nd International Conference on Computer Science and Information Technology (ICCSIT'2012)* (pp. 28-29). Academic Press.

Kaur, S., & Verma, A. (2012). An efficient approach to genetic algorithm for task scheduling in cloud computing environment. *International Journal of Information Technology and Computer Science, 4*(10), 74–79. doi:10.5815/ijitcs.2012.10.09

Kokilavani, T., & Amalarethinam, D. G. (2011). Load balanced min-min algorithm for static meta-task scheduling in grid computing. *International Journal of Computers and Applications, 20*(2), 43–49.

Kopaneli, A., Kousiouris, G., Velez, G. E., Evangelinou, A., & Varvarigou, T. (2015). A model driven approach for supporting the Cloud target selection process. *Procedia Computer Science, 68*, 89–102. doi:10.1016/j.procs.2015.09.226

Kruekaew, B., & Kimpan, W. (2014). Virtual machine scheduling management on cloud computing using artificial bee colony. In *Proceedings of the International MultiConference of Engineers and Computer Scientists* (*Vol. 1*, pp. 12-14). Academic Press.

Lau, S. M., Lu, Q., & Leung, K. S. (2006). Adaptive load distribution algorithms for heterogeneous distributed systems with multiple task classes. *Journal of Parallel and Distributed Computing, 66*(2), 163–180. doi:10.1016/j.jpdc.2004.01.007

LD, D. B., & Krishna, P. V. (2013). Honey bee behavior inspired load balancing of tasks in cloud computing environments. *Applied Soft Computing, 13*(5), 2292–2303. doi:10.1016/j.asoc.2013.01.025

Li, W., Tordsson, J., & Elmroth, E. (2011, December). Virtual machine placement for predictable and time-constrained peak loads. In *International Workshop on Grid Economics and Business Models* (pp. 120-134). Springer.

Liao, J. S., Chang, C. C., Hsu, Y. L., Zhang, X. W., Lai, K. C., & Hsu, C. H. (2012, September). Energy-efficient resource provisioning with SLA consideration on cloud computing. In *Proceeding of Parallel Processing Workshops (ICPPW), 2012 41st International Conference on* (pp. 206-211). IEEE.

Lin, W., Wang, J. Z., Liang, C., & Qi, D. (2011). A threshold-based dynamic resource allocation scheme for cloud computing. *Procedia Engineering, 23*, 695–703. doi:10.1016/j.proeng.2011.11.2568

Lu, C., & Lau, S. M. (1995). An adaptive algorithm for resolving processor thrashing in load distribution. *Concurrency and Computation, 7*(7), 653–670. doi:10.1002/cpe.4330070706

Lu, F., Parkin, S., & Morgan, G. (2006, October). Load balancing for massively multiplayer online games. In *Proceedings of 5th ACM SIGCOMM workshop on Network and system support for games* (p. 1). ACM. 10.1145/1230040.1230064

Maini, E., & Mazzocca, N. (2014, December). A compositional modeling approach for live migration in Software Defined Networks. In *Network of the Future (NOF), In Proceedings of the 2014 International Conference and Workshop on the* (pp. 1-6). IEEE.

Malik, V., & Barde, C. R. (2015). Live migration of Virtual Machines in Cloud Environment using Prediction of CPU Usage. *International Journal of Computers and Applications, 117*(23).

Meera, A., & Swamynathan, S. (2013). Agent based resource monitoring system in iaas cloud environment. *Procedia Technology, 10*, 200–207. doi:10.1016/j.protcy.2013.12.353

Nathan, S., Kulkarni, P., & Bellur, U. (2013, April). Resource availability based performance benchmarking of virtual machine migrations. In *Proceedings of the 4th ACM/SPEC International Conference on Performance Engineering* (pp. 387-398). ACM. 10.1145/2479871.2479932

Nayak, S., & Patel. (2015). A Survey on Load Balancing Algorithms in Cloud Computing and Proposed a model with Improved Throttled Algorithm. *International Journal for Scientific Research & Development, 3*(1).

Patel. N, H., & Shah. J. (2016). Improved Throttling Load Balancing Algorithm With Respect To Computing Cost and Throughput For Cloud Based Requests. *IJARIIE, 2*(3), 2192-2198.

Radojevic, B., & Zagar, M. (2011). Analysis of issues with load balancing algorithms in hosted (cloud) environments. In *Proceedings of 34th International Convention on MIPRO*. IEEE.

Rastogi, G., & Sushil, R. (2016). Performance Analysis of Live and Offline VM Migration Using KVM. *International Journal of Modern Education and Computer Science, 8*(11), 50–57. doi:10.5815/ijmecs.2016.11.07

Rathore, N., & Chana, I. (2014). Load balancing and job migration techniques in grid: A survey of recent trends. *Wireless Personal Communications, 79*(3), 2089–2125. doi:10.100711277-014-1975-9

Rotithor, H. G. (1994). Taxonomy of dynamic task scheduling schemes in distributed computing systems. *Proceeding of IEEE -Computers and Digital Techniques, 141*(1), 1-10.

Sammy, K., Shengbing, R., & Wilson, C. (2012). Energy efficient security preserving vm live migration in data centers for cloud computing. *IJCSI International Journal of Computer Science Issues, 9*(2), 1694–0814.

Saraswathi, A. T., Kalaashri, Y. R. A., & Padmavathi, S. (2015). Dynamic resource allocation scheme in cloud computing. *Procedia Computer Science, 47*, 30–36. doi:10.1016/j.procs.2015.03.180

Sim, K. M. (2012). Agent-based cloud computing. *IEEE Transactions on Services Computing, 5*(4), 564–577. doi:10.1109/TSC.2011.52

Singh, A., Juneja, D., & Malhotra, M. (2015). Autonomous agent based load balancing algorithm in cloud computing. *Procedia Computer Science, 45*, 832–841. doi:10.1016/j.procs.2015.03.168

Upadhyay, A., & Lakkadwala, P. (2015, September). Migration of over loaded process and schedule for resource utilization in Cloud Computing. In *Proceedings of the Reliability, Infocom Technologies and Optimization (ICRITO)(Trends and Future Directions), 2015 4th International Conference on* (pp. 1-4). IEEE. 10.1109/ICRITO.2015.7359325

Vinothina, V., Sridaran, R., & Ganapathi, P. (2012). A survey on resource allocation strategies in cloud computing. *International Journal of Advanced Computer Science and Applications, 3*(6), 97–104. doi:10.14569/IJACSA.2012.030616

Wickremasinghe, B., Calheiros, R. N., & Buyya, R. (2010, April). Cloudanalyst: A CloudSim-based visual modeller for analysing cloud computing environments and applications. In *Proceeding of Advanced Information Networking and Applications (AINA), 2010 24th IEEE International Conference* (pp. 446-452). IEEE.

Xianqin, C., & Xiaopeng, G. (2012). Application-Transparent Live Migration for Virtual Machine on Network Security Enhanced Hypervisor. *China Communications.*

Xiao, Z., Jiang, J., Zhu, Y., Ming, Z., Zhong, S., & Cai, S. (2015). A solution of dynamic VMs placement problem for energy consumption optimization based on evolutionary game theory. *Journal of Systems and Software, 101*, 260–272. doi:10.1016/j.jss.2014.12.030

Xu, Z., Han, J., & Bhuyan, L. (2007, April). Scalable and Decentralized Content-Aware Dispatching in Web Clusters. In *Proceedings of the Performance, Computing, and Communications Conference, 2007. IPCCC 2007. IEEE International* (pp. 202-209). IEEE. 10.1109/PCCC.2007.358896

Yang, C. T., Liu, Y. T., Liu, J. C., Chuang, C. L., & Jiang, F. C. (2013, December). Implementation of a cloud iaas with dynamic resource allocation method using openstack. In *Proceedings of the Parallel and Distributed Computing, Applications and Technologies (PDCAT), 2013 International Conference on* (pp. 71-78). IEEE. 10.1109/PDCAT.2013.18

Ye, Z., Zhou, X., & Bouguettaya, A. (2011, April). Genetic algorithm based QoS-aware service compositions in cloud computing. In *International Conference on Database Systems for Advanced Applications* (pp. 321-334). Springer. 10.1007/978-3-642-20152-3_24

Zaw, E. P., & Thein, N. L. (2012). Improved live VM migration using LRU and splay tree algorithm. *International Journal of Computer Science and Telecommunications, 3*(3), 1–7.

Zhang, Q., Cheng, L., & Boutaba, R. (2010). Cloud computing: State-of-the-art and research challenges. *Journal of Internet Services and Applications, 1*(1), 7–18. doi:10.100713174-010-0007-6

Compilation of References

Abbache, A., Meziane, F., Belalem, G., & Belkredim, F. Z. (2018). Arabic query expansion using WordNet and association rules. In *Information Retrieval and Management: Concepts, Methodologies, Tools, and Applications* (pp. 1239–1254). Hershey, PA: IGI Global. doi:10.4018/978-1-5225-5191-1.ch054

Abdelfattah, A., & Abdelkader, T., & EI-Horbaty, E. (2017). RSAM: An enhanced architecture for achieving web services reliability in mobile cloud computing. *Computer and Information Sciences, 30*, 164–174. doi:10.1016/j.jksuci.2017.03.002

Abderrahim, M. A. (2013). Utilisation des ressources externes pour la reformulation des requêtes dans un système de recherche d'information. The PBML 99: The Prague Bulletinof Mathematical Linguistics, 87-99. doi:10.2478/pralin-2013-0006

Abdi, M. K., Lounis, H., & Sahraoui, H. (2009, July). Predicting change impact in object-oriented applications with bayesian networks. In *Computer Software and Applications Conference, 2009. COMPSAC'09. 33rd Annual IEEE International* (Vol. 1, pp. 234-239). IEEE. 10.1109/COMPSAC.2009.38

Abeer Al-Arfaj, A. A.-S. (2015). Ontology Construction from Text: Challenges and Trends. *International Journal of Artificial Intelligence and Expert Systems, 6*(2).

Abinaya, C. &. (2013). Semi-Automatic Ontology Merging of Domain Specific Ontologies. International Journal of Science and Research.

Achemoukh, F., & Ahmed-Ouamer, R. (2012). Modélisation d'évolution de profil utilisateur en recherche d'information personnalisée. CORIA 2012, 83-97.

Ahmad, F., & Kondrak, G. (2005). Learning a spelling error model from search query logs. In *Proceedings of the Conference on Human Language Technology and Empirical Methods in Natural Language Processing* (pp. 955-962). Stroudsburg, PA: ACL. 10.3115/1220575.1220695

Ahn, J., Kim, C., Han, J., Choi, Y. R., & Huh, J. (2012, June). Dynamic Virtual Machine Scheduling in Clouds for Architectural Shared Resources. HotCloud.

Ai, H., Litman, D. J., Forbes-Riley, K., Rotaru, M., Tetreault, J., & Purandare, A. (2006). Using system and user performance features to improve emotion detection in spoken tutoring systems. Proceedings of Interspeech, 797–800.

Akoush, S., Sohan, R., Rice, A., Moore, A. W., & Hopper, A. (2010, August). Predicting the performance of virtual machine migration. In *Proceedings of the Modeling, Analysis & Simulation of Computer and Telecommunication Systems (MASCOTS), 2010 IEEE International Symposium on* (pp. 37-46). IEEE. 10.1109/MASCOTS.2010.13

Al Kabary, I., & Schuldt, H. (2014). Enhancing sketch-based sport video retrieval by suggesting relevant motion paths. In *Proceedings of the 37th international ACM SIGIR conference on Research & development in information retrieval* (pp. 1227-1230). New York: ACM. 10.1145/2600428.2609551

Al-Ameen, Z., Sulong, G., Rehman, A., Al-Dhelaan, A., Saba, T., & Al-Rodhaan, M. (2015). An innovative technique for contrast enhancement of computed tomography images using normalized gamma-corrected contrast-limited adaptive histogram equalization. *EURASIP Journal on Advances in Signal Processing*, *2015*(1), 32. doi:10.118613634-015-0214-1

Alani, H. (2006). Position Paper: Ontology Construction from Online Ontologies. *WWW2006*.

Al-Ani, A. (2005). Ant Colony Optimization for feature subset selection. In *Proceedings Of World Academy Of Science. Engineering and Technology*.

Alaoui, A., & Elberrichi, Z. (2018). Feature Subset Selection Using Ant Colony Optimization for a Decision Trees Classification of Medical Data. *International Journal of Information Retrieval Research*, *8*(4), 39–50. doi:10.4018/IJIRR.2018100103

Albornoz, E. M., Milone, D. H., & Rufiner, H. L. (2011). Spoken emotion recognition using hierarchical classifiers. *Computer Speech & Language*, *25*(3), 556–570. doi:10.1016/j.csl.2010.10.001

Alexandre, S. (2004). *Textual Information Extraction Using Structure Induction*. LIRIS-CNRS.

Ali, S. A., Zehra, S., & Arif, A. (2013). Performance evaluation of learning classifiers for speech emotions corpus using combinations of prosodic features. *International Journal of Computers and Applications*, *76*(2).

Al-Khiaty, M., Abdel-Aal, R., & Elish, M. O. (2017). Abductive network ensembles for improved prediction of future change-prone classes in object-oriented software. *The International Arab Journal of Information Technology*, *14*(6), 803–811.

Andreia, D. P. N., & Parente de Oliveira, J. M. (2012). Simple Method for Ontology Automatic Extraction from Documents. *International Journal of Advanced Computer Science and Applications*, *3*(12). doi:10.14569/IJACSA.2012.031206

Andreolini, M., Casolari, S., Colajanni, M., & Messori, M. (2009, October). Dynamic load management of virtual machines in cloud architectures. In *Proceedings of the International Conference on Cloud Computing* (pp. 201-214). Springer.

Ang, J., Dhillon, R., Krupski, A., Shriberg, E., & Stolcke, A. (2002). Prosody-based automatic detection of annoyance and frustration in human-computer dialog. *Proceedings of international conference on spoken language processing*, 2037-2039.

Anzbock, R., & Dustdar, S. (2005). Modeling and implementing medical Web services. *Data & Knowledge Engineering*, *55*(2), 203–236. doi:10.1016/j.datak.2005.03.009

Arabshian, K., P. D. (2012). LexOnt: A Semi-Automatic Ontology Creation Tool for Programmable Web. In *AAAI Spring Symposium: Intelligent Web Services Meet Social Computing*, (pp. 2-8). AAAI.

Asher, N., Venant, A., Muller, P., & Afantenos, S. (2011). Complex discourse units and their semantics. *Nation (New York, N.Y.)*, *2*(3), 7.

Association Lalla Salma de lutte contre le cancer. (2011). Guide de détection précoce des cancers du sein et du col de l'utérus. Author.

Aswathi, M., & Nisha, N., & Mahesh A. S. (2016). An Enhancement of Throttled Load Balancing Algorithm in Cloud using Throughput. *IJCTA*, *9*(15), 7603–7611.

Bacchelli, A., D'Ambros, M., & Lanza, M. (2010). Are popular classes more defect prone? In *Fundamental Approaches to Software Engineering* (pp. 59–73). Springer Berlin Heidelberg. doi:10.1007/978-3-642-12029-9_5

Balaji, J., Geetha, T. V., & Parthasarathi, R. (2016). Abstractive summarization: A hybrid approach for the compression of semantic graphs. *International Journal on Semantic Web and Information Systems*, 12(2), 76–99. doi:10.4018/IJSWIS.2016040104

Balakumaran, Vennila, & Shankar. (2010). Detection of Microcalcification in Mammograms Using Wavelet Transform and Fuzzy Shell Clustering. *International Journal of Computer Science and Information Security*, 7(1).

Bamberger, R. H., & Smith, M. J. T. (1992). A filter bank for the directional decomposition of images: Theory and design. *IEEE Trans. Signal Processing*, 40(4), 882–893.

Bansal, A., & Jajoria, S. (2019). Cross-Project Change Prediction Using Meta-Heuristic Techniques. *International Journal of Applied Metaheuristic Computing*, 10(1), 43–61. doi:10.4018/IJAMC.2019010103

Bansal, A., Modi, K., & Jain, R. (2019). Analysis of the Performance of Learners for Change Prediction Using Imbalanced Data. In *Applications of Artificial Intelligence Techniques in Engineering* (pp. 345–359). Singapore: Springer. doi:10.1007/978-981-13-1819-1_33

Bansal, R., Arora, P., Gaur, M., Sehgal, P., & Bedi, P. (2009). Fingerprint Image Enhancement Using Type-2 Fuzzy Sets. *2009 Sixth International Conference on Fuzzy Systems and Knowledge Discovery*. 10.1109/FSKD.2009.396

Banse, R., & Scherer, K. R. (1996). Acoustic profiles in vocal emotion expression. *Journal of Personality and Social Psychology*, 70(3), 614–636. doi:10.1037/0022-3514.70.3.614 PMID:8851745

Batliner, A., Steidl, S., & Nöth, E. (2008, May). Releasing a thoroughly annotated and processed spontaneous emotional database: the FAU Aibo Emotion Corpus. *Proc. of a Satellite Workshop of LREC*, 28.

Belkhodja, L., & Benamrane, N. (2009) Approche d'extraction de la région globale d'intérêt et suppression des artefacts radiopaques dans une image mammographique. IMAGE'09 Biskra.

Bellifemine, F., Caire, G., Poggi, A., & Rimassa, G. (2008, January). JADE: A software framework for developing multi-agent applications. Lessons learned. *Information and Software Technology*, 50(1-2), 10–21. doi:10.1016/j.infsof.2007.10.008

Beloglazov, A., & Buyya, R. (2015). OpenStack Neat: A framework for dynamic and energy efficient consolidation of virtual machines in OpenStack clouds. *Concurrency and Computation*, 27(5), 1310–1333. doi:10.1002/cpe.3314

Benjamin, B. J. (1981). Frequency variability in the aged voice. *Journal of Gerontology*, 36(6), 722–726. doi:10.1093/geronj/36.6.722 PMID:7299089

Bergenti, F., & Poggi, A. (2000, July). Improving UML designs using automatic design pattern detection. In *12th International Conference on Software Engineering and Knowledge Engineering (SEKE)* (pp. 336-343). Academic Press.

Beura, S., Majhi, B., & Dash, R. (2015). Mammogram classification using two dimensional discrete wavelet transform and gray-level co-occurrence matrix for detection of breast cancer. *Neurocomputing*, 154, 1–14. doi:10.1016/j.neucom.2014.12.032

Bhavana Dalvi, A. M. (2016). Hierarchical Semi-supervised Classification with Incomplete Class Hierarchies. In WSDM'16. San Francisco, CA: ACM.

Bing, X., Mengjie, Z., & Will, B. (2014). Particle swarm optimization for feature selection in classification: Novel initialization and updating mechanisms. *Applied Soft Computing*, (18): 261–276.

Biniz, M., & El Ayachi, R. (2018). Optimizing Ontology Alignments by Using Neural NSGA-II. *Journal of Electronic Commerce in Organizations*, 16(1), 29–42. doi:10.4018/JECO.2018010103

Biniz, M., El Ayachi, R., & Fakir, M. (2017). Ontology Matching Using BabelNet Dictionary and Word Sense Disambiguation Algorithms. *Indonesian Journal of Electrical Engineering and Computer Science, 5*(1), 196–205. doi:10.11591/ijeecs.v5.i1.pp196-205

Bird, R. E., & Wallace, T. W. (1992). *Yankaskas BC Radiology.* PMID:1509041

Bitam, S. (2012 Feb) Bees life algorithm for job scheduling in cloud computing. In *Proceedings of the Third International Conference on Communications and Information Technology,* (pp. 186-191). Academic Press.

Bitouk, D., Verma, R., & Nenkova, A. (2010). Class-level spectral features for emotion recognition. *Speech Communication, 52*(7-8), 613–625. doi:10.1016/j.specom.2010.02.010 PMID:23794771

Blake, C., & Merz, C. (1998). *UCI Repository of machine learning DataBases.* Irvine, CA: University of California.

Boiman, O., Shechtman, E., & Irani, M. (2008). In defense of nearest neighbor based image classification. *Proceedings of the IEEE Conference on Computer Vision and Pattern Recognition (VPR).*

Bonnet. (n.d.). Image processing courses. USTL.

Bora, D. J. (2017). *Importance of image enhancement techniques in color image segmentation: a comprehensive and comparative study.* arXiv preprint arXiv:1708.05081

Bora, D. J. 2019. HE Stain Image Segmentation Using an Innovative Type-2 Fuzzy Set-Based Approach. In Histopathological Image Analysis in Medical Decision Making (pp. 276-299). IGI Global. doi:10.4018/978-1-5225-6316-7.ch012

Bora, A., & Bezboruah, T. (2014). Testing and Evaluation of a Hierarchical SOAP based Medical Web Service. *International Journal of Database Theory and Application, 7*(4), 169–188. doi:10.14257/ijdta.2014.7.4.13

Bora, A., & Bezboruah, T. (2016). *Some Aspects of QoS for High Performance of Service Oriented Computing in Load Balancing Cluster Based Web server. In Handbook of Research on Recent Developments in Intelligent Communication Application* (pp. 566–603). IGI- Global. doi:10.4018/978-1-5225-1785-6

Bora, A., & Bezboruah, T. (2018b). Some aspects of reliability evaluation of multi service multi functional SOAP based web services. *International Journal of Information Retrieval Research, 8*(4), 24–39. doi:10.4018/IJIRR.2018100102

Bora, A., Bhuyan, M. K., & Bezboruah, T. (2013). Investigations on Hierarchical Web service based on Java Technique. *Proceedings of the World Congress on Engineering (WCE).*

Bora, A., Medhi, S., & Bezboruah, T. (2018a). *Investigations on Failure and Reliability Aspects of Service Oriented Computing Based On Different Deployment Technique. In Advanced Computational and Communication Paradigms. Lecture Notes in Electrical Engineering* (Vol. 475). Springer. doi:10.1007/978-981-10-8240-5_60

Bora, D. (2017). AERSCIEA: An efficient and robust satellite color image enhancement approach. *Proceedings of the Second International Conference on Research in Intelligent and Computing in Engineering.* 10.15439/2017R53

Bora, D. J. (2017). Performance Comparison of K-Means Algorithm and FCM Algorithm with Respect to Color Image Segmentation. *International Journal of Emerging Technology and Advanced Engineering, 7*(8), 460–470.

Bora, D. J. (2018). An Efficient Innovative Approach Towards Color Image Enhancement. *International Journal of Information Retrieval Research, 8*(1), 20–37. doi:10.4018/IJIRR.2018010102

Bora, D. J. (2018). An Ideal Approach for Medical Color Image Enhancement. In *Advanced Computational and Communication Paradigms* (pp. 351–361). Singapore: Springer. doi:10.1007/978-981-10-8237-5_34

Bosch, L. (2003). Emotions, speech and the ASR framework. *Speech Communication, 40*(1-2), 213–225. doi:10.1016/S0167-6393(02)00083-3

Bosma, W. (2005). Query-based summarization using rhetorical structure theory. *LOT Occasional Series, 4*, 29–44.

Bothma, J. D. (2010). Ontology learning from Swedish text. *International Conference on Computer Science and Education.*

Boudia, M. A., Hamou, R. M., & Amine, A. (2016). A New Approach Based on the Detection of Opinion by Senti-WordNet for Automatic Text Summaries by Extraction. *International Journal of Information Retrieval Research, 6*(3), 19–36. doi:10.4018/IJIRR.2016070102

Boughammoura, R., & Omri, M. N. (2011). SeMQI: A New Model for Semantic Interpretation of Query Interfaces. *Proceedings of NGNS.*

Boughammoura, R., Omri, M. N., & Hlaoua, L. (2012). VIQI: A New Approach for Visual Interpretation of Deep Web Query Interfaces. *Proceedings ICITeS.* 10.1109/ICITeS.2012.6216656

Boughammoura, R., Omri, M. N., & Hlaoua, L. (2013). Information Retrieval from Deep Web based on Visuel Query Interpretation *International Journal of Information Retrieval Research, 2*(4), 45–59. doi:10.4018/ijirr.2012100104

Bouramoul, A., Kholladi, M.-K., & Doan, B.-L. (2011, May). Using Context to Improve the Evaluation of Information Retrieval Systems. *International Journal of Database Management Systems, 3*(2), 22–39. doi:10.5121/ijdms.2011.3202

Bousquet. (2001). Introduction to Vector Machine Support (SVM). Academic Press.

Brezocnik, L., Fister, I., & Podgorelec, V. (2018). *Swarm Intelligence Algorithms for Feature Selection: A Review.* Applied Sciences Journal. doi:10.3390/app8091521

Bryhni, H., Klovning, E., & Kure, O. (2000). A Comparison of Load Balancing Techniques for Scalable Web Servers. *IEEE Network, 14*(4), 58–64. doi:10.1109/65.855480

Bumans, G. (2010). *Mapping between Relational Databases and OWL Ontologies: An Example. In Computer Science and Information Technologies, Scientific Papers* (Vol. 756). University of Latvia.

Bura, D., Choudhary, A., & Singh, R. K. (2017). A Novel UML Based Approach for Early Detection of Change Prone Classes. *International Journal of Open Source Software and Processes, 8*(3), 1–23. doi:10.4018/IJOSSP.2017070101

Burges, J. C. (1998). A tutorial on support vector machines for pattern recognition. *Data Mining and Knowledge Discovery, 2*(2), 121–167. doi:10.1023/A:1009715923555

Burkhardt, F., Paeschke, A., Rolfes, M., Sendlmeier, W. F., & Weiss, B. (2005). A database of German emotional speech. *Ninth European Conference on Speech Communication and Technology.*

Burt, P. J., & Adelson, E. H. (1983). The Laplacian pyramid as a compact image code. *IEEE Trans. Comm., 31*, 532–540.

Buyya, R., Ranjan, R., & Calheiros, R. N. (2010, May). Intercloud: Utility-oriented federation of cloud computing environments for scaling of application services. In *Proceeding of International Conference on Algorithms and Architectures for Parallel Processing* (pp. 13-31). Springer. 10.1007/978-3-642-13119-6_2

Cabanac, G. (2008). Annotation collective dans le contexte RI: définition d'une plate-forme pour expérimenter la validation sociale. In *Conférence en Recherche d'Information et Applications* (pp. 385–392). CORIA.

Cady, B., & Michaelson, J. S. (2001). The life-sparing potential of mammographic screening. *Cancer, 91*(9), 1699–1703. doi:10.1002/1097-0142(20010501)91:9<1699::AID-CNCR1186>3.0.CO;2-W PMID:11335893

Calheiros, R. N., Ranjan, R., Beloglazov, A., De Rose, C. A., & Buyya, R. (2011). CloudSim: A toolkit for modeling and simulation of cloud computing environments and evaluation of resource provisioning algorithms. *Software, Practice & Experience*, *41*(1), 23–50. doi:10.1002pe.995

Cao, J., Spooner, D. P., Jarvis, S. A., Saini, S., & Nudd, G. R. (2003, April). Agent-based grid load balancing using performance-driven task scheduling. In *Proceedings of Parallel and Distributed Processing Symposium*. IEEE.

Cao, Z., An, S., & Gorodetsky, C., & Yu. (Eds.). (2014). *Agents and Data Mining Interaction. 10th International workshop, ADMI 2014*, Paris, France.

Carpineto, C., & Romano, G. (2012). A survey of automatic query expansion in information retrieval. *ACM Computing Surveys*, *44*(1), 1–50. doi:10.1145/2071389.2071390

Casalicchio, E., & Colajanni, M. (2001). A client-aware dispatching algorithm for web clusters providing multiple services. *Proceedings of the 10th International World Wide Web Conference*, 535-544. 10.1145/371920.372155

Castro, V., Sanz, M., & Marcos, E. (2006). Business Process Development based on Web Services: a Web Information System for Medical Image Management and Processing. *IEEE International Conference on Web Services*, 807 – 814. 10.1109/ICWS.2006.41

Catolino, G., & Ferrucci, F. (n.d.). An extensive evaluation of ensemble techniques for software change prediction. Journal of Software: Evolution and Process, e2156.

Catolino, G., Palomba, F., De Lucia, A., Ferrucci, F., & Zaidman, A. (2018). Enhancing change prediction models using developer-related factors. *Journal of Systems and Software*, *143*, 14–28. doi:10.1016/j.jss.2018.05.003

Chahal, P., Singh, M., & Kumar, S. (2017). Semantic Analysis Based Approach for Relevant Text Extraction Using Ontology. *International Journal of Information Retrieval Research*, *7*(4), 19–36. doi:10.4018/IJIRR.2017100102

Chaira, T. (2013) Contrast enhancement of medical images using type II fuzzy set. *2013 National Conference on Communications (NCC)*. 10.1109/NCC.2013.6488016

Chaira, T. (2014). An improved medical image enhancement scheme using Type II fuzzy set. *Applied Soft Computing*, *25*, 293–308. doi:10.1016/j.asoc.2014.09.004

Chandrasekar, P., Chapaneri, S., & Jayaswal, D. (2014, April). Automatic speech emotion recognition: A survey. In *2014 International Conference on Circuits, Systems, Communication and Information Technology Applications (CSCITA)* (pp. 341-346). IEEE. 10.1109/CSCITA.2014.6839284

Chang, Y. K., Cirillo, C., & Razon, J. (1971). Evaluation of feedback retrieval using modified freezing, residual collection and test and control groups. In The SMART retrieval system- experiments in automatic document processing (pp. 355-370). Academic Press.

Chaudhari, J. S., & Kagalkar, R. M. (2015A). Methodology for Gender Identification, Classification and Recognition of Human Age. *International Journal of Computer Applications*.

Chaudhari, S. J., & Kagalkar, R. M. (2015B). Automatic speaker age estimation and gender dependent emotion recognition. *International Journal of Computers and Applications*, *117*(17), 5–10. doi:10.5120/20644-3383

Chebil, W., Soualmia, L. F., Omri, M. N., & Darmoni, S. J. (2015). Biomedical Concepts Extraction Based on Possibilistic Network and Vector Model. *Artificial Intelligence in Medicine*, *9105*, 227–231.

Cheikhrouhou. (2012). Description et classification des masses mammaires pour le diagnostic du cancer du sein. Universite D'evry Val D'essonne Laboratoire d'Informatique, Biologie Intégrative et Systèmes Complexes.

Chen, J., Qin, Y., Ye, Y., & Tang, Z. (2015, August). A Live Migration Algorithm for Virtual Machine in a Cloud Computing Environment. In *Proceedings of the Ubiquitous Intelligence and Computing and 2015 IEEE 12th Intl Conf on Autonomic and Trusted Computing and 2015 IEEE 15th Intl Conf on Scalable Computing and Communications and Its Associated Workshops (UIC-ATC-ScalCom), 2015 IEEE 12th Intl Conf on* (pp. 1319-1326). IEEE. 10.1109/UIC-ATC-ScalCom-CBDCom-IoP.2015.239

Cheng, H. D., Shi, X. J., Min, R., Hu, L. M., Cai, X. P., & Du, H. N. (2006). Approaches for automated detection and classification of masses in mammograms. *IEEE Transactions on Systems, Man, and Cybernetics*, (6): 610–621.

Cheng, X. M., Cheng, P. Y., & Zhao, L. (2009). A study on emotional feature analysis and recognition in speech signal. In *Proc. International Conference on Measuring Technology and Mechatronics Automation* (pp. 418-420). IEEE. 10.1109/ICMTMA.2009.89

Chen, H., Kang, H., Jiang, G., & Stage, Y. Z. (2012). *Network-aware migration control and scheduling of differentiated virtual machine workloads.* IEEE Computer Society.

Chen, Q., Li, M., & Zhou, M. (2007). Improving query spelling correction using web search results. In *Proceedings of the 2007 Joint Conference on Empirical Methods in Natural Language Processing and Computational Natural Language Learning* (pp. 181-189). Stroudsburg, PA: ACL.

Christophe Debruyne, T.-K. T. (2013). Grounding Ontologies with Social Processes and Natural Language. *Journal on Data Semantics*, 2(2-3), 89–118. doi:10.100713740-013-0023-3

Chul Min Leeand Shrikanth, S. N. (2005). Toward Detecting Emotions in Spoken Dialogs. *IEEE Transactions on Speech and Audio Processing*, 13(2), 293–303. doi:10.1109/TSA.2004.838534

Cohan, A., & Goharian, N. (2017). *Scientific article summarization using citation-context and article's discourse structure.* arXiv preprint arXiv:1704.06619

Colace, F., De Santo, M., Greco, L., & Napoletano, P. (2015). Weighted word pairs for query expansion. *Information Processing & Management*, 51(1), 179–193. doi:10.1016/j.ipm.2014.07.004

Cosenza, B., Cordasco, G., De Chiara, R., & Scarano, V. (2011, February). Distributed load balancing for parallel agent-based simulations. In *Parallel, Distributed and Network-Based Processing (PDP), 2011 19th Euromicro International Conference on* (pp. 62-69). IEEE. 10.1109/PDP.2011.22

Cotta, C., & Moscato, P. (2003). The k-feature set problem is w[2]-complete. *Journal of Computer and System Sciences*, 686-690. doi:10.1016/S0022-0000(03)00081-3

Dam, S., Mandal, G., Dasgupta, K., & Dutta, P. (2015, February). Genetic algorithm and gravitational emulation based hybrid load balancing strategy in cloud computing. In *Computer, Communication, Control and Information Technology (C3IT), 2015 Third International Conference on* (pp. 1-7). IEEE. 10.1109/C3IT.2015.7060176

Daoud, M., & Huang, J. X. (2013). Modeling geographic, temporal, and proximity contexts for improving geotemporal search. *Journal of the American Society for Information Science and Technology*, 34(1), 190–212. doi:10.1002/asi.22648

Darwish, A., Sayed, G. I., & Aboul Hassanien, E. (2018). Meta-Heuristic Optimization Algorithms Based Feature Selection For Clinical Breast Cancer Diagnosis. *Journal of the Egyptian Mathematical Society*, 26(3).

Das, B., Mandal, S., Mitra, P., & Basu, A. (2013). Effect of aging on speech features and phoneme recognition: A study on Bengali voicing vowels. *International Journal of Speech Technology*, 16(1), 19–31. doi:10.100710772-012-9147-3

Davis, S. B., & Mermelstein, P. (1980, August). Comparison of Parametric Representations for Monosyllabic Word Recognition in Continuously Spoken Sentences. *IEEE Transactions on Acoustics, Speech, and Signal Processing, 28*(4), 357–366. doi:10.1109/TASSP.1980.1163420

Dellaert, F., Polzin, T., & Waibel, A. (1996), Recognizing emotion in speech, *Proceedings of international conference on spoken language processing*, 3, 1970-1973.

Deng, W., Liu, F., Jin, H., Li, B., & Li, D. (2014). Harnessing renewable energy in cloud datacenters: Opportunities and challenges. *IEEE Network, 28*(1), 48–55. doi:10.1109/MNET.2014.6724106

Devillers, L., & Vidrascu, L. (2006). Real-life emotions detection with lexical and paralinguistic cues on human–human call center dialogs. Proceedings of Interspeech, 801-804.

Dhal, K. G., Ray, S., Sen, M., & Das, S. 2018. Proper Enhancement and Segmentation of the Overexposed Color Skin Cancer Image. In Intelligent Multidimensional Data and Image Processing (pp. 240-258). IGI Global. doi:10.4018/978-1-5225-5246-8.ch009

Dif, N., & Elberrichi, Z. (2019). An Enhanced Recursive Firefly Algorithm for Informative Gene Selection. *International Journal of Swarm Intelligence Research, 10*(2), 21–33. doi:10.4018/IJSIR.2019040102

Do, MN., & Vetterli, M. (2005). The contourlet transform: an efficient directional multiresolution image representation. IEEE Trans. Image Proc., 14(12).

Domingos, H. P. (2014). *Unsupervised Ontology Induction from Text*. Academic Press.

Dorigo, M. (2007). *Ant colony optimization*. Retrieved from http://www.scholarpedia.org/article/Ant_colony_optimization

Drymonas, K. Z. (2010). Unsupervised Ontology Acquisition from Plain Texts: The OntoGain System. *LNCS, 6177*, 277–287.

Duggan, M., Duggan, J., Howley, E., & Barrett, E. (2016, September). An autonomous network aware vm migration strategy in cloud data centres. In *Proceedings of the Cloud and Autonomic Computing (ICCAC), 2016 International Conference on* (pp. 24-32). IEEE. 10.1109/ICCAC.2016.9

Dupuis, K., & Pichora-Fuller, M. K. (2011). Recognition of emotional speech for younger and older talkers: Behavioural findings from the Toronto Emotional Speech Set. *Canadian Acoustics, 39*(3), 182–183.

Dupuis, K., & Pichora-Fuller, M. K. (2014). Intelligibility of emotional speech in younger and older adults. *Ear and Hearing, 35*(6), 695–707. doi:10.1097/AUD.0000000000000082 PMID:25127327

Durrett, G., Berg-Kirkpatrick, T., & Klein, D. (2016). *Learning-based single-document summarization with compression and anaphoricity constraints.* arXiv preprint arXiv:1603.08887

Eisenstein, J., O'Connor, B., Smith, N. A., & Xing, E. P. (2012). Mapping the geographical diffusion of new words. *Workshop on Social Network and Social Media Analysis: Methods, Models and Applications.*

El Ayadi, M., Kamel, M. S., & Karray, F. (2011, March). Survey on speech emotion recognition: Features, classification schemes, and databases. *Pattern Recognition, 44*(3), 572–587. doi:10.1016/j.patcog.2010.09.020

El Houby, E.M.F., Yassin, N., & Omran, S. (2017). A Hybrid Approach From Ant Colony Optimization And K-Nearest Neighbor For Classifying Datasets Using Selected Features. *Informatica, 41*(4).

Elish, M. O., & Al-Zouri, A. A. (2014, January). Effectiveness of Coupling Metrics in Identifying Change-Prone Object-Oriented Classes. In *Proceedings of the International Conference on Software Engineering Research and Practice (SERP)* (p. 1). The Steering Committee of The World Congress in Computer Science, Computer Engineering and Applied Computing (WorldComp).

Ellouzi, H., Ltifi, H., & Ben Ayed, M. (2017, April). Multi-agent modelling of decision support systems based on visual data mining. *Multiagent Grid Syst., 13*(1), 31–45. doi:10.3233/MGS-170260

Eltoukhy, M.M., Faye, I., & Samir, B.B. (2010). Breast cancer diagnosis in digital mammogram using multiscale curvelet transform. Comput. Med. Imag.Graphics, 34.

Emam, K., Benlarbi, S., Goel, N., & Rai, S. (1999). *A validation of object-oriented metrics*. Technical Report ERB-1063, National Research Council of Canada.

Emden Gansner, E. K. (2006). *Drawing graphs with dot*. Academic Press.

Engberg, I. S., Hansen, A. V., Andersen, O., & Dalsgaard, P. (1997). Design, recording and verification of a Danish emotional speech database. *Fifth European Conference on Speech Communication and Technology.*

Ensafi, P., & Tizhoosh, H. (2005). Type-2 Fuzzy Image Enhancement. *Lecture Notes in Computer Science, 3656,* 159–166. doi:10.1007/11559573_20

Eski, S., & Buzluca, F. (2011, March). An empirical study on object-oriented metrics and software evolution in order to reduce testing costs by predicting change-prone classes. In *Software Testing, Verification and Validation Workshops (ICSTW), 2011 IEEE Fourth International Conference on* (pp. 566-571). IEEE. 10.1109/ICSTW.2011.43

Fan, S., Tang, J., Tian, Q., & Wu, C. (2019). A robust fuzzy rule based integrative feature selection strategy for gene expression data in TCGA. *BMC Medical Genomics, 12*(1), 14. doi:10.118612920-018-0451-x PMID:30704464

Farahnakian, F., Liljeberg, P., & Plosila, J. (2013, September). LiRCUP: Linear regression based CPU usage prediction algorithm for live migration of virtual machines in data centers. In *Proceedings of the Software Engineering and Advanced Applications (SEAA), 2013 39th EUROMICRO Conference on* (pp. 357-364). IEEE.

Farhoudi, Z., Setayeshi, S., & Rabiee, A. (2017). Using learning automata in brain emotional learning for speech emotion recognition. *International Journal of Speech Technology, 20*(3), 553–562. doi:10.100710772-017-9426-0

Farrell, Mammone, & Assaleh. (1994). Speaker Networks Recognition Using Neural and Conventional Classifiers. *IEEE Transactions on Acoustics, Speech, and Signal Processing, 2*(1), 194–205.

Fekade Getahun, K. W. (2017). Integrated Ontology Learner: Towards Generic Semantic Annotation Framework. In *MEDES'17.* Bangkok, Thailand: ACM.

Feld, M., Burkhardt, F., & Müller, C. (2010). *Automatic speaker age and gender recognition in the car for tailoring dialog and mobile services.* Interspeech.

Feldman, R. (2007). *The Text Mining Handbook Advanced Approaches in Analyzing Unstructured Data.* Cambridge University Press.

Feng, T., Xuezheng, F., Yanqing, Z., & Bourgeois, G. (2007). *A genetic algorithm-based method for feature subset selection.* Springer-Verlag.

Fernández-Reyes, F. C., Hermosillo-Valadez, J., & Montes-y-Gómez, M. (2018). A prospect-guided global query expansion strategy using word embeddings. *Information Processing & Management, 54*(1), 1–13. doi:10.1016/j.ipm.2017.09.001

Ferreto, T. C., Netto, M. A., Calheiros, R. N., & De Rose, C. A. (2011). Server consolidation with migration control for virtualized data centers. *Future Generation Computer Systems*, *27*(8), 1027–1034. doi:10.1016/j.future.2011.04.016

Fkih, F., & Omri, M. N. (2012). Complex Terminology Extraction Model from Unstructured Web Text Based Linguistic and Statistical Knowledge. *International Journal of Information Retrieval Research*, *2*(3), 1–18. doi:10.4018/ijirr.2012070101

Forsman, M., Glad, A., Lundberg, L., & Ilie, D. (2015). Algorithms for automated live migration of virtual machines. *Journal of Systems and Software*, *101*, 110–126. doi:10.1016/j.jss.2014.11.044

Fragopanagos, N., & Taylor, J. G. (2005). Emotion recognition in human–computer interaction. *Neural Networks*, *18*(4), 389–405. doi:10.1016/j.neunet.2005.03.006 PMID:15921887

Freund, Y. (1995). Boosting a weak learning algorithm by majority. *Information and Computation*, *121*(2), 256–285. doi:10.1006/inco.1995.1136

Freund, Y., & Schapire, R. (1996). Experiments with a New Boosting Algorithm. *Machine Learning: Proceedings of the Thirteenth International Conference*.

Fulmare, N. S., Chakrabarti, P., & Yadav, D. (2013). Understanding and estimation of emotional expression using acoustic analysis of natural speech. *International Journal on Natural Language Computing*, *2*(4), 37–46. doi:10.5121/ijnlc.2013.2503

Gao, K., Zhang, Y., Zhang, D., & Lin, S. (2013). Accurate off-line query expansion for large-scale mobile visual search. *Signal Processing*, *93*(8), 2305–2315. doi:10.1016/j.sigpro.2012.10.011

Garcia, E. (2016). *The Extended Boolean Model*. Retrieved from www.minerazzi.com

Garrouch, K., Omri, M. N., & Kouzana, A. (2012). A New Information Retrieval Model Based on Possibilistic Bayesian Networks. *Proceedings ICCRK'12*, 9105, 1-7.

Gillam, K. A. (2005). *Automatic Ontology Extraction from Unstructured Texts*. On the Move to Meaningful Internet.

Gillani Andleeb, S. (2015). *From text mining to knowledge mining: An integrated framework of concept extraction and categorization for domain ontology*. Budapesti Corvinus Egyetem.

Glisky, E. L. (2007). Changes in cognitive function in human aging. Brain aging: Models, Methods, and Mechanisms, 3-20.

Godara, D., Choudhary, A., & Singh, R. K. (2018). Predicting Change Prone Classes in Open Source Software. *International Journal of Information Retrieval Research*, *8*(4), 1–23. doi:10.4018/IJIRR.2018100101

Godara, D., & Singh, R. K. (2015). Enhancing Frequency Based Change Proneness Prediction Method Using Artificial Bee Colony Algorithm. In *Advances in Intelligent Informatics* (pp. 535–543). Cham: Springer. doi:10.1007/978-3-319-11218-3_48

Godara, D., & Singh, R. K. (2017). Exploring the relationships between design measures and change proneness in object-oriented systems. *International Journal of Software Engineering, Technology and Applications*, *2*(1), 64–80.

Goel, A. L. (1985). Software Reliability Models: Assumptions, Limitations, and Applicability. *IEEE Transaction of Software Computing*, *SE-11*(12), 1411–1423. doi:10.1109/TSE.1985.232177

Gokhan, T., & Renato, D. (2011). *Spoken Language Understanding: Systems for Extracting Semantic Information from speech*. John Wiley & Sons, Ltd.

Goldberg, E. (1989). *Genetic algorithms in search: optimization and machine learning*. Addison-Wesley.

Gopinath, P. G., & Vasudevan, S. K. (2015). An in-depth analysis and study of Load balancing techniques in the cloud computing environment. *Procedia Computer Science*, *50*, 427–432. doi:10.1016/j.procs.2015.04.009

Gordon, M. S., & Hibberts, M. (2011). Audiovisual speech from emotionally expressive and lateralized faces. *Q J Exp Psychol (Hove)*, *64*(4), 730–750. doi:10.1080/17470218.2010.516835 PMID:20945268

Greene, W. A. (2001, November). Dynamic load-balancing via a genetic algorithm. In *Tools with Artificial Intelligence, Proceedings of the 13th International Conference on* (pp. 121-128). IEEE.

Grishman, R. (1997). Information Extraction: Techniques and Challenges. *Computer Science*, *1299*, 10–27.

Grose, J. H., Mamo, S. K., & Hall, J. W. III. (2009). Age effects in temporal envelope processing: Speech unmasking and auditory steady state responses. *Ear and Hearing*, *30*(5), 568–575. doi:10.1097/AUD.0b013e3181ac128f PMID:19633565

Gu, J., Hua, L., Wu, X., Yang, H., & Zhou, Z. (2015). Color medical image enhancement based on adaptive equalization of intensity numbers matrix histogram. *International Journal of Automation and Computing*, *12*(5), 551–558. doi:10.100711633-014-0871-9

Gupta, D. B., & Lehal, G. S. (2010). A Survey of Text Summarization Extractive Techniques. doi:10.4304/jetwi.2.3.258-268

Gupta, D., Cherkasova, L., Gardner, R., & Vahdat, A. (2006, November). Enforcing performance isolation across virtual machines in Xen. In *Proceedings of the ACM/IFIP/USENIX 2006 International Conference on Middleware* (pp. 342-362). Springer-Verlag. 10.1007/11925071_18

Gurcan, Yardımcı, & Cetin, Enis¸, & Ansari. (1997). Detection of Microcalcifications in Mammograms Using Higher Order Statistics. *IEEE Signal Processing Letters*, *4*(8).

Hämäläinen, A., Meinedo, H., Tjalve, M., Pellegrini, P., Trancoso, I., & Dias, M. S. (2011). Improving speech recognition through automatic selection of age group–Specific Acoustic Models. ADFA, 1.

Han, A. R., Jeon, S. U., Bae, D. H., & Hong, J. E. (2008, July). Behavioral dependency measurement for change-proneness prediction in UML 2.0 design models. In Computer Software and Applications, 2008. COMPSAC'08. 32nd Annual IEEE International (pp. 76-83). IEEE.

Han, D. (2013).Comparison of Commonly Used Image Interpolation Methods. *Proceedings of the 2nd International Conference on Computer Science and Electronics Engineering (ICCSEE 2013)*. 10.2991/iccsee.2013.391

Han, Kamber, & Pei. (2011). Data Mining: Concepts and Techniques. *Lecture Notes in Computer Science*, 9145.

Harb, M., & Desuky, A. (2014). Feature Selection on Classification of Medical Datasets based on Particle Swarm Optimization. *International Journal of Computers and Applications*, *104*(5).

Hayes, M. H. (1996). *Statistical Digital Signal Processing and Modeling*. John Wiley and Sons.

Haykin, S. (2005). Neural Networks: A comprehensive foundation (2nd ed.). Essex, UK: Pearson Education.

HE Stain. (n.d.). Retrieved from https://en.wikipedia.org/wiki/H\%26E_stain

Hearst, M. A. (1992). Automatic Acquisition of Hypernyms from Large Text Corpora. Proc. of Collins.

He, L., Lech, M., Maddage, N. C., & Allen, N. B. (2011). Study of empirical mode decomposition and spectral analysis for stress and emotion classification in natural speech. *Biomedical Signal Processing and Control*, *6*(2), 139–146. doi:10.1016/j.bspc.2010.11.001

Hermansk, H. (1990). Perceptual linear predictive (PLP) analysis of speech. *The Journal of the Acoustical Society of America*, *87*(4), 1739–1752. PMID:2341679

Hitam, M., Yussof, W., Awalludin, E., & Bachok, Z. (2013). Mixture contrast limited adaptive histogram equalization for underwater image enhancement. *2013 International Conference On Computer Applications Technology (ICCAT)*. 10.1109/ICCAT.2013.6522017

Hlaoua, L. (2006). *Reformulation de requêtes par structure en RI dans les documents XML*. Lyon: CORIA.

Hongbin, Z., & Guangyu, S. (2002). Feature selection using Tabu Search method. *Pattern Recognition*, 701–711.

Horowitz, S. L., & Pavlidis, T. (1976). Picture segmentation by a directed split and merge procedure. Computer Methods in Images Analysis.

Hosmer, D. W. Jr, & Lemeshow, S. (2004). *Applied logistic regression*. John Wiley & Sons.

Hristo Tanev Tanev, B. M. (2008). *Weakly Supervised Approaches for Ontology Population*. Academic Press.

Hsu, W., & Chou, C. (2015). Medical Image Enhancement Using Modified Color Histogram Equalization. *Journal of Medical and Biological Engineering*, 35(5), 580–584. doi:10.100740846-015-0078-8

Hu, B., Lei, Z., Lei, Y., Xu, D., & Li, J. (2011). A Time-series Based Precopy Approach for Live Migration of Virtual Machines. *Proceedings of the 17th International Conference on Parallel and Distributed Systems (ICPADS)*. 10.1109/ICPADS.2011.19

Huber, R., Batliner, A., Buckow, J., No¨th, E., Warnke, V., & Niemann, H. (2000). Recognition of emotion in a realistic dialogue scenario. *Proceedings of international conference on spoken language processing*, 665-668.

Idrissi, N. (2008). *La navigation dans des bases d'images: prise en compte des attributs de texture* (PhD thesis). Université de Nantes.

Institut National du Cancer. (2016). *Cancers du sein*. Author.

Ismail, H., Issa, K., & Abdallah, K. (2015). Designing High Performance Web-Based Computing Services to Promote Telemedicine Database Management System. *IEEE Transactions on Services Computing*, 8(1), 47–64. doi:10.1109/TSC.2014.2300499

Jacewicz, E., Fox, R. A., & Wei, L. (2010). Between-speaker and within-speaker variation in speech tempo of American English. *The Journal of the Acoustical Society of America*, 128(2), 839–850. doi:10.1121/1.3459842 PMID:20707453

Jackson, P., & Haq, S. (2014). *Surrey audio-visual expressed emotion (savee) database*. Guildford, UK: University of Surrey.

Jain, R. (2012). *The art of computer systems performance analysis: Technique for experimental Design, Measurement, Simulation and Modeling*. Wiley Professional Computing.

Jameel, S., & Rehman, S. U. (2018). An Optimal Feature Selection Method Using A Modified Wrapper Based Ant Colony Optimization. *Journal of the National Science Foundation of Srilanka*, 46(2), 143 – 151.

Janes, A., Scotto, M., Pedrycz, W., Russo, B., Stefanovic, M., & Succi, G. (2006). Identification of defect-prone classes in telecommunication software systems using design metrics. *Information Sciences*, 176(24), 3711–3734. doi:10.1016/j.ins.2005.12.002

Janowicz, K. (2005). Extending Semantic Similarity Measurement with Thematic Roles GeoS'05. In *Proceedings of the First international conference on GeoSpatial Semantics* (pp. 137-152). Springer-Verlag Berlin Heidelberg. 10.1007/11586180_10

Javidi, M. M., & Roshan, E. F. (2013). Speech emotion recognition by using combinations of C5. 0, neural network (NN), and support vector machines (SVM) classification methods. Journal of mathematics and computer. *Science, 6*(3), 191–200.

Javidi, M. M., & Roshan, E. F. (2013, April). Speech Emotion Recognition by Using Combinations of C5.0, Neural Network (NN), and Support Vector Machines (SVM) Classification Methods. *Journal of Mathematics and Computer Science, 6*, 191–200.

Jenifer, S., Parasuraman, S., & Kadirvelu, A. (2016). Contrast enhancement and brightness preserving of digital mammograms using fuzzy clipped contrast-limited adaptive histogram equalization algorithm. *Applied Soft Computing, 42*, 167–177. doi:10.1016/j.asoc.2016.01.039

Jiang, P., Elag, M., Kumar, P., Peckham, S. D., Marini, L., & Rui, L. (2017). A service-oriented architecture for coupling web service models using the Basic Model Interface (BMI). *Environmental Modelling & Software, 92*, 107–118. doi:10.1016/j.envsoft.2017.01.021

Jiazheng, Sahiner, Chan, Ge, Hadjiiski, Helvie, … Cui. (2010). Characterization of Mammographic Masses Based on Level Set Segmentation with New Image Features and Patient Information. *Medical Physics*.

Joseph, C. T., Chandrasekaran, K., & Cyriac, R. (2015). A novel family genetic approach for virtual machine allocation. *Procedia Computer Science, 46*, 558–565. doi:10.1016/j.procs.2015.02.090

Joshi, D. D., & Zalte, M. B. (2013), Speech Emotion Recognition: A Review. *IOSR Journal of Electronics and Communication Engineering, 4*(4), 34-37.

Julia Hoxha, A. S. (2010). An Approach to Formal and Semantic Representation of Logistics Services. In *Proceedings of the ECAI'10 Workshop on Artificial Intelligence and Logistics*, (pp. 73-78). Academic Press.

Kabalan, K. Y., Smari, W. W., & Hakimian, J. Y. (2002). Adaptive load sharing in heterogeneous systems: Policies, modifications, and simulation. *International Journal of Simulation, Systems, Science and Technology, 3*(1-2), 89–100.

Kalita, M., & Bezboruah, T. (2011a). Investigations on performance testing and evaluation of PReWebD: A. NET technique for implementing web application. *IET Software, 5*(4), 357–365. doi:10.1049/iet-sen.2010.0139

Kalita, M., Khanikar, S., & Bezboruah, T. (2011b). Investigation on performance testing and evaluation of PReWebN: A JAVA technique for implementing web application. *IET Software, 5*(5), 434–444. doi:10.1049/iet-sen.2011.0030

Kalra, M., & Singh, S. (2015). A review of metaheuristic scheduling techniques in cloud computing. *Egyptian Informatics Journal, 16*(3), 275-295.

Kanagaraj, G., Shanmugasundaram, N., & Prakash, S. (2012). Adaptive Load Balancing Algorithm Using Service Queue. In *2nd International Conference on Computer Science and Information Technology (ICCSIT'2012)* (pp. 28-29). Academic Press.

Kasture, N. R., Yargal, N., Nityan, N., Kulkarni, N., & Mathur, V. (2014). A Survey on Methods of Abstractive Text Summarization. *International Journal for Research in Emerging Science and Technology, 1*(6).

Kaur, J., & Vashish, S. (2013). Analysis of different clustering techniques for detecting human emotions variation through data mining. *International Journal of Computer Science Engineering and Information Technology Research, 3*(2), 27–36. doi:10.5815/ijitcs.2013.07.03

Kaur, S., & Verma, A. (2012). An efficient approach to genetic algorithm for task scheduling in cloud computing environment. *International Journal of Information Technology and Computer Science, 4*(10), 74–79. doi:10.5815/ijitcs.2012.10.09

Kaya, H., Salah, A. A., Gürgen, S. F., & Ekenel, H. (2014, April). Protocol and baseline for experiments on Bogazici University Turkish emotional speech corpus. In *2014 22nd Signal Processing and Communications Applications Conference (SIU)* (pp. 1698-1701). IEEE. 10.1109/SIU.2014.6830575

Kenneth Clarkson, A. L. (2018). User-Centric Ontology Population. *ESWC-Conferences.*

Keys, R. (1981). Cubic convolution interpolation for digital image processing. *IEEE Transactions on Acoustics, Speech, and Signal Processing, 29*(6), 1153–1160. doi:10.1109/TASSP.1981.1163711

Kgotatso Desmond Mogotlane, J. V.-D. (2016). Automatic Conversion of Relational Databases into Ontologies: A Comparative Analysis of Protégé Plug-ins Performances. *International Journal of Web and Semantic Technology.*

Khan, A., & Baig, A. (2016). Multi-objective feature subset selection using MRMR based enhanced ant colony optimization algorithm. *Journal of Experimental & Theoretical Artificial Intelligence, 28*(6), 1061–1073. doi:10.1080/09528 13X.2015.1056240

Khare, P., & Burse, K. (2016). Feature Selection Using Genetic Algorithm and Classification using Weka for Ovarian Cancer. *International Journal of Computer Science and Information Technologies, 7*(1), 194–196.

Khennak, I., & Drias, H. (2017). Bat-Inspired Algorithm Based Query Expansion for Medical Web Information Retrieval. *Journal of Medical Systems, 41*(2), 34. doi:10.100710916-016-0668-1 PMID:28054196

Khomh, F., Penta, M. D., & Gueheneuc, Y. G. (2009, October). An exploratory study of the impact of code smells on software change-proneness. In *Reverse Engineering, 2009. WCRE'09. 16th Working Conference on* (pp. 75-84). IEEE. 10.1109/WCRE.2009.28

Kilintzis, V., Beredimas, N., & Chouvarda, I. (2014). *Evaluation of the performance of open-source RDBMS and triplestores for storing medical data over a web service.* doi:10.1109/EMBC.2014.6944623

Kokilavani, T., & Amalarethinam, D. G. (2011). Load balanced min-min algorithm for static meta-task scheduling in grid computing. *International Journal of Computers and Applications, 20*(2), 43–49.

Kolodyazhniy, V., Kreibig, S. D., Gross, J. J., Roth, W. T., & Wilhelm, F. H. (2011). An affective computing approach to physiological emotion specificity: Toward subject-independent and stimulus-independent classification of film induced emotions. *Psychophysiology, 48*, 908–922. PMID:21261632

Kopaneli, A., Kousiouris, G., Velez, G. E., Evangelinou, A., & Varvarigou, T. (2015). A model driven approach for supporting the Cloud target selection process. *Procedia Computer Science, 68*, 89–102. doi:10.1016/j.procs.2015.09.226

Koru, A. G., & Liu, H. (2007). Identifying and characterizing change-prone classes in two large-scale open-source products. *Journal of Systems and Software, 80*(1), 63–73. doi:10.1016/j.jss.2006.05.017

Kreßel, U. (1999). Pairwise classification and support vector Machines. In *Advances in Kernel Methods: Support Vector Learnings* (pp. 255–268). Cambridge, MA: MIT Press.

Kruekaew, B., & Kimpan, W. (2014). Virtual machine scheduling management on cloud computing using artificial bee colony. In *Proceedings of the International MultiConference of Engineers and Computer Scientists* (*Vol. 1*, pp. 12-14). Academic Press.

Kumar, S., & Mewada, P. (2011). ACO based Feature subset Selection for multiple K-Nearest Neighbor Classifiers. *International Journal on Computer Science and Engineering.*

Kumar, Y. J., Goh, O. S., Basiron, H., Choon, N. H., & Suppiah, P. C. (2016). A Review on Automatic Text Summarization Approaches. *Journal of Computational Science, 12*(4), 178–190. doi:10.3844/jcssp.2016.178.190

Kummerfeld, D. H. (2012). Parser Showdown at the Wall Street Corral: An Empirical Investigation of Error Types in Parser Output. In *Proceedings of the 2012 Joint Conference on Empirical Methods in Natural Language Processing and Computational Natural Language Learning,* (pp. 1048–1059). Jeju Island, South Korea: Academic Press.

Kuru, K. (2014). Optimization and enhancement of H&E stained microscopical images by applying bilinear interpolation method on lab color mode. *Theoretical Biology & Medical Modelling, 11*(1), 9. doi:10.1186/1742-4682-11-9 PMID:24502223

Kwary, D. A. (2017). A corpus and a concordancer of academic journal articles. *Data in Brief, 16,* 94–100. doi:10.1016/j. dib.2017.11.023 PubMed

Kyriakakis, P., Chatzigeorgiou, A., Ampatzoglou, A., & Xinogalos, S. (2019). Exploring the frequency and change proneness of dynamic feature pattern instances in PHP applications. *Science of Computer Programming, 171,* 1–20. doi:10.1016/j.scico.2018.10.004

Lahbib. (2013). Algorithm KNN: K-nearest neighbor. Academic Press.

Laukka, P., Neiberg, D., Forsell, M., Karlsson, I., & Elenius, K. (2011). Expression of affect in spontaneous speech: Acoustic correlates and automatic detection of irritation and resignation. *Computer Speech & Language, 25*(1), 84–104. doi:10.1016/j.csl.2010.03.004

Laukka, P., Patrik, J., & Roberto, B. (2005). A dimensional approach to vocal expression of emotion. *Cognition and Emotion, 19*(5), 633–653. doi:10.1080/02699930441000445

Lau, S. M., Lu, Q., & Leung, K. S. (2006). Adaptive load distribution algorithms for heterogeneous distributed systems with multiple task classes. *Journal of Parallel and Distributed Computing, 66*(2), 163–180. doi:10.1016/j.jpdc.2004.01.007

LD, D. B., & Krishna, P. V. (2013). Honey bee behavior inspired load balancing of tasks in cloud computing environments. *Applied Soft Computing, 13*(5), 2292–2303. doi:10.1016/j.asoc.2013.01.025

Lee, C. M., & Narayanan, S. (2003). Emotion recognition using a data driven fuzzy inference system. Proceedings of Eurospeech, 157-160.

Lee, C. M., Narayanan, S., & Pieraccini, R. (2001). Recognition of negative emotions from the speech signal. In *IEEE Workshop on Automatic Speech Recognition and Understanding, 2001. ASRU'01* (pp. 240-243). IEEE. 10.1109/ASRU.2001.1034632

Lee, A., & Chau, M. (2011). The impact of query suggestion in e-commerce websites. In *Workshop on E-Business* (pp. 248-254). Berlin: Springer.

Lee, C. M., & Narayanan, S. (2003). Emotion recognition using a data-driven fuzzy inference system. *Eighth European conference on speech communication and technology.*

Lehnert, W., Cardie, C., Fisher, D., Riloff, E., & Williams, R. (1991). Description of the CIRCUS, System as Used for MUC-3. In *Proceedings of Third Message Understanding Conference (MUC-3)* (pp. 223-233). University of Massachusetts.

Leturia, I., Gurrutxaga, A., Areta, N., Alegria, I., & Ezeiza, A. (2013). Morphological query expansion and language-filtering words for improving Basque web retrieval. *Language Resources and Evaluation, 47*(2), 425–448. doi:10.100710579-012-9208-x

Levin, I., Richard, S., & Rubin, D. (2009). Statistics for management, Pearson education, Inc. *South Asia.*

Li, J. H. (2013). *An Entropy-Based Weighted Concept Lattice for Merging Multi-Source Geo-Ontologies.* doi:10.3390/e15062303

Liam, C., Bing, X., Mengjie, Z., & Lin, S. (2012). Binary Particle Swarm Optimization for Feature Selection: A Filter Based Approach. *Proceedings of the IEEE World Congress on Computational Intelligence.*

Liao, J. S., Chang, C. C., Hsu, Y. L., Zhang, X. W., Lai, K. C., & Hsu, C. H. (2012, September). Energy-efficient resource provisioning with SLA consideration on cloud computing. In *Proceeding of Parallel Processing Workshops (ICPPW), 2012 41st International Conference on* (pp. 206-211). IEEE.

Li, L., Si, Y., & Jia, Z. (2018). Medical image enhancement based on CLAHE and unsharp masking in NSCT domain. *Journal of Medical Imaging and Health Informatics, 8*(3), 431–438. doi:10.1166/jmihi.2018.2328

Lin, P., & Lin, B. (2016). Fuzzy automatic contrast enhancement based on fuzzy C-means clustering in CIELAB color space. *2016 12th IEEE/ASME International Conference on Mechatronic and Embedded Systems and Applications (MESA).* doi: 10.1109/mesa.2016.7587156

Lindqvist, N., & Price, T. (2018). *Evaluation of Feature Selection Methods for Machine Learning Classification of Breast Cancer.* Academic Press.

Lin, H., Wang, L., & Chen, S.-M. (2006). Query expansion for document retrieval based on fuzzy rules and user relevance feedback techniques. *Expert Systems with Applications, 31*(2), 397–405. doi:10.1016/j.eswa.2005.09.078

Lin, W., Wang, J. Z., Liang, C., & Qi, D. (2011). A threshold-based dynamic resource allocation scheme for cloud computing. *Procedia Engineering, 23,* 695–703. doi:10.1016/j.proeng.2011.11.2568

Lioma, C., Moens, M. F., & Azzopardi, L. (2008). Collaborative annotation for pseudo relevance feedback. In *ECIR workshop on exploiting semantic annotation in information retrieval.* ESAIR.

Li, P., Wang, H., & Li, X. (2017). Improved ant colony algorithm for global path planning. *Advances in Materials, Machinery, Electronics,* I.

Liscombe, J., Hirschberg, J., & Venditti, J. J. (2005). Detecting certainness in spoken tutorial dialogues. *Proceeding of European conference on speech communication and technology,* 1837-1840.

Litman, D. J., & Forbes-Riley, K. (2006). Recognizing student emotions and attitudes on the basis of utterances in spoken tutoring dialogues with both human and computer tutors. *Speech Communication, 48*(5), 559–590. doi:10.1016/j.specom.2005.09.008

Liu, F., Flanigan, J., Thomson, S., Sadeh, N., & Smith, N. A. (2018). *Toward abstractive summarization using semantic representations.* arXiv preprint arXiv:1805.10399

Liu, Y., & Zheng, F. (2005). FS_SFS: A novel feature selection method for support vector machines. *The Journal of Pattern Recognition Society.*

Liu, A. U., & Bing, P. (2011). *Information Retrieval and Web Search. In Web Data Mining* (pp. 211–268). Springer-Verlag Berlin Heidelberg.

Liu, X., Chen, F., Fang, H., & Wang, M. (2014). Exploiting entity relationship for query expansion in enterprise search. *Information Retrieval, 17*(3), 265–294. doi:10.100710791-013-9237-0

Li, W., Tordsson, J., & Elmroth, E. (2011, December). Virtual machine placement for predictable and time-constrained peak loads. In *International Workshop on Grid Economics and Business Models* (pp. 120-134). Springer.

Li, Y., & Zhao, Y. (1998). Recognizing emotions in speech using short-term and long-term features. *Fifth International Conference on Spoken Language Processing.*

Loizou, P. C. (2007). *Speech enhancement: theory and practice.* CRC Press. doi:10.1201/9781420015836

Lopes, C. T. (2013). *Context-Based Health Information Retrieval* (PhD dissertation). University of Porto. Retrieved from http://www.carlalopes.com/pubs/lopes_PhD_2013.pdf

Lotfi, H. (2012). *Contribution à l'analyse de textures de radiographies Osseuses pour le diagnostic précoce de l'ostéoporose*. Thèse de Doctorat.

Lu, C., & Lau, S. M. (1995). An adaptive algorithm for resolving processor thrashing in load distribution. *Concurrency and Computation, 7*(7), 653–670. doi:10.1002/cpe.4330070706

Lu, F., Parkin, S., & Morgan, G. (2006, October). Load balancing for massively multiplayer online games. In *Proceedings of 5th ACM SIGCOMM workshop on Network and system support for games* (p. 1). ACM. 10.1145/1230040.1230064

Lu, H., Zhou, Y., Xu, B., Leung, H., & Chen, L. (2012). The ability of object-oriented metrics to predict change-proneness: A meta-analysis. *Empirical Software Engineering, 17*(3), 200–242. doi:10.100710664-011-9170-z

Luhn, H. (1958). The automatic creation of literature abstracts. IBM Journal of Research and Development, 2(2), 159–165.

Luhn, H. P. (1958). The Automatic Creation of Literature Abstracts. *IBM Journal of Research and Development, 2*(2), 159–165. doi:10.1147/rd.22.0159

Lyakso, E., Frolova, O., Dmitrieva, E., Grigorev, A., Kaya, H., Salah, A. A., & Karpov, A. (2015A). EmoChildRu: emotional child Russian speech corpus. *Speech and Computer, 17th International Conference*, 144-152.

Lyakso, E., & Frolova, O. (2015B, September). Emotion state manifestation in voice features: chimpanzees, human infants, children, adults. In *International Conference on Speech and Computer* (pp. 201-208). Springer. 10.1007/978-3-319-23132-7_25

Maca, V. M. M., Espada, J. P., Diaz, V. G., & Semwal, V. B. (2016). Measurement of viewer sentiment to improve the quality of television and interactive content using adaptive content. *International conference on electrical, electronics, and optimization techniques*, 4445-4450.

Magudeeswaran, V., & Singh, J. F. (2017). Contrast limited fuzzy adaptive histogram equalization for enhancement of brain images. *International Journal of Imaging Systems and Technology, 27*(1), 98–103. doi:10.1002/ima.22214

Maimon, O. (2015). Ontology Learning from Text: Why the Ontology Learning Layer Cake is not Viable. *International Journal of Signs and Semiotic Systems, 4*(2), 1–14. doi:10.4018/IJSSS.2015070101

Maini, E., & Mazzocca, N. (2014, December). A compositional modeling approach for live migration in Software Defined Networks. In *Network of the Future (NOF), In Proceedings of the 2014 International Conference and Workshop on the* (pp. 1-6). IEEE.

Makhoul, J. (1975). Linear prediction: A tutorial review. *Proceedings of the IEEE, 63*(4), 561–580. doi:10.1109/PROC.1975.9792

Malhotra, R., & Chug, A. (2013). An empirical study to redefine the relationship between software design metrics and maintainability in high data intensive applications. In *Proceedings of the World Congress on Engineering and Computer Science* (Vol. 1). Academic Press.

Malhotra, R., & Jangra, R. (2015). Prediction & Assessment of Change Prone Classes Using Statistical & Machine Learning Techniques. Journal of Information Processing Systems, 1-26.

Malhotra, R., & Khanna, M. (2013). Investigation of relationship between object-oriented metrics and change proneness. *International Journal of Machine Learning and Cybernetics, 4*(4), 273–286. doi:10.100713042-012-0095-7

Malhotra, R., & Khanna, M. (2018). Prediction of change prone classes using evolution-based and object-oriented metrics. *Journal of Intelligent & Fuzzy Systems, 34*(3), 1755–1766. doi:10.3233/JIFS-169468

Malik, V., & Barde, C. R. (2015). Live migration of Virtual Machines in Cloud Environment using Prediction of CPU Usage. *International Journal of Computers and Applications, 117*(23).

Mallat, S. G. (1989). A theory for multiresolution signal decomposition: The wavelet representation. *IEEE Transactions on Pattern Analysis and Machine Intelligence, 11*(7), 674–693. doi:10.1109/34.192463

Mann, W. C., & Thompson, S. A. (1988). Rhetorical structure theory: Toward a functional theory of text organization. *Text-Interdisciplinary Journal for the Study of Discourse, 8*(3), 243–281. doi:10.1515/text.1.1988.8.3.243

Marée. (2005). *Automatic classification of images by decision tree.* Academic Press.

Mari Carmen Sua'rez-Figueroa, A. G.-P.-L. (2012). *The NeOn Methodology for Ontology. In Ontology Engineering in a Networked World.* Springer-Verlag Berlin Heidelberg. doi:10.1007/978-3-642-24794-1

Marie-Catherine de Marneffe, M. C. (2013). *More constructions, more genres: Extending Stanford Dependencies.* Academic Press.

Marius-Gabriel. (2016). *Semantically Enriching Content Using OpenCalais.* Thomsan Reuters.

Marneffe, M. (2015). *Stanford dependency parser.* Retrieved from nlp.stanford.edu/software/stanford-dependencies

Martin, D. J. (2015). *Speech and Language Processing.* Copyright.

Mata, F., & Claramunt, C. (2011). GeoST: Geographic, thematic and term-poral information retrieval from heterogeneous web data sources. In *Proceedings of the 10th International Conference on Web and Wireless Geographical Information Systems (W2GIS'11),* (pp. 5–20). Heidelberg, Germany: Springer.

Matthew, M. C., Laskey, K., McCabe, F., Brown, P., & Metz, R. (2005). *Reference Model for Service Oriented Architectures. Published on the internet.* OASIS Working Draft.

Medhi, S., & Bezboruah, T. (2014). Investigations on implementation of e-ATM Web Services based on. NET technique. *International Journal of Information Retrieval Research, 4*(2), 42–51. doi:10.4018/ijirr.2014040103

Medhi, S., Bora, A., & Bezboruah, T. (2017). Investigations On Some Aspects of Reliability of Content Based Routing SOAP based Windows Communication Foundation Services'. *International Journal of Information Retrieval Research, 7*(1), 17–31. doi:10.4018/IJIRR.2017010102

Medisp.bme.teiath.gr. (2018). Available at: http://medisp.bme.teiath.gr/hicl/Images/staining/HE.png

Meera, A., & Swamynathan, S. (2013). Agent based resource monitoring system in iaas cloud environment. *Procedia Technology, 10,* 200–207. doi:10.1016/j.protcy.2013.12.353

Menard, S. (2002). *Applied logistic regression analysis* (Vol. 106). Sage. doi:10.4135/9781412983433

Mendel, J., & John, R. (2002). Type-2 fuzzy sets made simple. *IEEE Transactions on Fuzzy Systems, 10*(2), 117–127. doi:10.1109/91.995115

Mercury LoadRunner. (n.d.). Available at: https://qageek.files.wordpress.com/2007/05/loadrunner_tutorial.pdf

Mihir Narayan Mohanty, H. K. P., & Chandra, M. (2014). Design of Neural Network Model for Emotional Speech Recognition. *Artificial Intelligence and Evolutionary Algorithms in Engineering Systems, 325,* 291–300.

Missikoff, A. D. (2016). A Lightweight Methodology for Rapid Ontology Engineering. *ACM, 59*(3), 79-86.

Mitchell, R. L. C. (2007). Age-related decline in the ability to decode emotional prosody: Primary or secondary phenomenon? *Cognition and Emotion, 21*(7), 1435–1454. doi:10.1080/02699930601133994

Mohanty, Routray, & Kabisatpathy. (2010, December). Voice Detection using Statistical Method. *Int. J. Engg. Techsci.*, 2(1), 120–124.

Mohanty, M. N., & Jena, B. (2011). Analysis of stressed human speech. *International Journal of Computational Vision and Robotics, 2*(2), 180–187. doi:10.1504/IJCVR.2011.042273

Mohanty, M. N., & Routray, A. (2014, December). Machine Learning Approach for Emotional Speech Classification. In *International Conference on Swarm, Evolutionary, and Memetic Computing* (pp. 490-501). Springer.

Mohanty, Mishra, & Routray. (2009). A Non-rigid Motion Estimation Algorithm for Yawn Detection in Human Drivers. *International Journal of Computational Vision and Robotics, 1*(1), 89–109.

Mokhtari, N., & Dieng-Kuntz, R. (2008). Extraction et exploitation des annotations contextuelles. In Proceedings of Extraction et gestion des connaissances (EGC'2008). Academic Press.

Monika Rani, A. K. (2017). *Ontology Learning Based on Topic Modeling*. Semi-Automatic Terminology.

Morales, M. R., & Levitan, R. (2016). Mitigating confounding factors in depression detection using an unsupervised clustering approach. *Proceedings of the 2016 Computing and Mental Health Workshop*.

Morris, M. R., & Horvitz, E. (2007). Search Together: An interface for collaborative Web Search. *Proceedings of the 20th annual ACM symposium on User interface software and technology.*

Morton, J. B., & Trehub, S. E. (2001). Children's understanding of emotion in speech. *Child Development, 72*(3), 834–843. doi:10.1111/1467-8624.00318 PMID:11405585

Munivar, P. (1991). *Nannool Kandikaiyurai-Ezhuthathikaram*. Chennai, India: Mullai Nilayam.

Naderi, H., Rumpler, B., & Pinon, J. M. (2007). An Efficient Collaborative Information Retrieval System by Incorporating the User Profile. In *Adaptive Multimedia Retrieval* (Vol. 4398, pp. 247–257). User, Context, and Feedback Lecture Notes in Computer Science. doi:10.1007/978-3-540-71545-0_19

Nagi, J., Sameem, A., Nagi, F., & Syed, K. (2011). *Automated breast profile segmentation for ROI detection using digital mammograms*. In *IEEE Biomedical Engineering and Sciences*. IECBES.

Nahm. (2004). *Doctoral Dissertation: Text mining with information extraction*. University of Texas at Austin.

Nallapati, R., Zhou, B., Santos, C. N., Gulcehre, C., & Xiang, B. (2016). Abstractive Text Summarization Using Sequence-to-Sequence RNNs and Beyond. ArXiv:1602.06023 [Cs]

Naouar, F., Hlaoua, L., & Omri, M. N. (2013a). Relevance Feedback for Collaborative Retrieval Based on Semantic Annotations. In *The International Conference on Information and Knowledge Engineering IKE'13,* (pp.54-60). Las Vegas, NV: Academic Press.

Naouar, F., Hlaoua, L., & Omri, M. N. (2015). Collaborative Information Retrieval Model Based on Fuzzy Confidence Network. Journal of Intelligent and Fuzzy Systems.

Naouar, F., Hlaoua, L., & Omri, M. N. (2017). Information retrieval model using uncertain confidence's network. International Journal of Information Retrieval Research, 7(2), 34-50. doi:10.4018/IJIRR.2017040103

Naouar, F., Hlaoua, L., & Omri, M. N. (2012). Possibilistic Model for Relevance Feedback in Collaborative Information Retrieval. *International Journal of Web Applications, IJWA, 4*(2), 78–86.

Naouar, F., Hlaoua, L., & Omri, M. N. (2013b). Relevance Feedback in Collaborative Information Retrieval based on Validated Annotation. *International Conference on Reasoning and Optimization in Information Systems ROIS'2013.*

Nathan, S., Kulkarni, P., & Bellur, U. (2013, April). Resource availability based performance benchmarking of virtual machine migrations. In *Proceedings of the 4th ACM/SPEC International Conference on Performance Engineering* (pp. 387-398). ACM. 10.1145/2479871.2479932

Navaneethakrishnan, S. C., & Parthasarathi, R. (2015). Building a Language-Independent Discourse Parser using Universal Networking Language. *Computational Intelligence, 31*(4), 593–618. doi:10.1111/coin.12037

Nayak, S., & Patel. (2015). A Survey on Load Balancing Algorithms in Cloud Computing and Proposed a model with Improved Throttled Algorithm. *International Journal for Scientific Research & Development, 3*(1).

Nematzadeh, H., Enayatifar, R., Mahmud, M., & Akbari, E. (2019). Frequency based feature selection method using whale algorithm. *Genomics.* doi:10.1016/j.ygeno.2019.01.006 PMID:30660788

Neto, J., Moreira, A., & Musicante, M. (2018). Semantic Web Services testing: A Systematic Mapping study. *Computer Science Review, 28*, 140–156. doi:10.1016/j.cosrev.2018.03.002

Niazalizadeh Moghadam, A., & Ravanmehr, R.. (2018, January). Multi-agent distributed data mining approach for classifying meteorology data: Case study on Iran's synoptic weather stations. *International Journal of Environmental Science and Technology, 15*(1), 149–158. doi:10.100713762-017-1351-x

Nishio, M., & Niimi, S. (2008). Changes in speaking fundamental frequency characteristics with aging. *Folia Phoniatrica et Logopaedica, 60*(3), 120–127. doi:10.1159/000118510 PMID:18305390

Nithya, R., & Santhi, B. (2011). *Comparative study on feature extraction method for breast cancer classification.* Academic Press.

Ntalampiras, S., & Fakotakis, N. (2012). Modelling the Temporal Evolution of Acoustic Parameters for Speech Emotion Recognition. *IEEE Transactions on Affective Computing, 3*(1), 116–125. doi:10.1109/T-AFFC.2011.31

Nwe, T. L., Foo, S. W., & De Silva, L. C. (2003). Speech emotion recognition using hidden Markov models. *Speech Communication, 41*(4), 603–623. doi:10.1016/S0167-6393(03)00099-2

Omri, M. N. (1994). *Système interactif flou d'aide à l'utilisation de dispositifs techniques: SIFADE* (PhD thesis). l'université Pierre et Marie Curie, Paris, France.

Omri, M. N. (2004). Pertinent Knowledge Extraction from a Semantic Network: Application of Fuzzy Sets Theory. *International Journal of Artificial Intelligence Tools, 13*(3), 705–719. doi:10.1142/S0218213004001752

Omri, M. N. (2012). Effects of Terms Recognition Mistakes on Requests Processing for Interactive Information Retrieval. *International Journal of Information Retrieval Research, 2*(3), 19–35. doi:10.4018/ijirr.2012070102

Pacifici, G., Spreitzer, M., Tantawi, A. N., & Youssef, A. (2005). Performance Management for Cluster-Based Web Services. *IEEE Journal on Selected Areas in Communications, 23*(12), 2333–2343. doi:10.1109/JSAC.2005.857208

Pal, D., Mitra, M., & Datta, K. (2014). Improving query expansion using WordNet. *Journal of the Association for Information Science and Technology, 65*(12), 2469–2478. doi:10.1002/asi.23143

Palo, H. K., & Sagar, S. (2018E, September). Comparison of Neural Network Models for Speech Emotion Recognition. In *2018 2nd International Conference on Data Science and Business Analytics (ICDSBA)* (pp. 127-131). IEEE. 10.1109/ICDSBA.2018.00030

Palo, H. K., Mohanty, M. N., & Chandra, M. (2016A). Sad state analysis of speech signals using different clustering algorithm. In *2016 2nd International Conference on Next Generation Computing Technologies (NGCT)* (pp. 714-718). IEEE. 10.1109/NGCT.2016.7877504

Palo, H. K., Mohanty, M. N., & Chandra, M. (2017A). Emotion Analysis from Speech of Different Age Groups. *Proceedings of the Second International Conference on Research in Intelligent and Computing in Engineering*, 283–287. 10.15439/2017R21

Palo, Mohanty, & Chandra. (2015). Novel Feature Extraction Technique for Child Emotion Recognition. In *International Conference on Electrical, Electronics, Signals, Communication and Optimization (EESCO)* (pp. 1848-1852). IEEE. 10.1109/EESCO.2015.7253839

Palo, H. K., Chandra, M., & Mohanty, M. N. (2017B). Emotion recognition using MLP and GMM for Oriya language. *International Journal of Computational Vision and Robotics*, 7(4), 426–442. doi:10.1504/IJCVR.2017.084987

Palo, H. K., Chandra, M., & Mohanty, M. N. (2018C). Recognition of Human Speech Emotion Using Variants of Mel-Frequency Cepstral Coefficients. In *Advances in Systems, Control and Automation* (pp. 491–498). Singapore: Springer. doi:10.1007/978-981-10-4762-6_47

Palo, H. K., & Mohanty, M. N. (2016). Modified-VQ Features for Speech Emotion Recognition. *Journal of Applied Sciences (Faisalabad)*, 16(9), 406–418. doi:10.3923/jas.2016.406.418

Palo, H. K., & Mohanty, M. N. (2016C). Performance analysis of emotion recognition from speech using combined prosodic features. *Advanced Science Letters*, 22(2), 288–293.

Palo, H. K., & Mohanty, M. N. (2017). *Wavelet based feature combination for recognition of emotions. Ain Shams Engineering Journal.*

Palo, H. K., & Mohanty, M. N. (2018A). Comparative analysis of neural networks for speech motion recognition. *IACSIT International Journal of Engineering and Technology*, 7(4), 112–116.

Palo, H. K., & Mohanty, M. N. (2018B). Wavelet based feature combination for recognition of emotions. *Ain Shams Engineering Journal*, 9(4), 1799–1806. doi:10.1016/j.asej.2016.11.001

Palo, H. K., Mohanty, M. N., & Chandra, M. (2015). Design of neural network model for emotional speech recognition. In *Artificial intelligence and evolutionary algorithms in engineering systems* (pp. 291–300). New Delhi: Springer. doi:10.1007/978-81-322-2135-7_32

Palo, H. K., Mohanty, M. N., & Chandra, M. (2015). *Statistical feature based child emotion analysis.* Academic Press.

Palo, H. K., Mohanty, M. N., & Chandra, M. (2015). Use of different features for emotion recognition using MLP network. In *Computational Vision and Robotics* (pp. 7–15). New Delhi: Springer. doi:10.1007/978-81-322-2196-8_2

Palo, H. K., Mohanty, M. N., & Chandra, M. (2018). Speech Emotion Analysis of Different Age Groups Using Clustering Techniques. *International Journal of Information Retrieval Research*, 8(1), 69–85. doi:10.4018/IJIRR.2018010105

Pan, Y., Shen, P., & Shen, L. (2012). Speech emotion recognition using support vector machine. *International Journal of Smart Home*, 6(2), 101–108.

Park, J. H., & Croft, W. B. (2015). Using key concepts in a translation model for retrieval. In *Proceedings of the 38th International ACM SIGIR Conference on Research and Development in Information Retrieval* (pp. 927-930). New York: ACM. 10.1145/2766462.2767768

Patel. N, H., & Shah. J. (2016). Improved Throttling Load Balancing Algorithm With Respect To Computing Cost and Throughput For Cloud Based Requests. *IJARIIE, 2*(3), 2192-2198.

Paxton, S., Peckham, M., & Adele, K. (2003). *The Leeds Histology Guide.* Academic Press.

Pedersen, T. S. P. (2004). WordNet: Similarity - Measuring the Relatedness of Concepts. In Human Language Technology Conference of the North American Chapter of the Association for Computational Linguistics Demonstrations (pp. 38-41). Boston: Academic Press.

Peiris, C., Mulder, D., Cicoria, S., Bahree, A., & Pathak, N. (2007). *Pro WCF: Practical Microsoft SOA Implementation.* Apress Press.

Pereira & Ramos . (2014). Segmentation and detection of breast cancer in mammograms combining wavelet analysis and genetic algorithm. *Marcelo Zanchetta do Nascimento., 114,* 88–101.

Pérez-Espinosa, H., Reyes-García, C. A., & Villaseñor-Pineda, L. (2011). EmoWisconsin: an emotional children speech database in Mexican Spanish. In *Affective Computing and Intelligent Interaction* (pp. 62–71). Berlin: Springer. doi:10.1007/978-3-642-24571-8_7

Perner, P. (2017). *Advances in Data Mining. Applications and Theoretical Aspects. 17th Industrial Conference, ICDM 2017,* New York, NY.

Polzehl, T., Schmitt, A., Metze, F., & Wagner, M. (2011). Anger recognition in speech using acoustic and linguistic cues. *Speech Communication, 53*(9-10), 1198–1209. doi:10.1016/j.specom.2011.05.002

Porat, R., Lange, D., & Zigel, Y. (2010). *Age recognition based on speech signals using weights super vector.* Interspeech.

Princeton University, . (2010). *About WordNet.* Princeton University.

Pritam, N., Khari, M., Kumar, R., Jha, S., Priyadarshini, I., Abdel-Basset, M., & Long, H. V. (2019). Assessment of Code Smell for Predicting Class Change Proneness using Machine Learning. *IEEE Access: Practical Innovations, Open Solutions, 7,* 37414–37425. doi:10.1109/ACCESS.2019.2905133

Pujol. (2009). Contribution à la classification sémantique d'imageAcademic Press..

Purcell, D. W., John, S. M., Schneider, B. A., & Picton, T. W. (2004). Human temporal auditory acuity as assessed by auditory steady state responses. *The Journal of the Acoustical Society of America, 116,* 3581–3593. doi:10.1121/1.1798354 PMID:15658709

Quatieri, T. F. (1996). *Discrete-Time Speech Signal Processing* (3rd ed.). Prentice-Hall.

Quinlan, R. (1988). Decision Trees and Multivalued Attributes. *Machine Intelligence,* (11), 305 – 318.

Quinlan, R. (1986). Induction of decision trees. *Machine Learning, 1*(1), 81–106. doi:10.1007/BF00116251

Quinlan, R. (1993). *C4.5: Programs for machine learning.* Morgan Kaufmann Publishers.

Radojevic, B., & Zagar, M. (2011). Analysis of issues with load balancing algorithms in hosted (cloud) environments. In *Proceedings of 34th International Convention on MIPRO.* IEEE.

Rahmani, M., Azadmanesh, A., & Siy, H. (2014). Architectural reliability analysis of framework-intensive applications: A web service case study. *Journal of Systems and Software, 94,* 186–201. doi:10.1016/j.jss.2014.03.070

Rahmati & Ayatollahi. (2009). Maximum Likelihood Active Contours Specialized for Mammography Segmentation. *Biomedical Engineering and Informatics. BMEI '09. 2nd International Conference.*

Ramakrishnan, S. (2012). Recognition of emotion from speech: A review. In *Speech Enhancement, Modeling and recognition-algorithms and Applications*. IntechOpen. doi:10.5772/39246

Ram, Palo, & Mohanty. (2013). Emotion Recognition with Speech for Call Centres using LPC and Spectral Analysis. *International Journal of Advanced Computer Research*, 3(11), 189–194.

Ram, R., Palo, H. K., Mohanty, M. N., & Suresh, L. P. (2016). Design of FIS-Based Model for Emotional Speech Recognition. *Proc. of the International Conference on Soft Computing Systems, Advances in Intelligent Systems and Computing*, 77-88. 10.1007/978-81-322-2671-0_8

Rao, V. S. (n.d.). Multi Agent-Based Distributed Data Mining: An Over View. *Lecture Notes in Computer Science, 10357.*

Rastogi, G., & Sushil, R. (2016). Performance Analysis of Live and Offline VM Migration Using KVM. *International Journal of Modern Education and Computer Science*, 8(11), 50–57. doi:10.5815/ijmecs.2016.11.07

Rathina, X. A., Mehata, K. M., & Ponnavaikko, M. (2012). Basic analysis on prosodic features in emotional speech. *International Journal of Computer Science Engineering and Applications*, 2(4), 99.

Rathore, N., & Chana, I. (2014). Load balancing and job migration techniques in grid: A survey of recent trends. *Wireless Personal Communications*, 79(3), 2089–2125. doi:10.100711277-014-1975-9

Ravi Kumar, G., Ramachandra, G. A., & Nagamani, K. (2014). An Efficient Feature Selection System to Integrating SVM with Genetic Algorithm for Large Medical Datasets. *International Journal of Advanced Research in Computer Science and Software Engineering*, 4(2).

Reynolds, D. A., & Rose, R. C. (1995, January). Robust Text-Independent Speaker Identification Using Gaussian Mixture Speaker Models. *IEEE Transactions on Speech and Audio Processing*, 3(1), 72–83. doi:10.1109/89.365379

Rizwan, M., Waseem, S., & Ejaz, A. (2017). Maximum Relevancy Minimum Redundancy Based Feature Subset Selection using Ant Colony Optimization. *Journal of Applied Environmental and Biological Sciences*, 7(4), 118–130.

Robertson, S. E., & Walker, S. (1997). On relevance weights with little relevance information. In *20th annual international ACM SIGIR conference on Research and development in information retrieval*, (pp. 16–24). ACM Press. 10.1145/258525.258529

Robertson, S. E., & Jones, K. S. (1976). Relevance weighting of search terms. *Journal of the American Society for Information Science*, 27(3), 129–146. doi:10.1002/asi.4630270302

Rocchio, J. (1971). Relevance feedback in information retrieval. In The SMART retrieval system-experiments in automatic document processing. Prentice Hall Inc.

Rocchio, J. J. (1971). Relevance feedback in information retrieval. In G. Salton (Ed.), *The Smart retrieval system - experiments in automatic document processing* (pp. 313–323). Englewood Cliffs, NJ: Prentice-Hall.

Rodrıguez-Aranda, C., & Jakobsen, M. (2011). Differential contribution of cognitive and psychomotor functions to the age-related slowing of speech production. *Journal of the International Neuropsychological Society, 17*, 1–15.

Romano, D., & Pinzger, M. (2011, September). Using source code metrics to predict change-prone java interfaces. In *Software Maintenance (ICSM), 2011 27th IEEE International Conference on* (pp. 303-312). IEEE. 10.1109/ICSM.2011.6080797

Ronan Collobert, P. K. (2011). Natural Language Processing (Almost) from Scratch. *Journal of Machine Learning Research, 12*, 2461–2505.

Ronen, M., & Jacob, Z. (2004). Using simulated annealing to optimize feature selection problem in marketing applications. *European Journal of Operational Research*, 171(3), 842–858.

Rotithor, H. G. (1994). Taxonomy of dynamic task scheduling schemes in distributed computing systems. *Proceeding of IEEE -Computers and Digital Techniques, 141*(1), 1-10.

Rouse & Hemami. (n.d.). The Role of edge information to estimate the perceived utility of natural images. Visual Communications Lab, School of Electrical and Computer Engineering. *Cornell University.*

Ruthven, I., & Lalmas, M. (2003). A survey on the use of relevance feedback for information access systems. *The Knowledge Engineering Review, 18*(2), 95–145. doi:10.1017/S0269888903000638

Ryan, M., Murray, J., & Ruffman, T. (2010). Aging and the perception of emotion: Processing vocal expressions alone and with faces. *Experimental Aging Research, 36*(1), 1–22. doi:10.1080/03610730903418372 PMID:20054724

Saddik, A. E. (2006). Performance measurement of Web Service based application. *IEEE Transactions on Instrumentation and Measurement, 55*(5), 1599–1605. doi:10.1109/TIM.2006.880288

Safi, H. (2014). AXON: Un Système de RI Personnalisée dans des Textes Arabes basée sur le profil utilisateur et l'expansion de requêtes. *Proceedings of CORIA 2014.*

Samal, Parida, Satpathy, & Mohanty. (2014). On the use of MFCC Feature Vectors Clustering for Efficient Text Dependent Speaker Recognition. Advances in Intelligence System and Computing Series, 247, 305-312.

Sammy, K., Shengbing, R., & Wilson, C. (2012). Energy efficient security preserving vm live migration in data centers for cloud computing. *IJCSI International Journal of Computer Science Issues, 9*(2), 1694–0814.

Sangam, S., & Shinde, S. (2019). Most Persistent Feature Selection Method for Opinion Mining of Social Media Reviews. Information and Communication Technology for Competitive Strategies, 213 – 221.

Sant'Ana, R., & Rosângela, C. A. A. (2006, May). Text-Independent Speaker Recognition Based on the Hurst Parameter and the Multidimensional Fractional Brownian Motion Model, IEEE Transactions on Audio. *Speech And Language Processing, 14*(3), 931–940. doi:10.1109/TSA.2005.858054

Saranya, R., & Bharathi Ph, M. D. (2014). Automatic Detection and Classification of Microcalcification on Mammographic Images. *IOSR Journal of Electronics and Communication Engineering, 9*(3), 65-71.

Saraswathi, A. T., Kalaashri, Y. R. A., & Padmavathi, S. (2015). Dynamic resource allocation scheme in cloud computing. *Procedia Computer Science, 47*, 30–36. doi:10.1016/j.procs.2015.03.180

Sauter, D. A., Eisner, F., Calder, A. J., & Scott, S. K. (2010). Perceptual cues in nonverbal vocal expressions of emotion. *Quarterly Journal of Experimental Psychology, 63*(11), 2251–2272. doi:10.1080/17470211003721642 PMID:20437296

Schenkel, R., & Thbobald, M. (2005). Relevance Feedback for Structural Query Expansion. In INEX 2005 Workshop Pre-Proceedings (pp. 260-272). Academic Press.

Scholkopfand, B. A., & Smola, J. (2002). *Learning with Kernels.* MIT Press.

Schuller, B., Batliner, A., Seppi, D., Steidl, S., Vogt, T., Wagner, J., ... Aharonson, V. (2007). The relevance of feature type for the automatic classification of emotional user states: low level descriptors and functionals. *Eighth Annual Conference of the International Speech Communication Association.*

Seehapoch, T., & Wongthanavasu, S. (2013, January). Speech emotion recognition using support vector machines. In *2013 5th international conference on Knowledge and smart technology (KST)* (pp. 86-91). IEEE. 10.1109/KST.2013.6512793

Seki, Y. (2002). *Sentence Extraction by tf/idf and Position Weighting from Newspaper Articles.* Academic Press.

Shah, C., Marchionini, G., & Kelly, D. (2009). Learning Design Principles for a Collaborative Information Seeking System. In *Proceedings of ACM SIGCHI Conference 2009*. Boston, MA: ACM. 10.1145/1520340.1520496

Shahzad, W. (2010). Classification and Associative Classification Rule Discovery Using Ant Colony Optimization, these. Islamabad, Pakistan: Academic Press.

Shami, M., & Verhelst, W. (2007). Automatic classification of expressiveness in speech: a multi-corpus study. In *Speaker classification II* (pp. 43–56). Berlin: Springer. doi:10.1007/978-3-540-74122-0_5

Shamir, L., Orlov, N., Eckley, D. M., Macura, T. J., & Goldberg, I. G. (2008). IICBU 2008: A proposed benchmark suite for biological image analysis. *Medical & Biological Engineering & Computing, 46*(9), 943–947. doi:10.100711517-008-0380-5 PMID:18668273

Sheikhan, M., Bejani, M., & Gharavian, D. (2012). *Modular neural-SVM scheme for speech emotion recognition using ANOVA feature selection method. In Neural Comput & Applic.* Springer-Verlag London. doi:10.100700521-012-0814-8

Sheldon, S., Pichora-Fuller, M. K., & Schneider, B. A. (2008). Effect of age, presentation method, and learning on identification of noise-vocoded words. *The Journal of the Acoustical Society of America, 123*(1), 476–488. doi:10.1121/1.2805676 PMID:18177175

Shoaih, M., & Shah, A. A. (2006). *A new indexing technique for information retrieval systems using rhetorical structure theory.* RST.

Shooman, M. L. (2002). *Reliability of Computer Systems and Networks: Fault Tolerance, Analysis, and Design.* New York: John Wiley & Sons. doi:10.1002/047122460X

Sim, K. M. (2012). Agent-based cloud computing. *IEEE Transactions on Services Computing, 5*(4), 564–577. doi:10.1109/TSC.2011.52

Singh & Gupta. (2015). A Novel Approach for Breast Cancer Detection and Segmentation in a Mammogram. Eleventh International Multi-Conference on Information Processing-2015.

Singh, J., & Sharan, A. (2015). Information retrieval. Context Window Based Co-occurrence Approach for Improving Feedback Based Query Expansion in Information Retrieval. International Journal of Information Retrieval Research, 5(4), 31-45.

Singh, A., Juneja, D., & Malhotra, M. (2015). Autonomous agent based load balancing algorithm in cloud computing. *Procedia Computer Science, 45*, 832–841. doi:10.1016/j.procs.2015.03.168

Singh, J., & Sharan, A. (2015). Context window based co-occurrence approach for improving feedback based query expansion in information retrieval. *International Journal of Information Retrieval Research, 5*(4), 31–45. doi:10.4018/IJIRR.2015100103

Singh, J., & Sharan, A. (2017). A new fuzzy logic-based query expansion model for efficient information retrieval using relevance feedback approach. *Neural Computing & Applications, 28*(9), 2557–2580. doi:10.100700521-016-2207-x

Sivanandam, S. N., & Deepa, S. N. (2011). *Principles of Soft Computing* (2nd ed.). Wiley India.

Skoog Waller, S., Eriksson, M., & Sörqvist, P. (2015). Can you hear my age? Influences of speech rate and speech spontaneity on estimation of speaker age. *Frontiers in Psychology, 6*, 978. doi:10.3389/fpsyg.2015.00978 PMID:26236259

Slaney, M., & McRoberts, G. (2003). BabyEars: A recognition system for affective vocalizations. *Speech Communication, 39*(3-4), 367–384. doi:10.1016/S0167-6393(02)00049-3

Smart, C. R., Hendrick, R. E., Rutledge, J. H., & Smith, R. A. (1995). Benefit of mammography screening in women ages 40 to 49 years: Current evidence from randomized controlled trials. *Cancer, 75*(7), 1619–1626. doi:10.1002/1097-0142(19950401)75:7<1619::AID-CNCR2820750711>3.0.CO;2-T PMID:8826919

Smruti, S., Sahoo, J., Dash, M., & Mohanty, M. N. (2015). An approach to design an intelligent parametric synthesizer for emotional speech. In *Proceedings of the 3rd International Conference on Frontiers of Intelligent Computing: Theory and Applications (FICTA) 2014* (pp. 367-374). Springer. 10.1007/978-3-319-12012-6_40

SOAP. (n.d.). Available at http://www.w3.org/TR/soap12-part1/]

Soares, F. M., & Souza, A. M. F. (2016). *Neural network programming with Java: unleash the power of neural networks by implementing professional Java code.* Birmingham, UK: Packt Publishing.

Sourish Dasgupta, A. P. (2018). *Formal Ontology Learning from English IS-A Sentences.* arXiv:1802.03701v1 [cs.AI]

Souza, P. E., & Boike, K. T. (2006). Combining temporal-envelope cues across channels: Effects of age and hearing loss. *Journal of Speech, Language, and Hearing Research: JSLHR, 49*(1), 138–149. doi:10.1044/1092-4388(2006/011) PMID:16533079

Sripada, S., & Jagarlamudi, J. (2009). Summarization Approaches Based on Document Probability Distributions. *Proceedings of the 23rd Pacific Asia Conference on Language, Information and Computation,* 521–529.

Srivenkatesha Subba Yajva Shastri. (1934). *Bhatta Deepika with Bhatta Chintamani Commentary by Vancheshwara.* Chennai: Madras Law Journal Press.

Stephen Roller, D. K. (2018). Hearst Patterns Revisited:Automatic Hypernym Detection from Large Text Corpora. In *Proceedings of the 56th Annual Meeting of the Association for Computational Linguistics (Short Papers)* (pp. 358–363). Melbourne, Australia: Academic Press.

Subalalith1a, C. N., & Parthasarathi, R. (2017). Query Focused Summary Generation System using Unique Discourse Structure. International Journal of Information Retrieval Research, 7(1), 49-69.

Subalalitha, C. N., & Parthasarathi, R. (2012). An approach to discourse parsing using sangati and rhetorical structure theory. In *Proceedings of the Workshop on Machine Translation and Parsing in Indian Languages* (pp. 73-82). Academic Press.

Subalalitha, C. N., & Ranjani, P. (2013). A Unique Indexing Technique for Indexing Discourse Structures. *Journal of Intelligent Systems., 23*(3), 231–243.

Subalalitha, C. N., & Ranjani, P. (2014). A Unique Indexing Technique for Discourse Structures. *Journal of Intelligent Systems, 23*(3), 231–243. doi:10.1515/jisys-2013-0034

Subanya, B., & Rajalaxmi, R. (2014). A Novel Feature Selection Algorithm for Heart Disease Classification. *International Journal of Computational Intelligence and Informatic, 4*(2).

Subramaniam, L. V., Roy, S., Faruquie, T. A., & Negi, S. (2009). A survey of types of text noise and techniques to handle noisy text. In *Proceedings of the 3rd Workshop on Analytics for Noisy Unstructured Text Data* (pp. 115-122). New York: ACM. 10.1145/1568296.1568315

Suckling, J. (1994). The mammographic image analysis society digital mammogram database, Exerpta Medica. *International Congress Series, 1069,* 375–378.

Sun, H. M. (2010). A study of the features of internet English from the linguistic perspective. *Studies in Literature and Language, 1*(7), 98–103.

Suresh Kumar, G. Z. (2015). Concept relation extraction using Naïve Bayes classifier for ontology-based question answering systems. Journal of King Saud University – Computer and Information Sciences, 13–24.

Tabár, L., Fagerberg, C. J., Gad, A., Baldetorp, L., Holmberg, L. H., Gröntoft, O., ... Eklund, G. (1985, April 13). Reduction in mortality from breast cancer after mass screening with mammography. *Lancet, 1*(8433), 829–832. doi:10.1016/S0140-6736(85)92204-4 PMID:2858707

Taher, R. (2004). Soutien Personnalisé pour la Recherche d'Information Collaborative. In *2ème Congrès MAJECSTIC 2004*. Manifestation de JEunes Chercheurs Sciences et Technologies de l'Information et de la Communication.

Tamine, L., Boughanem, M., & Daoud, M. (2010). Evaluation of contextual information retrieval effectiveness: Overview of issues and research. *Journal of Knowledge and Information Systems, 24*(1), 1–34. doi:10.100710115-009-0231-1

Tang, X., Dai, Y., & Xiang, Y. (2019). Feature selection based on feature interactions with application to text categorization. *Expert Systems with Applications, 120*, 207–216. doi:10.1016/j.eswa.2018.11.018

Tanner, D. C., & Tanner, M. E. (2004). *Forensic aspects of speech patterns: voice prints, speaker profiling, lie and intoxication detection.* Lawyers & Judges Publishing.

Tan, X. J.-H. (2010, January). CRCTOL: A semantic-based domain ontology learning system. *Journal of the American Society for Information Science and Technology, 61*(1), 150–168. doi:10.1002/asi.21231

Thierry, P., Horacio, S., Jakub, P., & Roman, Y. (2013). *Multi-source. In Multilingual Information Extraction and Summarization. Theory and Applications of Natural Language Processing* (pp. 27–28). Springer Publishing Company.

Tizhoosh, H. R., & Fochem, M. (1995). Image Enhancement with Fuzzy Histogram Hyperbolization. Proceedings of EUFIT'95, 3, 1695 - 1698.

Tizhoosh, H. (2005). Image thresholding using type II fuzzy sets. *Pattern Recognition, 38*(12), 2363–2372. doi:10.1016/j.patcog.2005.02.014

Tizhoosh, H. R., Krell, G., & Michaelis, B. (1997). Locally adaptive fuzzy image enhancement. In B. Reusch (Ed.), Lecture Notes in Computer Science: Vol. 1226. *Computational Intelligence Theory and Applications. Fuzzy Days 1997.* Berlin: Springer.

Tolkmitt, F. J., & Scherer, K. R. (1986). Effect of experimentally induced stress on vocal parameters. *Journal of Experimental Psychology. Human Perception and Performance, 12*(3), 302–313. doi:10.1037/0096-1523.12.3.302 PMID:2943858

Torres, M., & Juan, M. (2014). Automatic Text Summarization. doi:10.1002/9781119004752.fmatter

Trabelsi, I., Ayed, D. B., & Ellouze, N. (2016). Comparison between GMM-SVM sequence kernel and GMM: Application to speech emotion recognition. *Journal of Engineering Science and Technology, 11*(9), 1221–1233.

Uchida, H., Zhu, M., & Della Senta, T. (1999). *A gift for a millennium.* Tokyo: IAS/UNU.

Udhan, T. (2016). Emotion Recognition using Fuzzy Clustering Analysis. Georgia Southern University.

Upadhyay, A., & Lakkadwala, P. (2015, September). Migration of over loaded process and schedule for resource utilization in Cloud Computing. In *Proceedings of the Reliability, Infocom Technologies and Optimization (ICRITO)(Trends and Future Directions), 2015 4th International Conference on* (pp. 1-4). IEEE. 10.1109/ICRITO.2015.7359325

Vanderwende, L., Suzuki, H., Brockett, C., & Nenkova, A. (2007). Beyond SumBasic: Task-focused summarization with sentence simplification and lexical expansion. *Information Processing & Management, 43*(6), 1606–1618. doi:10.1016/j.ipm.2007.01.023

Verma, D., & Mukhopadhyay, D. (2016, April). Age driven automatic speech emotion recognition system. In *2016 International Conference on Computing, Communication and Automation (ICCCA)* (pp. 1005-1010). IEEE. 10.1109/CCAA.2016.7813862

Ververidis, D., & Kotropolos, C. (2004, May). Automatic emotional speech classification. *Proceedings of the IEEE International Conference on Acoustics, Speech, and Signal Processing, 1*, 593–596.

Ververidis, D., & Kotropoulos, C. (2006). Emotional speech recognition: Resources, features, and methods. *Speech Communication, 48*(9), 1162–1181. doi:10.1016/j.specom.2006.04.003

Vetterli, M., & Herley, C. (1992). Wavelets and filter banks: Theory and design. *IEEE Trans. Signal Processing, 40*, 2207–2232.

Vinothina, V., Sridaran, R., & Ganapathi, P. (2012). A survey on resource allocation strategies in cloud computing. *International Journal of Advanced Computer Science and Applications, 3*(6), 97–104. doi:10.14569/IJACSA.2012.030616

Vogt, T., & André, E. (2005, July). Comparing feature sets for acted and spontaneous speech in view of automatic emotion recognition. In *2005 IEEE International Conference on Multimedia and Expo* (pp. 474-477). IEEE. 10.1109/ICME.2005.1521463

Wan, J. B. (2011). *A New Semantic Model for Domain-Ontology Learning.* Springer-Verlag Berlin Heidelberg.

Wang, G., & Song, Q. (2012). Selecting Feature Subset via Constraint Association Rules. Advances in Knowledge Discovery and Data Mining. doi:10.1007/978-3-642-30220-6_26

Wang, H., Fan, H., Li, J., & Wang, J. (2014). Research on the method of semantic query expansion in civil aviation emergency domain ontology. International Journal of Digital Content Technology and its Applications, 8(5), 128.

Wang, K., Zhu, Z., Wang, S., Sun, X., & Li, L. (2016, June). A database for emotional interactions of the elderly. In *2016 IEEE/ACIS 15th International Conference on Computer and Information Science (ICIS)* (pp. 1-6). IEEE. 10.1109/ICIS.2016.7550902

Wang, L., & Ling, W. (2016). *Neural network-based abstract generation for opinions and arguIments.* arXiv preprint arXiv:1606.02785

Wang, Y., & Ma, L. (2009). Feature selection for medical dataset using rough set theory. In *Proceedings of 3rd WSEAS international conference on Computer engineering and applications,* (pp. 68 – 72). Academic Press.

Wen, H., Qi, W., & Shuang, L. (2016). Medical X-Ray Image Enhancement Based on Wavelet Domain Homomorphic Filtering and CLAHE. *2016 International Conference On Robots & Intelligent System (ICRIS)*, 249-254. 10.1109/ICRIS.2016.50

Wickremasinghe, B., Calheiros, R. N., & Buyya, R. (2010, April). Cloudanalyst: A CloudSim-based visual modeller for analysing cloud computing environments and applications. In *Proceeding of Advanced Information Networking and Applications (AINA), 2010 24th IEEE International Conference* (pp. 446-452). IEEE.

Wilkie, F. G., & Kitchenham, B. A. (2000). Coupling measures and change ripples in C++ application software. *Journal of Systems and Software, 52*(2), 157–164. doi:10.1016/S0164-1212(99)00142-9

Williams, H. E., & Zobel, J. (2005). Searchable words on the web. *International Journal on Digital Libraries, 5*(2), 99–105. doi:10.100700799-003-0050-z

Winkler, R. (2007). Influences of pitch and speech rate on the perception of age from voice. *Proc. of ICPhS*, 1849-1852.

Wirth, M., & Nikitenko, D. (2005). *Suppression of stripe artifacts in mammograms using weighted median filtering.* Springer Link. doi:10.1007/11559573_117

Wosiak, A., & Zakrzewska, D. (2014). Feature Selection for Classification Incorporating Less Meaningful Attributes in Medical Diagnostics. In *Proceedings of the 2014 Federated Conference on Computer Science and Information Systems,* (pp.235–240). Academic Press. 10.15439/2014F296

WSDL. (n.d.). Available at http://www.w3.org/TR/wsdl20-primer/

Wu, S., Falk, T. H., & Chan, W. Y. (2011). Automatic speech emotion recognition using modulation spectral features. *Speech Communication, 53*(5), 768–785. doi:10.1016/j.specom.2010.08.013

Xiang, B., & Berger, T. (2003, September). Efficient Text-Independent Speaker Verification with Structural Gaussian Mixture Models and Neural Network. *IEEE Transactions on Acoustics, Speech, and Signal Processing, 11*(5), 447–456.

Xianqin, C., & Xiaopeng, G. (2012). Application-Transparent Live Migration for Virtual Machine on Network Security Enhanced Hypervisor. *China Communications.*

Xiao, Z., Jiang, J., Zhu, Y., Ming, Z., Zhong, S., & Cai, S. (2015). A solution of dynamic VMs placement problem for energy consumption optimization based on evolutionary game theory. *Journal of Systems and Software, 101,* 260–272. doi:10.1016/j.jss.2014.12.030

Xie, H., Zhang, Y., Tan, J., Guo, L., & Li, J. (2014). Contextual query expansion for image retrieval. *IEEE Transactions on Multimedia, 16*(4), 1104–1114. doi:10.1109/TMM.2014.2305909

Xu, Z., Han, J., & Bhuyan, L. (2007, April). Scalable and Decentralized Content-Aware Dispatching in Web Clusters. In *Proceedings of the Performance, Computing, and Communications Conference, 2007. IPCCC 2007. IEEE International* (pp. 202-209). IEEE. 10.1109/PCCC.2007.358896

Xu, B., Lin, H., & Lin, Y. (2016). Assessment of learning to rank methods for query expansion. *Journal of the Association for Information Science and Technology, 67*(6), 1345–1357. doi:10.1002/asi.23476

Xue, S. A., & Hao, G. J. (2003). Changes in the human vocal tract due to aging and the acoustic correlates of speech production: A pilot study. *Journal of Speech, Language, and Hearing Research: JSLHR, 46*(3), 689–701. doi:10.1044/1092-4388(2003/054) PMID:14696995

Yacoub, S., Simske, S., Lin, X., & Burns, J. (2003). Recognition of emotions in interactive voice response systems. *Proceeding of European conference on speech communication and technology,* 729–732.

Yadav, G., Maheshwari, S., & Agarwal, A. (2014). Contrast limited adaptive histogram equalization based enhancement for real time video system. *2014 International Conference on Advances in Computing, Communications and Informatics (ICACCI),* 2392-2397. 10.1109/ICACCI.2014.6968381

Yamada, T., Suzuki, K., & Ninagawa, C. (2018). Scalability Analysis of Aggregation Web Services for Smart Grid Fast Automated Demand Response. *2018 IEEE International Conference on Industrial Technology (ICIT).* 10.1109/ICIT.2018.8352363

Yang, C. T., Liu, Y. T., Liu, J. C., Chuang, C. L., & Jiang, F. C. (2013, December). Implementation of a cloud iaas with dynamic resource allocation method using openstack. In *Proceedings of the Parallel and Distributed Computing, Applications and Technologies (PDCAT), 2013 International Conference on* (pp. 71-78). IEEE. 10.1109/PDCAT.2013.18

Yang, B., & Lugger, M. (2010). Emotion recognition from speech signals using New Harmony features. *Signal Processing, 90*(5), 1415–1423. doi:10.1016/j.sigpro.2009.09.009

Ye, Z., Zhou, X., & Bouguettaya, A. (2011, April). Genetic algorithm based QoS-aware service compositions in cloud computing. In *International Conference on Database Systems for Advanced Applications* (pp. 321-334). Springer. 10.1007/978-3-642-20152-3_24

Yong Nahm, U., & Raymond, J. (2002). *Text Mining with Information Extraction. In Mooney Department of Computer Sciences* (p. 2). Austin, TX: University of Texas.

Yue, Lu., & Minh, N. (2006). A new contourlet transform with sharp frequency localization. *Proc. of IEEE International Conference on Image Processing.*

Yusra, Al-Najjar, & Soong. (2012). Comparison of Image Quality Assessment:PSNR, HVS, SSIM, UIQI. *International Journal of Scientific & Engineering Research, 3*(8).

Zadeh, L. (1965). Fuzzy sets. *Information and Control, 8*(3), 338–353. doi:10.1016/S0019-9958(65)90241-X

Zadeh, L. A. (1975). The concept of a linguistic variable and its application to approximate reasoningâ€"I. *Information Sciences, 8*(3), 199–249. doi:10.1016/0020-0255(75)90036-5

Zão, L., Cavalcante, D., & Coelho, R. (2014). Time-Frequency Feature and AMS-GMM Mask for Acoustic Emotion Classification. *IEEE Signal Processing Letters, 21*(5), 620–624. doi:10.1109/LSP.2014.2311435

Zaw, E. P., & Thein, N. L. (2012). Improved live VM migration using LRU and splay tree algorithm. *International Journal of Computer Science and Telecommunications, 3*(3), 1–7.

Zbancioc, M., & Ferarua, M. (2012). *A Study about the Statistical Parameters Used in the Emotion Recognition.* In 11th International Conference on development and application systems, Suceava, Romania.

Zeng, Z., Pantic, M., Roisman, G. I., & Huang, T. S. (2009). A survey of affect recognition methods: Audio, visual, and spontaneous expressions. *IEEE Transactions on Pattern Analysis and Machine Intelligence, 31*(1), 39–58.

Zhang, Q., Cheng, L., & Boutaba, R. (2010). Cloud computing: State-of-the-art and research challenges. *Journal of Internet Services and Applications, 1*(1), 7–18. doi:10.100713174-010-0007-6

Zhang, Y., Tomuro, N., Furst, J., & Stan Raicu, D. (2010). *A Contour-based Mass Segmentation in Mammograms.* Scientific Commons.

Zhang, Z., & Fan, W. (2008). Stochastics and Statistics Web server load balancing: A queueing analysis. *European Journal of Operational Research, 186*, 681–693. doi:10.1016/j.ejor.2007.02.011

Zhao, Z., & Zhou, Y. (2016) PLIP based unsharp masking for medical image enhancement. *2016 IEEE International Conference on Acoustics, Speech and Signal Processing (ICASSP).* 10.1109/ICASSP.2016.7471874

Zheng, L., Wang, H., & Gao, S. (2018). Sentimental feature selection for sentiment analysis of Chinese online reviews. *International Journal of Machine Learning and Cybernetics, 9*(1), 75–84. doi:10.100713042-015-0347-4

Zhou, B., Zhang, Q., Shi, Q., Yang, Q., Yang, P., & Yu, Y. (2017). Measuring webservice security in the era of Internet of Things. *Computers & Electrical Engineering*, 1–11. doi:10.1016/j.compeleceng.2017.06.020

Zhou, Y., Leung, H., & Xu, B. (2009). Examining the potentially confounding effect of class size on the associations between object-oriented metrics and change-proneness. *Software Engineering. IEEE Transactions on, 35*(5), 607–623.

Zhu, X., Song, Q., & Sun, Z. (2013). Automated identification of change-prone classes in open source software projects. *Journal of Software, 8*(2), 361–366. doi:10.4304/jsw.8.2.361-366

Zingla, M. A., Latiri, C., Mulhem, P., Berrut, C., & Slimani, Y. (2018). Hybrid query expansion model for text and microblog information retrieval. *Information Retrieval Journal, 21*(4), 337–367. doi:10.100710791-017-9326-6

Zouaq, A., Gasevic, D., & Hatala, M. (2011). Towards open ontology learning and filtering. *Information Systems, 36*(7), 1064–1081. doi:10.1016/j.is.2011.03.005

About the Contributors

Muhammad Sarfraz is a Professor and Director of MSIT in the Department of Information Science, Kuwait University, Kuwait. His research interests include Computer Graphics, Pattern Recognition, Computer Vision, Image Processing, Soft Computing, Data Science, Intelligent Systems, Information Technology and Information Systems. He is currently working on various projects related to academia and industry. Prof. Sarfraz has been keynote/invited speaker at various platforms around the globe. He has advised/supervised more than 85 students for their MSc and PhD theses. He has published more than 350 publications as journal and conference papers. His publications include around 60 Books as Autor and Editor. He is also Editor of Proceeding Books of various Conferences around the globe. Prof. Sarfraz is member of various professional societies including IEEE, ACM, IFAC, IVS, INSTICC and ISOSS. He is a Chair, member of the International Advisory Committees and Organizing Committees of various international conferences, Symposiums and Workshops. He is also Editor-in-Chief, Editor and Guest Editor of various International Journals. He is the reviewer, for many international Journals, Conferences, meetings, and workshops around the world. He has achieved various awards in education, research, and administrative services.

* * *

Amita Arora is presently working as an Assistant Professor at Department of Computer Engineering in JC Bose University of Science and Technology, YMCA, Faridabad. She has twelve years of experience in teaching. She has supervised Nine M. Tech. Thesis. Her current research interests are Semantic Web, Information Retrieval, Natural language Processing. She has been teaching subjects like Analysis and Design of Algorithm, Compiler Design, Computer Graphics. She has published Ten articles in International/National Journals and Conferences.

Debasis Behera has completed his M-Tech in Enginerring and presently pursuing his Ph. D. from V.S.S.U.T. burla, Odisha, India. He has been working as an Assistant Professor in the Department of Electronics and Communication Engineering, C. V. Raman College of Engineering, Khorda, Odisha, India. He is having 14 years of experience in teaching to both undergraduate and post graduate students. His area of interest is VLSI, Signal Processing and Internet of Things.

Tulshi Bezboruah (M'12) received the B.Sc. degree in physics with electronics from the University of Dibrugarh, Dibrugarh, India, in 1990, and the M.Sc. and Ph.D. degrees in electronics and radio physics from the University of Gauhati, Guwahati, India, in 1993 and 1999, respectively. In 2000, he joined in the Department of Electronics Science, Gauhati University, as a Lecturer. He is currently the Professor & Head, Department of Electronics and Communication Technology, Gauhati University. His current research interests include instrumentation and control, distributed computing, and computer networks. Prof. Bezboruah is a member of the IEEE Geoscience and Remote Sensing Society as well as an Associate Member of the International Center for Theoretical Physics, Trieste, Italy.

Abhijit Bora, Department of Electronics and Communication Technology, Gauhati University, India received Master of Computer Applications (MCA) degree from Jorhat Engineering College (Under Dibrugarh University), India in 2008 and Ph.D degree from University of Gauhati in the year 2017. His research interests include web service, web security and software engineering.

Dibya Bora, PhD in Computer Science, Master of Science in Information Technology (University 1st Rank Holder, B.U., Bhopal), B.Sc. Honors in Mathematics (University Distinction Holder, Dibrugarh University, Assam). Actively involved in Image Processing And Machine Learning Research. Google Scholar: https://scholar.google.co.in/citations?user=FY7bIDsAAAAJ&hl=en. Research Gate: https://www.researchgate.net/profile/Dibya_Bora4.

Deepa Bura received her B.E. degree in Electronics & Communication Engineering from Maharishi Dayanand University, Rohtak, India. She completed her M.Tech. in Information Technology from Guru Gobind Singh Indraprastha University, Delhi, India. She has done Ph.D. degree from Uttarakhand Technical University, Dehradun, India. Her field of research includes Software Engineering, Database systems and Datawarehouse and data mining. She is working as Assistant Professor in Manav Rachna International Institute of Research & Studies, India. She has published many papers in reputed national and international journals.

Subalalitha C. N. is working as An Associate Professor at SRM Institute of Science and Technology. Their area of expertise is Natural Language Processing.

Imane Chakour is a PhD student within the Moroccan faculty of Sultan Moulay Slimane University.

Amit Choudhary is currently working as an Associate Professor and Head in the Department of Computer Science at Maharaja Surajmal Institute, New Delhi, India for the last 11 years. He has done MCA, M.Tech and M.Phil in Computer science and doctoral degree in Computer Science and Engineering from M. D. University, Rohtak, India. His research interest is focused on Machine Learning, Pattern Recognition and Artificial Intelligence. He has many international publications to his credit.

Habiba Drias received the M.S. degree in computer science from CWRU Cleveland OHIO USA in 1984 and the Ph.D. degree in computer science from USTHB, Algiers, Algeria in collaboration with UPMC Paris, France, in 1993. She is a full professor at USTHB since 1999 and directs the Laboratory of Research in Artificial Intelligence (LRIA). By the past, she was the head of the Computer Science Institute of USTHB from 1995 to 1998 and the general director of the Algerian National Institute of Informatics -INI from 2003 to 2008. She has published around 200 papers in well-recognized international conference proceedings and journals and has directed 20 Ph.D. Theses, 38 master theses and 31 engineer projects. In 2013, she won the Algerian Scopus award in computer science and in 2015, she was selected by a jury of international academicians as a funding member of the Algerian Academy of Science and Technology (AAST).

Zakaria Elberrichi is a Professor at Djillali Liabes University.

Mohamed Fakir is currently with the department of computer sciences at university Sultan Moulay Slimane, Morocco. He received his Master degree from Nagaoka University of Technology, Japan (1991), and PHD from Cadi Ayad University, Morocco (2001). He was staff with the air conditioning department, Hitachi ltd, Japan from 1991 to 1994. He is currently working on various projects related to academia and industry. His research interests, in general, are data-mining, pattern recognition, computer vision, image processing, and web mining. He has published more than 100 publications in the form of book chapters, journal papers, and conference papers. He is a general chair, co-chair, and member of the International scientific Committees and Organizing Committees of various international conferences, symposiums and workshops. He is a Guest Editor of Journal of Electronics Commerce in Organisations and International journal of Information Technology Research (IGI global).

Rohit Kumar Gupta is working Assistant Professor in Department of Information Technology, Manipal University Jaipur. He has more than 6 year teaching experience. He is currently doing Ph.D. from MNIT, Jaipur. He completed M.tech. for MNNIT, Allahabad. His research interest are Cloud Computing, CDN, Peer-2 Peer network, and video streaming.

Najlae Idrissi received the M.S. degree in Computer Science from Faculty of Sciences, Rabat, Morocco in 2003. Then her PHD in 2008, from the University Mohammed V, Morocco and University of Nantes, France. She joined the Faculty of Sciences and Techniques of Béni Mellal in 2009 as Assistant Professor in Computer Science Department, University Sultan Moulay Slimane. In 2014, she became Associate Professor. Her areas of interest are image (natural & medical) processing, speech recognition (Tamazight) and wireless sensor networks. She has many publications in these fields. Also, she reviewed several international conference papers and journals.

Tarun Jain is an Assistant Professor in Computer Science & Engineering Department at Manipal University Jaipur, India. He is pursuing his Ph.D degree in Natural Language Processing in Computer Science & Engg from the MNIT, Jaipur India. He received the M.Tech degree in Computer Science & Engg from the NSIT, New Delhi India, 2015. The Bachelor in Technology degree in Computer Science & Engg from the UP Technical University, India, in 2013. His research interests cover the NLP & Machine Learning. He has published 2 article in refereed international journal and 5 publications in international conferences (i.e. IEEE, Springer).

Rida Khalloufi, physics and chemistry teacher, received master degree on business intelligence on 2017 University Sultan Moulay Slimane. Studies Laboratory of Information Processing and Decision Support (TIAD), Sultan Moulay Slimane University,

Ilyes Khennak received the Master degree in intelligent computer systems from USTHB, Algiers, Algeria in 2011 and the Ph.D. degree in computer science from USTHB, Algiers, Algeria in 2017. He is a professor at USTHB since 2017 and member of the Laboratory of Research in Artificial Intelligence (LRIA). His research interests include Artificial Intelligence and Information Retrieval.

Ichrak Khoulqi was born on 14/10/1995 in Marrakech and is a PhD student in Computer Science and they are working especially on the processing of Mammographic images.

Mihir Narayan Mohanty is presently working as a Professor in the Department of Electronics and Communication Engineering, Institute of Technical Education and Research, Siksha 'O' Anusandhan (Deemed to be University), Bhubaneswar, Odisha. He has published over 300 papers in International/ National Journals and Conferences along with approximately 20 years of teaching experience. He is the active member of many professional societies like IEEE, IET, IETE, EMC & EMI Engineers India, IE (I), ISCA, ACEEE, IA Eng etc. He has received his M.Tech. degree in Communication System Engineering from the Sambalpur University, Sambalpur, Odisha. Now he has done his Ph.D. work in Applied Signal Processing. He is currently working as Associate Professor and was Head in the Department of Electronics and Instrumentation Engineering, Institute of Technical Education and Research, Siksha 'O' Anusandhan University, Bhubaneswar, Odisha. His area of research interests includes Applied Signal and image Processing, Digital Signal/Image Processing, Biomedical Signal Processing, Microwave Communication Engineering and Bioinformatics.

Ankit Mundra is working as an Assistant Professor in the Department of Information Technology, School of Computer Science and IT, Manipal University Jaipur. Previously, he has worked at Department of CSE, Central University of Rajasthan for two years. He has completed his M.Tech in Computer Science and Engineering from Jaypee University of Information Technology (JUIT), Waknaghat, India and awarded with Gold Medal for scoring highest grades during M.Tech program. His research interest includes Online Fraud Detection, Distributed Computer Networks, Parallel Computing, Cyber Physical Systems, Sensor Networks, Network Algorithms, and Parallel Algorithms. He has supervised 8 M.Tech Scholars and published 21 research papers in peer-reviewed International Journals, Book series and IEEE/Springer/Elsevier conference.

Mohamed Nazih Omri received the PhD degree in Computer Science from the University of Jussieu in 1994, Paris, France. He is an Associate Professor in Computer Science at the Faculty of Sciences of Monastir, in Monastir University, Tunisia. He's the Director of MARS (Modeling of Automated Reasonin Systems) Research Unit. He's also the General Secretary of TCS (Tunisian Computing society). His group conducts research on data mining, text mining, web mining, and information retrieval, indexing methods and semantic web.

Hemanta Kumar Palo completed his 'A.M.I.E.' from Institute of Engineers, India in 1997, Master of Engineering from Birla Institute of Technology, Mesra, Ranchi in 2011 and Ph.D. in 2018 from the Siksha 'O' Anusandhan (Deemed to be University), Bhubaneswar, Odisha, India. He is having 20 years of experience in the field of Electronics and Communication Engineering from 1990 to 2010 in Indian Air Force. Currently he is serving as an Associate Professor in the department of Electronics and Communication Engineering in the Institute of Technical Education and Research, Siksha 'O' Anusandhan University, Bhubaneswar, Odisha, India. He had been an Assistant Professor in Gandhi Academy of Technology and Engineering, Odisha, in the Department of ECE from 2011 to 2012. He has been awarded with Sikshasree Sanman-2017 as a young scientist by the Saheed Raghu-Divakar Smruti Sansad, Odisha. He is the life member of IEI, India and is the member of IEEE. He has published around 40 research papers in reputed international and national highly indexed journals and conferences and is an organizing member of number of such conferences. His area of research includes signal processing, speech and emotion recognition.

Geeta Rani is working as an Assistant Professor in Computer & Communication Engineering at Manipal University Jaipur. Previously, she worked at Department of Computer Science and Engineering department at GD Goenka University, Gurugram, TIAS, Delhi and NIT, Delhi, India. She has completed his PhD in Computer Engineering from NSIT, Delhi University, M.Phil from CDLU, M.Tech and MCA from MDU with Distinction. Her research interest covers the Data Science, Machine Learning, E-Governance, Image Processing. She 18 publications in Journals, national and internals conferences, 2 chapters in the CCIS book series published by springer.

Said Safi is currently with the Department of Mathematics and Informatics,· LIRST Laboratory Morocco, · Beni Mellal at University Sultan Moulay Slimane, Morocco.

Khaddouj Taifi received his Master degree in Computer Science (2011), and PHD from the University Sultan Moulay Slimane Beni Mellal (2017), her research focuses on the Detection and Classification of Medical Image.

Naima Taifi is currently with the Department of Physics at university Sultan Moulay Slimane, Morocco. SHe received his PHD from Ibn Zohr Agadir Morocco (2006).

Pradeep Kumar Tiwari is working as an Assistant Professor in Manipal University Jaipur. Previously, he has worked at Department of Computer Science and Engineering, Vindhya Institute of Technology, and Aditya College of Technology, India. He has completed his Ph.D in Faculty of Engineering from Manipal University Jaipur, M.Phil in Computer Science from Mahatma Gandhi Chitrakoot Gramodaya Vishwavidyalaya, M.P., India and M.C.A degree in Computer Application from the Rajiv Gandhi Proudyogiki Vishwavidyalaya, M.P., India. His research intrest cover the Distributed Computing, Cloud Computing, Virtualization, Grid and Cluster Computing and Network Security. He has published 6 articles in refereed international journal, 7 book chapters in international book publishers, and 10 publications in international conferences (IEEE/ Springer). He reviewed the several international conferences papers and at present, he is reviewer and editorial member of 4 journals.

Index

T

term co-occurrence 1-5, 15
term proximity 1-2, 4-5, 15
text mining 70-73

U

Universal Networking Language 87-88

V

virtual machine 301-304, 306-307, 311
vote 210-211, 219, 223, 225

W

WBCD 210, 221
Web Services 198

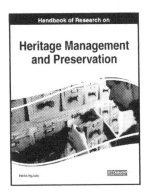

Ensure Quality Research is Introduced to the Academic Community

Become an IGI Global Reviewer for Authored Book Projects

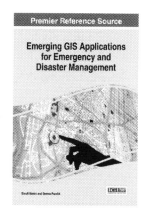

The overall success of an authored book project is dependent on quality and timely reviews.

In this competitive age of scholarly publishing, constructive and timely feedback significantly expedites the turnaround time of manuscripts from submission to acceptance, allowing the publication and discovery of forward-thinking research at a much more expeditious rate. Several IGI Global authored book projects are currently seeking highly-qualified experts in the field to fill vacancies on their respective editorial review boards:

Applications and Inquiries may be sent to:
development@igi-global.com

Applicants must have a doctorate (or an equivalent degree) as well as publishing and reviewing experience. Reviewers are asked to complete the open-ended evaluation questions with as much detail as possible in a timely, collegial, and constructive manner. All reviewers' tenures run for one-year terms on the editorial review boards and are expected to complete at least three reviews per term. Upon successful completion of this term, reviewers can be considered for an additional term.

If you have a colleague that may be interested in this opportunity, we encourage you to share this information with them.

IGI Global Proudly Partners With eContent Pro International

Receive a 25% Discount on all Editorial Services

Editorial Services

IGI Global expects all final manuscripts submitted for publication to be in their final form. This means they must be reviewed, revised, and professionally copy edited prior to their final submission. Not only does this support with accelerating the publication process, but it also ensures that the highest quality scholarly work can be disseminated.

English Language Copy Editing

Let eContent Pro International's expert copy editors perform edits on your manuscript to resolve spelling, punctuaion, grammar, syntax, flow, formatting issues and more.

Scientific and Scholarly Editing

Allow colleagues in your research area to examine the content of your manuscript and provide you with valuable feedback and suggestions before submission.

Figure, Table, Chart & Equation Conversions

Do you have poor quality figures? Do you need visual elements in your manuscript created or converted? A design expert can help!

Translation

Need your documjent translated into English? eContent Pro International's expert translators are fluent in English and more than 40 different languages.

Printed in the United States
By Bookmasters